RIGHT TO DIE AND EUTHANASIA

REVISED EDITION

LIBRARY IN A BOOK

RIGHT TO DIE AND EUTHANASIA
REVISED EDITION

Lisa Yount

Facts On File
An imprint of Infobase Publishing

Right to Die and Euthanasia, Revised Edition

Facts On File, Inc.
An imprint of Infobase Publishing
132 West 31st Street
New York NY 10001

Library of Congress Cataloging-in-Publication Data

Yount, Lisa.
    Right to die and euthanasia / Lisa Yount.—Rev. ed.
      p. cm.—(Library in a book)
    Previously published; Physician-assisted suicide and euthanasia.
New York : Facts on File, 2000.
    Includes bibliographical references and index.
    ISBN-13: 978-0-8160-6275-1 (alk. paper)
    1. Assisted suicide—Moral and ethical aspects. 2. Assisted suicide—
Law and legislation. 3. Euthanasia—Moral and ethical aspects.
I. Yount, Lisa. Physician-assisted suicide and euthanasia. II. Title.
R726.Y673 2007
179.7—dc22   2006033424

Facts On File books are available at special discounts when purchased in bulk quantities for businesses, associations, institutions, or sales promotions. Please call our Special Sales Department in New York at (212) 967-8800 or (800) 322-8755.

You can find Facts On File on the World Wide Web at http://www.factsonfile.com

Text design by Ron Monteleone

Printed in the United States of America

MP Hermitage 10 9 8 7 6 5 4 3 2 1

This book is printed on acid-free paper.

To everyone I love:
May we never need
to investigate this subject further

CONTENTS

PART III
APPENDICES

PART I

OVERVIEW OF THE TOPIC

CHAPTER 1

INTRODUCTION TO
EUTHANASIA

Supporters call it the ultimate civil right. Opponents link it with the Holocaust. As the 21st century dawns, euthanasia (from Greek words meaning "good death") has joined abortion as one of the most painfully divisive issues in the developed world. The ethical issues raised by the debate about euthanasia reach to the very roots of human mortality and compassion. Federal Ninth Circuit Court judge Stephen Reinhardt, in his historic 1996 decision on the right-to-die case *Compassion in Dying et al. v. State of Washington*, said that this debate

> *requires us to confront the most basic of human concerns—the mortality of self and loved ones—and to balance the interest in preserving human life against the desire to die peacefully and with dignity. . . . [This] controversy . . . may touch more people more profoundly than any other issue the courts will face in the foreseeable future.[1]*

The movement to legalize some form of euthanasia has often been called the right-to-die movement. The name seems strange, since nothing is more unquestionably guaranteed to everyone than death. What the movement's supporters want to protect is not really the right to die but the right to have some degree of control over the time and manner of one's death—as one group puts it, "the right to choose to die." They believe that competent adults with less than six months to live should be legally permitted not only to refuse life-sustaining medical treatment but also to receive a physician's help in ending their lives if they request it. Some right-to-die supporters feel that people who have an incurable degenerative or disabling condition should also be allowed to ask for aid in dying, even though their illness is not terminal.

3

Right to Die and Euthanasia

People who oppose the movement, on the other hand, say that no individual's right outweighs the state's duty to protect life and the physician's duty not to harm patients. They fear that if physician-assisted suicide or euthanasia is legalized, society will slide down a "slippery slope" toward coercing and even perhaps forcing vulnerable members—the elderly, chronically ill, disabled, poor, and minorities—to die against their will. The so-called right to die, they say, will become a duty to die.

Aid in dying can take several forms. Distinguishing among them is important because some individuals or groups support some forms but not others, and state and national laws also often make such distinctions. One form is passive euthanasia, or "letting die": ceasing or not starting medical treatment that keeps a person alive, such as attachment to a respirator or provision of food and water through a tube. Another is assisted suicide, in which a physician or, sometimes, a family member or friend provides the means for a person with a terminal or incurable illness to end life, but the patient is still the one who performs the final act. The third is active euthanasia, in which someone (usually a physician) causes the death of a sick person without that person's participation. Active euthanasia can be either voluntary (done at the sick person's request) or involuntary (done without the person's concurrent request or permission). Some groups also distinguish between nonvoluntary and involuntary euthanasia, using *nonvoluntary euthanasia* to refer to euthanasia of people incompetent to consent to the act (though they may have given permission for it or requested it at an earlier time, when they were competent) and *involuntary euthanasia* to refer to the "mercy killing" of competent adults who are suffering but have not requested death.

The right of competent adults to refuse medical treatment, including medical treatment that sustains life, is legally recognized today in all states of the United States and in most other Western countries. The right of designated surrogates to refuse such treatment on behalf of incompetent but formerly competent adults who left prior instructions to do so in the form of living wills or other advance directives is also widely recognized. Some states allow surrogates to refuse life-sustaining treatment on behalf of never-competent individuals as well. Physician-assisted suicide, on the other hand, is legal in only one state (Oregon) and legal or openly practiced in only a few other countries, chiefly the Netherlands. Active euthanasia, even if voluntary, is even more rarely legalized. It is not legal anywhere in the United States.

Even though they seldom have an explicit legal right to do so, survey after survey makes clear that, under certain circumstances, physicians regularly if clandestinely do assist death, just as they surely have throughout history. According to an article published in the *Journal of Medical Ethics* in

4

October 2004, between 4 and 10 percent of physicians admit (anonymously) in surveys that they have deliberately helped patients die. The percentage may be higher among doctors whose specialties bring them many patients who are terminally ill. Of 355 American oncologists (cancer specialists) interviewed in 1998, for example, 56 (15.8 percent) admitted having carried out physician-assisted suicide or euthanasia. Many of these assisted deaths take the form of terminal sedation or what is often called the "double effect," in which a physician gives high doses of narcotics primarily for the purpose of controlling pain but knows that such doses will also shorten or perhaps even end a terminally ill patient's life. "This is the dirty little secret of medicine," says internist Howard Grossman of the St. Lukes-Roosevelt Hospital at Columbia University. "This is the tremendous burden that physicians have carried with them for a long, long time, the fact that they already help people [to die]."[2]

HISTORICAL ATTITUDES TOWARD SUICIDE AND EUTHANASIA

Feelings and laws about euthanasia, especially in the form of physician-assisted suicide, are closely related to those concerning suicide in general. Both have changed considerably throughout history. The ancient Greeks, for example, believed that suicide could be acceptable or even honorable under certain conditions, one of which was escaping the pain of an untreatable illness. In some Greek city-states, including Athens, people could request government help in killing themselves. The state could also order suicide as a punishment for crimes, as happened most notably in the case of the philosopher Socrates, whom Athenian magistrates commanded to drink poison hemlock in 399 b.c. after convicting him of corrupting the city's youth with his teachings. Socrates accepted his death sentence calmly; indeed, in *Phaedo*, the account his student Plato wrote of Socrates' death, the philosopher is quoted as saying, "True philosophers make dying their profession."[3]

In spite of such statements, neither Socrates nor Plato encouraged people to seek death. They disapproved of suicide under most circumstances, although they agreed that it might be forgiven as a kind of temporary insanity if it was a response to "intolerable . . . misfortune" such as incurable illness.[4] Plato's student Aristotle spoke out even more strongly against suicide, calling it an act of cowardice in his *Ethics*.

On the other hand, a school of Greek and Roman philosophers called the Stoics offered eight different motives for which suicide was acceptable, including terminal or degenerative illness. Seneca, a Roman Stoic philosopher, wrote, "I will not relish old age unless it leaves my mind intact. . . . If I know when I will suffer forever, I will depart. . . . Just as I choose a ship to sail in or a house to live in, so I choose a death for my passage from life."[5] Even the Stoics, however, considered only a few motives for suicide to be heroic, and the desire to escape painful illness was not one of them.

This relative tolerance for suicide ended when Christianity became the dominant religion of the Western world. Although nothing in the Bible explicitly forbids suicide, Judaism condemns it (as does Islam), and such condemnation became part of the doctrine of the early Christians as well. St. Augustine, bishop of Hippo in the early fifth century, expressed the Church's attitude very plainly when he called suicide a "detestable and damnable wickedness."[6] Unless done at the specific command of God, Augustine wrote, self-murder violated the sixth commandment, "Thou shalt not kill."

St. Thomas Aquinas, drawing on the writings of Aristotle as well as Augustine, expanded on this position in the 13th century by claiming that suicide was a sin against God because only God had the right to take back the gift of life that He had given. Indeed, he wrote, suicide was the worst of sins because it left no time for repentance. Aquinas said that suicide was also a sin against society because it deprived the community of useful people. The writings of Aquinas, along with those of Augustine and other church leaders, defined the prevailing Western view of suicide for hundreds of years. They still underlie most Christian objections to assisted suicide and euthanasia.

The Renaissance, with its reemphasis on the culture of the ancient world and on the importance of human beings and earthly life, brought the first stirrings of a return to the idea that people might be entitled to exert some control over the manner of their death. The ideal society described in Sir Thomas More's *Utopia* (1516), for example, encouraged assisted suicide to end painful and incurable illness. Ethicist Michael M. Uhlmann points out, however, that *Utopia* was partly satirical, so statements in the book may not have represented the personal feelings of More, who was a devout Catholic and thus was unlikely to favor an action of which the Catholic Church so strongly disapproved.

Some Enlightenment intellectuals also accepted suicide, at least under some circumstances. The 16th-century French essayist Michel de Montaigne and the 17th-century English poet John Donne are among those whose writings suggest that they condoned suicide. In *Biathanatos*, Donne offered an explicit defense of suicide and a refutation of the reasoning behind the Christian prohibition of the act.

In an essay published in 1777, a year after his death, Scottish philosopher David Hume stated even more clearly than Donne that suicide "is no transgression of our duty to God," especially in the case of people who are already dying. Regarding Aquinas's claim that suicide shirked one's duty to the community, Hume wrote, "I am not obliged to do a small good to society at the expense of a great harm to myself: when then should I prolong a miserable existence because of some frivolous advantage which the public may perhaps receive from me?"[7] According to Hume, suicide to end a life of severe illness or disability, in which one can contribute little or nothing to society and is enduring intolerable suffering, not only is acceptable but may even confer a net social benefit.

On the other hand, Hume's contemporary, German philosopher Immanuel Kant, opposed suicide because, he said, its motive was self-interest, which he did not consider a justifiable reason for an action. Kant also believed that suicide showed a disrespect for life. He agreed with Aquinas that the act usurped a power that belonged only to God and violated one's duty as a created being: "Human beings are sentinels on earth and may not leave their posts until relieved by another beneficent hand. God is our owner; we are His property."[8]

For centuries, suicide was against the law in most countries as well as proscribed by religion. Antisuicide laws usually required the heirs of a suicide to forfeit some or all of the person's property to the state. Such laws began to be withdrawn in the 19th century, not because people found suicide any more morally acceptable than before, but because they came to feel that punishing the suicide's family was unfair. Suicide was further decriminalized in the 20th century because the act came to be seen primarily as a result of mental illness. Suicide and attempted suicide are no longer against the law in any state of the United States.

On the other hand, assisting in a suicide, even that of a terminally or incurably ill person, has always been illegal in most states. In 1872, for example, the Ohio Supreme Court ruled in the case of a man who had made poison available to such a person:

> *It is immaterial whether the party taking the poison took it willingly . . . or was overcome by force. . . . The li[ves] of those to whom life has become a burden—of those who are hopelessly diseased or fatally wounded . . . are under the protection of the law equally as the lives of those who are in the full tide of life's enjoyment.*[9]

Euthanasia, in its modern meaning of "mercy killing," was even more surely illegal: technically, it was simply a form of murder. The term was coined by the English philosopher and statesman Sir Francis Bacon in the early 17th century, but Bacon used it only to describe the painless, peaceful natural death that people hoped to have. Its meaning changed in the 20th century.

Illegal and nameless though it might have been, euthanasia in its present meaning has no doubt always existed. Although family members or friends might occasionally have killed sick people to end their suffering, that unhappy task, in ancient times as well as today, was most likely to be performed by a physician. Physicians are uniquely well placed to assist suicide or perform euthanasia for their patients because of their medical skills and access to painlessly lethal drugs. Whether doing so is an extension of the physician's role as healer and comforter or the ultimate violation of it has been hotly debated.

By far the best known ancient statement about such activity is found in the Hippocratic Oath, which many doctors still take when they graduate from medical school. Part of the oath reads, "I will [not] give a deadly drug to anybody if asked for it, nor will I make a suggestion to that effect."[10] Although this oath is often considered to be the ultimate statement of the physician's moral creed, Michael Uhlmann points out that Hippocrates, the Greek physician of the fourth century B.C. to whom the oath is credited, was not expressing the common medical viewpoint of his time. Hippocrates' views were probably derived from those of the philosopher Pythagoras, who held (as Christian theologians also later would) that human souls contained sparks of divinity and thus should not be wantonly destroyed.

During the Christian era, physicians probably were as repelled as anyone else by the idea of deliberately hastening death under most circumstances. Nonetheless, despite the official disapproval of church, law, and their profession, some doctors—perhaps even a majority—once in a while quietly speeded a suffering patient's dying process by drugs or other means. Beginning in the late 19th century and increasingly as the 20th century progressed, a few physicians dared to mention this hidden practice in print and even to demand that it be given legal sanction.

ASSISTED SUICIDE AND EUTHANASIA IN THE 20TH CENTURY

The first attempt to legalize voluntary euthanasia performed by physicians in the United States was a bill introduced into the Ohio legislature in 1906. According to a contemporary newspaper, the bill proposed that

> *when an adult of sound mind has been fatally hurt and is so ill that recovery is impossible or is suffering extreme physical pain without hope of relief, his physician, if not a relative and if not interested in any way in the person's estate, may ask his patient in the presence of three witnesses if he or she is ready to die. . . . Three other physicians are to be consulted.*[11]

If the patient acquiesced and the other physicians agreed about the person's medical condition, the doctor could provide a painless death. The bill called this act *euthanasia*, applying the term, perhaps for the first time, to the deliberate causing of death in order to relieve suffering.

The bill met powerful opposition. An editorial warned of many of the same dangers that opponents bring up in connection with physician-assisted suicide and euthanasia today, including the possibility that people would use such a law to rid themselves of burdensome relatives or gain inheritances. It also claimed that such a law would destroy the trusting relationship between patient and doctor, so that "the patient would look forward to the visit of the physician with dread."[12] When the bill was sent to the legislature's Committee on Medical Jurisprudence, it failed by a vote of 78 to 22.

Another important effort to legalize voluntary euthanasia was made in Great Britain in the 1930s. C. Killick Millard, health officer for the city of Leicester, drew up a draft bill for this purpose in 1931, and the British Voluntary Euthanasia Society was formed in 1935 to promote the bill. Although it did not use the term, the society was essentially the world's first right-to-die organization. Its members included such prominent figures as H. G. Wells, George Bernard Shaw, and Bertrand Russell. Nonetheless, when the bill was introduced into Parliament in 1936, the House of Lords voted it down by 35 to 14. The society continued its advocacy efforts but was unable to bring another euthanasia bill into Parliament until 1950.

Charles Potter, a Unitarian minister, formed a similar group, the Euthanasia Society of America, in the United States in 1938. Some of its members proposed legalizing euthanasia not only for terminally or incurably ill people who requested it but also for infants with severe mental and physical defects ("nature's mistakes") and even "criminals and hopeless lunatics."[13] The society tried to introduce a bill legalizing voluntary euthanasia for terminally ill adults into the New York legislature in 1939 but could find no legislator to sponsor it. Later attempts, continuing until about 1960, met with similar failure.

In opinion polls taken in the 1930s, about 40 percent of Americans and as much as 69 percent of Britons favored euthanasia for the terminally or incurably ill under at least some circumstances. Even when family members were arrested for assisted suicide or euthanasia of terminally ill people, they were seldom convicted or punished. In 1938, for example, a New York grand jury refused to indict Harry C. Johnson for gassing his cancer-stricken wife (at her request, he said) after three psychiatrists testified that he had committed the act while temporarily insane. Several parents who killed children with severe mental retardation were also acquitted or given suspended sentences. Such cases lent support to the claim in a 1939 *Time* article that there were "unwritten laws condoning mercy killings," although judges invariably reminded juries that the written laws said otherwise.[14]

During World War II, however, Nazi Germany gave the word *euthanasia* a sinister connotation that it has yet to shake. Between 1939 and 1941, the Hitler government carried out a program of so-called euthanasia for people possessing what the Nazis deemed *lebensunwerten leben*, or "life unworthy of life."[15] The program started with mentally disabled children, then expanded to include mentally and physically disabled adults. The rationale behind the program was partly economic—a desire to spare the state the expense of caring for "useless" people—and partly biological, stemming from a belief in eugenics, which claimed that only the healthy should reproduce.

The Nazi "euthanasia" program is estimated to have killed as many as 100,000 disabled people, all Aryan Germans. The infamous "final solution" to the problem of Jews and other minority groups, whom the Nazis also eventually dubbed unworthy of life, grew out of this program. Indeed, the euthanasia program was a sort of dress rehearsal for the Holocaust, featuring the same combination of gas-emitting fake shower stalls, ever-running crematoria, and—most tellingly, modern opponents of euthanasia say—the full cooperation of many German physicians. Leo Alexander, an investigator for the Nuremberg War Crimes Tribunal, wrote in 1949:

> *It started with the [German physicians'] acceptance of the attitude, basic in the euthanasia movement, that there is such a thing as life not worthy to be lived. This attitude in its early stages concerned itself merely with the severely and chronically sick. Gradually the sphere of those to be included in this category was enlarged to encompass the socially unproductive, the ideologically unwanted, the racially unwanted and finally all non-Germans. But it is important to realize that the infinitely small wedged-in lever from which this entire trend of mind received its impetus was the attitude toward the nonrehabilitable sick.[16]*

Needless to say, modern supporters of the right-to-die movement disavow any similarity between the Nazi program and the activities they propose to legalize. They emphasize that their programs, even at their furthest extension, would approve only euthanasia requested by competent adults or, in the case of incompetent people, by written directives made at an earlier date when the people were competent. In the case of never-competent people, family members or other legally recognized surrogates would have to request euthanasia for them. The Nazi program, by contrast, made no pretense of fulfilling sick people's requests or asking anyone's permission.

Introduction to Euthanasia

Although some details of the Nazi euthanasia program were not revealed until 20 years after it occurred, enough emerged after the war to make the American public leery of the subject. In a 1947 Gallup poll, only 37 percent of those polled answered yes when asked, "When a person has a disease that cannot be cured, do you think doctors should be allowed by law to end the patient's life by some painless means if the patient and his family request it?" By contrast, 46 percent had answered yes to a similar question in 1937 and 1939 Gallup polls.

Demand for a way to control events at the end of life began to build again in industrialized countries during the 1950s and 1960s, however, chiefly because of the unexpected effects of medical technology's success in extending life expectancy. As antibiotics and other advances did away with many infectious diseases and other formerly common causes of a relatively quick death, more people lived into old age and began to suffer from chronic conditions such as cancer, heart disease, diabetes, and Alzheimer's disease. Death from such illnesses was often preceded by years of slow and sometimes painful decline in physical or mental functions.

For the first time, too, technology became able to prolong—sometimes for years—the process of dying. Dying people began to be "rescued" by respirators or ventilators and by machines that used electric shock to restart the heart. These devices sometimes restored people to normal life, but at other times they returned them only to coma or a few extra days of pain. Tubes that carried water and nutritive solutions into the stomach could maintain the life of a comatose person for decades. A doctor noted in a *New York Times* article, "Our medical inventions have invented our own dilemma. Sometimes the machines are a blessing. And sometimes they are a curse. But we haven't invented laws or rules yet to tell the difference."[17]

An important indication of a change in feelings about some forms of euthanasia came in a statement that Pope Pius XII made in 1957. The pope continued to oppose active euthanasia, but he told a conference of anesthesiologists that Catholics and their families did not have to continue extraordinary treatments such as the use of artificial respirators in seemingly hopeless cases. He also sanctioned the "double effect," in which pain-controlling narcotics might ease someone into death. In short, the pope said that passive euthanasia was acceptable.

Another factor that encouraged public thinking about a right to die was the rise of what has been called the "rights culture" in the late 1960s and early 1970s. Students in America and Europe envisioned, and indeed tried to insist on, a society in which all people could "do their thing" without interference, so long as they did not harm others. They expressed, sometimes violently, a distrust of and resistance to all forms of authority.

11

Women, African Americans, and other minority groups demanded an end to discrimination and unequal treatment and a recognition of their individual rights, and many of their demands were put into law. Individual liberty and autonomy, always high on the list of American values, began to be celebrated almost to the exclusion of everything else.

A combination of increasing technology and specialization, which tended to depersonalize medicine, and people's growing demand to have a say in decisions that affected them eroded the worshipful respect with which most Americans had regarded the medical profession in the 1950s. Instead, the public began to view doctors as paternalistic, greedy, and indifferent to the feelings of patients and their families. The result was the patients' rights movement of the 1970s. One of the medical rights that people demanded was the right to have a voice in end-of-life decisions involving themselves or loved ones. At very least, they wanted to be able to refuse medical treatment that they considered futile or excessively painful, even if it (after a fashion) preserved life.

THE 1970s: THE RIGHT-TO-DIE MOVEMENT BEGINS

Death had been a taboo subject in the United States during much of the century, but in the early 1970s it instead became almost an obsession. Beginning with Swiss-born psychiatrist Elisabeth Kübler-Ross's *On Death and Dying* (1969), books about death became best-sellers. The number of new books and popular magazine articles on the subject in the United States doubled each year between 1968 and 1973, then doubled again between 1973 and 1975. Some people even began to talk about the possibility of hastening death for the terminally ill. During the early 1970s, bills that would have legalized some form of voluntary euthanasia were introduced in Montana, Florida, Washington, Oregon, and Wisconsin. None came even close to passing; the time was not yet ripe.

Public concern was growing, however, as medical technology continued to change the face of death. Traditionally, most people had died at home, but by 1978, about 71 percent died in hospitals, nursing homes, or other medical institutions. The figure had risen to more than 80 percent in the late 1990s. In his 1994 best-seller *How We Die*, physician-writer Sherwin Nuland described the typical modern death scene as filled with

> *beeping and squealing monitors, the hissing of respirators and pistoned mattresses, the flashing multicolored electronic signals—the whole technological panoply is background for the tactics by which we are deprived of the tran-*

quillity we have every right to hope for, and separated from those few who would not let us die alone.[18]

The 1970s saw the first appearance of an alternative to this kind of death: the hospice, an institution devoted to palliative or "comfort" care for the dying. The World Health Organization defines palliative care as care that

affirms life and regards dying as a normal process; neither hastens nor postpones death; provides relief from pain and other distressing symptoms; integrates the psychological and spiritual aspects of patient care; offers a support system to help patients live as actively as possible until death; [and] offers a support system to help the family cope during the patient's illness and in their own bereavement.[19]

Hospice, which has the same root as *hospital*, meant a way station for people on religious pilgrimages during the Middle Ages. Dame Cicely Saunders, a British physician, established St. Christopher's, the world's first modern hospice, in London in 1967. The first American hospice opened in New Haven, Connecticut, in 1974. Today, although some hospices are separate institutions like these, hospice has come to mean more a philosophy of end-of-life care than a set of buildings; in most cases, hospice workers help people die comfortably at home. In the 1970s, however, neither hospice organizations nor their philosophy was common.

Public concern about modern dying came to a head because of a series of events in 1975 and 1976—events that some historians place at the root of the right-to-die movement. On April 14, 1975, a 21-year-old New Jersey woman named Karen Ann Quinlan went into a coma after consuming a mixture of drugs and alcohol at a party. A respirator had to be inserted in her throat to keep her breathing.

When Quinlan showed no signs of returning consciousness after a month and a half, Robert Morse, the neurologist who was acting as her physician, told Joe and Julia Quinlan, her grieving parents, that she was in a persistent vegetative state (PVS). This meant that her brain stem, which is responsible for automatic bodily functions, remained active, producing tracings on an electroencephalogram as well as causing her to open her eyes and sometimes thrash about and make sounds. Her higher brain, however, had been damaged beyond repair. Only the respirator, feeding tubes, and other medical machinery kept her alive.

After spending agonized months at their daughter's bedside, watching her weight drop from 115 to 90 pounds and her contracting muscles draw her body into a contorted posture, Joseph and Julia Quinlan concluded that, for all purposes that mattered, Karen was dead. Both Catholics, they asked their priest, Tom Trapasso, for advice. He told them about Pope Pius XII's 1957 statement that doctors did not have to employ "extraordinary means" such as respirators to keep patients alive. On July 31, therefore, the Quinlans signed a form directing Morse to remove the respirator. Morse and St. Clare's, the large Catholic hospital where Quinlan was being treated, refused. "You have to understand our position," Sister Urban, the president of the St. Clare's board of trustees, later told Julia Quinlan. "In this hospital we don't kill people."[20]

The Quinlans and their attorney, Paul W. Armstrong, appeared before Judge Robert Muir, Jr., in probate court in Morristown, New Jersey, on October 20, 1975. Armstrong not only asked for Joe Quinlan to be named Karen's guardian but directly requested permission to disconnect Karen's respirator. This made the case a precedent-setting one, and it immediately attracted wide media attention. "Whatever the decision," wrote *Washington Post* reporter B. D. Colen, "it is one that will haunt us for years to come."[21] The attention was increased because the case featured an attractive young woman (Karen was usually shown staring out thoughtfully from her high school yearbook photo). The media and the public pictured her as a sort of tragic Sleeping Beauty.

In court, Julia Quinlan testified that Karen had twice, after seeing people she knew die slowly from cancer, said that she would not want to be "kept alive like that," although Mrs. Quinlan admitted that she was not using Karen's exact words. Armstrong claimed that the case was covered under the rights to medical privacy and to control over one's body that the Supreme Court had recognized in several decisions, most notably in *Roe v. Wade*, the landmark 1973 ruling that legalized abortion. On the other hand, Thomas R. Curtin, appointed by Muir as Karen's temporary guardian, said that his job was "to do every single thing that I can do as a skilled professional to keep Karen Quinlan alive."[22] He and Ralph Porzio, Morse's lawyer, insisted that what the Quinlans wanted to do was euthanasia and, as such, was both legally and morally wrong.

After hearing four days of testimony and reviewing the 745-page hearing transcript, Muir gave his decision on November 10, 1975. He refused to make Joe Quinlan Karen's guardian because, he said, doing so would not be in her best interest. He also refused permission to turn off the respirator. Although he agreed that if she had been conscious, Karen, like any competent adult, would have had the right (long recognized both in common law and in Supreme Court decisions) to refuse any medical treatment for herself, he maintained that "there is no constitutional right to die that can be asserted by a parent for his incompetent adult child."[23] Karen's wishes, he believed, were not clearly known, and he felt that in such situations physicians rather than family members should make "substituted judgments" about the health care of incompetent patients.

Armstrong and the Quinlans appealed their case to the New Jersey Supreme Court, which heard it beginning on January 26, 1976. On March 31, the state high court unanimously reversed Muir's decision. The justices ruled that the right to privacy could in fact cover situations like the Quinlans', making theirs the first state court to apply the right to a case of "letting die." The court appointed Joseph Quinlan as Karen's guardian and gave Morse and the hospital immunity from prosecution if they disconnected her respirator. In the written opinion of the court, Justice Richard J. Hughes said that whatever the Quinlans decided to do about their daughter "should be accepted by society, the overwhelming majority of whose members would, we think, in similar circumstances exercise such a choice in the same way for themselves or for those closest to them."[24]

Tragically for the Quinlans, their story by no means ended with their court victory. In spite of the justices' decision, Morse and St. Clare's still refused to remove Karen's respirator, and while the family was searching for a more cooperative long-term-care home to which she could be transferred, the hospital staff began to "wean" her from the respirator by turning it off for longer and longer periods of time. On June 9, 1976, the Quinlans transferred Karen to Morris View Nursing Home and turned the respirator off, but by then she was able to breathe on her own. Her parents refused to authorize removal of the feeding tubes and antibiotics that now sustained her ("That would be euthanasia" and therefore against his religion, Joseph Quinlan had said during the trial), so Karen lingered on in her medical twilight for another decade, finally dying of pneumonia on June 13, 1986.[25]

One of the most immediate consequences of the Quinlan case was an uprush of interest in living wills, the first type of advance health care directive to be introduced. A living will specifies which medical treatments a competent adult wishes to have or to refuse if he or she should become incompetent. Louis Kutner had coined the term in an article in the summer 1969 *Indiana Law Review*. Such a document, he wrote, would be "analogous to a revocable or conditional trust with the patient's body as the *res*, the patient as the beneficiary and grantor, and the doctor and the hospital as trustees."[26] Before the Quinlan case, however, few people knew about living wills and fewer still had filled them out.

Living wills were supposed to serve as guidelines to family and hospital staff, but they were not legally binding. For reasons ranging from paternalism to fear of lawsuits, doctors and hospitals frequently ignored them. In the early 1970s, therefore, groups who supported living wills, such as the Society for the Right to Die (originally the Euthanasia Society of America), began to work toward giving them legal standing. Barry Keene, a California assemblyman from Eureka, introduced a state bill for this purpose in 1974. The bill might have seemed destined for easy passage, since an opinion poll taken at the time showed that 87 percent of California adults supported the right of incurably ill people to refuse life-prolonging medical treatment, but three powerful groups—the California Medical Association, the California Catholic Conference, and the California Pro-Life Council—opposed the bill, and it was defeated. Similar bills were introduced in four other states that year, but they also failed.

When the California bill was reintroduced in 1976 in the wake of the Quinlan case, however, it passed, albeit narrowly and after much debate. (Ironically, the bill would not have helped the Quinlan family even if it had been in effect where they lived and Karen had made a living will, because it allowed refusal of life-prolonging medical treatment only for patients who were terminally ill, which Karen was not.) Governor Jerry Brown signed the bill, called the Natural Death Act, into law on September 30, 1976, saying, "This bill gives recognition to the human right that people have to let their life come to its natural conclusion."[27] It was the first living-will law in the country. Fifty similar bills were introduced in 38 states the following year, and they passed in seven. During the next decade, a total of 36 states followed California's lead.

The Quinlan case also increased people's knowledge of hospital ethics committees, a fairly new type of body designed to settle difficult cases such as the Quinlans' without reference to the courts. The New Jersey court required the Quinlans to consult such a committee, which is composed of physicians, social workers, attorneys, theologians, and others, before disconnecting Karen's respirator. Most hospitals would eventually establish ethics committees.

Above all, the case galvanized the public into trying to make sure that they and their loved ones would never find themselves in the horrible situation that the Quinlan family faced. Wrenched by the fact that Karen's life and her family's emotional ordeal did not end when her respirator was turned off, some people began to demand the right not only to refuse medical treatment but also to hasten an unduly prolonged death.

THE 1980s: THE MOVEMENT EXPANDS

The right-to-die movement, as it was beginning to be called, gained increasing prominence during the 1980s. To begin with, right-to-die supporters encouraged the expansion of advance health care directives to include not only living wills but also a new type of directive called a durable power

16

of attorney for health care, or a health care proxy. This directive allowed people to specify a surrogate to make health care decisions for them if they should become incompetent. By 1986, all 50 states had made durable powers of attorney legally binding, although in some states, an appointed surrogate could not order the withholding of life-sustaining treatment without "clear and convincing" evidence, such as a living will, that the patient would have wanted such an action. The health care proxy was thus a complement to the living will, not a substitute for it.

At the same time advance directives were becoming more common and accepted, several influential groups softened their position on the withdrawal of medical treatment that such directives often mandated. In 1986 the American Medical Association revised its position on patients with PVS, stating that the group now felt that it was ethically permissible for a physician to remove both respirator and feeding tubes from someone in irreversible PVS if the person's family wished. The Catholic Church, too, abandoned attempts to distinguish between "ordinary" and "extraordinary" treatment. Pope John Paul II stated in 1980 that patients might refuse any type of medical treatment without violating church doctrine, provided that death is imminent and treatment is futile.

The chief leader in "pushing the envelope" of death rights beyond advance directives and refusal of medical treatment into active hastening of death during the 1980s was Derek Humphry, a British-born journalist. In 1973, while Humphry was living in England, his first wife, Jean, developed breast and bone cancer. Treatment failed, leaving her in tremendous pain, and she asked Humphry to help her end her life. Such an act was illegal in England, but charges could be brought only with the permission of the Director of Public Prosecutions, a man Humphry knew from his reporting work and felt would be unlikely to pursue this course. Humphry therefore consulted a physician he later identified only as "Dr. Joe" and obtained a prescription for a lethal dose of medication. In March 1975, when Jean decided that the time had come, Humphry prepared the mixture. She drank it and died about an hour later. Humphry published a book about this experience, *Jean's Way*, in 1978. It attracted considerable media attention, and the police investigated, but, as Humphry had predicted, the prosecutor declined to press charges.

In August 1980, Humphry and his second wife, Ann Wickett, then living in southern California, founded the Hemlock Society, a group whose purpose was to legalize physician-assisted suicide and voluntary euthanasia for terminally ill people. This was a much more active approach to the right to die than that taken by the existing American euthanasia societies, Concern for Dying (formerly the Euthanasia Education Council) and the Society for the Right to Die (formerly the Euthanasia Society of America), which concentrated strictly on promoting advance directives. His approach was more similar to that of Britain's Voluntary Euthanasia Society, or EXIT, as it was then called.

Humphry published a second book, *Let Me Die Before I Wake*, in early 1981. It consisted primarily of accounts by family members who had helped terminally ill people die, but drug dosages and other specific details of suicide methods were embedded in the stories. The other American right-to-die societies protested Humphry's activist approach, both because they thought that people who were not terminally ill might misuse the information he provided and because they feared that his book and campaign to legalize physician-assisted suicide would turn public opinion against their own less controversial efforts. Ann Jane Levinson, Concern for Dying's executive director, wrote to Humphry, "I only hope the backlash [caused by your activities] doesn't sink us all."[28]

Active right-to-die efforts like Humphry's gained support during the 1980s from an unexpected source: sufferers in the AIDS epidemic. After observing the often protracted and painful deaths of friends and lovers, some people infected with HIV, the virus that causes AIDS, began "saving pills" for the day when their own suffering might become unendurable. They also brought discussion of the right to die out of the shadows. "Instead of broken and weary 80-year-old citizens dealing with life-threatening diseases. . . , affluent 25- to 35-year-old men—eager and able to extend their political clout and organization—suddenly joined the debate" on assisted suicide and euthanasia, Gary Thomas noted in *Christianity Today*. "Almost immediately, prolonged deaths became a matter of public discussion."[29]

Meanwhile, by fits and starts, American courts were expanding both the range of incompetent people for whom surrogates might refuse life-sustaining treatment and the types of treatment that might be rejected. Right-to-life groups and some other critics claimed that these court decisions bore out predictions that they had made in the 1970s when they stated that seemingly harmless advance directives and the surrogate rights granted to Karen Quinlan's parents marked the first steps down the slippery slope to Nazi-style involuntary euthanasia.

A 1977 Massachusetts case involving a severely retarded man, Joseph Saikewicz, had established a precedent for the right of surrogates to refuse life-extending medical treatment on behalf of never-competent adults in some cases. That case, however, caused nothing like the stir that surrounded another in the early 1980s, in which the never-competent person was a baby. The child, a boy, was born on April 9, 1982, in Bloomington, Indiana.

Known to courts and public only as Baby Doe, the Bloomington baby had Down's syndrome, which is caused by an extra chromosome 21 and produces moderate to severe mental retardation. He also had an opening between his esophagus and his windpipe that prevented him from eating without choking. Surgery to close the opening would not have been difficult, but Walter Owens, the family's obstetrician, emphasized the extremely limited mental activity of most children with Down's syndrome (as it was understood at the time) and the high economic and emotional cost of caring for such a child. He advised the baby's parents to refuse the surgery, and they did so. They also decided against having the baby fed intravenously.

Hospital administrators and other pediatricians who disagreed with Owens's prognosis set up an emergency session with a local judge, John Baker, to try to force the baby's treatment and feeding. Baker ruled that Baby Doe's parents had the right to decide its fate. The district attorney appealed the decision to the county circuit court and then, when that appeal failed, to the Indiana Supreme Court. The higher court, too, found for the parents. The district attorney even asked the U.S. Supreme Court for an emergency intervention, but the baby died before this appeal could be ruled upon.

The Baby Doe case caused far more outcry against the parents than Karen Quinlan's had. In *In the Arms of Others: A Cultural History of the Right-to-Die in America*, Peter G. Filene speculates that this may have been partly because Baby Doe's parents, unlike the Quinlans, insisted on preserving their anonymity and because they had reached their decision very quickly. Another factor may have been that many people who saw a respirator as "extraordinary" treatment did not feel the same way about provision of food. The helplessness of an infant, who obviously (unlike a formerly competent adult such as Karen Quinlan) never could have consented to withdrawal of treatment, also tugged powerfully on people's emotions. As a Virginia man wrote to the *Washington Post*, "the cries of a starving infant are apt to haunt my nightmares."[30] The uproar increased when evidence surfaced that Baby Doe's case was anything but unique. On the contrary, failing to treat severely brain-damaged infants (with the parents' consent) was a fairly common practice in neonatal intensive care units.

The publicity surrounding Baby Doe's death attracted the attention of the conservative Reagan administration. On April 30, two weeks after the child died, President Ronald Reagan directed the Justice Department and the Department of Health and Human Services (HHS) to require treatment in future cases of this type. The administration used as its justification Section 504 of the Rehabilitation Act of 1973, which stated that discrimination on the basis of disability was illegal.

A little less than a year later, HHS sent a notice to all hospitals, requiring them to post large signs in every infant care facility reading "Discriminatory failure to feed and care for handicapped infants in this facility is prohibited by federal law."[31] The signs also had to include a toll-free "Baby

Doe hotline" phone number via which anyone could report instances of such discrimination. When calls were placed to this number, "Baby Doe squads" of physicians, lawyers, and government workers would fly to the offending hospitals, seize relevant medical records, and enforce the rule. Irritated pediatricians called these squads the "Baby Doe Gestapo."

The "interim final" Baby Doe rules took effect on March 21, 1983. The American Academy of Pediatrics, however, resented this interference with physicians' right to decide on treatment and sued immediately in a federal district court to have the rules blocked. Federal District judge Gerhard Gesell did so in April. Gesell said he had made his decision partly on procedural grounds, but he also had harsh words for the regulations themselves, calling them "arbitrary and capricious" and the hotline "ill-considered."[32]

After HHS made some minor modifications, the final Baby Doe rules took effect on February 12, 1984. Less than two weeks later, however, they were rendered unenforceable by the decision of the Second Circuit Court of Appeals in a second "Baby Doe" case. This ruling, confirmed by the U.S. Supreme Court in a different case (*Bowen v. American Hospital Association et al.*) in 1986, denied the government access to the medical records that it would need in order to prove discrimination.

During its year or so of existence, the Baby Doe hotline received 1,633 calls, and the government squads (which had continued to operate even while the rules mandating them were being contested and revised) investigated 49 of these. In only six of those cases did the investigations result in babies receiving medical treatment that they might not otherwise have had. Adrian Peracchio reported in *Newsday*, a Long Island, New York, newspaper, that "in some [of these six] cases, intervention has saved a baby with a fair chance of living a useful life; in others, extraordinary surgical measures have given babies no more than a few extra days of life at enormous financial and emotional costs."[33]

Despite the court defeats, the federal government did not lose its determination to protect the lives of babies born with birth defects. In 1985 it established a new set of regulations that classified refusal of treatment for such babies as a form of child abuse or neglect. The new rules required any state receiving federal funds for prevention of child abuse to make sure that all infants received life-supporting treatment unless they were clearly terminally ill, irreversibly comatose, or suffering from conditions that made life support both futile and inhumane. Even in those cases, basic nutrition and liquids had to be provided. These rules are still in place, leading to the strange legal situation that food and water can be refused on behalf of an incompetent adult but not on behalf of a baby who is expected never to be competent.

The case of Claire Conroy in 1983 further expanded the types of medical treatment that could be refused on an incompetent person's behalf. Conroy, an 82-year-old woman, had suffered from diabetes, hardening of the arteries, and other debilitating conditions before falling into an irreversible semiconscious state somewhere between dementia and coma. She could breathe on her own but could not eat or drink, so her life was maintained by nutrition delivered to her stomach through a tube. Thomas Whittemore, her nephew and guardian, asked the doctor in her nursing home to remove her feeding tube, citing her independence and fear of doctors as evidence that she would not want to go on living in her present condition. The doctor refused on ethical grounds. Whittemore then appealed to the New Jersey Superior Court on January 24, 1983, for permission to order the tube removed.

Judge Reginald Stanton concluded that, given her medical condition, Conroy's life "had become impossibly and permanently burdensome for her" and that the tube could be removed.[34] Conroy died before the order could be carried out, but because of its importance as a precedent, her case continued on its way through the court system. The New Jersey Court of Appeals reversed the lower court, but in January 1985 the New Jersey Supreme Court reversed the appeals court. The state supreme court ruled 6 to 1 that "a competent person has the right to decline any medical treatment, including artificial feeding, and should retain that right when and if he becomes incompetent."[35] At the same time, however, the court said that this general ruling would not necessarily have applied to Conroy because she had not left a living will or other written document describing her wishes, and Whittemore had not, in the justices' opinion, provided enough evidence about her beliefs and opinions to allow a judgment on the matter.

Not only right-to-life supporters but others, including famed bioethicist Daniel Callahan, protested the Conroy decision, both because starvation and dehydration seemed such an inhumane way to die and because removal of food and water tubes, far more than removal of a respirator, seemed to hover on the line between letting die and actively killing. Similarly, some states that accepted living wills did not allow the stopping of food and hydration unless death was imminent. As time went on, however, more and more ethicists, physicians, and members of the public came to see feeding tubes as being just as artificial and "extraordinary" as respirators and removal of them just as acceptable. Callahan, for instance, expressed such an opinion in 1993.

The range of conditions under which one could refuse medical treatment or even ask for help in dying was broadened by another case, that of Elizabeth Bouvia in California. Bouvia had severe cerebral palsy, which left her with only a little use of her right hand, plus some control of her face; she also had arthritis, which caused her considerable pain. Nonetheless, her request for aid in dying shocked many because she was neither in uncontrollable agony nor terminally ill. She had simply decided that she no longer found her life worth living.

Bouvia's difficulties in life had included not only severe disability but the divorce of her parents, a stint in a children's home, a miscarriage, and a failing marriage. In September 1983, when she was 26 years old, she entered the emergency room of Riverside General Hospital in California and announced that she wanted to kill herself at the hospital— "just to be left alone and not bothered by friends or family or anyone else and to ultimately starve to death."[36]

Bouvia was admitted to the hospital's psychiatric ward as a voluntary patient. When Donald Fisher, the hospital's chief of psychiatry, refused to let her carry out her plan, she called a reporter and the American Civil Liberties Union (ACLU) and asked for help in gaining legal permission to refuse medical treatment—that is, her feeding tube. Her story was publicized, and it brought her a variety of visitors, including other disabled people and organizations such as Advocates for the Developmentally Disabled.

Bouvia's first court hearing was before John Hews, a probate judge. At the hearing, Fisher claimed that Bouvia would eventually change her mind about wanting to die and said he would force-feed her if necessary to keep her alive. In December 1983, Hews ruled that Fisher could carry out the force-feeding if Bouvia would not eat. The judge agreed that Bouvia was rational, sincere, and mentally competent but ruled against her because of the effect her death would have on the hospital staff and on other disabled people.

Bouvia appealed her case. Meanwhile, physicians, law professors, newspaper columnists, and others argued about it—and the force-feeding, a gruesome procedure, went on. She lost her first court appeal, and in April 1984 she left Riverside Hospital. She changed hospitals several times and eventually appeared in court again. Her second court hearing also denied her right to what the judge, Warren Deering, interpreted as assistance in suicide. In 1986, however, the California Court of Appeal reversed the second decision and affirmed Bouvia's right to refuse medical treatment, including a feeding tube, even if doing so shortened her life. "A desire to terminate one's life is probably the ultimate exercise of one's right to privacy," the judges wrote.[37]

In fact, however, Elizabeth Bouvia did not starve herself. In 1995 she was still living in a California hospital, supported by Medicaid, the combined state and federal program that pays for medical care for the poor. Morphine controlled the pain of her arthritis. She told a reporter that she spent most of her time watching television. "I wouldn't say I'm happy, but I'm physically comfortable, more comfortable than before. There is nothing really to do. I just kind of lay here."[38] She was still reported to be alive in 2002.

Introduction to Euthanasia

The impact of all these 1980s court cases, great as it was, was dwarfed by that of another case that began just as the decade was ending. Because it produced the U.S. Supreme Court's first ruling regarding a possible constitutional right to die, *Cruzan v. Director, Missouri Department of Health* became even more of a landmark than *In re Quinlan.*

This case, too, involved an unconscious young woman and her grieving family. The young woman, Nancy Beth Cruzan, was 25 years old when her car spun off the road on the night of January 11, 1983. Cruzan spent at least 15 minutes face down in a water-filled ditch before police and paramedics found her. They were able to restart her breathing and pulse, but lack of oxygen had permanently damaged her brain, and she never regained consciousness. Unlike Karen Quinlan, Cruzan was always able to breathe on her own, but she had to receive food and water through a tube.

After waiting four years for improvement that never came, Nancy's parents, Lester (known as Joe) and Joyce Cruzan, asked the nursing home caring for her to remove her feeding tube so that she could die. The facility refused. Like the Quinlans, the Cruzans then sought legal help.

Accompanied by William Colby, a young attorney, the Cruzans appeared in probate court in Jasper County, Missouri, early in 1988. The presiding judge, Charles E. Teel, granted them permission to have Nancy's feeding tube removed, but the state appealed. When the Missouri Supreme Court reviewed the decision in November 1988, it reversed the lower court on a vote of 4 to 3. The justices ruled that the only testimony provided regarding Nancy's feelings about medical treatment, a housemate's recollection of a conversation with her, did not meet the state's requirement for "clear and convincing" evidence of her wishes. Lacking such evidence, they said, the state's "unqualified interest in [preserving] life" should prevail.[39]

The Cruzans and Colby then took the matter to the U.S. Supreme Court. The high court agreed to hear the case, which the justices said was "the first case in which we have been squarely presented with the issue of whether the U.S. Constitution grants what is in common parlance referred to as a right to die."[40] The hearing took place on December 6, 1989, and the Court announced its decision on June 25, 1990. Its ruling was both a victory and a loss for the Cruzans and for the right-to-die movement as a whole.

"For purposes of this case, we assumed that the United States Constitution would grant a competent person a constitutionally protected right to refuse life-saving nutrition and hydration," Chief Justice William Rehnquist wrote in the majority opinion, stating also that such a right "can be inferred from our [the Supreme Court's] previous decisions."[41] The right also extended to presently incompetent people such as Cruzan, provided that they had made their wishes clear while they were competent. These statements were certainly a step forward for the right to die, albeit a tentative one.

On the other hand, the justices ruled that the Missouri law requiring "clear and convincing evidence" of an incompetent person's prior wishes was also constitutional because "there can be no gainsaying" the state's "interest in the protection and preservation of human life."[42] They agreed with the Missouri high court that such evidence had not been provided in the Cruzan case and held that Nancy Cruzan's feeding tube could not be removed unless convincing new evidence was produced. The justices returned the case to Missouri for further adjudication.

Fortunately for the Cruzans, several friends of Nancy's, who had known her only under her married name of Davis and therefore had not realized that the "Cruzan" case concerned her, came forward after the massive publicity surrounding the Supreme Court decision linked the names. In a new hearing in the Missouri lower court in November 1990, they reported conversations in which Cruzan had expressed a wish not to be kept alive by a respirator or artificial nutrition. This new evidence, combined with the Missouri attorney general's decision to withdraw the state from the case, allowed Judge Teel to reassert his original ruling that Cruzan's feeding tube could be removed. The tube was removed on December 14, 1990, and Cruzan died on December 26.

Like the Quinlan case, that of Nancy Cruzan had many repercussions. As with Quinlan, one of the first was a reemphasis on advance directives. In her concurring opinion on the case, Justice Sandra Day O'Connor recommended that people fill out such directives in order to avoid Nancy Cruzan's situation. This time the emphasis occurred at a federal as well as a state level. Inspired by the Cruzan case, Missouri Republican Senator John Danforth introduced the Patient Self-Determination Act, which required all hospitals and other health care delivery institutions receiving federal funds (primarily Medicare and Medicaid) to tell patients about their right to fill out advance directives and refuse medical care and to explain the state's laws and the institution's policies concerning such documents. The bill passed in November 1990 and became law on December 1, 1991. Many states also amended their living-will laws to permit withdrawal of food and water from patients in PVS if they had signed advance directives requesting this.

Even more important, the *Cruzan* decision firmly established the legality of refusing life-sustaining medical treatment, including nutrition—that is, passive euthanasia—at least for competent adults or incompetent ones who had left previous clear indications of their wishes. About 75 percent of the American public accepted that terminally ill people, or the families of irreversibly unconscious people who had left records of their desires, could ethically make such a choice.

THE 1990s: FOCUS ON PHYSICIAN-ASSISTED SUICIDE

In the last decade of the 20th century, the ante in the right-to-die debate was raised from termination of medical treatment (passive euthanasia) to the next most active form of aid in dying: physician-assisted suicide. The person who unquestionably did the most to bring this issue to public attention was a new player on the right-to-die scene, retired Michigan pathologist Jack Kevorkian. Abrasive and eccentric in personality, devotedly wooing the media, he made physician-assisted suicide impossible to ignore. Indeed, many Americans came to see his name as almost synonymous with it.

Kevorkian's crusade to make assisted suicide an accepted part of a physician's treatment options began in the late 1980s. By 1989 he was appearing on television talk shows, describing a machine he had built out of scrap metal that would allow terminally or incurably ill people to inject a sequence of sedatives and lethal drugs into themselves under the supervision of a physician like himself. Newsmagazines such as *Newsweek* also covered Kevorkian and his "Mercitron."

One of the people who heard about Kevorkian was Janet Adkins, a 54-year-old Oregon woman. Adkins was physically healthy, but she had just learned that she was in the early stages of Alzheimer's disease. Her husband said later that this news hit her "like a bombshell" because "her mind was her life."[43] Rather than face years of irreversible mental degeneration, Adkins, a member of the Hemlock Society, decided to seek Kevorkian's help in ending her life. Since Kevorkian would not leave his home state, Adkins, her husband, and her three sons flew to Michigan to meet him at his tiny apartment in Royal Oak, a suburb of Detroit.

After meeting with Adkins and her family for two hours, having her sign consent documents, and making a videotape of her requesting death, Kevorkian agreed to help her die. The following day—June 4, 1990—he set up his Mercitron and a cot in the back of his elderly Volkswagen camper van in a city park, having been unable to find any better place to go. There, just a few weeks before the Supreme Court ruled that Nancy Cruzan had at least a theoretical right to die, Janet Adkins became the first person to receive what he called "medicide" at the hands of Jack Kevorkian. She died six minutes after she pressed the button to start his machine.

Kevorkian's subsequent career in assisting suicide spanned the decade. He later claimed that he helped some 150 people to die. After November 1991, when Michigan suspended his medical license, Kevorkian could no longer obtain lethal drugs, so he began having clients breathe carbon monoxide through a mask instead of using the Mercitron. As with the earlier machine, the clients themselves activated the carbon monoxide system.

Kevorkian was put on trial for his activities four times during the early and middle years of the decade, but he was acquitted on three of those occasions, and the fourth was declared a mistrial. The acquittals were the result of a combination of the ambiguous legal status of assisted suicide in Michigan (the state did not have a clear, permanent law against this activity until late 1998); the work of Kevorkian's flamboyant and skillful lawyer, Geoffrey Fieger; and the fact that juries generally were in sympathy with Kevorkian, or at least with his clients and their families. "I don't feel it's our obligation to choose for someone else how much pain and suffering that they can go through," one juror said.[44]

Not surprisingly, opponents of assisted death have pictured Kevorkian as practically satanic. "Dr. Death" and "Jack the Dripper" were some of the more printable names given him. Kevorkian's arch-foe, Oakland County prosecutor Richard Thompson, called him "Jeffrey Dahmer in a lab coat."[45] Even among those who believed that physician-assisted suicide should be legalized, Kevorkian was controversial, to say the least. For instance, Derek Humphry, ironically echoing comments that the more conservative right-to-die organizations made about Humphry himself when he founded the Hemlock Society in 1980, praised Kevorkian for bringing the issue into the open but feared that his maverick methods would backfire and discredit the entire movement. Famed ethicist Arthur Caplan summarized these contradictory feelings when he wrote that Kevorkian's "place in the right-to-die debate should be as the John Brown of the movement—a loony fanatic who stirred a nation to confront an important issue."[46] (Kevorkian, for his part, said that Hemlock and similar groups were too cautious. He disdained their efforts to change laws, preferring instead to defy the legal system outright.)

Several features distinguished Kevorkian from most other right-to-die crusaders and offered easy points for foes to attack. First, many, if not most, of the people the Michigan doctor helped to die were not terminally ill, although most, like Adkins, were incurably so. They suffered from such conditions as amyotrophic lateral sclerosis (ALS, or Lou Gehrig's disease) and multiple sclerosis, both of which cause progressive loss of neurological function, in some cases accompanied by pain, dementia, or both. Many (though by no means all) people who were willing to accept physician-assisted dying for the terminally ill were not ready to accept it for those who were not near death, no matter how distressing their condition. Kevorkian's willingness to help such people die especially concerned advocates for the disabled, who had always been fearful that the nonterminally ill disabled would be pressured to kill themselves or even killed against their will if any kind of euthanasia became legal.

26

People on both sides of the euthanasia debate also criticized Kevorkian because he did not know his patients well and did not take any steps to confirm their diagnoses. This criticism became especially sharp when autopsies on several of the people he had helped to kill themselves showed no sign of physical disease at all. Such people presumably were suffering from depression, which probably could have been treated.

On the other hand, even Kevorkian's harshest critics had to admit that all the people on whom he committed his "medicide" left copious evidence (including videotapes) of their feelings of intolerable suffering and their desire to die, and all appeared competent, even if possibly depressed or misinformed. In no case had Kevorkian sought them out or tried to persuade them to kill themselves (though he also did not try to dissuade them or suggest alternative solutions to their medical problems), nor had he accepted money from them. The family members of many of Kevorkian's clients supported their intention and defended Kevorkian fiercely. They and some others saw him as a true deliverer of mercy—as one said, "an angel."[47]

Soon after Kevorkian began making headlines, a more moderate spokesman for physician-assisted suicide entered the scene. He was Timothy E. Quill, then a 42-year-old internist working for the University of Rochester (New York) School of Medicine and Genesee Hospital. In a March 1991 issue of the prestigious *New England Journal of Medicine*, Quill described how he had prescribed a fatal dose of barbiturates for "Diane," a 45-year-old woman with acute leukemia, knowing she planned to use them to kill herself. "I wrote the prescription with an uneasy feeling about the boundaries I was exploring—spiritual, legal, professional and personal," Quill wrote. "Yet I also felt strongly that I was setting [Diane] free to get the most out of the time she had left, and to maintain dignity and control on her own terms until her death."[48]

Unlike most of Kevorkian's clients, Diane was terminally ill, and unlike Kevorkian, Quill had known his patient for eight years. Quill wrote that the only thing he ultimately regretted was that, because assisting suicide was illegal, neither he nor Diane's family had been able to be with her when she died. He decided to write his article, he said later, to bring the issue into the open and present an alternative approach to that of the notorious Kevorkian. In doing so he risked a prison term of five to 15 years.

At first the Rochester district attorney declined to prosecute Quill because the article did not fully identify Diane. After an anonymous tipster revealed Diane's last name (Trumbull) and the location of her body and an autopsy on her revealed a lethal dose of barbiturates, however, the district attorney felt he had to take the case before a grand jury. The grand jury met on July 22, 1991, but, after four days of testimony and deliberation, it decided not to indict Quill.

Quill's experience with Diane and the reaction to his article turned him into a vigorous advocate for physician-assisted suicide, though he believes it should be a last resort called upon only after all attempts at palliative or other treatment have failed. "I'm not really an advocate of assisted suicide," he has said. "I'm an advocate of not abandoning people."[49] He has expressed his ideas in several books as well as innumerable articles and lectures. He was the chief plaintiff in one of two right-to-die cases that reached the U.S. Supreme Court in 1997.

Because Quill lacked Kevorkian's eccentricity and had better medical credentials (Kevorkian had never actually treated patients, whereas Quill did so regularly), many right-to-die supporters and members of the general public found Quill a much more acceptable advocate for the cause. Derek Humphry, for example, wrote that "Quill presented the gentle, thoughtful face of compassionate medicine. . . . His philosophy seemed to be the one most likely to succeed in the long term in the United States."[50] Nursing ethics specialist Carol Tauer said, "Quill enjoys great respect even among hospice people, though they don't agree with him on suicide."[51]

Unlike Kevorkian, who made a point of saying that he did not care whether his actions were illegal, Quill focused his efforts on trying to change state laws that banned physician-assisted death. He shared this aim with many others in the right-to-die movement, particularly Derek Humphry, whose Hemlock Society spearheaded several attempts to legalize physician-assisted death during the early 1990s. All of these legalization efforts took place on the West Coast, a part of the country known for its independence and liberal politics, and all were in states where the people could vote directly on laws through initiative measures. Indeed, Oregon, the state in which the society's work finally succeeded, had originated the initiative process in 1902.

Humphry himself was living in Eugene, Oregon, at the time of these voter contests. He was able to help finance them partly because of an extremely successful book that he published in 1991. This book, *Final Exit*, was much more explicit in its instructions about what Humphry called "'nuts and bolts' of voluntary euthanasia" than *Let Me Die Before I Wake*; for instance, it had a lethal dosage table that covered 18 different drugs.[52] *Final Exit* not only appeared on the *New York Times* bestseller list—a phenomenal achievement for a privately published book—but remained there for 18 weeks. It reached the number-one spot on the list on August 18, 1991.

The chief opponents of these and all other attempts to legalize physician-assisted suicide and euthanasia were, and are, the Catholic Church, Protestant fundamentalist groups, and most especially the Right to Life movement, which had been formed in response to the legalization of abortion. These groups have vowed to protect the "sanctity of life" at life's end as well as its beginning. The American Medical Association, the American Nurses Association, and other large medical groups also have usually opposed legalization of physician-assisted suicide.

The Hemlock Society's plans to legalize physician-assisted death began even before the success of *Final Exit*. Around 1985, Robert Risley and Michael White, two Los Angeles law partners who were also Hemlock Society members, began drafting a model law that they called the Humane and Dignified Death Act. Humphry (then still living in Los Angeles) and Curt Garbesi, a member of the society's board and a professor at Loyola Law School in Los Angeles, soon joined them. The final model, published in 1986, would have legalized not only physician-assisted suicide but also voluntary euthanasia, and it would have made these options available not only to terminally ill but also to irreversibly but nonterminally ill adults, such as those who had ALS. It would even have permitted competent people with early Alzheimer's disease to nominate a surrogate to end their lives when they became incompetent. Right-to-die advocates were to learn that such a law represented far more changes than the American public was willing to accept.

As a tax-exempt organization, the Hemlock Society could not work for political change, so it created a new group, Americans Against Human Suffering, to be its political action arm. This group tried to put the proposed law on the California ballot as an initiative in 1988, but it was able to gather only about a third of the signatures needed to qualify. The experience taught Humphry and his supporters useful, albeit painful, lessons about managing a political campaign and about which portions of their proposal (such as the Alzheimer's provision) were least acceptable to voters.

Applying this hard-won knowledge, the group was more successful in a second initiative campaign in Washington state in 1990–91. This time, employing a signature-gathering firm, it collected almost twice the number of signatures it needed to qualify its measure for the ballot. Polls taken early in the campaign showed that a majority of those polled favored the measure, which was known as Measure 119 or the Death with Dignity Act. When Washingtonians cast their votes on November 4, 1991, however, the measure was defeated, 54 to 46 percent. It had proved vulnerable to attack because it lacked important safeguards, such as a required evaluation for depression and a waiting period between a request for death and granting of the request.

The next attempt to legalize physician-assisted suicide, in 1992, again took place in California. The result was much the same as in Washington: an early lead, followed by massive opposition and failure at the voting booth, 54 to 46 percent. Although better drafted than the Washington initiative, the California measure, Proposition 161, still lacked some of the safeguards that voters demanded. Fund-raising problems and dissention among the groups supporting the measure may also have contributed to its defeat.

The final contest took place in Oregon in 1994. This time, having learned what the public would and would not accept, right-to-die groups moved to legalize only physician-assisted suicide, not euthanasia. This eliminated the image of a stealthy doctor with a hypodermic that apparently had terrified many voters in previous campaigns. The measure also contained more safeguards than any of the previous ones, including a requirement for two opinions about the person's medical condition, psychiatric evaluation if depression or other mental problems are suspected, and a waiting period of 15 days between a patient's initial and final requests for a fatal prescription. Technically, the proposal did not even legalize assisted suicide. Rather, it defined activities that fit within its guidelines as not being assisted suicide and, therefore, not breaking the state's existing law against assisting a suicide.

This time the right-to-die supporters' efforts were successful. On November 8, 1994, Oregon Measure 16, also known as the Death with Dignity Act, passed, although just barely: 52 percent in favor to 48 percent against. Oregon thus became the first state in the country to legalize actively assisted dying.

Such actions did not stay legal for long, however. Lawyers for the National Right to Life Committee persuaded Michael Hogan, a federal district court judge in Salem, to pass a temporary restraining order that blocked the law just six hours before it was scheduled to go into effect on December 5. They claimed that the law was unconstitutional because it denied terminally ill Oregonians the protection of laws intended to prevent suicide and forbid manslaughter. Five plaintiffs also joined the appeal, claiming that they would be injured if the law took effect. Hogan ruled the law unconstitutional on August 4, 1995. The law's supporters immediately appealed the ruling.

In the first half of 1997, while the Oregon law was still on hold, the U.S. Supreme Court ruled on two cases that forced it to go beyond the refusal of medical treatment dealt with in *Cruzan* and address the question of actively hastened death for the first time. One case had begun in Washington state in 1994, where it was known as *Compassion in Dying et al. v. State of Washington* and, later, *Glucksberg v. Washington*. (Compassion in Dying was a Seattle-based organization, founded in 1993 to help competent, terminally ill adults achieve a "good death," including advising them about assisted suicide if appropriate. Glucksberg was cancer specialist Harold Glucksberg, one of five physicians who agreed to be plaintiffs in Compassion in Dying's suit.) The other came from New York, where it was first filed in the federal court for the southern district on July 29, 1994, as *Timothy E. Quill v. G. Oliver Koppell* or *Quill v. N.Y. Attorney General.* (Quill was the physician and right-to-die advocate who had achieved fame after describing his role in the assisted suicide of "Diane." Koppell was New York's state attorney general at the time of the first filing; his name was later replaced in the suit by that of Dennis C. Vacco, the subsequent state attorney general. The case is usually referred to as *Quill v. Vacco.*) In both cases, a group of physicians and a group of terminally ill patients filed suit against the state, claiming that the state's law against assisted suicide was unconstitutional because it violated the rights guaranteed under both the Due Process Clause and the Equal Protection Clause of the Fourteenth Amendment. Compassion in Dying sponsored and helped to pay for the litigation in both cases.

Ruling on *Compassion in Dying et al. v. State of Washington* in Seattle on May 3, 1994, Barbara Rothstein, chief judge of the federal district court for western Washington, held that the Washington law violated both clauses of the Fourteenth Amendment and was therefore unconstitutional. The state appealed the decision, however, and on March 9, 1995, a three-judge panel of the federal Ninth Circuit Court of Appeals, whose decisions are binding in Alaska, Arizona, California, Hawaii, Idaho, Montana, Nevada, Oregon, and Washington, reversed the lower court's ruling by a vote of two to one.

As stated by Judge John T. Noonan, Jr., the majority of the appeals court panel held that assisted suicide was not protected by either the Due Process Clause or the Equal Protection Clause. If a right to ask for assistance in suicide was part of the "liberty interests" protected by the Due Process Clause, Noonan wrote, it could not be limited to the terminally ill but would have to apply to every competent adult, a notion that the judges found ridiculous. The panel's decision cited five important state interests that they said outweighed any personal right to physician-assisted suicide, including protection of the disabled, elderly, poor, and minorities from pressure to kill themselves and prevention of physicians from taking on the role of killers. The judges also denied that refusing medical treatment and requesting assistance in suicide were equivalent acts that deserved equal protection.

Because both Noonan and Diarmuid F. O'Scannlain, the judge who concurred with him, were Catholics, the plaintiffs claimed possible religious bias and asked for a rehearing. On October 26, 1995, therefore, the full 11-judge panel of the appeals court heard the case, and on March 6, 1996, they ruled 8 to 3 to reverse Noonan's decision. Stephen Reinhardt, a judge famous for liberal rulings that the Supreme Court often later reversed, wrote the appeals court's 112-page majority opinion. Reinhardt held that the Supreme Court's two rulings about abortion, *Roe v. Wade* (1973) and *Planned Parenthood v. Casey* (1992), established precedents for considering the right to make private decisions about one's body to be part of protected liberty interests. Nothing, he wrote, could be more private and personal than a decision about when and how to end one's life. By abridging the freedom to make that decision, he claimed, the Washington law violated the Due Process Clause and was unconstitutional.

Ruling on *Quill v. Vacco*, New York federal judge Thomas Griesa declared on December 15, 1994, that there was no constitutional right to assisted suicide and that the New York laws forbidding this activity therefore were constitutional. Neither court decisions permitting abortion nor those permitting termination of medical treatment applied, he wrote. When Quill and the other plaintiffs appealed, however, three judges of the Second Circuit Court of Appeals, whose decisions cover New York, Connecticut, and Vermont, came to the same conclusion on April 2, 1996, that Reinhardt and his fellow Ninth Circuit Court judges had a month earlier.

The Second Circuit Court's opinion, written by Judge Roger J. Miner, followed a line of reasoning different from Reinhardt's. The New York court based its decision on a different clause of the Fourteenth Amendment, which guarantees equal protection under the law for groups that are similarly situated. The 1991 *Cruzan* case, Miner wrote, had established that patients and their surrogates had the right to refuse medical treatment, even if doing so would end their lives. The circuit court judges maintained that there was no significant distinction between, say, removing a respirator and giving a lethal prescription to a terminally ill person. Therefore, they concluded, people who were terminally ill but not on life support should have the same right to end their lives as people who could do so by refusing life-sustaining medical treatment.

The combination of these two circuit court decisions theoretically made assisted suicide available to qualifying people in about a quarter of the United States. Shortly after the decisions were handed down, however, Supreme Court Justice Sandra Day O'Connor blocked doctors in the affected states from helping anyone die until the high court decided whether to hear the cases, which the respective states had appealed. On October 1, 1996, the Court agreed to hear the two cases (now *Washington v. Glucksberg* and *New York v. Quill*) together.

On January 8, 1997, the Supreme Court heard two hours of oral arguments, one hour for each case. The time was divided evenly between pro and con presentations, both frequently interrupted by questions from the justices. These arguments were supplemented by 60 *amicus curiae* (friend of the court) briefs, filed by individuals ranging from the solicitor general of the United States (expressing the Clinton administration's opposition to legalization of assisted suicide) to six well-known philosophers (offering arguments in favor of legalization) and groups ranging from the Hemlock

Society to the militant disabled group Not Dead Yet. Some of these groups staged demonstrations outside the courthouse as well.

From the beginning, it was clear to even the most ardent supporters of assisted suicide that the Supreme Court was unlikely to agree with their claim that there was a "constitutional right to die." For one thing, the relatively conservative justices had no desire to preempt a societal debate that was obviously just beginning, as the Court had been widely criticized for doing with the abortion issue. The justices also saw no compelling reason to overturn laws that existed in almost every state. Few observers were surprised, therefore, that the Court's unanimous decision, released on June 26, 1997, overturned both appeals court rulings and upheld the constitutionality of the Washington and New York laws. The justices ruled out both arguments that the Fourteenth Amendment could be construed as including a right to die.

In *Washington v. Glucksberg,* the high court ruled unanimously that there was no liberty interest in the right to commit suicide or to be assisted in doing so, as the Ninth Circuit court had implied. On the contrary, the justices said, "We are confronted with a consistent and almost universal tradition that has long rejected the asserted right, and continues explicitly to reject it today, even for terminally ill, mentally competent adults."[53] The Court reaffirmed the state's interest in preserving life and preventing suicide and accepted the view of the American Medical Association and others that assisted suicide was incompatible with a physician's healing role. It agreed with disabled groups and others that if physician-assisted suicide was legalized, vulnerable people might be pressured into accepting it for economic or other reasons and that the practice might eventually lead to involuntary euthanasia.

Similarly, in *New York v. Quill,* the Supreme Court affirmed that the distinction between refusing medical treatment and asking for assistance in suicide was "both important and logical; it is certainly rational."[54] The distinction was based on the physician's purpose or intent in each case. Groups demanding these two actions, therefore, were not similarly situated and did not need to be treated equally.

The Supreme Court's rulings were not a complete defeat for right-to-die forces, however. Nothing in the rulings indicated that laws permitting assisted suicide, such as Oregon's, were any less constitutional than those forbidding it. The justices also required all states to ensure that any laws against physician-assisted suicide not prohibit or unreasonably burden provision of adequate palliative care, especially aggressive alleviation of pain and other physical symptoms, even if such treatment hastened patients' deaths. In concurring opinions, furthermore, five of the eight justices left the door open for finding a limited right to assisted suicide in future cases.

Primarily, the high court stated that it wished to return the issue to the states for further debate in individual legislatures and experimentation with different laws.

While the Supreme Court was still deliberating its two right-to-die cases, supporters of Oregon's stalled assisted suicide law won a victory. On February 28, 1997, a three-judge panel of the U.S. Ninth Circuit Court of Appeals, the same court that had declared the Washington law against assisted suicide unconstitutional, voted 3-0 to reverse Michael Hogan's ruling against the Oregon law. The appeals court stated that the plaintiffs had failed to prove that they would be harmed by the law. James Bopp, the chief attorney for the National Right to Life Committee, appealed to the U.S. Supreme Court, but on October 14 the high court announced its refusal to hear the case.

Having survived all its judicial challenges, the Oregon law finally took effect on October 27, 1997. By then, however, its opponents, after failing to persuade the state legislature to repeal it, had succeeded in putting a repeal measure on the November ballot. Some legislators and Governor John Kitzhaber had protested that asking citizens to vote again on a law that had not been altered not only was highly unusual but smacked of insulting their intelligence ("We shall be remembered as the legislature which stuck its finger in the eye of the voters," said Rep. Floyd Prozanski), but Measure 51 went on the ballot anyway.[55]

Rather than attacking the morality of assisted suicide directly, the Measure 51 advertising campaign stressed what it claimed were flaws in the law. It also played up the chance that suicides, even with physician-prescribed drugs, would fail, leaving patients worse off than before. In spite of these efforts, the attempt to reverse the law backfired. Oregon voters not only defeated Measure 51 but did so by 60 percent to 40 percent, a much wider margin than the one by which Measure 16 had passed in 1994.

The country had a chance to study the early results of the controversial law when the Oregon Health Department published a report in the February 18, 1999, *New England Journal of Medicine* describing the law's use during its first year. The report stated that during that time, 23 people had received lethal prescriptions and 15 had used them to commit suicide. Six of the remaining eight people died of their disease before using the medication, and two were still alive as of January 1. Eighteen of the 23 had cancer. The average age of the patients was 69 years. In those who had died from the ingested drugs, unconsciousness had occurred within five minutes and death within an hour for most, although one took 11 hours to die. There were no failed suicide attempts in the group.

Both sides of the right-to-die issue claimed confirmation for their views in this report. "It's what we expected—a year of impeccable implementation," said Barbara Coombs Lee, coauthor and chief sponsor of the Oregon law.[56] She and other supporters of the law pointed out that, contrary to some opponents' predictions, it had not brought on a massive number of suicides. The torturous failed suicides dramatized in the 1997 preelection campaign also had not occurred.

On the other hand, opponents of physician-assisted suicide such as psychiatrist Herbert Hendin, head of the American Foundation for Suicide Prevention in New York City, noted that information in the report had come only from the physicians who wrote the lethal prescriptions. Hendin said there was no way to tell whether the doctors had told the whole truth or whether other assisted suicides that were less in compliance with the guidelines had gone unreported. Ezekiel Emanuel, a specialist in end-of-life ethics and another critic of physician-assisted suicide, said the report showed that

> *either there is very little demand and hence little need for legalized physician-assisted suicide in the United States or there is a lot of euthanasia and physician-assisted suicide going on outside the law, undermining the notion that legalization is the only way to ensure regulation and enforcement of safeguards.*[57]

Furthermore, although the Oregon report mentions no complications during assisted suicides, a study from the Netherlands (where assisted suicide and euthanasia, though technically illegal, were widely and openly practiced), summarized in the February 24, 2000, issue of the *New England Journal of Medicine*, suggested that the clean record was unlikely to continue if the number of suicides grew. Dutch physicians reported that complications, including vomiting and failure to induce a coma, occurred in 7 percent of 114 assisted-suicide cases and delayed death in 16 percent. Physicians, which Dutch standards (unlike the rules in Oregon) require to be present during assisted suicides, had to step in and administer lethal medication directly in 21 cases that began as assisted suicides.

Meanwhile, having failed to block the Oregon law in the courtroom and at the ballot box, its opponents have tried to do so through the federal government. These efforts bore their first fruit in April 1997, before the second vote on the law occurred. In that month Congress passed the Assisted Suicide Funding Restriction Act, which prohibited federally funded health programs from participating in assisted suicide. To be sure, the *Congressional Quarterly Weekly Report* for March 22, describing hearings on the bill, noted that the measure would have no current impact because using federal money to fund assisted suicide was already prohibited.

Right to Die and Euthanasia

On November 5, 1997, the day after the Oregon election, federal Drug Enforcement Administrator Thomas Constantine wrote to the Senate and House Judiciary Committees that, state law or no, prescribing controlled substances (which include most, if not all, of the powerful narcotics likely to be prescribed by doctors to end life) to help people kill themselves violated the Controlled Substances Act (1971) because suicide was not a legitimate medical purpose for using such drugs. He warned that physicians who made prescriptions for suicide under the Oregon law therefore could lose their registration, which would prevent them from prescribing controlled substances for any purpose, even if they followed the state guidelines meticulously.

Constantine's statement effectively put the Death with Dignity Act on hold yet again until June 5, 1998, when U.S. Attorney General Janet Reno overruled Constantine, stating that doctors who followed the state law would not be liable to federal prosecution. In response to Reno's statement, which opponents of physician-assisted suicide felt had overstepped her authority, Don Nickles (R-Okla.) introduced a bill termed the Lethal Drug Abuse Prevention Act (S. 2151) into the Senate the following month. Henry Hyde (R-Ill.) introduced the same bill (H.R. 4006) into the House. If passed, these bills would have amended the Controlled Substances Act to require federal prosecution of doctors who prescribed a controlled substance with the knowledge that it would be used for suicide, even if the doctors lived in a state where such an act was legal.

The Nickles and Hyde bills drew strong opposition, not only from supporters of physician-assisted suicide but from a coalition of medical and palliative care organizations that included the American Medical Association and the National Hospice Organization. These groups protested that the proposed law would make control of severe pain difficult or impossible because doses of narcotics high enough to alleviate such pain might also shorten or even end patient's lives. This "double effect" is currently permitted, legally as well as in most religions, as long as the doctor's intention is not to cause death. If the Lethal Drug Abuse Prevention Act was passed, however, critics said that doctors would not dare to prescribe such high doses for fear of having their motives put under intense scrutiny.

Chiefly because of this opposition, the Nickles and Hyde bills were withdrawn on October 14, 1998. The bills' supporters then set about redrafting them to meet the objections of the hospice groups. Among other things, they added a $5 million annual appropriation for improvements in pain management and palliative care. After seeing the changes, the American Hospice Association, the American Medical Association, and most of the other opposing groups declared themselves basically satisfied. In June 1999, Nickles and Hyde reintroduced the bills (S. 1272 and H. R. 2260) under the new title of the Pain Relief Promotion Act.

On October 27, 1999, the House of Representatives passed its part of the act by a resounding vote of 271 to 156. However, physicians protested its harsh penalties—ranging from a mandatory minimum of 20 years in prison to possible life imprisonment—and its emphasis on the difficult task of determining a doctor's precise motive. In addition, the Clinton administration, although opposed to physician-assisted suicide, protested the bill's effect on states' right to legislate. Although the Senate Judiciary Committee approved the Senate's version of the bill in April 2000, efforts by Oregon Democratic senator Ron Wyden and others kept the bill from being passed by the full Senate during the fall term. The Pain Relief Promotion Act was not reintroduced in later terms.

In spite of the bill's eventual defeat, House passage of the Pain Relief Promotion Act was not the only sign that support for assisted death was cooling at the end of the century. Another was that the luck of the controversial Jack Kevorkian finally ran out. On September 17, 1998, Kevorkian (whose support in public opinion polls had been dropping throughout the decade) administered a lethal injection to 52-year-old Thomas Youk, who suffered from ALS. Kevorkian captured most of the experience, including Youk's request for death and his own giving of the injection, on videotape. He then sent the tape to CBS's news program *60 Minutes*, which broadcast it to more than 15 million households on November 22.

On the Youk tape and in interviews, Kevorkian dared Michigan to prosecute him for euthanasia. Authorities obliged, charging Kevorkian with first-degree murder on November 25. A permanent law against assisted suicide had taken effect in the state at the beginning of September, but prosecutors said that it did not apply in this case because the tape clearly showed that Kevorkian, not Youk, had administered the fatal drug dose.

From a legal standpoint, that fact was the most important difference between the Youk trial and Kevorkian's three earlier ones, in which he had been acquitted. Two other factors also made unusual difficulties for the maverick doctor in this trial. One was the broadcasting of the tape, which had offended many people, even those who supported the idea of physician-assisted suicide. The other was Kevorkian's decision to represent himself in the courtroom. "There are certain points I can bring out better than any attorney," he told Oakland County Circuit Court judge Jessica Cooper in a pretrial session. "I've been planning this all along."[58]

Kevorkian's murder trial began on March 22, 1999. According to a *Washington Post* news account, Cooper often seemed "exasperated" by Kevorkian's "hesitant and at times obviously befuddled" defense and repeatedly advised him to let a lawyer represent him.[59] Worse still from Kevorkian's point of view, Cooper refused to let him introduce evidence of Youk's wish to die or to present the testimony of Youk's wife, Melody, about his suffering; she ruled that neither Youk's intentions nor Kevorkian's were relevant. Thus, although Kevorkian tried in his closing argument to produce the emotional effects that had helped him to win acquittals before, he was left with little legal defense.

On March 26, after 13 hours of deliberation, the jury found Kevorkian guilty of second-degree murder (rather than the first-degree murder charge demanded by the prosecutor) and delivery of a controlled substance. Cooper sentenced Kevorkian on April 13 to 10 to 25 years in prison for the crimes. "This trial was not about the political or moral correctness of euthanasia," she told him. "It was all about you, sir. . . . You had the audacity to go on national television, show the world what you did and dare the legal system to stop you. Well, sir, consider yourself stopped."[60] The 70-year-old Kevorkian was sent to Southern Michigan Prison in Jackson. He will not be eligible for parole until June 2007. Kevorkian has asked the Michigan parole board several times to commute his sentence on the grounds that he is dying of liver disease, but the parole board has always denied the request, most recently in June 2006.

THE EARLY 2000s: OLD ISSUES, POWERFUL EMOTIONS

Discussions of the right to die in the early 2000s (through 2006) broke little new ground in terms of ethical or practical arguments. Supporters continued to speak of autonomy, "dignity," and the desire to spare themselves or loved ones needless suffering and physical or mental degeneration. Opponents stressed the importance of preserving all human life without judging its quality and warned that the disabled, elderly, or other vulnerable groups might be forced by economic or psychological pressure into accepting a "duty to die." Groups on both sides of the issue called for better care of the dying, chronically ill, and disabled, but the increasing cost of health care combined with the growing needs of an aging population made funding for such care hard to obtain.

What the debate lacked in intellectual advancement, it more than made up for in emotion. The most intense feelings were aroused by the case of Theresa Marie (Terri) Schindler Schiavo, a Florida woman who made headlines around the world in early 2005. Schiavo's story had begun much earlier, on February 25, 1990, when her heart stopped beating because of a chemical imbalance in her body, possibly resulting from an eating disorder. She was 26 years old at the time. Schiavo was revived, but lack of oxygen during her cardiac arrest had severely damaged her brain, and she never regained consciousness. After a month, doctors concluded that she was in a persistent vegetative state (PVS).

Michael Schiavo, Terri's husband, and her parents, Robert and Mary Schindler, worked together to manage Terri's care at first, but in early 1993 they began to disagree about the direction that the care should take. Michael Schiavo had come to believe that his wife's condition would never improve, but the Schindlers still thought that aggressive treatment could restore Terri to some degree of function. In 1994, the Schindlers filed the first of many lawsuits attempting to take legal guardianship of Terri from Michael Schiavo. Their efforts were unsuccessful.

The family battle escalated in 1998, when Michael Schiavo petitioned a Florida court to let him remove the tube that provided Terri with food and water. Terri had left no advance directives, but Schiavo claimed that she had said she would not want to be kept alive "on anything artificial." The Schindlers bitterly opposed Schiavo's proposal, saying that Terri's religious beliefs (she and the Schindlers were devout Catholics) would have kept her from accepting hastened death. They also produced videotapes that, they believed, proved that Terri was at least dimly conscious of her environment and, therefore, was not in a persistent vegetative state.

After several years of legal arguments and judicial reviews, circuit court judge George Greer approved Michael Schiavo's request on February 11, 2000, but Terri's tube remained in place while the Schindlers appealed Greer's ruling. The Florida Supreme Court denied their appeal early in 2001, and the U.S. Supreme Court declined to hear the case.

As their war in the courts continued during the next few years, both sides of this unhappy family acquired vocal and powerful supporters. The ACLU and other supporters of individual rights in general and the right to die in particular sided with Michael Schiavo, whereas disabled-rights activists and the conservative Christian "right-to-life" movement backed the Schindlers. Moved by the emotional appeals of these latter groups, the Florida legislature passed a special law dealing exclusively with the case on October 21, 2003. "Terri's Law," as it was known, authorized Florida's governor, Jeb Bush (brother of President George W. Bush), to order the reinsertion of Terri's feeding tube, which had been removed six days before. Bush gave his order, but the Florida Supreme Court unanimously declared Terri's Law unconstitutional on September 23, 2004.

On March 20, 2004, just as publicity and feelings on the Schiavo case were building, Pope John Paul II issued an official statement (allocution) to an international congress on "Life-Sustaining Treatments and Vegetative State: Scientific and Ethical Dilemmas," which clarified the Catholic position regarding situations like Terri's. The allocution, "Care for Patients in a 'Permanent' Vegetative State," classified provision of food and water, even through a tube, as "a natural means of preserving life, not a medical act."[61] It therefore was "normal care," and Catholics had a "moral obligation" not to deny it to anyone, including people in a permanent vegetative state (PVS).[62] Some commentators, including renowned Catholic theologian Thomas A. Shannon, professor of religion and social ethics at Worcester Polytechnic Institute in Massachusetts and author of many books on bioethics, said that this statement went against earlier Catholic teaching, which would have determined whether artificial nutrition and hydration were "ordinary care" (which must be provided) or "extraordinary care" (which can be discontinued) by considering whether their burden to a particular patient outweighed their benefits.

The endgame of the Schiavo story played out on newspaper front pages and in wrenching television footage during the early months of 2005. On January 24, the U.S. Supreme Court declined to hear Governor Bush's appeal against the Florida Supreme Court's decision. Judge Greer again authorized removal of Terri Schiavo's feeding tube, and the tube was taken out on March 18.

This time, no less than the U.S. Congress stepped in. After an all-night emergency session on March 21, the legislators passed a bill (An Act for the Relief of Parents of Theresa Marie Schiavo) that gave jurisdiction of the Schiavo case to the federal courts, and President Bush flew back from a vacation in Texas to sign it. ("In extraordinary circumstances like this, it is wise to always err on the side of life," he said.[63]) The change of jurisdiction did not affect the case's outcome, however. A federal district judge and a three-judge panel of the 11th Circuit Court of Appeals rejected the Schindlers' request to have the tube reinserted, and the Supreme Court again refused to intervene.

On March 31, ending weeks of vigils and impassioned statements outside her hospice (the time was just before Easter, and protesters supporting the Schindlers compared Terri to Christ), Terri Schiavo died. The results of an exhaustive autopsy, released on June 15, showed that the centers of consciousness in her brain had been completely destroyed. The autopsy also revealed that she was blind, so she could not have deliberately followed people or objects with her eyes, as her parents had claimed.

Legally, the Schiavo case brought up no issues that had not been settled long before in the rulings concerning Karen Quinlan and Nancy Cruzan. As what *Los Angeles Times* reporter John-Thor Dahlburg called "one of the most celebrated right-to-die cases in U.S. history," however, it certainly revealed the depth of feelings for and against assisted death.[64] It also demonstrated, once again, the damage that could result when a formerly competent adult left no clear indications about the kind of treatment he or she would want if competence ended. The California Medical Association reported that during the last two weeks of the Schiavo saga its web site, which contains forms and information on advance health care directives, received an average of 1,750 hits a day, as compared to a usual average of 50 hits.

The almost unprecedented intervention of the legislative and executive branches at both the state and the federal level also drew strong reactions. Whatever public opinion about Terri Schiavo's treatment might have been, polls taken at the time showed that a high percentage of those polled—more than 80 percent in some cases—felt that the government should not involve itself in such private decisions.

A few years earlier, a California Supreme Court decision in a case resulting from another family conflict, *Wendland v. Wendland,* had highlighted the somewhat obscure medical distinction between a persistent vegetative state and a so-called minimally conscious state. A minimally conscious state can result from defects or damage at birth, severe head injuries, or the last stages of neurodegenerative illnesses such as Alzheimer's disease. People whose minimally conscious state results from recent head injuries sometimes gain further improvements in brain functioning, but major recovery is considered unlikely after a year. Unlike people in a persistent vegetative state, such as Terri Schiavo, people in a minimally conscious state are aware of themselves and their environment to a limited degree. For example, their eyes can track moving objects consistently. They can communicate a little and can feel pain.

Robert Wendland, a California resident, was left minimally conscious by head injuries resulting from a car accident in 1993. Like Schiavo, he was kept alive by food and water sent to his stomach through a tube, but unlike Schiavo, he was said to be able to operate a wheelchair, to signal "yes" and "no" with a communication board, and even to paint and play wheelchair bowling. He had not left an advance directive or designated a surrogate to make medical decisions for him.

In 1995, Wendland's wife, Rose, petitioned a trial court to allow removal of his feeding tube. Like Michael Schiavo, she claimed that her husband had said on several occasions that he would not want to be kept alive artificially if he were permanently unconscious or severely disabled. (The Wendlands' daughter, Katie, and Robert Wendland's brother reported similar conversations.) Also similar to the Schiavo case, Rose Wendland's actions were opposed by Robert Wendland's mother and sister. The court appointed Rose Wendland as her husband's conservator but denied her request regarding the feeding tube, claiming that she had not supplied sufficient evidence of Wendland's wishes. The state court of appeals reversed the lower court's decision on February 24, 2000.

On August 9, 2001, the California Supreme Court ruled that Rose Wendland could not have Robert Wendland's feeding tube removed because she had not provided clear and convincing evidence that he would have wanted such an action or that removing the tube was in his best interest. "Clear and convincing evidence" was the same strict standard of proof that a Missouri court had required of Nancy Cruzan's family in the late 1980s. The California court said that "a proponderance of the evidence," a less rigorous requirement, would have been acceptable for terminally ill or permanently unconscious patients, but the more demanding standard was necessary for Robert Wendland because he was minimally conscious and, therefore, had a stronger interest in avoiding a possibly harmful decision. The court also invoked the more severe standard because Wendland had not left written evidence of his wishes or chosen his own surrogate decision maker.

The case was academic for the Wendland family by the time of the court ruling because Robert Wendland had died of pneumonia in July, but the decision was important because it specified the level of proof that would be required in future California cases involving minimally conscious patients who have neither left advance directives nor chosen surrogates. Courts in some other states have reached similar conclusions, setting the stage for battles over the health care of minimally conscious people that could prove even harder to settle than the Schiavo case.

The only right-to-die case to reach the U.S. Supreme Court during this period was a continuation of earlier federal attempts to (in effect) nullify the Oregon assisted-suicide law by means of the Controlled Substances Act (CSA). Citing a 2001 Supreme Court ruling that invalidated a California law permitting use of marijuana for medical purposes, John Ashcroft, then-U.S. attorney general, issued a memorandum to Asa Hutchinson, the head of the Drug Enforcement Administration, on November 6, 2001, that essentially reinstated the order that Thomas Constantine had made in November 1997 and that Janet Reno had revoked in 1998.

Like Constantine, Ashcroft, drawing on an opinion by the U.S. Office of Legal Counsel, concluded that assisting suicide was not a "legitimate medical purpose" within the meaning of the CSA and, therefore, physicians who prescribed controlled substances in accordance with the Oregon law could be prosecuted for violation of the act and lose their federal prescription licenses. The same applied to pharmacists who knowingly filled such prescriptions.

Oregon attorney general Hardy Myers and others filed suit in federal court to block Ashcroft's order on November 20, 2001, and U.S. district judge Robert Jones of Portland issued a temporary restraining order against Ashcroft. Jones made the injunction permanent on April 17, 2002. Ashcroft appealed Jones's ruling, but on May 26, 2004, a three-judge panel of the Ninth Circuit Court of Appeals voted 2 to 1 to uphold the lower court's decision. The court rejected the Bush administration's request for a rehearing of the case, *Oregon v. Ashcroft*, with all 11 judges in August.

The government appealed again, and on February 22, 2005, the U.S. Supreme Court agreed to hear the case, now called *Gonzales v. Oregon*. (Alberto Gonzales had replaced Ashcroft as attorney general on November 15, 2004.) The Court heard oral arguments on the case on October 5. Unlike the 1997 *Glucksberg* and *Quill* cases, this case did not discuss a possible right to die directly. Rather, it centered on whether the federal government or the states had the right to regulate medical practice. Specifically, the justices had to decide whether Congress, in formulating the Controlled Substances Act, had granted the attorney general the authority to determine what constituted "legitimate medical practice."

On January 17, 2006, the high court voted 6 to 3 to uphold the judicial decision blocking Ashcroft's order. In essence, therefore, the Court's decision also upheld the Oregon law. Justice Anthony Kennedy wrote in the Court's majority opinion that Congress had intended the Controlled Substances Act to stop drug abuse and illegal drug trafficking, not to take away states' traditional right to regulate the practice of medicine. He claimed that the act did not give the attorney general the authority to determine the legitimacy of any medical practice. In a dissenting opinion, Justice Antonin Scalia disagreed with Kennedy's analysis of the Controlled Substances Act and held that the act did provide the attorney general with the power to determine which medical practices were legitimate and in the public interest.

Meanwhile, both friends and foes of assisted suicide continued to watch closely the yearly reports on the Death with Dignity Act that the Oregon Department of Human Services produced. The seventh report, issued on March 9, 2006, provided statistics for 2005. Like all the department's previous accounts, this one was based solely on information from physicians and death certificates.

The department stated that 39 physicians wrote 64 prescriptions for lethal doses of medication during 2005, a slight increase over the 60 prescriptions in 2004 but less than the highest number, 68, written in 2003. Thirty-five people died from the medication. The authors of the report said that the number of people dying under the assisted suicide law has remained relatively stable since 2002. Assisted suicide accounted for about one out of every 800 deaths in Oregon in 2005, the same figure as in 2004.

Patients who committed assisted suicide under the Oregon law in 2005 had characteristics similar to those of people who had used the law in previous years. Their median age was 70 years. Almost all were white. Most of the people who requested aid in dying had cancer; four had amyotrophic lateral sclerosis. They were younger than the average person who died in

Oregon, better educated (37 percent had at least a bachelor's degree, as opposed to 14 percent of all deaths), and more likely to be divorced or never married. Almost all died at home. Most (92 percent) were enrolled in hospice care, and all had some form of health insurance.

Most of the people who died under the law in 2005 gave multiple reasons for wishing to end their lives, the report stated. Interviewers had asked about seven possible end-of-life concerns: loss of autonomy, loss of ability to engage in activities that made life enjoyable, loss of dignity, loss of control of bodily functions, being a burden to family or other caregivers, experience of or concern about pain, and concern about financial issues. Of these, the ones patients mentioned most often were loss of ability to take part in activities that made life enjoyable (87 percent), loss of dignity (89 percent), and loss of autonomy (79 percent). People who had committed assisted suicide in previous years had frequently cited these same issues. Concerns about pain (expressed by 24 percent of the people who died in 2005) and financial problems (3 percent), aspects most often brought up in defenses and criticisms of assisted suicide, were mentioned least frequently by patients in Oregon.

PHYSICIAN-ASSISTED SUICIDE AND EUTHANASIA IN OTHER COUNTRIES

Although most Western countries have been as conservative as the United States about accepting physician-assisted suicide and euthanasia, there was one notable exception: the Netherlands. As medical ethicist Edmund Pellegrino says, that country is "a living laboratory of what happens when a society accepts the legitimacy of [physician-assisted suicide and euthanasia]. You've got direct, empirical evidence" of the consequences.[65] Both friends and foes of these activities have studied the Dutch experience closely.

Assisted death was first widely discussed in the Netherlands in 1973, when Geertruida Postma, a physician, granted her terminally ill mother's request for death by giving her a fatal injection. In a highly publicized trial, Postma was found guilty of murder but given only a very short suspended sentence and a year's probation. Then, although physician-assisted suicide and euthanasia remained illegal, a Dutch Supreme Court decision in 1984 produced an informal agreement not to prosecute doctors who committed these activities provided that the physicians followed guidelines drawn up by the Royal Dutch Medical Society. The Ministry of Justice made this agreement official in 1990, and in 1993 the Dutch Parliament accepted a reporting system based on the guidelines. The legal argument used to permit assisted suicide and euthanasia, even though these acts were still technically against the law, was that they took place under "necessity or duress" arising from the physician's duty not to let a patient suffer, even though fulfilling that duty violated the competing duty of preserving the patient's life.[66]

In the early 2000s, the Netherlands moved from winking at euthanasia and physician-assisted suicide to making these acts fully legal, provided that certain guidelines were followed. The lower house of the country's parliament voted 104 to 40 to legalize voluntary euthanasia and physician-assisted suicide on November 28, 2000, and the upper house followed on April 11, 2001. The new law, called the Termination of Life on Request and Assisted Suicide (Review Procedures) Act, went into effect on April 1, 2002.

The Dutch guidelines are generally similar to the requirements of Oregon's physician-assisted suicide law. In both places the patient must make a free, informed, and explicit request for the act, and the request must be repeated over time. The patient also must be experiencing unbearable and unrelievable suffering. The physician must consult another doctor to confirm the medical diagnosis and, after the death occurs, must report it to the coroner. In Oregon, however, the patient must be suffering from a terminal illness, whereas in the Netherlands the cause of the patient's suffering need not be terminal or, indeed, even physical. The rules in the Netherlands also differ from those in Oregon in that the Netherlands permits voluntary euthanasia as well as assisted suicide. Indeed, euthanasia apparently is the more preferred of the two forms of assisted death because it is faster and more certain to be effective.

The Dutch have issued three major reports describing the practice of physician-assisted suicide and euthanasia in the Netherlands. The first of these, called the Remmelink Report, was published in 1991. It stated that out of about 130,000 deaths that occurred in the country in 1990, some 2,300 (1.8 percent) were caused by euthanasia. This figure did not include 1,350 cases (1 percent) in which high doses of narcotics given for pain relief may have shortened life (the "double effect"). Another 400 deaths (0.3 percent) were physician-assisted suicides. The report claimed that most or all of the required guidelines were followed in the reported cases except for the one requiring reporting to authorities. (Statistics for the Remmelink Report were gathered through questionnaires anonymously answered by physicians as well as through coroners' reports.)

As with the report on the suicides that took place during the first year of the Oregon law, both sides in the euthanasia debate found evidence in the Remmelink Report to validate their point of view. Supporters of assisted death, for example, pointed out the small percentage of euthanasia and assisted suicide cases among total deaths, the fact that almost all (more than 99 percent) of them euthanized people were terminally ill (on average, patients' lives were estimated to have been shortened by only two or three weeks), and the information that doctors granted fewer than a third of the requests for euthanasia that they received.

Critics of euthanasia, on the other hand, noted with alarm the 1,000 cases (0.8 percent of total deaths) in which patients had not explicitly requested euthanasia near the time of death. The Remmelink Report did not include these deaths in the euthanasia category because it defined euthanasia as including a voluntary request; instead, it placed them in a separate classification. The physicians who performed these acts of apparent involuntary euthanasia claimed that 79 percent of the patients were incompetent at the time and that more than half had expressed an interest in euthanasia at an earlier date, when they were competent. In cases where euthanasia had not been discussed with the patients themselves, the doctors claimed to have consulted the patients' families or other doctors. Critics pointed out that these physicians may not have been totally reliable sources, and they may well have not reported cases in which they committed euthanasia without consulting anyone. The report also did not explain why doctors committed euthanasia without discussion with the patient in the 21 percent of cases in which patients were competent.

In an attempt to answer some of the questions raised by the Remmelink Report, the Dutch government commissioned a follow-up report in 1995. This update was intended both to show how the pattern of euthanasia had changed over the four years since the original report and to evaluate the notification procedure introduced in 1993. According to this second report, there was little change in the practice of euthanasia during the four years between the two reports. Slightly fewer cases occurred in which people were euthanized without their explicit request (900 as compared to 1,000). The number of euthanasia cases reported to authorities had increased from 18 percent of the total cases estimated (on the basis of the anonymous questionnaires) to have occured in 1990 to 41 percent in 1995, but that still left 59 percent of the cases unreported.

"We found no signs of an unacceptable increase in the number of decisions [to commit euthanasia] or of less careful decision making," the authors of the 1995 report stated.[67] They claimed that their data "do not support the idea that physicians in the Netherlands are moving down a slippery slope."[68] Critics such as Herbert Hendin, who has frequently described what he sees as the dangers illustrated by the Dutch system, strongly disagreed, however. They pointed out that although the change between the 2,300 euthanasia cases reported in 1991 and the 3,200 reported in 1995 (a figure that questionnaire estimates raised to 3,600) was not very great in absolute numbers, it represented a jump of about 40 percent of the lower figure. "Double effect" cases, which do not require patient consent, had gone up by a similar percentage (from 1,350 cases, or 1 percent of total deaths, to 1,896 cases, or 1.4 percent of total deaths). Adding together the deaths from euthanasia, assisted suicide, ending the life of a patient without consent, and double effect, Hendin says that total deaths caused by intervention of physicians in the Netherlands increased from 4,813, or 3.7 percent of all deaths, in 1990 to 6,368, or 4.7 percent of all deaths, in 1995, a jump of 27 percent. "The reports . . . provide ample evidence that the slippery slope is no myth but a reality," says a second critic, Edmund Pellegrino.[69] "Virtually every guideline established by the Dutch to regulate euthanasia has been modified or violated with impunity," Hendin adds.[70] Raphael Cohen-Almagor, after interviewing leading authorities on Dutch euthanasia policy in 1999, reported that most of them seemed unconcerned about violations of the guidelines requiring patient consent for euthanasia.

The Dutch government issued a third report in 2003, based on information gathered in 2001, before physician-assisted suicide and euthanasia became legal. As with the earlier documents, data on deaths in the 2003 report came only from death certificates and physicians' voluntary responses. Summarizing the report in the August 2, 2003, issue of the British medical journal *Lancet*, the study's authors stated that "since 1995, the demand for physician-assisted death has not risen among patients and physicians."[71] They claimed that the number of explicit requests for euthanasia or assisted suicide (9,700) remained the same as in 1995 and that about 5,900 of these requests were rejected or not carried out. (In April 2006, the Regional Oversight Boards for Euthanasia, a Dutch watchdog agency, stated that total number of euthanasia and assisted-suicide deaths reported by physicians had risen slightly for the third year in a row: the figures were 1,933 death in 2005, 1,866 in 2004, and 1,815 in 2003.)

The most disturbing figure in the earlier Dutch government reports, the number of cases in which euthanasia was performed without a patient's explicit request, was said to be 1,000 in 2001, the same number as in the original Remmelink report. Richard Fenigsen, a critic of the new report, claimed in the Summer 2004 *Issues in Law and Medicine* that the true number may have been substantially higher because patient consent—or lack of it—was not recorded for deaths caused by narcotic overdose not specifically intended as euthanasia (terminal sedation or the "double effect").

Critics in both the United States and the Netherlands have complained that the Dutch system puts too much power in the hands of physicians. Herbert Hendin, for example, says that in the Netherlands, "doctors can suggest euthanasia, ignore patient ambivalence, not present suitable alternatives, and even end the lives of patients who have not requested it."[72] Joost Schudel, chairman of the Royal Dutch Medical Society, stated in 1997 that the physician decides whether a demented patient should be given euthanasia, usually without consulting family members. These decisions are based on what the doctors themselves would want done for them if they were in the patient's position—not necessarily a valid guide to the patient's own wishes. "There is a certain paternalism built into our system," an anonymous Dutch doctor admitted.[73]

Some examples of Dutch physicians' decision making mentioned by Hendin do seem disturbing. In one case, a physician ended the life of a nun a few days before she would have died naturally because she was in excruciating pain. Her religious convictions did not permit her to ask for death, but the doctor felt free to override them. Another woman with metastatic breast cancer did not want euthanasia, but her doctor provided it anyway because, he said bluntly, "It could have taken another week before she died. I . . . needed this [hospital] bed."[74]

Hendin and other critics say that progressive broadening of both the types of life-ending activities permitted and the categories of illness considered acceptable for such activities are proof of a Dutch slide down the "slippery slope." Hendin wrote in 1997:

> *The Netherlands has moved from considering assisted suicide . . . to giving legal sanction to both physician-assisted suicide and euthanasia, from euthanasia for terminally ill patients to euthanasia for those who are chronically ill, from euthanasia for physical illness to euthanasia for psychological distress, and from voluntary euthanasia to nonvoluntary and involuntary euthanasia.*[75]

Perhaps the most controversial change (or at least clarification) in the guidelines during the 1990s resulted from a 1994 Dutch Supreme Court decision in the case of psychiatrist Boudewijn Chabot. Chabot had given drugs for suicide to Hilly Bosscher, a physically healthy 50-year-old woman who was severely depressed after being abused by her alcoholic husband and losing two sons, one to cancer and one to suicide. After coming to Chabot and asking for assistance in suicide, Bosscher tried two months of therapy for depression, but at the end of that time she said it had not helped her and repeated her earlier request. After consulting with seven colleagues (none of whom actually examined Bosscher), Chabot granted her request in September 1991. The high court found Chabot guilty of violating the medical society guidelines because he had not had another doctor examine Bosscher, but the court did not penalize him.

The Dutch guidelines had always left open the possibility of granting assistance in suicide on the basis of mental suffering alone, but this aspect of them had never been tested in court. "The [court] ruling recognizes the right of patients experiencing severe psychic pain to choose to die with dignity," Chabot's attorney said.[76] The decision nonetheless shocked many

Americans who read about it, just as they were shocked to learn that some of Jack Kevorkian's patients had apparently suffered only from mental problems (although neither the patients nor Kevorkian were aware of this). Permitting assistance in suicide for mental suffering without physical disease "is a morally frightening place for the public policy of any nation to be," renowned American ethicist Arthur Caplan maintains.[77]

Criteria for euthanasia in the Netherlands have been broadened further in the early 2000s, to the dismay of some critics. Although "anticipated suffering" from brain-destroying diseases such as Alzheimer's disease and Huntington's disease is not an acceptable reason for requesting euthanasia according to the current Dutch guidelines, for example, several physicians who performed euthanasia at the request of people diagnosed with these illnesses were not prosecuted, according to a 2004 report in the *Lancet*.

The legislation that legalized euthanasia specified that children as young as 12 years of age could request it, and those 16 years old or older could obtain it even if their parents disapproved. In 2004, furthermore, physicians at the Groningen University Medical Center drew up guidelines for euthanasia of terminally and incurably ill babies held to be in great pain. By mid-2006 the Dutch government had not officially adopted the guidelines, called the Groningen Protocol, but doing so would not require any change in the current law, and the Dutch Pediatric Society accepted the guidelines in May 2006. Spokespeople for the hospital said they expected the guidelines to apply to only about 10 cases per year. (Although deliberate euthanasia of incurably ill newborns is admitted only in the Netherlands and France, a study published in the *Lancet* in 2000 claimed that withholding or withdrawal of medical treatment such as mechanical ventilation for such infants is extremely common in neonatal intensive care units in many European countries.)

Most controversial of all, some euthanasia supporters in the Netherlands, including Els Borst, the Dutch health minister, who spearheaded the drive to legalize euthanasia, are seeking to make a "suicide pill" available to elderly people who wish to end their lives, regardless of their state of health. A poll taken in 2004 found that only 15 percent of the public and an even smaller percentage of physicians favored this idea, however.

Opponents and even some supporters of physician-assisted suicide say that however well euthanasia and assisted suicide may function in the Netherlands, differences between the countries and their cultures all but guarantee that such activities will work much less well in the United States. Probably the most important difference is that the Netherlands provides health care to all its citizens, whereas the United States has no national health care system. A substantial proportion of Americans lack private health insurance and thus have limited access to health care.

Patients in the Netherlands do not run the risk of being forced into accelerated death because they cannot afford good health care, but poor or marginalized people in the United States might.

The Netherlands is much more homogeneous in race, class, income, and culture than the United States, so differences in point of view and inequities in treatment caused by these factors are much less likely to influence discussions on euthanasia in Holland. Unlike frequently contentious Americans, too, the Dutch pride themselves on open and calm discussion of controversial subjects and on being obedient to law and government. Finally, most Dutch physicians live close to their patients and develop longterm personal relationships with them and their families (a doctor who helps a patient die in the Netherlands has, on average, known the patient eight years), whereas in the United States, with its increasing reliance on managed health care and medical specialization, many doctors cannot come to know their patients well or spend much time with them. All these factors make the potential for mistakes, misunderstandings, or abuses in assisting suicide or performing euthanasia much greater in the United States than in the Netherlands. Speaking to Americans thinking of copying the Dutch system, Herbert Cohen, a physician who practices in the Netherlands and has frequently carried out euthanasia, warns, "For goodness sakes, don't do it. You'll be in trouble."[78]

The parliament of Belgium voted to decriminalize voluntary euthanasia for people with "hopeless" illnesses on May 16, 2002, making Belgium the second country in the world in which euthanasia is legal. The law went into effect on October 1 of that year. A report released about a year later stated that only 170 people had made use of the law during its first year, but about 400 euthanasia deaths were reported in 2005.

Euthanasia is not legal in Switzerland, but assisting in suicide is (or at least is almost never prosecuted), unless the assistance is given for selfish motives. Unlike in the Netherlands, Belgium, and Oregon, assistance does not even need to come from a physician. The Swiss right-to-die organization Dignitas drew widespread controversy both within and outside that country in the early 2000s by offering to provide lethal prescriptions for members, including those from other countries, if they came to the organization's headquarters in Zurich. Critics referred to such travelers as "suicide tourists." In March 2004, a *National Right to Life News* article claimed that more than 200 foreigners had used the services of Dignitas since its founder, Ludwig Minelli, announced the group's policy in 1999.

When people seeking death come to Dignitas, Minelli says, they are screened by a local physician to determine whether their condition is "hopeless." Their illness does not have to be terminal or even physical, however. Dignitas does not require repeated requests issued over a period of time, nor does it test for depression or other mental illness.

If the examining physician accepts a person's request for death, the person is taken to an apartment and given a lethal dose of barbiturates (which may be either swallowed or taken through intravenous injection). A member of the Dignitas staff and a relative or friend of the dying person stay in the apartment as witnesses to be sure that the person takes the fatal dose by him- or herself. A German woman who went to Zurich to help her terminally ill mother die with the aid of Dignitas described the procedure as "bittersweet and peaceful."[79]

Australia also experimented with open practice of physician-assisted suicide, but only briefly and on a scale more like that in Oregon than that in the Netherlands. The law in question applied only in the Northern Territory, one of the three territories and five states that make up the country. As of June 2005, the Northern Territory contained 202,800 people, the smallest number of any Australian state or territory (about 1 percent of the country's total population). Some 27 percent were native people, or Aborigines, the highest proportion in any state or territory. These indigenous people account for almost half of the territory's yearly deaths.

In 1994, just before his retirement, Marshall Perron, then the Northern Territory's chief minister, drafted a law that would permit physician-assisted suicide under limited conditions. The law, called the Rights of the Terminally Ill Act, passed in the territorial legislature by one vote (13 to 12) on May 25, 1995, and went into effect on July 1, 1996. Like the Oregon assisted-suicide law, the Northern Territory one required a patient requesting help in suicide to be a competent, terminally ill adult, although the Australian law did not define terminal illness. The patient had to be experiencing "unacceptable" pain, suffering, and distress and had to make the decision to request death freely, voluntarily, and after due consideration. Both laws also required that two physicians evaluate a patient's illness, competence, and emotional state. The Australian law required a waiting period of seven days between initial and final requests, and the death had to be reported to the coroner. The Australian law differed from the Oregon one in requiring the administering physician to be present during the death and in permitting lethal injections. (The injections were to be triggered by the patient, so they did not constitute euthanasia.)

An opinion poll taken soon after the Rights of the Terminally Ill Act passed showed that 46 percent of the public, 33 percent of nurses, and 14 percent of doctors supported it. Nonetheless, only one Northern Territory physician proved willing to carry out assisted suicide and publicly acknowledge it. That doctor, Philip Nitschke, has become known as the Australian equivalent of Jack Kevorkian. Like Kevorkian, Nitschke built his own machine to administer lethal drugs. It consisted of an intravenous line connected to supplies of the drugs and to a laptop computer. The computer contained a program that basically asked the patient in three different ways, "Do you know that what you are about to do will cause your death and, knowing this, do you still want to proceed?" The patient used a computer mouse to click "yes" or "no." At the third "yes," the machine injected the drugs.

During the lifetime of the law, seven patients requested aid in dying under its provisions. Nitschke provided such aid for four, beginning with Bob Dent, a 66-year-old man with terminal cancer, on September 22, 1996. As described in interviews with Nitschke and public records, all seven people had cancer, although medical opinions differed about whether their conditions were terminal. Three were socially isolated, and four had symptoms of depression.

Nitschke and those who sought his services did not have much time in which to work. The Australian central government cannot overrule laws passed by full states, but it can do so for laws passed by territories, and opponents of physician-assisted suicide quickly began a campaign to have the Northern Territory law repealed. These opponents included advocates for the Aborigines, who, already distrustful of mainstream government and medicine, feared that the law would be used or expanded to kill them against their will if they entered a hospital.

After an appeal to the Australian Supreme Court failed, the groups turned to the country's legislature. On September 9, 1996, just two weeks before Bob Dent's death, Kevin Andrews, a Liberal member from Victoria, introduced the Euthanasia Laws Bill into the Australian Parliament. If passed, the bill would repeal the Northern Territory law and prevent territories from legislating about assisted death in the future.

On March 24, 1997, just nine months after the Northern Territory law had gone into effect, the Australian Parliament voted in favor of the Andrews bill, 38 to 33. This was the first time Parliament had struck down a law passed by a territory. Philip Nitschke, like Jack Kevorkian, has refused to let questions of legality interfere with what he sees as his medical duty, however. In early 1999 he said that he had helped 60 people die after the law was repealed. He advised on and witnessed the suicide of Nancy Crick, a 69-year-old Queensland woman, on May 22, 2002, in a highly publicized case. (Crick had had bowel cancer, but it was said to be in remission at the time of her death.) Nitschke continues to give workshops on methods for committing suicide.

A surprise addition to the small list of places that legally permitted euthanasia came in June 1997, when a ruling by the highest court in Colombia made that country the only one in the Americas to legalize euthanasia. The ruling allowed euthanasia only for terminally ill, competent adults who request it. "What the court did was simply to recognize what is already consecrated in the constitution: the autonomy of a person to decide whether to opt for euthanasia," said the court's chief justice, Carlos Gavira.[80] In 1999, however, the Colombian Senate reviewed the court's regulation and declined to pass legislation supporting it. As a result, euthanasia remains a punishable offense in Colombia.

Most other Western countries have followed patterns similar to that in most of the United States. In Canada and Britain, as well as the United States, for example, opinion polls generally show that around three quarters of the public support availability of physician-assisted suicide at least for competent, terminally ill adults, and courts rarely hand down convictions or severe sentences for assisted suicide or "mercy killing." Nonetheless, laws against assisting in suicide or committing euthanasia, even for the terminally ill, remain unshakably in place.

Physician-assisted suicide remains illegal in Canada, despite a widely publicized but unsuccessful 1993 appeal for its legalization from Sue Rodriguez, a British Columbia ALS victim, that went all the way to the country's supreme court. In the wake of the Rodriguez case, the Canadian legislature created a seven-member Senate Special Committee on Euthanasia and Assisted Suicide, which decided by a four-to-three vote in June 1995 that the national law did not need to be changed. Since that time, several legislators have introduced private members' bills into the Canadian Parliament to legalize assisted suicide, but none has passed. Francine Lalonde, a Parliament member from Quebec, introduced the most recent bill, C-407, on June 15, 2005. It did not pass in that year, but Lalonde, reelected in 2006, vowed to reintroduce it.

Canadians' conflicting feelings about euthanasia were demonstrated in the different outcomes of two widely publicized cases. One involved a Saskatchewan farmer, Robert Latimer, who in 1993 used carbon monoxide from his truck exhaust to kill his 12-year-old daughter, Tracy. Tracy had been gravely retarded since birth (she was said to have the mental development of a three-month-old baby) and also suffered from severe cerebral palsy and pain from a dislocated hip. Latimer claimed that he killed her to end her pain.

In 1994 a Canadian court convicted Latimer of second-degree murder and sentenced him to the 10-year mandatory minimum prison term. In an unusual move in 1997, however, a judge invoked a constitutional exemption to reduce Latimer's sentence to only two years. The Crown appealed this relatively light sentence, and, in December 1997, the Saskatchewan Court of Appeal reinstated the original 10-year term. The Canadian Supreme Court upheld the 10-year sentence by unanimous vote on January 18, 2001. In mid-2006, Latimer was still in prison.

On the other hand, in March 1998 a Nova Scotia court dismissed charges against Nancy Morrison, a physician who injected potassium chloride into the heart of a cancer patient who was dying in agony after huge doses of narcotics had failed to affect him. Potassium chloride stops the heart but has no direct effect on pain. Part of Morrison's acquittal stemmed from questions about whether a possibly defective intravenous line actually transmitted either the narcotics or the potassium chloride into the man's body. Nonetheless, the verdict was considered something of a victory for supporters of euthanasia.

Similarly, a court judgment in Britain in 1993 legalized removal of feeding and hydration tubes from permanently comatose patients at their families' request, but all attempts to change England's 1961 law against assisting suicide so far have failed. (Assisting suicide is legal in Scotland.) The most recent effort was the Assisted Dying for the Terminally Ill Bill, which Lord Joel Goodman Joffe introduced into the British Parliament. The bill, which would legalize assisted suicide but not euthanasia, was debated in the House of Lords in October 2005. After a seven-hour debate on May 12, 2006, the House of Lords voted 148 to 100 to delay the second reading of the bill, which guaranteed that the bill would not become law during the current parliamentary session. News stories attributed the bill's defeat at least partly to an intensive campaign against it by the Catholic Church.

Two highly publicized cases during the early 2000s demonstrated the conflicting feelings about assisted dying that prevail in the British government. In the first case, which took place in 2001, Diane Pretty, a woman suffering from motor neurone disease (amyotrophic lateral sclerosis, or ALS), asked the Department of Public Prosecutions to exempt her husband from prosecution if he helped her kill herself. When the department refused to make such a promise and the refusal was sustained in court reviews, she appealed the case to the European Court of Human Rights, claiming that Britain's suicide law violated the European Convention on Human Rights. That court also rejected her suit on April 29, 2002. Diane Pretty died naturally on May 11, less than two weeks later.

The other case, which recalled the Elizabeth Bouvia case in the United States in the 1980s, ended quite differently. In early 2002, a 43-year-old quadriplegic woman known only as Ms. B became the first Briton to petition a court to have her ventilator turned off. Ms. B was not terminally ill, but, like Bouvia, she apparently felt that her life was not worth continuing. After an interview, Dame Elizabeth Butler-Sloss, president of the family division of the British High Court, concluded that Ms. B was competent to refuse medical treatment and therefore granted her request. Unlike Bouvia, Ms. B did not change her mind, and she died on April 29.

The British public has shown considerable support for assisted suicide, at least as applied to terminally ill people. A poll taken by YouGov and published in the *Daily Telegraph* in August 2005, for example, reported that

87 percent of those polled favored such action. Even the powerful British Medical Association, which had previously opposed attempts to legalize assisted suicide and euthanasia, declared in mid-2005 that it would take a neutral position on assisted suicide for the terminally ill. It returned to a position of opposing assisted suicide and euthanasia in 2006, however.

In the rest of the world, physician-assisted suicide and euthanasia are either illegal or, if legal, very seldom publicly practiced. Germany, for example, has had no law against assisting suicide for altruistic motives since 1751, but, perhaps because of lingering memories of Nazi forced euthanasia, assistance in suicide is rarely performed openly; euthanasia is illegal.

Since November 2004, France has permitted ending of futile medical treatment and passive euthanasia, but it does not allow assisted suicide or active euthanasia. Nonetheless, people engaging in these activities may not be punished if they clearly were acting on the wishes of the person who died. In the famous case that spawned the 2004 law, the mother and doctor of Vincent Humbert, a 22-year-old man left deaf, mute, and paralyzed by an automobile accident in 2000, killed him with sedative overdoses in September 2003 after he repeatedly asked to die (he communicated and even dictated a book with movements of one thumb). They were charged in his death, but in February 2006, acting on the advice of prosecutors, the judge in the case dropped all charges against them.

Euthanasia has been legal in Japan since a landmark ruling by the High Court of Central Japan in 1962. In a highly publicized 1992 case, a physician was convicted of murder after euthanizing a dying cancer patient at the request of the patient's family, but he received a suspended sentence. According to Noritoshi Tanida, chairman of the department of medical humanities at Yamaguchi University, surveys have shown that 40 to 70 percent of Japanese laypeople think euthanasia is permissible under some circumstances, but they are reluctant to discuss the subject publicly. Tanida says that the traditional Japanese religions of Shinto and Buddhism support allowing people to die naturally rather than struggling to keep them alive, and unlike traditional Christian (especially Catholic) religion, these religions do not take a strong position against euthanasia. However, most Japanese health care professionals oppose euthanasia and do everything in their power to sustain the life of dying patients. Traditions in Japan see suicide as honorable under some conditions, but they do not support suicide as a response to incurable illness.

He Huaihong, a philosophy professor at Peking University, reported at a bioethics conference in 2003 that although euthanasia is illegal in China, it is widely practiced in secret. He said that the most common reasons for euthanasia requests from patients or their families were the physical suffering of the patients and the burdens, financial and otherwise, that their care imposed on their relatives. He stated that, unlike the case in Japan, 95 percent of Chinese medical workers approve of euthanasia. Traditionally, he said, "the Chinese believe that while life is valuable, it is not to be clung to."

THE FUTURE

"Throughout the nation, Americans are engaged in an earnest and profound debate about the morality, legality and practicality of physician-assisted suicide," Chief Justice William Rehnquist wrote in the majority opinion in the June 1997 Supreme Court decision on two right-to-die cases. "Our holding permits this debate to continue, as it should in a democratic society."[81]

As Rehnquist noted, the debate about physician-assisted suicide and euthanasia, intense as it has been during the 1990s and early 2000s, is clearly just beginning. "There is no question that the struggle over euthanasia will be one of the most dominant issues into the next century," says Burke Baulch, director of the department of medical ethics at the National Right to Life Committee.[82] The chief factor likely to make it so is the aging of the population: a 1997 study in the prestigious British science journal *Nature*, for example, predicted that the percentage of the earth's population that is over the age of 60 will double during the next 50 years. This means that ever-increasing numbers of people will suffer from incurable chronic diseases. Furthermore, although it actually affects only a tiny number of people, the assisted suicide/euthanasia debate touches on common and deeply held beliefs about the sanctity of life and the importance of self-determination and fears of being controlled by impersonal technology or being abandoned because one's care costs too much money or effort.

The legal right of patients or their surrogates to refuse life-sustaining treatment was hotly debated in the 1970s, yet it is almost universally accepted today. Whether physician-assisted suicide and even, eventually, euthanasia will follow the same path remains to be seen. In the United States, the federal government may preclude this possibility by legislation. If that does not happen, at least a few other states most likely will sooner or later follow Oregon's lead in legalizing physician-assisted suicide, at least for competent, terminally ill adults. (In 2005, for example, California and Vermont were considering such a possibility.) The courts, too, may continue to play a role if physicians who assist in suicide in states where doing so is illegal appeal their convictions or if terminally ill patients again file suit to challenge the constitutionality of laws forbidding assisted suicide. The Supreme Court left open the possibility of such a challenge succeeding if it did not demand as sweeping a right as the 1997 cases did. The results of experiments in legalization, like the present results from the Netherlands, Belgium, and Oregon, will no doubt provide ammunition for both sides of the discussion and help to determine the likelihood of further legalization.

If physician-assisted suicide does become an accepted option for competent, terminally ill adults, the debate surely will not stop there. Demands to broaden the category of eligible people have already arisen. Compassion in Dying, for example, said in a December 1997 fund-raising letter, "We have expanded our mission to include not only terminally ill individuals, but also persons with incurable illnesses which will eventually lead to a terminal diagnosis."[83]

Every new category of people whose eligibility for physician-assisted suicide or euthanasia is considered will bring its own debate and, if accepted, will introduce the possibility of further expansion. Discussions on these topics will raise increasingly thorny and painful questions: Should competent adults with incurable but not terminal illnesses or disabilities have the right to ask for assistance in dying if they find the quality of their lives unacceptable? If such a right is granted, would it add to the autonomy of disabled people or, instead, increase their marginalization and risk of being killed against their will? Should parents have the right to refuse treatment for "Baby Does" born with severe mental or physical disabilities? Should people be allowed to request active euthanasia in advance directives? Should family members or other surrogates be allowed to ask for euthanasia for incompetent patients who have not left such directives? Should people be allowed to ask for help in dying if they find their lives intolerable for strictly psychological reasons, as Hilly Bosscher did? Should doctors, hospital ethics committees, or other agencies ever have the right to end medical treatment they consider "futile," or even administer euthanasia, against the wishes of patients or their families?

Each broadening of categories is sure to be considered a step down the "slippery slope" to moral disaster by some and a logical extension of autonomy and equal protection by others. *New England Journal of Medicine* executive editor Marcia Angell claims, "It is impossible to avoid slippery slopes in medicine (or in any aspect of life)."[84] Where, if anywhere, should the "bright line" finally be drawn, and how can safeguards be installed at each step to minimize potential abuse?

In discussing these options, both supporters and critics of physician-assisted suicide and euthanasia will have to face the fact that the "poster" case for demanding these alternatives—a terminally ill adult in uncontrollable physical pain—actually represents only a very small (perhaps vanishingly small, if state-of-the-art pain control and other palliative care were available to all) percentage of the sick people who ask to die. In virtually every Western country where the issue has been examined, most of the people asking for (though not necessarily most of those receiving) aid in dying gave as their chief reason not pain or other physical symptoms but fear of being dependent, losing "dignity," and being a burden to their families. The Netherlands' Remmelink Report, for example, stated that pain was the sole motivating factor in only 5 percent of the people who requested aid in dying in that country. By contrast, 57 percent of the requests mentioned loss of dignity as a motivating factor, 46 percent cited "unworthy dying," and 33 percent referred to fear of being dependent on others. Similarly, a Canadian study published in 2001 reported that the main reasons people with HIV/AIDS requested assisted suicide or euthanasia were loss of physical functioning and loss of community (the power to have close personal relationships with other people). For these patients, these two losses added up to a loss of their sense of self. In the Netherlands, too, according to a 2003 article in the *British Medical Journal,* pain became less common as a reason for seeking death and loss of physical function became more so in the years between 1977 and 2001, as euthanasia was increasingly accepted in that country. Both the state government reports and independent studies of people who died under Oregon's assisted suicide law cited loss of physical abilities and loss of autonomy as the most common reasons for seeking death.

Does this emphasis on psychological rather than physical reasons for seeking assisted death mean that most sick people who ask to die are suffering from treatable depression, as critics of assisted death claim? Or does it mean that, perhaps because of personal or social stress on autonomy and independence, many people really do consider helplessness and social isolation worse than death? Answering these questions will require more studies to learn whether treating depression in incurably ill or disabled people increases their desire to live. It will also require probing, and perhaps changing, of personal, family, and societal attitudes toward disability, dependence, and caregiving. People will need to explore what they mean by terms such as *dignity* and *autonomy*—what they mean by a good death and a good life—and what practical steps can be taken to bring these goals within the reach of a greater part, or ideally all, of the world's population.

Most supporters and opponents of physician-assisted death can agree that, whatever the other outcomes of debates on this subject, two good things are likely to emerge from them. One is an end, or at least a diminution, to the societal taboo against facing up to and discussing death. Often forced by circumstances as they and their parents age, Americans are beginning to talk about issues related to death and end-of-life care more openly than in the past. Perhaps even more important, their doctors are learning to do so, too. Medical schools are adding courses on palliative and end-of-life care, subjects that until recently have been conspicuously absent from most doctors' education.

Both friends and foes of physician-assisted suicide and euthanasia hope that one fruit of this new honesty will be an increase in the number of citizens who fill out advance health care directives and discuss them both with their families or other designated surrogates and with their health care providers. Surveys show that more than four-fifths of Americans approve of advance directives, yet only a fifth to a quarter of them have actually completed such documents. This may change in coming years, as advance directives become more accessible and easier to fill out. Provision and possibly filling out of such directives may even be made mandatory for competent adults entering hospitals.

Even when advance directives have been completed, doctors still sometimes do not make them a permanent part of patients' medical records, and hospitals and other health care facilities sometimes do not implement them. A 1995 study by the University of Virginia Health Sciences Center, for instance, found that only 49 percent of 4,300 critically ill patients who requested do-not-resuscitate orders (a form of advance directive requiring health care personnel not to attempt to revive a patient if the person's heartbeat or breathing stops) actually got them, and 70 percent were not asked about their preferences. Institutions were rarely penalized for ignoring advance directives in the past, but several lawsuits against doctors or hospitals who did not follow such directives or the requests of designated surrogates were successful in the late 1990s. In the early 2000s, programs such as Respecting Choices in Wisconsin have increased compliance with advance directives in some places. These efforts combine clearer and more individualized directives, frequent discussions with patients and family members to revise treatment goals as patients' health status changes, transfer of directive information from one health care facility to another, and training of health care workers.

The second great benefit of the right-to-die movement has been, and likely will continue to be, better care at the end of life: relief of pain and other unpleasant physical symptoms such as nausea or difficulty in breathing, help with daily care and management of bodily functions, and emotional and spiritual comfort for the dying person and his or her family and friends. By the late 1990s, there were about 3,000 hospice programs in the United States, spread out among all 50 states, the District of Columbia, and Puerto Rico. They cared for about a fifth of the Americans who died in 1997, some 450,000 people. Medicare has covered hospice care since 1983, and Medicaid programs in 41 states also cover it.

Whether they see hospice care as an alternative or a complement to physician-assisted suicide and euthanasia, health care professionals as well as members of the public have been heartened by the growing availability of such care. As of 2004, more than 900,000 U.S. citizens were receiving care from more than 3,200 hospice programs. Studies have shown, however, that many dying people still suffer from pain and other unpleasant physical symptoms that could be relieved. Depression and other mental problems are even more often untreated or undertreated, especially among the elderly and ill.

Care for the terminally ill is only a small part of the health care needs highlighted by the physician-assisted suicide/euthanasia debate. A far greater need is—and will increasingly be—long-term care for the chronically sick or disabled who are not terminally ill. "We've made long-term care the step-child of medical care," says geriatrician Joanne Lynn. "We've never properly funded [it]."[85] Putting the problem in more specific terms, Lynn adds, "I can get elegant, $20,000 surgery for a patient at the drop of a hat, but I can't get her lunch."[86]

Unfortunately, as the population in the United States and other industrialized countries ages, this tremendous need is sure to collide with the need to control health care costs. On the positive side, cost cutting and the rise of managed care are likely to end the financial incentives that once drove some doctors and hospitals to force expensive, futile treatments on unwilling patients and their families. Health management organizations may even come to support physician-assisted suicide and euthanasia because these alternatives are cheaper than long-term or even hospice care. "In the final analysis," Derek Humphry predicted in 1998, "economics, not the quest for broadened individual liberties or increased autonomy, will drive assisted suicide to the plateau of acceptable practice."[87]

In the long term, opponents of physician-assisted suicide and euthanasia who worry that the right to die may become a socially approved, economically coerced, or even possibly forced "duty to die" for not only the terminally ill but the chronically ill, disabled, and even possibly healthy elderly, minorities, and poor people may well have reason for their fears. One sign of this is that the duty to die rather than exhaust familial or societal health care resources is increasingly being mentioned, not only as a possible danger by foes of assisted suicide, but as a possible benefit by supporters. Derek Humphry, for example, wrote in 1998:

A new study of seriously ill people in hospitals found that 30 percent of those surveyed said they would rather die than live permanently in a nursing home. This information begs the question: Why do we, as a nation, not allow these people to die, if they have no alternative to a nursing-home existence and this is what they want? Their lives would conclude with dignity and self-respect, and one measure of cost containment would be in place.[88]

Introduction to Euthanasia

The threat of a psychologically or externally imposed "duty to die" is likely to be greatest in the United States, with its lack of a nationalized health care system and many inequities in access to medical care, but reports indicate that the sick and disabled also feel economic pressures in countries such as Britain and the Netherlands, which have national health care systems.

In the long run, important as it is, the debate about physician-assisted suicide and euthanasia seems likely to be swallowed up by the larger debate about how to handle the health care needs of a growing and aging population without bankrupting society. Put another way, the search for a good death will come to be seen as only a small part of the search for a good life.

[1] Stephen Reinhardt, majority opinion in *Compassion in Dying et al. v. State of Washington*, 79 F3d 790 (9th Cir 1996), quoted in Maureen Harrison and Steve Gilbert, eds., *Life, Death, and the Law*. San Diego, Ca.: Excellent Books, 1997, p. 73.

[2] Howard Grossman, quoted in Sue Woodman, *Last Rights*. New York: Plenum, 1998, p. 174.

[3] Socrates, in Plato, *Phaedo*, quoted in Gregory E. Pence, *Classic Cases in Medical Ethics*. New York: McGraw-Hill, 1995, p. 34.

[4] Plato, *Laws*, Book IX, quoted in Michael M. Uhlmann, "Western Thought on Suicide: From Plato to Kant," in Michael M. Uhlmann, ed., *Last Rights: Assisted Suicide and Euthanasia Debated*. Washington, D.C.: Ethics and Public Policy Center/Grand Rapids, Mich.: William B. Eerdmans, 1998, p. 18.

[5] Seneca, quoted in Donald W. Cox, *Hemlock's Cup*. Buffalo, N.Y.: Prometheus Books, p. 44.

[6] Augustine, quoted in Derek Humphry and Ann Wickett, *The Right to Die: An Historical and Legal Perspective of Euthanasia*. Eugene, Ore.: Hemlock Society, 1990, p. 6.

[7] David Hume, quoted in Pence, *Classic Cases in Medical Ethics*, p. 38.

[8] Immanuel Kant, quoted in Pence, *Classic Cases in Medical Ethics*, p. 39.

[9] Ohio Supreme Court, *Blackburn v. State*, 23 Ohio SCt. 162–163 (1872), quoted in Edward J. Larson and Darrel W. Amundsen, *A Different Death: Euthanasia and the Christian Tradition*. Downers Grove, Ill.: Inter-Varsity Press, 1998, p. 161.

[10] Hippocratic Oath, quoted in Pence, *Classic Cases in Medical Ethics*, p. 63.

[11] Cleveland *Independent*, February 1, 1906, quoted in Humphry and Wickett, *The Right to Die*, p. 12.

[12] *Outlook*, February 3, 1906, quoted in Humphry and Wickett, *The Right to Die*, p. 12.

[13] Foster Kennedy and Alexis Carrel, quoted in Humphry and Wickett, *The Right to Die*, pp. 14–15.

[14] *Time*, January 23, 1939, quoted in Humphry and Wickett, *The Right to Die*, p. 17.

[15] Quoted in Humphry and Wickett, *The Right to Die*, p. 19.

[16] Leo Alexander, quoted in Humphry and Wickett, *The Right to Die*, p. 27.

[17] Quoted in Humphry and Wickett, *The Right to Die*, p. 129.

[18] Sherwin Nuland, quoted in Derek Humphry and Mary Clement, *Freedom to Die: People, Politics, and the Right-to-Die Movement*. New York: St. Martin's Press, 1998, p. 19.

[19] World Health Organization Expert Committee on Cancer Pain Relief and Palliative Care, quoted in Humphry and Clement, *Freedom to Die*, p. 50.

[20] Sister Urban, quoted in Peter G. Filene, *In the Arms of Others: A Cultural History of the Right-to-Die in America*. Chicago: Ivan R. Dee, 1998, p. 127.

[21] B. D. Colen, quoted in Filene, *In the Arms of Others*, p. 24.

[22] Thomas R. Curtin, quoted in Pence, *Classic Cases in Medical Ethics*, p. 13.

[23] Robert Muir, quoted in Humphry and Clement, *Freedom to Die*, p. 88.

[24] New Jersey Supreme Court, *In the Matter of Quinlan*, 355 A. 2d. 647, quoted in Albert R. Jonsen, Robert M. Veatch, and LeRoy Walters, eds., *Source Book in Bioethics: A Documentary History*. Washington, D.C.: Georgetown University Press, 1998, p. 149.

[25] Joseph Quinlan, quoted in Filene, *In the Arms of Others*, p. 132.

[26] Louis Kutner, quoted in Humphry and Wickett, *The Right to Die*, p. 87.

[27] Jerry Brown, quoted in Humphry and Wickett, *The Right to Die*, p. 99.

[28] Ann Jane Levinson, quoted in Humphry and Wickett, *The Right to Die*, p. 117.

[29] Gary L. Thomas, "Deadly Compassion," *Christianity Today*, June 16, 1997, pp. 14ff.

[30] Ronald P. Prishivalko, quoted in Filene, *In the Arms of Others*, p. 108.

[31] Health and Human Services Notice to Health Care Providers, quoted in Pence, *Classic Cases in Medical Ethics*, p. 179.

[32] Gerhard Gesell, *American Academy of Pediatrics v. Heckler*, U.S. District Court, D.C., No. 83-0774, quoted in Filene, *In the Arms of Others*, p. 117.

[33] Adrian Peracchio, quoted in Pence, *Classic Cases in Medical Ethics*, p. 180.

[34] Reginald Stanton, *In re Conroy*, 457 A. 2d 1232 (N.J. Super. Ct. 1983), quoted in Filene, *In the Arms of Others*, p. 141.

[35] *In re Conroy*, 486 A. 2d 1209 (N.J. 1985), quoted in Filene, *In the Arms of Others*, p. 142.

[36] Elizabeth Bouvia, quoted in Pence, *Classic Cases in Medical Ethics*, p. 41.

[37] *Bouvia v. Superior Court* ex rel. Glenchur (Cal. Reptr. 297 C. Ct. App. 1986), quoted in Pence, *Classic Cases in Medical Ethics*, p. 46.

[38] Elizabeth Bouvia, quoted in Pence, *Classic Cases in Medical Ethics*, p. 60.

[39] *Cruzan v. Harmon*, 760 S.W.2d 408 (Mo. banc 1988), quoted in Filene, *In the Arms of Others*, p. 171.

[40] *Cruzan v. Director, Missouri Department of Health*, 110 S. Ct. 2841 (1990), quoted in Harrison and Gilbert, *Life, Death, and the Law*, p. 26.

[41] *Cruzan v. Director*, quoted in Harrison and Gilbert, *Life, Death, and the Law*, pp. 26–27.

[42] *Cruzan v. Director,* quoted in Harrison and Gilbert, *Life, Death, and the Law,* p. 28.

[43] Ron Adkins, quoted in Pence, *Classic Cases in Medical Ethics,* p. 68.

[44] Quoted in Filene, *In the Arms of Others,* pp. 190–191.

[45] Richard Thompson, quoted in Pence, *Classic Cases in Medical Ethics,* p. 85.

[46] Arthur Caplan, quoted in Steve Hallock, "Physician-Assisted Suicide: 'Slippery Slope' or Civil Right?" *The Humanist,* July–August 1996, p.14.

[47] Christy Nichols, quoted in Woodman, *Last Rights,* p. 96.

[48] Timothy Quill, quoted in Woodman, *Last Rights,* p. 180.

[49] Timothy Quill, quoted in Humphry and Clement, *Freedom to Die,* p. 276.

[50] Humphry and Clement, *Freedom to Die,* p. 142.

[51] Carol Tauer, quoted in William Swanson, "Mortal Concern," *Minneapolis-St. Paul Magazine,* October 1996, pp. 52ff.

[52] Derek Humphry, quoted in Cox, *Hemlock's Cup,* p. 29.

[53] William Rehnquist, majority opinion in *Washington State v. Glucksberg,* 117 S. Ct. 2258 (1997), quoted in Harrison and Gilbert, *Life, Death, and the Law,* p. 190.

[54] *New York State v. Quill,* 117 S. Ct. 2293 (1997), quoted in Harrison and Gilbert, *Life, Death, and the Law,* p. 205.

[55] Floyd Prozanski, quoted in Humphry and Clement, *Freedom to Die,* p. 244.

[56] Barbara Coombs Lee, quoted in Associated Press, "15 Assisted Suicides Under New Oregon Law," *San Francisco Chronicle,* February 18, 1999, p. A3.

[57] Ezekiel J. Emanuel, "The End of Euthanasia? Death's Door," *New Republic,* May 17, 1999, p. 16.

[58] Jack Kevorkian, quoted in *The New York Times,* "Kevorkian Murder Trial Starts," reprinted in *San Francisco Chronicle,* March 23, 1999.

[59] Edward Walsh, "Kevorkian Stumbling Through Trial," *Washington Post,* reprinted in *San Francisco Chronicle,* March 24, 1999, A5.

[60] Jessica Cooper, quoted in "Consider Yourself Stopped," *National Right to Life News,* May 11, 1999, p. 12.

[61] Pope John Paul II, "Care for Patients in a 'Permanent' Vegetative State," quoted in Thomas A. Shannon and James J. Walter, "Artificial Nutrition, Hydration: Assessing Papal Statement," *National Catholic Reporter,* vol. 40, April 16, 2004, p. 9.

[62] Pope John Paul II, "Care for Patients in a 'Permanent' Vegetative State," quoted in Robert Barry, "The Papal Allocution on Caring for Persons in a 'Vegetative State,'" *Issues in Law and Medicine,* vol. 20, Fall 2004, p. 155.

[63] George W. Bush, quoted in Joe Garofoli, "Split Loyalty," *San Francisco Chronicle,* March 22, 2005, p. A10.

[64] John-Thor Dahlberg, "Florida Top Court Tosses Law Keeping Woman Alive," *Los Angeles Times,* reprinted in *San Francisco Chronicle,* September 24, 2004, p. A4.

[65] Edmund Pellegrino, quoted in Thomas, "Deadly Compassion," pp. 14ff.

[66] Humphry and Clement, *Freedom to Die,* p. 143.

[67] Paul J. van der Maas et al., "Euthanasia, Physician-Assisted Suicide, and Other Medical Practices Involving the End of Life in the Netherlands, 1990–1995," *New England Journal of Medicine*, November 28, 1996, p. 1,699.

[68] van der Maas, "Euthanasia, Physician-Assisted Suicide, and Other Medical Practices," p. 1,705.

[69] Edmund Pellegrino, quoted in Thomas, "Deadly Compassion," pp. 14ff.

[70] Herbert Hendin, quoted in Paul Wilkes, "The Next Pro-Lifers," *New York Times Magazine*, July 21, 1996, p. 26.

[71] Bregje D. Onwuteaka-Philipsen, et al., "Euthanasia and Other End-of-Life Decisions in the Netherlands in 1990, 1995, and 2001," *Lancet*, vol. 362, August 2, 2003, p. 395.

[72] Herbert Hendin, "Physician-Assisted Suicide: A Look at the Netherlands," *Current*, December 1997, pp. 25ff.

[73] Quoted in Michael J. Farrell, "As Assisted Suicide and Euthanasia Issues Simmer, Look at Holland," *National Catholic Reporter*, April 11, 1999, p. 15.

[74] Quoted in Herbert Hendin, Chris Rutenfrans, and Zbigniew Zylicz, "Physician-Assisted Suicide and Euthanasia in the Netherlands: Lessons from the Dutch," *Journal of the American Medical Association*, June 4, 1997, pp. 1,720ff.

[75] Ibid.

[76] Eugene Sutorius, quoted in Randall E. Otto, "Bottom of the Slope," *Commonweal*, May 19, 1995, pp. 5–6.

[77] Arthur Caplan, quoted in Humphry and Clement, *Freedom to Die*, p. 150.

[78] Herbert Cohen, quoted in Joseph P. Shapiro, "Euthanasia's Home: What the Dutch Experience Can Teach Americans About Assisted Suicide," *U.S. News & World Report*, January 13, 1997, p. 24.

[79] Johanna, quoted in Helena Bachmann, "One-Way Ticket," *Time International*, vol. 160, October 14, 2002, p. 40.

[80] Carlos Gavira, quoted in Humphry and Clement, *Freedom to Die*, p. 163.

[81] William Rehnquist, majority opinion in *Washington State v. Glucksberg*, quoted in Harrison and Gilbert, *Life, Death, and the Law*, p. 199.

[82] Burke Baulch, quoted in Woodman, *Last Rights*, p. 214.

[83] Compassion in Dying, quoted in Wesley J. Smith, "Death March," *National Review*, February 23, 1998, p. 33.

[84] Marcia Angell, "The Supreme Court and Physician-Assisted Suicide—The Ultimate Right," *New England Journal of Medicine*, January 2, 1997, p. 51.

[85] Joanne Lynn, quoted in Thomas, "Deadly Compassion," pp. 14ff.

[86] Ibid.

[87] Humphry and Clement, *Freedom to Die*, p. 313.

[88] Humphry and Clement, *Freedom to Die*, p. 319.

CHAPTER 2

THE LAW OF EUTHANASIA

This chapter presents detailed descriptions of laws and court cases important in determining the legal status of physician-assisted suicide and other aid in dying in the United States. Longer extracts from some of these laws and court decisions appear in the Appendices.

LAWS

Although suicide itself is not illegal, virtually all states in the United States have laws specifically forbidding assisting in a suicide. Euthanasia is universally considered simply a form of homicide, although it may not be punished as severely as other forms. Aside from this, only a few state or federal laws directly pertain to end-of-life decisions or deliberate hastening of death for the terminally ill. The most important are described below.

THE PATIENT SELF-DETERMINATION ACT
PUBLIC LAW 101-508, 1990

On November 5, 1990, President George H. W. Bush signed into law the Patient Self-Determination Act. This act modified several sections of Title 42 of the U.S. Code, which deals with health and welfare, to state that any health care institution receiving federal funds must, on admission of anyone as an inpatient or resident, provide written information to the person concerning the individual's "rights under State law . . . to make decisions concerning . . . medical care, including the right to accept or refuse medical or surgical treatment and the right to formulate advance directives." An advance directive is defined as "a written instruction, such as a living will or durable power of attorney for health care, recognized under State law . . . and relating to the provision of such care when the individual is incapacitated." The person must also be informed of "the written policies of the provider or organization respecting the implementation of such rights."

The act also requires health care facilities to document in the person's medical record whether or not the person had executed an advance directive, not to condition provision of care or otherwise discriminate against anyone for making or not making an advance directive, and to comply with state laws regarding implementation of advance directives. In addition, the facilities are supposed to educate staff and community on issues concerning advance directives. Health care facilities are not, however, required to provide forms for advance directives or to offer information about how to obtain such forms or fill them out. The law also mandates a national campaign to inform the public about advance directives and patients' right to participate in and direct health care decisions.

THE OREGON DEATH WITH DIGNITY ACT ORS 127.800-897, 1994

The controversial Oregon Death with Dignity Act, which in effect legalizes physician assistance in suicide for competent, terminally ill adults who meet certain conditions, was first passed as an initiative (Measure 16) by a narrow margin in 1994. Court rulings held up its implementation, however, until October 27, 1997. This was only a week before voting was to take place on Measure 51, which would have repealed Measure 16. Measure 51 was defeated by a much wider margin (60 percent against to 40 percent in favor) than that by which Measure 16 had been passed.

The Death with Dignity Act states:

An adult who is capable [of informed consent and making health care decisions], is a resident of Oregon, and has been determined by the attending physician and consulting physician to be suffering from a terminal disease [an incurable disease that is expected to end the person's life within six months], and who has voluntarily expressed his or her wish to die, may make a written request for medication for the purpose of ending his or her life in a humane and dignified manner in accordance with this Act.

The act requires the person's attending physician (regular doctor or primary-care physician) to make the initial determination of whether the person has a terminal disease, is capable of making health care decisions, and has made the request to die voluntarily. The physician must also inform the patient of his or her medical diagnosis and prognosis (the nature of the person's disease and its most likely future course, including its effect on the patient's life expectancy), the probable result and potential risks of taking the medication to be prescribed, and the available alternatives to assisted suicide, including (but not limited to) comfort care, hospice care, and pain control. After having done these things, the attending physician must refer the patient to a second (consulting) physician, a specialist in the person's disease, to confirm the diagnosis, the patient's capability for decision making, and the fact that he or she is acting voluntarily. If either of these physicians suspects that the patient "may be suffering from a psychiatric or psychological disorder, or depression causing impaired judgment," that physician must refer the patient to a mental health professional for counseling. Lethal medication cannot be prescribed for anyone determined to have mental problems. The attending physician must also advise the patient to inform next of kin of his or her decision, but the patient may refuse to do so without losing the right to request the medication. Finally, the physician must inform the patient that he or she can withdraw the request at any time.

A patient must make two oral requests for aid in dying that are at least 15 days apart. He or she must also make a written request that is signed by at least two witnesses, one of whom must be someone who is not related to the person, a beneficiary of the person's will, the attending physician, or an owner or employee of a health care facility where the person is living or receiving treatment. The witnesses must attest to the patient's identity and to the fact that "to the best of their knowledge and belief the patient is capable, acting voluntarily, and is not being coerced to sign the request." The medicine may not be prescribed until at least 48 hours after the written request is signed.

The attending physician is required to enter all relevant information about the proceeding in the patient's medical records. The law does not require the physician to report assisted suicides to the state health division, although it does specify that the division must "make rules to facilitate the collection of information regarding compliance with this Act." The information collected "shall not be a public record and may not be made available for inspection by the public," but the health division is required to publish an annual statistical report of information collected under the act.

The act states that no physician or other health care provider is required to assist in anyone's suicide. No one who assists a qualified patient and fulfils the requirements of the act is to be subject to criminal, civil, or professional liability or punishment. The act emphasizes that it does not authorize active euthanasia or assistance in suicide in any manner except that which it specifies. Indeed, technically it does not legalize assisted suicide, but rather exempts the medical action described from that category.

COURT CASES

Since the famous Karen Quinlan case in 1976, U.S. courts have rendered more than 200 judgments on the legality of intervening or failing to intervene in the dying process. In doing so, writes legal scholar Lawrence O. Gostin, "the judiciary has transformed not only the practice of medicine and the rights of patients, but has also shaped societal values."[1]

IN THE MATTER OF QUINLAN
THE SUPREME COURT, STATE OF NEW JERSEY
(355 A.2D 647, 1976)

Background

On April 14, 1975, after consuming a mixture of alcohol and drugs at a party, Karen Ann Quinlan, a 21-year-old New Jersey woman, became unconscious and later stopped breathing. Police restarted her breathing, but by then, lack of oxygen had permanently damaged her higher brain. Because she was unable to breathe on her own, physicians at St. Clare's Hospital in Danville, New Jersey, placed her on a respirator.

After a month and a half, when Karen showed no sign of returning consciousness, Robert Morse, the neurologist the hospital assigned to her, informed her parents, Joe and Julia Quinlan, that she appeared to be in a persistent vegetative state. Because her brain stem (which controls automatic functions) was still active, she could move and make sounds, but she showed no real awareness of or responsiveness to her environment. Morse said her condition was extremely unlikely to improve.

On July 31, after consultation with their priest, the Quinlans asked to have Karen's respirator disconnected. Morse and St. Clare's, however, refused on ethical grounds. The Quinlans then petitioned in probate court to have Joe Quinlan made Karen's guardian so that he could legally order the respirator turned off. The Morris County prosecutor opposed the action, saying that the state had a duty to preserve life.

During the October 20 hearing before Judge Robert Muir, Jr., in Morristown, New Jersey, Julia Quinlan testified that, after seeing two family friends die slowly from cancer, Karen had said she would not want to be "kept alive like that." On November 10, however, Muir ruled that Joe Quinlan should not be made Karen's guardian because doing so would not be in her best interest. "There is no constitutional right to die that can be asserted by a parent for his incompetent adult child," he wrote.[2] Karen's own feelings on the matter, said Muir, remained "theoretical" because she had not written them down and had not been speaking about her own imminent death. He believed that when clear indications of incompetent patients' wishes were lacking, physicians rather than family members should make decisions about their care. The Quinlans appealed their case to the New Jersey Supreme Court, which heard it on January 26, 1976.

The Law of Euthanasia

Legal Issues

The right of a competent adult to refuse medical treatment has been accepted for almost a century. It is grounded in common law, statutes, and both state and federal constitutions. In *Union Pacific Railroad Co. v. Botsford*, an 1891 case, the U.S. Supreme Court stated:

> *No right is held more sacred, or is more carefully guarded, by the common law, than the right of every individual to the possession and control of his own person, free from all restraint or interference of others, unless by clear and unquestionable authority of law.*

The right to refuse medical treatment is also included in the tort law requiring informed consent and in the Due Process Clause of the Fourteenth Amendment. In *Jacobson v. Massachusetts* (1905), the Supreme Court recognized a constitutionally protected liberty interest in refusing unwanted medical treatment, which it held to be equivalent to unlawful touching, or battery, because it is an unwanted invasion of the body.

In the 1960s and 1970s the Supreme Court extended the right to control one's body to include the right to make private decisions about the body, such as whom to marry, whether to use contraceptives, and, most famously, whether to have an abortion. The Supreme Court specifically recognized the right to privacy in the 1965 case *Griswold v. Connecticut*, in which it ruled that state laws against giving contraceptives to married couples were unconstitutional. The court extended this right to cover abortion in its landmark 1973 case, *Roe v. Wade*.

The question before the New Jersey courts, then, was not whether Karen Quinlan would have had the right to refuse the respirator if she had been conscious, but whether her parents had the right to make this decision for her. They claimed that, as her next of kin and the people who knew her best, they were entitled to substitute their judgment for hers. The lawyers opposing the Quinlans, however, said that the state had an interest in preserving life that outweighed the family's liberty interest in privacy. They pointed out that in *John F. Kennedy Memorial Hospital v. Heston*, a 1971 case, the New Jersey Supreme Court had ruled that the Jehovah's Witness parents of Delores Heston, a young woman injured in an accident, could be forced to allow her to have a blood transfusion even though their religion forbade it. The transfusion was necessary to keep Heston alive, and the court declared that the state's interest in preserving life outweighed the parents' right to privacy and freedom of religion. The state's lawyers in the Quinlan case maintained that turning off Karen's respirator was, in fact, euthanasia—and, therefore, homicide.

Right to Die and Euthanasia

Decision

The New Jersey high court issued its ruling on March 31, 1976. It reversed the lower court, appointing Joe Quinlan to be Karen's guardian and giving him permission to transfer her to a health care facility willing to remove her respirator.

Chief Justice Richard J. Hughes, writing the court's unanimous opinion, stated that the constitutional right to privacy was the issue that had concerned the court most. Like Muir, he affirmed that Karen Quinlan, had she been competent, would have had the right to refuse medical treatment for herself. Hughes agreed that the state had a responsibility to preserve life that could override the right to privacy and freedom of religion, but he said that the Quinlan case was very different from *Heston*. The blood transfusion required by Delores Heston involved only a minimal invasion of her body, and once she received it, she was "apparently salvable to long life and vibrant health—a situation not at all like the present case." In this case, therefore, Hughes held that the Quinlans' right to privacy should prevail.

> *We think the State's interest* contra *[against the request of the plaintiff] weakens and the individual's right to privacy grows as the degree of bodily invasion increases and the prognosis dims. Ultimately there comes a point at which the individual's rights overcome the State interest.*

Hughes agreed that the reported conversation about Karen's wishes was too "remote and impersonal" to be relevant, but, he said, the right that she would have had to refuse treatment for herself if she had been competent could reasonably be given to her parents now that she was permanently incompetent. Whatever the Quinlans, in their "best judgment," decided that Karen would have wanted done for herself, Hughes wrote,

> *should be accepted by society, the overwhelming majority of whose members would, we think, in similar circumstances exercise such a choice in the same way for themselves or for those closest to them. It is for this reason that we determine that Karen's right of privacy may be asserted in her behalf, in this respect, by her guardian and family under the particular circumstances presented by this record.*

This was the first time a state court had applied the right of privacy to a case of "letting die."

In removing legal liability from physicians like Morse if they discontinued treatment in accordance with a surrogate's wishes, Hughes made a distinction that would be important in future right-to-die cases:

The Law of Euthanasia

We are aware that . . . termination of treatment would accelerate Karen's death. The County Prosecutor and the Attorney General maintain that there would be criminal liability for such acceleration. . . . We conclude that there would be no criminal homicide in the circumstances of this case. We believe, first, that the ensuing death would not be homicide but rather expiration from existing natural causes. Secondly, even if it were to be regarded as homicide, it would not be unlawful. . . . There is a real . . . distinction between the unlawful taking of the life of another and the ending of artificial life-support systems as a matter of self-determination.

Impact

On a personal level, the impact of the court decision was tragically unexpected for the Quinlans. Joe and Julia Quinlan transferred Karen to a nursing home and there had her respirator turned off, but she proved able to breathe without it. They would not consider stopping her food, water, and antibiotics. Karen remained alive for another decade, finally dying of pneumonia on June 13, 1986.

Legal commentators' reactions to the Quinlan decision were mixed. McCarthy DeMere, a physician who had headed the American Bar Association committee that helped to work out a definition of brain death in 1967, called it "one of the worst decisions the country has seen in the last fifty years."[3] Other physicians, however, were happy to be relieved of the risk of being sued for malpractice if they discontinued futile treatment at a family's request. Several legal and ethical scholars said the court had made the right decision for the wrong reasons. Paul Ramsey of Princeton's Department of Religion, for example, supported the Quinlans' decision to turn off Karen's respirator but was distressed that the court had permitted this action on the basis of Karen's predicted poor quality of life, especially since she was not terminally ill. By using this criterion, he wrote, "the *Quinlan* case has gone a long way toward obliterating the distinction between voluntary and involuntary euthanasia."[4]

Socially, the most immediate effect of the Quinlan case, which had received tremendous publicity, was an upsurge of interest in living wills. These documents, the first form of advance health care directive to be introduced, allow competent adults to specify what kinds of medical treatment they would or would not want if they should become incompetent. The concept of the living will had existed since 1969, but the documents did not have legal force in any state, and health care providers usually ignored them even in the fairly rare cases in which patients had filled them out. Just six months after the New Jersey Supreme Court decision, however, the first state law giving advance directives legal standing took effect in California. Its sponsor, Barry Keene, may well have put his finger on the reason for the effort's success (the same bill had failed passage in 1974) when he said, "The image of Karen Quinlan haunts our dreams."[5]

The Quinlan case also gave great impetus to the fledgling right-to-die movement, which asked not only for the power to refuse life-sustaining medical treatment (or to have it refused for one by a surrogate) but for the right to ask for help in hastening death if what little remained of life would be marred by uncontrollable pain, degeneration, or unconsciousness. Noting that Karen Quinlan did not die after her respirator was turned off, right-to-die advocates pointed to the extremely poor quality of her life and the tremendous emotional and financial burdens that such a situation brought to families like the Quinlans.

Important as it was, the Quinlan ruling left many questions unanswered. Could surrogates refuse basic life care, such as food and water, as well as high-technology devices like a respirator? How clear an indication of a formerly competent adult's wishes was necessary to allow a surrogate to refuse treatment? Did a surrogate have the right to refuse treatment for a minor or for an adult who had never been competent, such as a severely retarded person? And, finally, could the right to refuse life-sustaining treatment be extended into a right to have help in hastening death? The courts and the public would have to face these issues in later cases.

BOUVIA V. SUPERIOR COURT EX REL. GLENCHUR CAL REPTR 297 C. CT. APP. (1986)

Background

Elizabeth Bouvia, a 26-year-old woman of normal intelligence, had been born with severe cerebral palsy, which left her with partial control of only her right hand and her head. She also suffered from arthritis, which caused her considerable pain. A difficult family situation, a miscarriage, and a failed marriage probably also influenced her psychological state.

Bouvia had been living in Oregon before her father, at her request, drove her to Riverside General Hospital in California in September 1983. She checked herself into the hospital and asked to have the tube by which she normally obtained nutrition removed and then "just to be left alone and not bothered by friends or family or anyone else and to ultimately starve to death."[6] She was admitted as a psychiatric patient and Donald Fisher, the hospital's chief of psychiatry, was assigned to be her physician. He refused to comply with her wishes. Bouvia called a reporter and the American Civil Liberties Union and instigated a court proceeding in which she demanded her right, as a mentally competent adult, to refuse medical treatment in the form of her feeding tube. Fisher, the hospital, and the county of Riverside opposed her. Fisher maintained that Bouvia would eventually change her mind about wanting to die and stated that he would have her force-fed, if necessary, to keep her alive.

Legal Issues

Both sides of the court dispute agreed that Bouvia was adult, competent to make health care decisions, rational, and consistent in her demands. Her decision to discontinue life-sustaining treatment caused controversy, however, because although her physical condition could not be cured or even substantially improved, she was by no means terminally ill. The pain of her arthritis, although significant, was treatable. She therefore did not fit the picture of the terminally ill patient in excruciating agony that right-to-die literature usually presented in its calls for permission to obtain assistance in suicide.

Supporters of Bouvia's position maintained that she had a right to refuse feeding and thereby end her life, regardless of whether anyone agreed with her decision. Opponents maintained that she should be given help in improving the quality of her life rather than in dying. Disabled rights activists claimed that allowing people like Bouvia, who were disabled but not terminally ill, to obtain even relatively passive help in dying would reinforce society's discriminatory belief that handicapped people's lives were not worth living. It might also open the door to pressuring such people to kill themselves as a way of avoiding the expense of their long-term care.

Decision

In Bouvia's first court hearing, which took place in December 1983, probate judge John Hews agreed that she was competent and rational. Nonetheless, he refused to grant her request because of the effect he felt that her dying would have on the hospital staff and on other disabled people. He ruled that Fisher could use force-feeding, which was carried out for a time.

Bouvia appealed, but in April 1984 an appeals court upheld Hews's ruling. She transferred to several hospitals, including one in Mexico, at times accepting feeding and at times being force-fed. A second court hearing early in 1986, before Judge Warren Deering, again denied Bouvia's right to what Deering considered assisted suicide, but later that year the California Court of Appeal reversed Deering's ruling. The appeals court held that Bouvia, as a competent adult, did have the right to refuse the feeding tube. The judges wrote:

The right to refuse medical treatment is basic and fundamental. It is recognized as part of the right of privacy protected by both the state and federal constitutions. . . . [A] precedent has been established that when a doctor performs treatment in the absence of informed consent, there is actionable battery. . . . In Elizabeth Bouvia's view, the quality of her life has been diminished to the point of hopelessness, uselessness, unenjoyability, and frustration. . . . She is not to be faulted for so concluding. . . . We do not believe it is the policy of this State that all and every life must be preserved against the will of the sufferer.

By then, however, Bouvia apparently had changed her mind and no longer insisted on removal of the tube.

Impact

Elizabeth Bouvia never exercised the right the court had given her to kill herself. She obtained medication (a morphine pump) that controlled the pain of her arthritis. In 1995 she was living in a California hospital. "I wouldn't say I'm happy, but I'm physically comfortable," she told a reporter. "There is nothing really to do. I just kind of lay here."[7] She was reported to be still alive in 2002.

The most basic importance of Bouvia's case lay in the appeals court's clear statement that any competent adult, terminally ill or not, had a constitutional right to refuse life-sustaining medical treatment. Bouvia's case and a similar one in 1989 involving a young Georgia man, Larry McAfee, who had been left a quadriplegic following a motorcycle accident, showed that disabled people could obtain the right to kill themselves by refusing life-sustaining treatment if they persisted through the court system long enough. This dismayed disabled advocacy groups, but such groups could also point to Bouvia's and McAfee's refusal to avail themselves of this permission after they had obtained it. Publicity from their cases put them in contact with people who were able to improve the quality of their lives enough to make them stop considering suicide.

CRUZAN V. DIRECTOR, MISSOURI DEPARTMENT OF HEALTH
497 U.S. 261 (1990)

Background

Nancy Beth Cruzan, a 25-year-old Missouri woman, lost control of her car on the night of January 11, 1983. Thrown from the vehicle when it crashed, she landed face down in a water-filled ditch. She had been there at least 15 minutes when police and paramedics found her. They restarted her breathing, but by then, damage to her brain from lack of oxygen had reduced her, like Karen Quinlan, to a persistent vegetative state. Unlike Quinlan, Cruzan was able to breathe on her own, but she had to be maintained by a tube that delivered food and water directly into her stomach.

Cruzan's parents, Lester (Joe) and Joyce Cruzan, faced the same type of agonizing decision that the Quinlans had, except that in Cruzan's case the treatment to be discontinued was not an artificial breathing machine but provision of basic nutrition. The Quinlans had firmly rejected such an action for Karen. The Cruzans waited four years, during which Nancy showed no signs of improvement, before deciding to ask for her feeding tube to be removed. Such removal was sure to cause Cruzan's death within a short time.

As had happened with the Quinlans, Cruzan's physician and hospital refused, and the Cruzans went to court. Nancy had not filled out an advance directive, but her housemate testified that, about a year earlier, Nancy had said in a "somewhat serious" conversation that if sick or injured, she would not want to be kept alive if she could not "live at least halfway normally."[8] Charles E. Teel, judge of a probate court in Jasper County, held that this testimony was sufficient evidence that Nancy would not have wished to continue nutrition and hydration in her present condition. He therefore granted the Cruzans the right to remove the feeding tube in early 1988.

The state appealed the decision, however, and in November 1988 the Missouri Supreme Court reversed Teel's ruling by a 4-to-3 vote. The justices granted that the common-law doctrine of informed consent would have given Cruzan the right to refuse treatment. However, they said, the family had not presented the "clear and convincing evidence" of Cruzan's wish to refuse medical treatment in case of incompetence that Missouri's Living Will law required. Given this fact and the state's "unqualified interest in [preserving] life," the justices ruled, they could not permit removal of Cruzan's feeding tube.[9]

The Cruzans appealed the case to the U.S. Supreme Court, which heard it on December 6, 1989. As the justices noted in their majority opinion, this was "the first case in which we have been squarely presented with the issue of whether the United States Constitution grants what is in common parlance referred to as a right to die."

Legal Issues

In some ways, *Cruzan* presented the same question as *Quinlan:* How much right do surrogates have to refuse life-sustaining medical treatment on behalf of incompetent, but formerly competent, adults who have left only ambiguous prior indications of their wishes? There were two important differences, however. First, *Cruzan* concerned provision of food and water, which many people saw as a much more basic kind of care than maintenance on a respirator. And second, *Cruzan*, unlike *Quinlan*, reached the U.S. Supreme Court. The ruling on *Cruzan*, therefore, would have a direct and important effect on right-to-die law throughout the country.

An additional issue in the Cruzan case was the question of how precise an indication of a formerly competent person's wishes a court could require before allowing a surrogate to refuse treatment. The Missouri law demanded "clear and convincing" evidence, which is the middle level of stringency in the three standards for evidence and the highest standard that can be applied in civil cases. It is more exacting than the loosest standard, "a preponderance of the evidence," but less so than the most rigorous standard, "beyond a reasonable doubt."

Decision

The Supreme Court made its ruling on June 25, 1990. The ruling, like the one in the Missouri Supreme Court, showed an almost even split (5–4) among the justices. Two concurring and two dissenting opinions were filed in addition to the majority opinion, which was written by Chief Justice William Rehnquist.

Rehnquist's majority opinion first reaffirmed the right of a competent adult to refuse medical treatment. It grounded this right in common law, which held that unwanted treatment was a form of battery (unlawful touching or bodily invasion); in the doctrine of informed consent and the right to control what happens to one's own body; and in the constitutionally protected right to liberty and privacy. It cited several other cases in which courts had defended this right even for incompetent people, including *Quinlan* and a 1985 case, *In re Conroy*, in which the New Jersey Supreme Court granted the right of a surrogate (a nephew) to order discontinuation of artificial nutrition and hydration for Claire Conroy, an incompetent elderly woman.

On the other hand, Rehnquist wrote, an individual's liberty interest in refusing treatment had to be balanced against the state's interest in preserving life and protecting the vulnerable, represented in this case by Missouri's demand for "clear and convincing evidence" of a formerly competent person's wishes. The court ruled that the state's requirement of clearer evidence than would be demanded for an ordinary civil proceeding was constitutional.

> *The choice between life and death is a deeply personal decision of obvious and overwhelming finality. We believe Missouri may legitimately seek to safeguard the personal element of this choice through the imposition of heightened evidentiary requirements. . . . A State is entitled to guard against potential abuse in such situations.*

___

Because Missouri's standard for evidence had not been met, the Supreme Court agreed that Nancy Cruzan's feeding tube could not be removed unless clearer evidence of her wishes was provided. The "substituted judgment" of her family, no matter how loving and well intentioned, was not sufficient: "We do not think the Due Process Clause requires the State to repose judgment on these matters with anyone but the patient herself," Rehnquist wrote. The high court therefore affirmed the Missouri Supreme Court's judgment.

Impact

The Cruzans returned to the Missouri courts. In a new hearing in Judge Teel's court in November 1990, some friends of Nancy's came forward and recounted conversations in which Nancy had indicated more clearly her wish not to be kept alive if she was rendered permanently unconscious. They had known her only under her married name of Davis and therefore had not connected her with the "Cruzan case" until the names were linked in the widespread publicity the case attracted when it went before the Supreme Court. The state then withdrew its opposition to the Cruzans. Nancy's feeding tube was removed on December 14, 1990, and she died on December 26.

As with the Quinlan case, the chief immediate effect of the *Cruzan* decision was to increase public interest in advance directives. (In her concurring opinion, Justice Sandra Day O'Connor urged people to fill out such directives in order to avoid the sort of problems that had arisen for the Cruzans.) This time, part of the legal effect was nationwide. In the same month the Cruzans finally won the right to disconnect Nancy's feeding tube, Congress passed the Patient Self-Determination Act, which requires all health care institutions receiving payments from federal programs to inform patients of their right to fill out advance directives and explain state laws and institutional policies concerning such directives. Many states also modified their advance directive laws to permit withdrawal of food and water from patients in persistent vegetative states if they had requested this in advance directives.

The right-to-die movement found victory in Chief Justice Rehnquist's statement that "the principle that a competent person has a constitutionally protected liberty interest in refusing unwanted medical treatment may be inferred from our prior decisions" and that "for the purposes of this case, we assume that the United States Constitution would grant a competent person a constitutionally protected right to refuse life-saving nutrition and hydration." These statements basically affirmed the constitutional right of a competent adult to refuse life-sustaining medical treatment, including provision of food and water, although their tentative phrasing kept them short of an explicit declaration of this right. The Court's decision also indicated that a surrogate could refuse life-sustaining treatment on an incompetent person's behalf, provided that the person had made his or her wishes clearly known while competent.

To some right-to-die supporters, Rehnquist's statement suggested that the Supreme Court might accept the notion that there was an overall "constitutional right to die." It was by no means clear, however, that such a right could be extended from refusal of medical treatment to the much more controversial actions of physician-assisted suicide and euthanasia, even in the case of competent, terminally ill adults.

According to medical ethicist Gregory Pence, legal scholars generally praised the *Cruzan* decision because of its conservative reluctance to find any new "rights" embedded in the Constitution, something the Supreme Court had been criticized for doing in, for example, *Roe v. Wade.* They approved the Court's insistence on clear demonstration of Cruzan's feelings rather than reliance on her family's "substituted judgment." Physician commentators, on the other hand, often complained that strict evidentiary requirements like those in Missouri put doctors and families alike under an intolerable burden. Neurologist and ethicist Ronald Cranford, for instance, called the Missouri standard

> *unworkable, unfair, and cruel to so many families who will experience the utter helplessness of the Cruzans. It will place an enormous burden on society, which will spend hundreds of millions of dollars each year for [maintenance of people in] a condition that no one in their right mind would ever want to be in.*[10]

COMPASSION IN DYING ET AL. V. STATE OF WASHINGTON 850 F. SUPP. 1454 (1994)/79 F. 3RD 790 (9TH CIR. 1996) GLUCKSBERG V. WASHINGTON

Background

Five physicians who regularly treated terminally ill patients, three terminally ill people, and a nonprofit group that counsels the terminally ill joined together on January 29, 1994, to bring suit against the state of Washington in an attempt to have the state's Promoting Suicide law declared unconstitutional as it applied to mentally competent, terminally ill adults who ask doctors for help in hastening their death. The physicians were Harold Glucksberg, a cancer specialist; Thomas Preston, a cardiologist; Abigail Halperin and John P. Geyman, family practitioners; and Peter Shalit, an internist. The patients, known in the court records only by pseudonyms, included a woman with cancer, a man with AIDS, and another man with heart and lung failure. (All died long before the case reached its conclusion.) The right-to-die group was Seattle-based Compassion in Dying, which provided counseling and assistance (although not medication) for terminally ill adults who wished to end their lives. (Compassion in Dying is now part of a new organization called Compassion and Choices.)

The physicians all testified that patients had "occasionally" asked them for medication to hasten death and end suffering but that the law prevented them from prescribing such medication, even when they deemed it medically appropriate. It thus hindered their right to practice medicine according to their best professional judgment, they claimed. The three patients described their suffering in detail and said that the law harmed them because it denied them the liberty to make health care decisions for themselves, specifically the liberty to ask for medical help in hastening their deaths in order to bring the suffering to an end. Compassion in Dying claimed that it feared prosecution for its efforts in helping dying people use their alleged constitutional right to hasten their deaths.

Legal Issues

Washington's Promoting Suicide Law states in part: "A person is guilty of promoting a suicide attempt when he knowingly causes or aids another person to attempt suicide. Promoting a suicide attempt is a felony punishable by imprisonment."[11] It traces its roots back to an 1854 statute against assisted suicide that was passed while Washington was still a territory. The plaintiffs did not question the state's overall interest in preventing suicide or the constitutionality of the law as a whole. Their suit referred only to the "or aids" part of the law's application to competent, terminally ill adults who ask for a physician's help in hastening their death.

The underlying legal issue in this case was whether a competent, terminally ill adult had a constitutional right to ask for active aid in hastening death. The coalition suing the state maintained that such a right could be inferred from two clauses in the Fourteenth Amendment, the Due Process Clause and the Equal Protection Clause. The Due Process Clause states that "No State shall deprive any person of life, liberty, or property without due process of law." In earlier decisions, including the famous *Roe v. Wade* abortion ruling in 1973, the Supreme Court had interpreted this clause as protecting the liberty to make certain personal decisions, including those involved in marriage, procreation, contraception, abortion, and the right to refuse medical treatment. The courts, however, have distinguished between due process liberty *interests* and more fundamental due process *rights*. In recent years the Supreme Court has been reluctant to find new fundamental rights, but it has been somewhat more permissive about interests.

Finding a liberty interest does not guarantee that that interest must predominate. Rather, individuals' liberty interests must be balanced against state interests in determining whether a law is constitutional. If a state's reasons for limiting or even blocking a liberty interest are deemed significant enough, the law may stand. The more important the individual's right or interest is held to be, however, the more persuasive the state's reasons for limiting it must be.

The Equal Protection Clause states that "No State shall deny to any person within its jurisdiction the equal protection of the laws." This has been interpreted to mean that similarly situated groups must be treated equally under the law. The plaintiffs in this suit maintained that terminally ill people who ask for medication to end their lives are similarly situated to terminally ill people who ask for discontinuation of life-sustaining treatment, such as a respirator or feeding tube. Because Washington law permits the action of the second group, they argued, it should permit that of the first group as well.

The state of Washington, represented by its attorney general, argued that the rights specified in these clauses were not great enough to outweigh several compelling state interests served by the law. These interests are preserving human life, preventing suicide, avoiding undue influence by third parties, protecting children and other family members, protecting the integrity of the medical profession, and preventing undesirable consequences.

Decision

Compassion in Dying et al. v. State of Washington was first heard before Barbara Rothstein, chief judge of the U.S. district court for western Washington, in Seattle on May 3, 1994. Rothstein ruled in favor of the patients, saying that the Washington law violated the rights guaranteed to them by both clauses of the Fourteenth Amendment. She denied the suit of the physicians and of Compassion in Dying "on the grounds that the basis for [their] claims has not been adequately addressed."

Rothstein quoted the U.S. Supreme Court's second abortion decision, in *Planned Parenthood of Southeastern Pennsylvania v. Casey* (1992), as establishing individuals' constitutionally protected liberty interest in making personal decisions, including those relating to marriage, contraception, reproduction, family relationships, and the rearing and education of children. The high court had stated:

> *These matters, involving the most intimate and personal choices a person may make in a lifetime, choices central to personal dignity and autonomy, are*

central to the liberty protected by the Fourteenth Amendment. At the heart of liberty is the right to define one's own concept of existence, of meaning, of the universe, and of the mystery of human life. Beliefs about these could not define the attributes of personhood were they formed under compulsion of the State.

Rothstein found the reasoning in *Casey* "highly instructive and almost prescriptive" on the issue of a terminally ill person's right to obtain assistance in suicide. The Supreme Court in *Casey* had written that the court's duty was not to assert a moral standard in a controversial issue such as abortion, even a standard that had support in the nation's history and culture. Similarly, Rothstein felt that the court was not obliged to set a moral standard in the hotly debated issue of physician-assisted suicide. Rather, as with abortion, individuals had the constitutionally protected right to make their own decisions in this matter.

This court concludes that the suffering of a terminally ill person cannot be deemed any less intimate or personal, or any less deserving of protection from unwarranted governmental interference, than that of a pregnant woman. Thus, consonant with the reasoning in Casey, *such an intimate personal decision falls within the realm of the liberties constitutionally protected under the Fourteenth Amendment.*

The Supreme Court's ruling in *Cruzan* was "instructive" to Rothstein as well. In that ruling, the Court had concluded that a competent adult's protected liberty interest in refusing unwanted, life-sustaining medical treatment could be inferred from its earlier decisions, and it had assumed such an interest for the purposes of the case. Rothstein maintained that this liberty interest could be expanded to include competent, terminally ill people who wished to hasten death by taking drugs prescribed for the purpose by a physician. She wrote:

There is no more profoundly personal decision, nor one which is closer to the heart of personal liberty, than the choice which a terminally ill person makes to end his or her suffering and hasten an inevitable death. From a constitutional perspective, the court does not believe that a distinction can be drawn between refusing life-sustaining medical treatment and physician-assisted suicide by an uncoerced, mentally competent, terminally ill adult.

In speaking of competing state interests that might override this liberty interest, Rothstein pointed out that, if anything, more competing interests were involved in abortion than in assisted suicide because the former involved the potential interest of an innocent third party, the fetus, whereas no other party would normally be harmed by the suicide of a terminally ill person. She granted that the state had a legitimate interest in preventing the suicide of people who had "a significant natural life span ahead of them," but she denied that this interest applied to those whose life would end in a short time anyway. She also said that the state legislature could devise regulations that would "define the appropriate boundaries of physician-assisted suicide for terminally ill individuals, and at the same time give due recognition to the important public policy concerns regarding the prevention of suicide."

Similarly, Rothstein granted that the state had a legitimate interest in preventing the abuse or coercion of vulnerable groups, but she said that this was just as much a risk with refusing medical treatment, especially when done by surrogates, as with asking for active assistance in suicide and that it, too, could be mitigated by regulations. She ruled that neither of these state interests would be significantly impeded by permitting physician-assisted suicide for competent, terminally ill adults.

Having already equated competent, terminally ill adults who wished to refuse life-sustaining medical treatment with those who asked for a prescription to hasten their deaths, Rothstein ruled that the Washington statute treated these two groups unequally by permitting refusal of medical treatment but denying requests for medical assistance in dying. She wrote:

> *This court is not persuaded that the distinction between "natural" and "artificial" death justifies disparate treatment of these similarly situated groups. . . . Therefore, this court finds that [the Washington law banning physician-assisted suicide] violates the equal protection guarantee of the Fourteenth Amendment.*

The state appealed Rothstein's decision, and a three-judge panel from the U.S. Ninth Circuit Court of Appeals heard the case on December 7, 1994. Rulings of this court affect Alaska, Arizona, California, Hawaii, Idaho, Montana, Nevada, Oregon, and Washington. Judge John T. Noonan delivered the majority opinion in the 2-to-1 ruling on March 9, 1995. Noonan reversed Rothstein's decision, saying that the state's interest in protecting human life in general and vulnerable groups in articular outweighed patients' liberty interest and that the Washington law therefore was constitutional. Noonan wrote that the right to privacy and to refuse unwanted medical treatment did not include "the right to have a second person collaborate in your death."

After reviewing the facts of the case and Rothstein's decision, Noonan made arguments against Rothstein's claim that the Washington law violated liberty interests protected by the Fourteenth Amendment. He wrote that "the language taken from *Casey* . . . should not be removed from the context in which it was uttered." If the general decision-making right described in *Casey* were applied to assisted suicide, Noonan maintained, there would be no logical reason to limit it to the terminally ill.

> *The depressed twenty-one year old, the romantically-devastated twenty-eight year old, the alcoholic forty year old who choose suicide are also expressing their views of the existence, meaning, the universe, and life; they are also asserting their personal liberty. If at the heart of the liberty protected by the Fourteenth Amendment is this uncurtailable ability to believe and to act on one's deepest beliefs about life, the right to suicide and the right to assistance in suicide are the prerogative of at least every sane adult. . . . The conclusion is a reductio ad absurdum [ridiculous].*

Noonan also disagreed with Rothstein's claim that the Supreme Court's *Cruzan* decision could be used to support a right to assisted suicide, even for the terminally ill. He pointed out that the Court in *Cruzan* stressed the state's interest in the protection and preservation of human life and specifically cited state laws criminalizing assistance in suicide as an example of this interest. "In the two hundred and five years of our [nation's] existence no constitutional right to aid in killing oneself has ever been asserted and upheld by a court of final jurisdiction," he emphasized.

The Washington law against assisted suicide served other state interests as well, Noonan wrote. These included "the interest in not having physicians in the role of killers of their patients," a role that the American Medical Association had called "fundamentally incompatible with the physician's role as healer" and with the Hippocratic Oath; an interest in "not subjecting the elderly and even the not-elderly but infirm to psychological pressure to consent to their own deaths," a pressure that could come from either physicians or family members; an interest in "protecting the poor and minorities from exploitation," for example by health care providers who might pressure them to commit suicide rather than pay the high cost of their care; and an interest in "protecting all of the handicapped from societal indifference and antipathy," which might force them to justify their continued existence or, as with the elderly, pressure them into dying to save money.

Noonan strongly disagreed with Rothstein's claim that refusing life-sustaining medical treatment and asking for assistance in suicide are the same. The first, he wrote, is a legally legitimate refusal based on the tort concept of battery: "You can be left alone if you want." However, he noted:

Right to Die and Euthanasia

When you assert a claim that another . . . should help you bring about your death, you ask for more than being let alone; you ask that the state . . . not prevent its licensee [the physician] from killing [you]. The difference is not of degree but of kind. . . . To protect all the interests enumerated [earlier in this decision] . . . the statute rightly and reasonably draws the line.

The right-to-die advocates protested that both Noonan and the judge who concurred with him, Diarmuid F. O'Scannlain, were Catholics and thus might have been influenced by religious bias. They therefore asked for a rehearing by the entire 11-judge appeals court panel. Because of "the extraordinary importance of the case," the court agreed to rehear it *en banc.* The new hearing took place on October 26, 1995.

On March 6, 1996, the full panel in turn reversed Noonan's decision. Judge Stephen Reinhardt, delivering the majority opinion, wrote: "We hold that insofar as the Washington statute prohibits physicians from prescribing life-ending medication for use by terminally ill, competent adults who wish to hasten their own deaths, it violates the Due Process Clause of the Fourteenth Amendment."

In the rest of his statement, Reinhardt essentially elaborated upon the reasoning in Rothstein's opinion, which he called "extremely thoughtful." Unlike Rothstein, however, Reinhardt focused strictly on the liberty interest and right to privacy protected by the Due Process Clause. He wrote that because the judges felt that the law violated this constitutional right, the question of whether it also violated the Equal Protection Clause did not need to be considered.

Reinhardt first offered evidence to support his conclusion that "there is a constitutionally-protected liberty interest in determining the time and manner of one's own death." Like Rothstein, he drew most of his reasoning on this point from analogies with the right to make decisions about abortion that the Supreme Court had granted in *Roe* and *Casey* and the right to refuse life-sustaining medical treatment that it had assumed in *Cruzan.* He quoted Justice John Marshall Harlan II's statement about broad liberty interests in the justice's dissenting opinion in *Poe v. Ullman* (1961):

The full scope of the liberty guaranteed by the Due Process Clause cannot be found in or limited by the precise terms of the specific guarantees elsewhere in the Constitution. . . . It is a rational continuum which, broadly speaking, includes a freedom from all substantial arbitrary impositions and purposeless restraints, . . . and which also recognizes . . . that certain interests require particularly careful scrutiny of the state needs asserted to justify their abridgement.

The Law of Euthanasia

The liberty interest he found was not in asking a physician or anyone else to assist in suicide, Reinhardt wrote, but rather in determining the time and manner of one's death. This interest encompassed "a whole range of acts that are generally not considered to constitute 'suicide,'" including the act of refusing or terminating unwanted medical treatment. The right to ask a physician for help in dying devolves from this more basic right. The same, he said, was true of the right to choose an abortion, from which the right to ask a physician to assist in the abortion devolved. "In short," he wrote, "it is the end and not the means that defines the liberty interest."

Reinhardt granted that the United States had a long history of prohibiting assistance in suicide, but he maintained that this alone was not enough to deny a liberty interest. He said the Supreme Court had often stated that "the limits of the substantive reach of the Due Process Clause are not frozen at any point in time." Laws against interracial marriage, for example, also had a long history but had nonetheless been overturned by the high court. Reinhardt then offered his own historical analysis to show that suicide, especially to end the suffering of terminal illness, had sometimes been considered acceptable. Furthermore, he claimed, "running beneath the official history of legal condemnation of physician-assisted suicide is a strong undercurrent of a time-honored but hidden practice of physicians helping terminally ill patients to hasten their deaths." He also cited polls showing that a majority of Americans currently favored allowing terminally ill people to ask doctors for help in dying.

Like Rothstein, Reinhardt pointed out that the substantive liberty interests protected by the Supreme Court in the past involved decisions that were important, personal, and intimate. "Few decisions are more personal, intimate or important than the decision to end one's life," he maintained.

A competent terminally ill adult, having lived nearly the full measure of his life, has a strong liberty interest in choosing a dignified and humane death rather than being reduced at the end of his existence to a childlike state of helplessness, diapered, sedated, incontinent. How a person dies not only determines the nature of the final period of his existence, but in many cases, the enduring memories held by those who love him. Prohibiting a terminally ill patient from hastening his death may have an even more profound impact on that person's life than forcing a woman to carry a pregnancy to term.

Interestingly, Reinhardt suggested that protected liberty interests might even include voluntary euthanasia:

For present purposes we view the critical line in right-to-die cases as the one between the voluntary and involuntary termination of an individual's life. . . .

Right to Die and Euthanasia

We consider it less important who administers the medication [that causes death] than who determines whether the terminally ill person's life shall end.

In this view he differed from most Americans, who had shown themselves in polls to be far less willing to accept euthanasia than physician-assisted suicide.

Having explained his reasons for believing that there was a substantive liberty interest in determining the time and manner of one's death, Reinhardt went on to weigh this interest against the state's interests in prohibiting such action (he accepted a state interest in regulating it). He identified six such interests: preserving life, preventing suicide, preventing undue influence of third parties, protecting family members and loved ones, protecting the integrity of the medical profession, and avoiding adverse consequences that might arise if the law in question was declared unconstitutional. He agreed that the state could assert an interest in preserving all life but held that its interest in preserving the lives of terminally ill or permanently comatose patients against their will was "dramatically diminished."

The state's interest in preventing suicide, Reinhardt maintained, was also greatly diminished in the case of terminally ill people. He showed how earlier distinctions involved in ending medical treatment, such as those between "extraordinary" and "ordinary" treatment and between refusing and terminating treatment, had vanished or changed when they had been found to be unworkable. He then rejected the three distinctions that the state maintained between ending of medical treatment and terminal sedation to control pain, both of which were legal, and physician-assisted suicide, which was not. Both groups of actions, he maintained, could require doctors to take an active role in causing death, could cause deaths that would not result from the patient's underlying disease, and could require doctors to provide the causal agent of patients' deaths. Because he equated these actions, Reinhardt found the state's interest in preventing suicide to be no greater in regard to one than in regard to the other. He also questioned whether any of them could really be considered suicide when applied to terminally ill people.

Regulations would be necessary to prevent third parties from coercing or influencing sick people to commit suicide, Reinhardt agreed, but he felt that the possibility of abuse was no greater with physician-assisted suicide than it was with refusal of life-sustaining treatment. He maintained that the interest in protecting children and family members was minimal in the case of people whose death was already imminent. Addressing the state interest in protecting physicians' integrity, he stated, "We do not believe that the integrity of the medical profession would be threatened in any way by the vindication of the liberty interest at issue here . . . given the similarity between what doctors are now permitted to do and what the plaintiffs assert they should be permitted to do."

Finally, Reinhardt rejected the "parade of horribles" that proponents of the "slippery slope" argument suggested would occur if physician-assisted suicide was legalized. He also noted, "The [Supreme] Court has *never* refused to recognize a substantive due process liberty right or interest merely because there were difficulties in determining when and how to limit its exercise or because others might someday attempt to use it improperly." Regulations, he reemphasized, should be able to ensure that the use of assisted suicide was appropriately limited.

Reinhardt concluded by stressing that removal of the Washington law would not force assisted suicide on anyone. Rather, it would leave this very personal choice to individuals.

Those who believe strongly that death must come without physician assistance are free to follow that creed, be they doctors or patients. They are not free, however, to force their views, their religious convictions, or their philosophies on all the other members of a democratic society, and to compel those whose values differ with theirs to die painful, protracted, and agonizing deaths.

The state of Washington appealed the Ninth Circuit Court's ruling. *Washington State v. Glucksberg*, as the case became known, was one of the two right-to-die cases that the U.S. Supreme Court heard on January 8, 1997. (The other was *Quill v. Vacco*)

Impact

Each of the rulings in this case produced the effect that would have been expected. Opponents of physician-assisted suicide applauded Noonan's decision, whereas supporters hailed Rothstein's and, later, Reinhardt's. Conversely, supporters claimed that Noonan's conclusions were spurred by religious bias, and opponents criticized Reinhardt's legal reasoning and historical accuracy.

One of the most common criticisms of Rothstein's and Reinhardt's rulings was that they took general philosophical comments such as those quoted from *Casey* out of context and overapplied them. Critics pointed out that no specific statements from the Supreme Court extended liberty interests in private decision making. Opponents of assisted suicide and euthanasia also questioned the assertion that there was no important distinction between removing a respirator or feeding tube, which they saw as "letting die," and deliberately prescribing or administering medication for the purpose of causing death, which they classified as killing, even if it was done at a patient's request.

QUILL V. KOPPELL (LATER VACCO)
870 F. SUPP. 78 (S.D.N.Y. 1994)
80 F. 3RD 716 (2ND CIR. 1996)

Background

This case was very similar to *Compassion et al. in Dying v. Washington,* and indeed was also sponsored by Compassion in Dying. The plaintiffs were a coalition of three physicians and three terminally ill patients. The group first filed its suit on July 29, 1994, in the U.S. Court for the Southern District of New York. The defendants in the suit were New York's attorney general and governor as well as the district attorney of New York County.

The physicians in the coalition were Timothy Quill, internist and advocate of physician-assisted suicide, and two New York City internists, Samuel C. Klagsbrun and Howard A. Grossman. The three claimed that their terminally ill patients had a constitutionally protected right to physician-assisted suicide and that they themselves, therefore, had a concomitant right not to be prosecuted under New York's laws forbidding aiding and promoting suicide. In one of his court declarations, Quill stated:

> *It is legally and ethically permitted for physicians to actively assist patients to die who are dependent on life-sustaining treatments. . . . Unfortunately, some dying patients who are in agony that can no longer be relieved, yet are not dependent on life-sustaining treatment, have no such option under current legal restrictions. It seems unfair, discriminatory, and inhumane to deprive some dying patients of such vital choices because of arbitrary elements of their condition which determine whether they are on life-sustaining treatment that can be stopped.*[12]

The pseudonymous patients included one woman with cancer and two men with AIDS. All were competent adults in the terminal stage of their illness who testified that they were suffering severely and had asked their doctors to prescribe drugs that they could use to commit suicide. They alleged that the New York laws prevented them from exercising a constitutional right to determine the time and manner of their death. None of the patients survived the litigation.

Legal Issues

New York's Aiding Suicide law states, "A person is guilty of manslaughter when he intentionally aids another person to commit suicide." The law against promoting suicide states, "A person is guilty of promoting a suicide attempt when he intentionally aids another person to attempt suicide."[13] A violation of either law is a felony punishable by a prison sentence. Like the Washington law, the New York ones have a long history, dating back originally to 1828. Indeed, the 1828 law was the earliest U.S. statute that explicitly criminalized assisting a suicide.

As in Washington, the plaintiffs claimed that New York's laws against assisted suicide violated terminally ill patients' constitutional right to determine the time and manner of their dying, including the right to ask for a physician's aid in hastening death. They maintained that this right was guaranteed by the Due Process Clause of the Fourteenth Amendment, the Equal Protection Clause, or both. The state of New York, represented by its attorney general, said that the laws protected state interests that outweighed these possible Fourteenth Amendment rights and were therefore constitutional. It cited the same six interests that had been considered in the Washington case.

Decision

Thomas Griesa, the district court's chief judge, issued his decision on December 15, 1994. After agreeing that, contrary to the state's claim, the doctors did have reason to fear prosecution and thus had a justiciable controversy, Griesa ruled against the physicians and dismissed the coalition's action. Neither clause of the Fourteenth Amendment guaranteed a right to physician-assisted suicide, he stated.

Griesa claimed that the plaintiffs' reading of *Casey* and *Cruzan*, which they had cited in support of their claim that there was a protected liberty interest in determining the time and manner of one's death, was too broad. He noted that the Supreme Court had been willing to find new fundamental rights protected by the Due Process Clause only when such rights were "implicit in the concept of ordered liberty so that neither liberty nor justice would exist if they were sacrificed" and were also "deeply rooted in the nation's history and traditions." A right to assisted suicide certainly did not meet the latter criterion, Griesa wrote, since most states had long histories of laws imposing criminal penalties on those who assisted suicide. No exception was made for physicians. Therefore, he held, New York's laws against assisted suicide did not violate a fundamental liberty interest protected by the Due Process clause.

Griesa also rejected the contention that the New York laws violated the Equal Protection Clause because they made an unreasonable and irrational distinction between refusal or termination of life-sustaining treatment and request for a physician's aid in committing suicide. He wrote:

Right to Die and Euthanasia

It is hardly unreasonable or irrational for the State to recognize a difference between allowing nature to take its course, even in the most severe situations, and intentionally using an artificial death-producing device.

The plaintiffs appealed the case, and on September 1, 1995, a three-judge panel of the U.S. Second Circuit Court of Appeals reviewed it. This court's decisions are binding in New York, Connecticut, and Vermont. The court ruled unanimously on April 2, 1996, to overturn the lower court and declare the New York laws unconstitutional as they applied to mentally competent, terminally ill patients who wished to self-administer lethal drugs provided by a physician. Justice Roger J. Miner wrote the court opinion.

Unlike Stephen Reinhardt's similar conclusion for the Ninth Circuit Court, Miner's opinion rejected the plaintiffs' Due Process arguments, citing the same reasons Griesa had given. Miner upheld the arguments based on the Equal Protection Clause, however, stating that "New York law does not treat equally all competent persons who are in the final stages of fatal illness and wish to hasten their deaths [and] the distinctions made by New York law with regard to such persons do not further any legitimate state purpose."

Miner pointed out that New York law explicitly recognizes the right of competent adults and the surrogates of incompetent ones to refuse life-sustaining medical treatment. Furthermore, he wrote, the Supreme Court had "all but" done the same in its *Cruzan* decision. He then maintained that there was no significant difference between refusing such treatment and asking for and ingesting lethal medication because both predictably resulted in the patient's death.

Countering Griesa's distinction between "allowing nature to take its course . . . and intentionally using an artificial death-producing device," Miner maintained that there was nothing natural about, for example, causing death from starvation and dehydration by withdrawing a tube that provides food and water. Indeed, he claimed that writing a prescription for lethal medication "involves a far less active role for the physician than is required in bringing about death through asphyxiation, starvation and/or dehydration." He counted both as "nothing more nor less than assisted suicide."

Miner then went on to consider whether the inequality of treatment applied to patients who wished to terminate life support as compared to those who wished a lethal prescription had any rational relationship to a legitimate state interest. The most likely interest was the preservation of life, but "what interest," Miner asked, "can the state possibly have in requiring the prolongation of a life that is all but ended?" In referring to the interest in preventing physicians from killing patients, he claimed that "physicians do not fulfill the role of 'killer' by prescribing drugs to hasten death any more than they do by disconnecting life-support systems." Similarly, he said, the potential for coercion or other abuse was the same for refusal of medical treatment as it was for assisted suicide. He concluded that the New York laws were not rationally related to any legitimate state interest and therefore violated the Equal Protection Clause. Therefore, he wrote:

> *We reverse [the lower court's decision] in part, holding that physicians who are willing to do so may prescribe drugs to be self-administered to mentally competent patients who seek to end their lives during the final stages of a terminal illness.*

After Miner's ruling, the state appealed the case to the Supreme Court. The high court heard oral arguments on this case, then known as *New York v. Quill* or *Vacco v. Quill* (Dennis Vacco was the New York attorney general at the time), along with arguments on *Washington v. Glucksberg* on January 8, 1997.

Impact

This decision, combined with the one made by the Ninth Circuit Court of Appeals, theoretically gave qualifying people in about one-fourth of the United States the right to ask for aid in dying. Soon after the decisions were handed down, however, Supreme Court Justice Sandra Day O'Connor blocked physicians in the affected states from carrying out any such action until after the Supreme Court ruled on the cases.

WASHINGTON STATE V. GLUCKSBERG
117 S. CT. 2258 (1997)
NEW YORK STATE V. QUILL
117 S. CT. 2293 (1997)

Background

Both of these cases involved constitutional challenges to state laws forbidding assisted suicide (in Washington and New York, respectively) as these laws applied to mentally competent, terminally ill adults who asked for a physician's aid in hastening their death. The plaintiffs in the original cases were physicians who regularly treated dying people and terminally ill patients who wished for a physician's help in dying. In both cases, lower courts had found the state laws to be constitutional, but federal appeals courts had reversed these rulings.

Right to Die and Euthanasia

Legal Issues

Plaintiffs in the original cases claimed that the state laws violated one or both of two clauses in the Fourteenth Amendment, the Due Process Clause and the Equal Protection Clause. The states, in turn, claimed that compelling state interests overrode any possible violation of individual rights.

The Supreme Court heard oral arguments on the two cases on January 8, 1997. They also reviewed 60 *amicus curiae* (friend of the court) briefs filed by individuals and organizations representing a wide spectrum of opinions on the right-to-die issue.

In oral arguments, Washington state assistant attorney general William Williams stated in regard to *Washington State v. Glucksberg:*

> *The issue here today is whether the Constitution requires that the social policy developed by Washington voters must be supplanted by a far different social policy, a constitutionally recognized right to physician-assisted suicide that is contrary to our traditions and overrides the important state interests that are served by the Washington statute [forbidding assistance in suicide].[14]*

Seattle attorney Kathryn Tucker, speaking for Glucksberg and the other defendants, maintained:

> *This case presents the question whether dying citizens in full possession of their mental faculties at the threshold of death due to terminal illness have the liberty to choose to cross that threshold in a humane and dignified manner.[15]*

In *New York State v. Quill,* Dennis Vacco, the state's attorney general, argued:

> *The question in this case is whether the State must remain neutral in the face of a decision of one of its citizens to help another kill herself. The [United States Court of Appeals for the] Second Circuit said "Yes" as a matter of equal protection. It is New York's view, however, that the Constitution does not require this to be the case.[16]*

Harvard Law School professor Lawrence Tribe, speaking for Quill and the other defendants, replied:

> *The liberty interest in this case is the liberty, when facing imminent and inevitable death, not to be forced by the government to endure a degree of pain and suffering that one can relieve only by being completely unconscious.*

The Law of Euthanasia

Not to be forced into that choice . . . is the freedom, at this threshold at the end of life, not to be a creature of the state but to have some voice in the question of how much pain one is really going through.[17]

Decision

The Supreme Court rendered its unanimous decisions on the two cases on June 26, 1997. It held that both state laws were constitutional and that neither clause of the Fourteenth Amendment protected a general "right to die." Chief Justice William H. Rehnquist wrote the majority opinion. Justices Sandra Day O'Connor, David H. Souter, Ruth Bader Ginsberg, John Paul Stevens, and Stephen G. Breyer wrote separate concurring opinions on *Washington v. Glucksberg*. Souter also wrote a concurring opinion on *New York v. Quill*.

In the *Washington v. Glucksberg* ruling, after reviewing the facts of the case, Rehnquist turned to history and noted that "in almost every State—indeed, in almost every western democracy—it is a crime to assist a suicide. The States' assisted-suicide bans . . . are longstanding expressions of the States' commitment to the protection and preservation of all human life." He added, "The well established common-law view . . . was . . . that the consent of a homicide victim is 'wholly immaterial to the guilt of the person who cause[d] [his death].'" Laws banning assisted suicide made no exceptions for those who were near death. Rather, "The life of those to whom life ha[d] become a burden—of those who [were] hopelessly diseased or fatally wounded . . . [was] under the protection of law, equally as the life of those who [were] in the full tide of life's enjoyment, and anxious to continue to live."

Rehnquist granted that recent advances in medical technology had changed the place and manner of many people's deaths, producing public concern about "how best to protect dignity and independence at the end of life." This concern resulted in new laws allowing advance health care directives and refusal or withdrawal of life-sustaining medical treatment. However, he noted, voters and legislators generally had maintained prohibitions against assisted suicide. He pointed out that both Washington and California had rejected initiatives permitting assisted suicide in the early 1990s and that an influential 1994 report by the New York State Task Force on Life and the Law had concluded that "[l]egalizing assisted suicide and euthanasia would pose profound risks to many individuals who are ill and vulnerable."

Turning to the question of rights protected by the Due Process Clause, Rehnquist said the Supreme Court had *held that, in addition to the specific freedoms protected by the Bill of Rights, the "liberty" specially protected by the Due Process Clause includes the rights to marry; to have children; to direct the education and upbringing of one's children; to marital privacy; to use contraception; to bodily integrity; and to abortion. We have also assumed, and strongly suggested, that the Due Process Clause protects the traditional right to refuse unwanted lifesaving medical treatment.*

Nonetheless, Rehnquist wrote, the Court had been reluctant to expand the list of substantive Due Process rights or liberty interests "because guideposts for responsible decisionmaking in this uncharted area are scarce and open-ended" and because rulings on these points "to a great extent, place the matter outside the arena of public debate and legislative action." In order for a new Due Process right to be granted, it must be shown to be "deeply rooted in this Nation's history and tradition" and "implicit in the concept of ordered liberty, . . . [such that] neither liberty nor justice would exist if [it] were sacrificed." The asserted right or liberty interest must also be carefully described.

In regard to the question of whether a right to commit suicide or to be assisted in doing so is deeply rooted in the history and tradition of the United States, Rehnquist reiterated his earlier point:

We are confronted with a consistent and almost universal tradition that has long rejected the asserted right [to assistance in suicide], and continues explicitly to reject it today, even for terminally ill, mentally competent adults. To hold for respondents, we would have to reverse centuries of legal doctrine and practice, and strike down the considered policy choice of almost every State.

Rehnquist then examined *Casey* and *Cruzan,* the decisions most often cited to support the idea of terminally ill people's liberty interest in asking for physician aid in dying. He wrote that the right to refuse medical treatment assumed in *Cruzan* "was not simply deduced from abstract concepts of personal autonomy" but rather was derived from the legal tradition that held unwanted medical treatment to be a form of battery.

The decision to commit suicide with the assistance of another may be just as personal and profound as the decision to refuse unwanted medical treatment, but . . . the two acts are widely and reasonably regarded as quite distinct. In Cruzan . . . *we certainly gave no intimation that the right to refuse unwanted medical treatment could be somehow transmuted into a right to assistance in committing suicide.*

94

Rehnquist stated that the general philosophical language about personal decision-making liberties that Rothstein and Reinhardt had cited from *Casey* did not mean that all major personal decisions were equally protected: "That many of the rights and liberties protected by the Due Process Clause sound in personal autonomy does not warrant the sweeping conclusion that any and all important, intimate, and personal decisions are so protected, and *Casey* did not suggest otherwise."

Rehnquist next took up the question of whether Washington's law against assisted suicide was rationally related to legitimate state interests. He concluded that "this requirement [for constitutionality] is unquestionably met." The most important state interest, he wrote, was the preservation of all human life, "from beginning to end, regardless of physical or mental condition." Rehnquist also asserted the importance of the state's interest in preventing suicide. "Legal physician-assisted suicide could make it more difficult for the State to protect depressed or mentally ill persons, or those who are suffering from untreated pain, from suicidal impulses," he wrote. Once depression and pain are treated, he noted, people who have requested a physician's aid in dying often change their minds.

The state's interest in protecting the ethics of the medical profession was also valid, Rehnquist ruled. He wrote that, further, the state needed to protect the poor, elderly, and disabled from coercion, neglect, and prejudice by laws showing that it valued their lives as highly as anyone else's. "Finally," he noted, "the State may fear that permitting assisted suicide will start it down the path to voluntary and perhaps even involuntary euthanasia." Rehnquist wrote that such concern was justified by the expansive wording in Reinhardt's opinion: "It turns out that what is couched as a limited right to 'physician-assisted suicide' is likely, in effect, a much broader license, which could prove extremely difficult to police and contain." Information from the Netherlands supported this concern, he noted. Rehnquist concluded his survey of state interests by saying that all the interests cited "are unquestionably important and legitimate, and Washington's ban on assisted suicide is at least reasonably related to their promotion and protection." Rehnquist ended his opinion on *Washington v. Glucksberg* by stating:

> *Throughout the Nation, Americans are engaged in an earnest and profound debate about the morality, legality, and practicality of physician-assisted suicide. Our holding permits this debate to continue, as it should in a democratic society.*

Justice John Paul Stevens, considered the Court's most liberal member at the time, agreed with the majority opinion, but his separate concurring opinion offered a hope for right-to-die advocates that was not found in Rehnquist's words. Stevens claimed that, although there was no constitutional support for a general right to assistance in suicide (even for terminally ill people), the Court might in the future find such a right in particular cases:

> *Today, the Court decides that Washington's statute prohibiting assisted suicide is not invalid "on its face," that is to say, in all or most cases in which it might be applied. That holding, however, does not foreclose the possibility that some applications of the statute might well be invalid.*

Stevens pointed out that by finding capital punishment constitutional, as it did in 1976, the Supreme Court had permitted states to place a lesser value on some lives than on others. In elaborating on this point, he made his willingness to accept the legitimacy of assisted suicide under some circumstances explicit:

> *A state, like Washington, that has authorized the death penalty and thereby has concluded that the sanctity of human life does not require that it always be preserved, must acknowledge that there are situations in which an interest in hastening death is legitimate. Indeed, not only is that interest sometimes legitimate, I am also convinced that there are times when it is entitled to constitutional protection.*

The Cruzan case offered support for the idea that an interest in actively hastening death might sometimes be constitutionally protected, Stevens maintained:

> *In finding that her best interests would be served by cutting off the nourishment that kept her alive, the trial court did more than simply vindicate Cruzan's interest in refusing medical treatment; the court, in essence, authorized affirmative conduct that would hasten her death.*

The right to control the manner and timing of one's death, Stevens stated, is even more basic than the right to refuse unwanted treatment:

> *I insist that the source of Nancy Cruzan's right to refuse treatment was not just a common-law rule. Rather, this right is an aspect of a far broader and more basic concept of freedom that is even older than the common law. This freedom embraces . . . her interest in dignity, and in determining the character of the memories that will survive long after her death.*

Although he agreed that the Supreme Court's ruling in *Cruzan* did not in itself guarantee a right to assisted suicide even for terminally ill people such as those who had originally been plaintiffs in the Washington case, Stevens found it more applicable to them than Rehnquist had.

The now deceased plaintiffs in this action may in fact have had a liberty interest even stronger than Nancy Cruzan's because, not only were they terminally ill, they were suffering constant and severe pain. . . . Cruzan [gave] recognition, not just to vague, unbridled notions of autonomy, but to the more specific interest in making decisions about how to confront an imminent death.

In cases such as Cruzan's or those of the terminally ill plaintiffs in the Washington and New York cases, Stevens said, the individual's interests might outweigh those of the state. Referring to state interests in preserving life and protecting vulnerable groups such as the disabled, Stevens wrote:

Although as a general matter the state's interest in the contributions each person may make to society outweighs the person's interest in ending her life, this interest does not have the same force for a terminally ill patient faced not with the choice of whether to live, only of how to die.

Stevens wrote that, although preventing people (even the terminally ill) from committing suicide because of coercion, depression, or inadequate pain management and other palliative care was important, he felt that some terminally ill people who requested aid in dying did not do so for any of these reasons, but rather were making a rational decision that should be respected. He implied that state regulation could exclude those who sought death for less legitimate or more treatable reasons.

Stevens questioned the idea that allowing doctors to prescribe lethal medication for terminally ill, suffering people who requested it would damage the profession's integrity or healing role. "For some patients, it would be a physician's refusal to dispense medication to ease their suffering and make their death tolerable and dignified that would be inconsistent with the healing role." Furthermore, he wrote,

because physicians are already involved in making decisions that hasten the death of terminally ill patients—through termination of life support, withholding of medical treatment, and terminal sedation—there is in fact significant tension between the traditional view of the physician's role and the actual practice in a growing number of cases.

The distinction between "letting die" and killing emphasized in Rehnquist's opinion might not always stand up, Stevens believed. Patients' and doctors' intentions might well be the same in both cases. Thus, Stevens concluded:

Although the differences the majority [Court opinion] notes in causation and intent between terminating life support and assisting in suicide support the Court's rejection of the respondents' facial challenge [general challenge to the constitutionality of the state laws], these distinctions may be inapplicable to particular terminally ill patients and their doctors.

In another concurring opinion, Justice David H. Souter also argued for a greater willingness to recognize substantive liberty interests under the Due Process Clause than Rehnquist's opinion had exhibited. Like Stevens, Souter left the door open for future changes in Supreme Court rulings on the right-to-die issue more than Rehnquist did, although he did not go as far as Stevens. He claimed that at present, legislatures were better equipped than the courts to deal with the issue of physician-assisted suicide.

Stephen Breyer, too, agreed that a substantive liberty interest in controlling the time and manner of one's imminent death might be found if the circumstances were different. Breyer thought that more support for such an interest might be discovered in the country's legal tradition if the alleged interest was defined, not as a "right to commit suicide with another's assistance," but as a "right to die with dignity." Breyer wrote: "At [the] core [of this right] would lie personal control over the manner of death, professional medical assistance, and the avoidance of unnecessary and severe physical suffering—combined."

Even if such a right were accepted, Breyer did not believe that the Washington and New York laws infringed upon it. However, he wrote, the same might not be true of other laws:

For example, were state law to prevent the provision of palliative care, including the administration of drugs as needed to avoid pain at the end of life—then the law's impact upon serious and otherwise unavoidable physical pain (accompanying death) would be more directly at issue.

Sandra Day O'Connor's concurring opinion also indicated that the question of whether "a mentally competent person who is experiencing great suffering" that cannot be controlled might have a constitutionally protected "interest in controlling the circumstances of his or her imminent death" was still open. In addition, she suggested that state laws permitting limited access to assisted suicide might be just as constitutional as those forbidding it.

In the Supreme Court ruling on *New York State v. Quill,* William Rehnquist maintained that the New York laws forbidding assistance in

suicide "neither infringe fundamental rights nor involve suspect classifications [protected groups, such as minorities]. These laws are therefore entitled to a 'strong presumption of validity.'" They also treat everyone
equally: "*Everyone*, regardless of physical condition, is entitled, if competent, to refuse unwanted lifesaving medical treatment; *no one* is permitted
to assist a suicide."

Rehnquist disagreed strongly with Roger Miner's equating of refusal of
medical treatment with requests for aid in suicide: "We think the distinction
between assisting suicide and withdrawing life-sustaining treatment, a distinction widely recognized and endorsed in the medical profession and in
our legal traditions, is both important and logical; it is certainly rational."

For Rehnquist, the most important distinction between the two acts was
in the intention of the physician committing them. A doctor who withdraws
or does not begin life-sustaining treatment at a patient's request intends
simply to fulfill the patient's wishes and avoid action that is both futile and
painful. One who medicates pain aggressively with drugs intends primarily
to relieve suffering, even though those drugs may also hasten the patient's
death. The intention of a physician who writes a prescription knowing that
it will be used for suicide, however, "must, necessarily and indubitably, . . .
[be] primarily that the patient be made dead." He noted, "The law has long
used actors' intent or purpose to distinguish between two acts that have the
same result."

Rehnquist maintained that the state interests discussed in *Glucksberg*
provide a rational and legitimate reason for keeping the distinction between
ending medical treatment and assisting suicide. If this distinction is valid,
then groups of terminally ill patients requesting these two actions are not
similarly situated, and treating them differently does not violate the Equal
Protection Clause, Rehnquist concluded.

Impact

Most commentators were not surprised by the justices' decision. The Supreme Court had been widely criticized for preempting a social debate on
abortion in its *Roe v. Wade* ruling, and legal scholars expected that the rather
conservative 1997 court would be careful not to repeat such an action in
regard to the controversy over physician-assisted suicide.

The ruling brought out important areas of agreement and disagreement
among the justices that could affect future Supreme Court decisions in
right-to-die cases. The justices agreed that there was no constitutionally
protected overall right to hasten death. They agreed that state legislatures
and voters, not the courts, should make the next attempts at the difficult task
of weighing the needs of the suffering terminally ill against the duties to
preserve life and protect vulnerable populations from abuse. They stressed

the importance of providing palliative care and accepted the legality of "double effect" or "terminal sedation." According to Derek Humphry's paraphrase of legal expert Michael S. Evans, however, the group of concurring opinions in *Glucksberg* showed that the justices had four significant areas of disagreement.

1. *They differed on what the issue really was. . . .*
2. *They differed on their views of the "double effect" and access to terminal sedation. . . .*
3. *They differed on how to draw the line between categories of people who should and should not have an assisted death available to them. . . .*
4. *Two opinions differ as to the physician's role as healer.*[18]

Law writer Stuart Taylor, speaking on *NewsHour with Jim Lehrer*, called the Supreme Court ruling "a mix—there's something for both sides in this decision."[19] Although dismayed at not being granted a clear and general "right to die," supporters of physician-assisted suicide found hope because, although the high court had found laws opposing assisted suicide to be constitutional, the justices had also hinted that they would find laws permitting assisted suicide to be constitutional as well. Several of the justices' concurring opinions, furthermore, had indicated that they might support the right of terminally ill people to ask for help in hastening their deaths "in a more particularized challenge." Justice Stevens's concurring opinion, in particular, "gave the right-to-die movement exactly what it wanted," according to Derek Humphry.[20]

Opponents of the legalization of physician-assisted suicide, including the Roman Catholic Church, the National Right to Life Committee, the Clinton administration, and the AMA, praised the Court's repeated insistence on a legal distinction between "letting die" (ceasing life-sustaining treatment at a patient's request) and killing (prescribing or administering lethal medication at a patient's request). They also were pleased at the justices' rejection of what they regarded as the spurious reasoning of the two appeals courts. President Bill Clinton called the decision a "victory for all Americans . . . [that] prevents us from going down a very dangerous and troubling path on this difficult and often agonizing issue."[21]

Both sides approved the Court's emphasis on the importance of improved palliative care for dying people. The Court required that state laws against assisted suicide not prohibit or "unreasonably burden" provision of adequate palliative care, including aggressive medication to control pain, even if such medication also shortened life.

The high court left the door open for future rulings on the right-to-die issue, including rulings that would partially reverse the current one. Mark

The Law of Euthanasia

Tushnet of Georgetown University Law School in Washington, D.C., said, "Beneath both sets of opinions are concurrences about how hard this question is, and about not foreclosing challenges that individuals may make."[22] *New York Times* reporter Linda Greenhouse wrote that the "Court's tone was that of a tentative first step rather than a definitive final ruling on the issue."[23]

Above all, the justices unanimously emphasized the need for state legislatures and voters to experiment with different approaches to the issue of assisted suicide for the terminally ill. Instead of ending the debate on whether there was a "right to die," the Supreme Court demanded that the discussion continue. The justices returned it from the courts to federal and state legislatures and, ultimately, the public forum and the ballot box.

MURDER TRIAL OF JACK KEVORKIAN (1999)

Background

On September 17, 1998, Jack Kevorkian, a retired Michigan pathologist, allegedly injected a lethal dose of a controlled narcotic into Thomas Youk. Youk, a 52-year-old man, suffered from amyotrophic lateral sclerosis (ALS) and had requested Kevorkian's help in dying. His family supported his request. Kevorkian videotaped Youk's death and sent it to the CBS television network, which broadcast it on the network's *60 Minutes* news program on November 22.

On the tape, Kevorkian, already well known for having assisted in (he claimed) about 150 suicides, dared the state of Michigan to prosecute him for euthanasia. The state obliged by filing first-degree murder charges against the controversial doctor on November 25. Kevorkian, whose license to practice medicine had been revoked in 1991, was also charged with illegal delivery of a controlled substance. Rather than relying on Geoffrey Fieger, the attorney who had helped him win acquittals in three previous cases, Kevorkian chose to act as his own lawyer in this trial. "There are certain points I can bring out better than any attorney," he told Oakland County circuit court judge Jessica Cooper in a pretrial hearing.

Legal Issues

Earlier in the same month that Thomas Youk died, Michigan passed a permanent law criminalizing assisted suicide. Because Kevorkian himself had allegedly injected the lethal substance in this case, however, the act was one of euthanasia rather than assisted suicide. In Michigan, as in other states, euthanasia is considered a form of homicide, or murder.

Decision

Kevorkian's trial began on March 22, 1999. His defense was rambling, and a *Washington Post* account said that Cooper often appeared "exasperated" with it.[24] She refused to allow Kevorkian to call Youk's wife as a witness or to present testimony about Youk's suffering and wish to die, claiming that Youk's and Kevorkian's intentions were irrelevant. The videotape, which was shown in court, clearly showed Kevorkian injecting a substance into Youk. The jury deliberated for 13 hours before finding Kevorkian guilty on March 26 of second-degree murder and delivery of a controlled substance.

On April 13, Cooper sentenced Kevorkian to 10 to 25 years in prison. She reminded Kevorkian that Michigan had laws against both euthanasia (a law that had been upheld in one of Kevorkian's own earlier trials) and assisted suicide (which Michigan voters had upheld by a vote of two and a half to one in a referendum held during the same month in which Kevorkian's controversial tape was broadcast). She also pointed out that, because his medical license had been revoked, Kevorkian had no right even to possess controlled substances, let alone inject them into anyone. She emphasized that she was giving him a full sentence because, based on his own statements, she saw little likelihood that he could be persuaded to obey the law in the future.

Above all, Cooper told Kevorkian,

> *We are not talking about assisted suicide here. When you purposely inject another human being with what you know to be a lethal dose of poison, that, sir, is murder. . . . This trial was not about the political or moral correctness of euthanasia. It was all about you, sir. It was about lawlessness. . . . You had the audacity to go on national television, show the world what you did and dare the legal system to stop you. Well, sir, consider yourself stopped.*

Impact

Kevorkian's trial broke no new legal ground, but it was important because of Kevorkian's often-criticized leading role in promoting and carrying out assisted suicide and euthanasia. It seemed likely to put a permanent end to Kevorkian's direct activities in aiding patients to die. This conviction, which stood in contrast to Kevorkian's earlier acquittals, suggested a public cooling of feelings toward the right-to-die movement or at least an unwillingness to extend acceptance of physician-assisted suicide to euthanasia. Alternatively, it may simply reflect the fact that the illegality of Kevorkian's actions was much more obvious in this case than in earlier ones, which involved assisted suicide at a time when Michigan law against that activity was either nonexistent or unclear.

The Law of Euthanasia

WENDLAND V. WENDLAND
26 CAL 4TH 519 (2001)

Background

Head injuries caused by an automobile accident in 1993 left Robert Wendland, a 42-year-old California man, with severe brain damage. About two years after the accident, he awoke from a coma into a "minimally conscious state." In this condition he could respond to his environment and communicate to a limited extent, but he could not speak, walk, swallow, or control his body functions, and his physicians felt that further improvement was unlikely. His wife, Rose, petitioned a trial court in 1995 to allow removal of the tube that provided him with food and water. Robert Wendland had left no advance directives, but Rose Wendland and Robert Wendland's brother, Michael, quoted several conversations in which Wendland had stated that he would not want to be kept alive if he was permanently unconscious or severely disabled. Wendland's mother, Florence, and his sister, Rebekah Vinson, opposed removal of the tube and filed a civil suit in 1997 to stop Rose Wendland's action.

Legal Issues

The *Quinlan* and *Cruzan* cases had established the right of surrogates to order discontinuation of life-sustaining treatment, including artificial provision of food and water, from people in a persistent vegetative state (PVS). Robert Wendland, however, retained a greater degree of brain function than a person in PVS, equivalent to someone in the last stages of Alzheimer's disease or some other form of advanced dementia. He was clearly incompetent to make medical decisions, but he could track objects with his eyes, manipulate a wheelchair, signal "yes" and "no," paint, and obey simple commands. Further complicating the case were the facts that Wendland had not chosen a surrogate to make health care decisions for him and that members of his family disagreed about what kind of care he would have wanted.

Decision

The trial court appointed Rose Wendland to be Robert Wendland's conservator but denied her petition to remove his feeding tube, saying that she had not provided "clear and convincing evidence" that Robert Wendland would have wanted his life support discontinued or that withdrawal of treatment would be in his best interest. She appealed the decision, and an appeals court reversed the lower court's decision on February 24, 2000. Florence Wendland and Rebekah Vinson then appealed the case to the California Supreme Court. During the oral arguments before that court, a number of medical and bioethical groups filed "friend of the court" briefs supporting Rose Wendland, and disability rights and right-to-life organizations filed similar briefs siding with Florence Wendland. On August 9, 2001, the high court unanimously upheld the original ruling that had denied Rose Wendland the right to withdraw her husband's feeding tube.

Most states require a relatively lax standard of evidence, "preponderance of the evidence" (more evidence supports the plaintiff's contention than opposes it), for civil cases like this one. The supreme court judges said that they would have accepted that standard for Robert Wendland if he had been in a coma or PVS, but because he possessed some degree of consciousness and might suffer during the process of dehydration and starvation, they felt justified in calling for the more stringent requirement of "clear and convincing evidence." (This was the standard used by the Missouri courts that had heard the Nancy Cruzan case, and the U.S. Supreme Court decision in that case affirmed Missouri's right to apply it.) "The decision to treat is reversible," Justice Kathryn Mickle Werdegar wrote in the court's decision. "The decision to withdraw treatment is not. The role of a high evidentiary standard in such a case is to adjust the risk of error to favor the less perilous result." The court did not specify exactly what evidence would have met the standard, but it ruled that general spoken comments of the type that Rose and Michael Wendland had quoted were not sufficient.

California's Health Care Decisions Law authorizes a conservator or surrogate named by a formerly competent person to withdraw medical treatment, including artificial nutrition and hydration, from that person if such a move fits with the person's wishes "to the extent known" or is in the patient's best interest. Rose Wendland, however, had been chosen as Robert Wendland's conservator by a court, not by Wendland himself. The supreme court cited this fact as another reason for requiring the "clear and convincing" evidence standard in this case. The court said that this high standard would be required "only when a conservator seeks to withdraw life-sustaining treatment from a conscious, incompetent patient who has not left legally cognizable instructions for health care or appointed an agent or surrogate for health care decisions."

Impact

Robert Wendland died of pneumonia in July 2001, before the California Supreme Court made its ruling, so the ruling was moot for the Wendland family. The court's decision was important, however, for future California cases involving people in a minimally conscious state. Right-to-life and disability rights groups praised the ruling, saying that it protected profoundly disabled people who could not speak for themselves. Right-to-die advocates, on the other hand, held that the "clear and convincing evidence" requirement was almost impossible to meet, condemning most severely brain-damaged people and their caregivers to an inescapable legal limbo. Norman L. Cantor, a professor at the Rutgers University School of Law, called use of that standard in cases like this "harsh and imprudent" and wrote in a 2001 article, "Very few people articulate their prospective wishes [for health care] with the precision demanded" by the standard.[25] Neutral commentators said that the decision (and similar ones in other states, such as the Michigan Supreme Court's ruling in an almost identical 1995 case, *In re Martin*) highlighted the importance of making advance directives, particularly powers of attorney for health care, which name a specific person as a surrogate for medical decision making. However, they noted that even some advance directives, such as living wills, are not precise enough to meet the "clear and convincing evidence" standard.

The court rulings in *Wendland v. Wendland*, *In re Martin*, and similar cases involving conscious but incompetent people suggest a developing legal consensus about treatment decisions concerning such people. "*Wendland* and the other state supreme court decisions indicate that courts will demand greater justification to authorize nontreatment for conscious incompetent patients who are not terminally ill," Rebecca Dresser, professor in the law and medical schools of Washington University in St. Louis, Missouri, wrote in 2002. "With an increasing number of dementia patients and aging Baby Boomers seeking control over their future care, cases presenting such questions will inevitably arise" in the 21st century.[26]

THE TERRI SCHIAVO CASE (1994–2005)

Background

On February 25, 1990, Theresa Marie ("Terri") Schindler Schiavo, then 26 years old and living in Florida, suffered a cardiac arrest because of a potassium imbalance in her body, possibly brought on by an eating disorder. She was revived, but lack of oxygen had destroyed the centers of consciousness in her brain. She remained in a vegetative state, which was eventually classified as persistent and, in all likelihood, permanent.

Schiavo's husband, Michael Schiavo, became her conservator. At first he and Terri's parents, Robert and Mary Schindler, worked together to care for her, but in early 1993 they began to disagree. Michael Schiavo believed that his wife's condition would never improve, but the Schindlers thought that she might recover some degree of consciousness if given the right therapy. In 1994, they filed the first of many suits that attempted to remove Michael from his position as Terri's conservator. All were unsuccessful.

Right to Die and Euthanasia

Michael Schiavo petitioned a Florida court in 1998 to allow him to have Terri Schiavo's feeding tube removed, claiming she had said that she would not want to be kept alive "on anything artificial." The Schindlers, devout Catholics (as was Terri), vehemently opposed this move. Terri had left no written directives and very little in the way of spoken comments, but on February 11, 2000, Florida circuit court judge George Greer ruled that Michael Schiavo had provided "clear and convincing" evidence of Terri's medical diagnosis (the Schindlers had claimed that she had more mental function than would appear in someone in a persistent vegetative state) and wishes and therefore could remove the feeding tube. The Schindlers appealed the decision, beginning the next stage of a long, bitter, and eventually very public personal and legal battle.

Legal Issues

The rulings in *Quinlan* and *Cruzan* had settled the basic legal issues in the long, contentious Schiavo case before that case even began. *Cruzan* established surrogates' right to refuse life-sustaining medical treatment, including artificial provision of food and water, for people in a persistent vegetative state as long as there was evidence that this was what the people would have wanted if they had been competent. The complicating factors in the Schiavo case were the bitterness of the family dispute (the families of Karen Quinlan and Nancy Cruzan had argued with the legal system but not with one another); disagreement about Terri Schiavo's neurological state and chances for improvement; and, above all, the extremely vocal and powerful supporters that both sides of the battle attracted. The American Civil Liberties Union and other advocates of individual autonomy, including the right to die, gathered around Michael Schiavo, while religious right-to-life groups and disability-rights organizations spoke out passionately in favor of the Schindlers.

The participation of these groups brought this individual family matter to the attention of the legislative and executive branches at the state and, eventually, the federal level. On October 21, 2003, the Florida legislature passed a bill that became known as "Terri's Law," the sole purpose of which was to give Florida governor Jeb Bush the authority to order Terri Schiavo's feeding tube reinserted. (It had been removed six days previously.) Bush gave the order, and the tube was replaced, but on September 23, 2004, the Florida Supreme Court ruled that this highly unusual legislative intervention was unconstitutional because it violated the separation of powers. "What is in the Constitution always must prevail over emotion," Chief Justice Barbara Pariente wrote in the court's ruling.

The U.S. Congress involved itself in the case in early 2005. Following an all-night emergency session on March 21, three days after Terri Schiavo's feeding tube had again been removed, the federal legislature passed its own one-person law, authorizing Terri's case to be transferred from state to federal court. President George W. Bush returned early from a Texas vacation to sign the bill.

Supporters claimed that these legislative and executive actions were necessary to rein in what House Majority Leader Tom DeLay (R-Texas) called "an arrogant, out of control, unaccountable judiciary."[27] However, many commentators, as well as a large percentage of the American public, saw them as an unwarranted intrusion that violated states' rights as well as the individual right to privacy. Some claimed that the special laws were part of a self-serving attempt to use the Schiavos' tragedy for political advantage.

Decision

The contest between Michael Schiavo and the Schindlers over Terri Schiavo's care eventually became what Michele Mathes, ethics education coordinator for the Center for Advocacy for the Rights and Interests of the Elderly in Philadelphia, Pennsylvania, called "the most litigated medical case in history."[28] It ended only with Terri Schiavo's death on March 31, 2005, two weeks after her feeding tube had been removed for the final time and 10 days after a three-judge panel of the 11th Circuit Court of Appeals, to which the congressional legislation had transferred the case, refused to order the tube reinserted. The Supreme Court also turned down a last-minute appeal.

Impact

The Schiavo case established no legal precedents, but commentators agreed that it set a precedent in depth of conflicting emotions, not only in the Schindler-Schiavo family but also in the country at large. Allan Lichtman, a professor of political history at American University in Washington, D.C., said the case showed that "our politics revolve around a new cultural polarization" concerning religious and racial rather than socioeconomic issues.[29] The case also brought a new degree of government intervention into what many felt should have remained a private or, at most, a judicial matter.

Some critics also claimed that the Schiavo case showed why end-of-life decisions should be kept out of the courts whenever possible. "When used in ways for which it was not designed, the law can cause great harm," Michele Mathes wrote. "When introduced into intimate personal relationships, whether between family members or friends or between doctor and patient, it can have devastating effects."[30] The legal system forces people into an adversarial framework in which compromise becomes very difficult, Mathes and others pointed out.

Right to Die and Euthanasia

GONZALES V. OREGON
04-623 (2006)

Background

On November 6, 2001, John Ashcroft, then U.S. attorney general, issued an "interpretive rule" in the form of a memorandum to Asa Hutchinson, head of the Drug Enforcement Agency (DEA), stating that physicians prescribing and pharmacists providing controlled substances (barbiturates) for patients to take as a way of killing themselves were not using the drugs for a "legitimate medical purpose" and therefore were violating the Controlled Substances Act (CSA). As violators, they could have their federal registration (which they needed in order to prescribe controlled drugs for any purpose) withdrawn and could be prosecuted for a criminal offense. Ashcroft's target was Oregon's Death with Dignity Act, which permitted doctors to make such prescriptions to terminally ill patients who met certain criteria. In essence, Ashcroft reinstated the order that Thomas Constantine, then administrator of the DEA, had issued in November 1997 and that then-attorney general Janet Reno had rescinded in June 1998 as being beyond the scope of federal authority. Ashcroft stated that his order was not intended to limit physicians' use of narcotics to treat pain or to affect medical practice outside of Oregon.

Oregon attorney general Hardy Myers, shortly joined by a physician, a pharmacist, and a group of terminally ill patients in that state, immediately filed suit to block the Ashcroft order. Robert E. Jones, a federal district court judge in Portland, Oregon, granted them first a temporary injunction and then, on April 17, 2002, a permanent injunction against the order. "Congress never intended, through the CSA or through any other current federal law, to grant blanket authority to the Attorney General or the DEA to define, as a matter of federal policy, what constitutes the legitimate practice of medicine," Jones wrote.

Legal Issues

The specific issue throughout the history of the case was whether the Controlled Substances Act, either in its original form, passed in 1970, or in the revision of the act made in 1984, gave the attorney general the authority to decide what constituted a "legitimate medical purpose." The 1984 revision gave the attorney general the right to deny, suspend, or revoke the registration of a practitioner if the issuance of such registration was deemed to be "inconsistent with the public interest."

The broader issue underlying this rather technical one was the degree to which the federal government had a right to overrule state laws governing the practice of medicine, traditionally a subject regulated by the states. John

The Law of Euthanasia

Adler, associate professor at the Case Western Reserve University School of Law, said that *Gonzales v. Oregon* was the current Supreme Court term's "premier federalism case."[31] In his November 6, 2001, order, Ashcroft cited the Supreme Court's 2001 decision in *United States v. Oakland Cannabis Buyers' Cooperative* as demonstrating that the Controlled Substances Act could be used to bar medical activities that individual states had legalized—use of marijuana for medical purposes in that case.

Unlike the *Glucksberg* and *Quill* cases in 1997, *Oregon v. Ashcroft* and its successor, *Gonzales v. Oregon* (Alberto Gonzales replaced Ashcroft as attorney general on November 15, 2004), did not bring up the "right to die" as such. "We take no position on the merits or morality of physician-assisted suicide. We express no opinion on whether the practice is inconsistent with the public interest or constitutes illegitimate medical care. This case is simply about who gets to decide," Judge Richard Tallman wrote in the Ninth Circuit Court of Appeals ruling on the case. Nonetheless, the disposition of the case was bound to have a powerful impact on the Oregon assisted-suicide law and any similar laws that other states might pass in the future.

Decision

The government appealed Robert Jones's decision. A three-judge panel of the Ninth Circuit Court of Appeals heard the case and voted 2 to 1 on May 26, 2004, to affirm the lower court's ruling. "The attorney general's unilateral attempt to regulate general medical practices historically entrusted to state lawmakers interferes with the democratic debate about physician-assisted suicide and far exceeds the scope of his authority under federal law," Richard Tallman wrote in the court's majority opinion. Ashcroft's order also altered the "usual constitutional balance between the States and the Federal Government," Tallman said.

The government requested a rehearing en banc, but the appeals court denied the request in August. The Supreme Court agreed to hear the case on February 22, 2005. It heard oral arguments on October 5 and rendered its decision on January 17, 2006. By a 6-3 vote, the high court ruled that the Controlled Substances Act did not give Ashcroft the authority he claimed.

Justice Anthony Kennedy's majority opinion analyzed the wording of the CSA in detail. It also discussed two standards, based on previous court rulings, under which an order like Ashcroft's might be given "deference," and concluded that neither standard applied. Kennedy stated that, under the CSA, the attorney general "is not authorized to make a rule declaring illegitimate a medical standard for care and treatment of patients that is specifically authorized under state law." The *Oakland Cannabis* case was different from *Gonzales v. Oregon*, Kennedy said, because Congress had expressly determined "that marijuana had no accepted medical use." It had not made a similar explicit determination about assisted suicide.

Like the lower court judges, Kennedy pointed out that the CSA focused on recreational drug abuse, not on the medical use of controlled substances. He pointed out that the attorney general shared authority for interpreting the act with the head of the Department of Health and Human Services and was supposed to defer to that official in connection with medical matters covered by the act. Kennedy therefore found it unlikely that Congress had intended to allow the attorney general to make unilateral judgments about medical practice.

Justice Antonin Scalia wrote a lengthy dissent, with which John Roberts, the new chief justice, and Clarence Thomas concurred. Like Kennedy, Scalia painstakingly examined the language of the Controlled Substances Act. Scalia's analysis disagreed with Kennedy's at almost every point.

Impact

The Supreme Court's decision means that the Oregon law permitting assisted suicide will stand unless Congress explicitly expands the attorney general's powers under the Controlled Substances Act to permit the kind of regulation that Ashcroft issued. (Congress twice attempted to do this after Janet Reno's ruling, but the legislation did not pass.) Right-to-die supporters therefore saw the decision as a victory. However, the decision did not make, or claim to make, any statement about the legitimacy (or lack of it) of prescribing medication for the purpose of committing suicide, an issue likely to be hotly debated well into the future.

---

[1] Lawrence O. Gostin, "Deciding Life and Death in the Courtroom," *Journal of the American Medical Association*, November 12, 1997, p. 1,523.

[2] Robert Muir, quoted in Derek Humphry and Mary Clement, *Freedom to Die: People, Politics, and the Right-to-Die Movement*. New York: St. Martin's Press, 1998, p. 88.

[3] McCarthy DeMere, quoted in Peter G. Filene, *In the Arms of Others: A Cultural History of the Right-to-Die in America*. Chicago: Ivan R. Dee, 1998, p. 94.

[4] Paul Ramsey, quoted in Filene, *In the Arms of Others*, p. 95.

[5] Barry Keene, quoted in Filene, *In the Arms of Others*, p. 104.

[6] Elizabeth Bouvia, quoted in Gregory E. Pence, *Classic Cases in Medical Ethics*. New York: McGraw-Hill, 1995, p. 41.

[7] Elizabeth Bouvia, quoted in Pence, *Classic Cases in Medical Ethics*, p. 60.

[8] Charles E. Teel, quoted in Maureen Harrison and Steve Gilbert, eds., *Life, Death, and the Law*. San Diego, Calif.: Excellent Books, 1997, p. 20.

The Law of Euthanasia

9 *Cruzan v. Harmon*, 760 S.W. 2d 408 (Mo. banc 1988), quoted in Filene, *In the Arms of Ohters*, p. 171.

10 Ronald Cranford, quoted in Pence, *Classic Cases in Medical Ethics*, p. 19.

11 Washington Promoting Suicide Law, quoted in Harrison and Gilbert, *Life, Death, and the Law*, p. 36.

12 Timothy Quill, quoted in Harrison and Gilbert, *Life, Death, and the Law*, p. 161.

13 New York laws against aiding and promoting suicide, quoted in Harrison and Gilbert, *Life, Death, and the Law*, p. 140.

14 William Williams, quoted in Harrison and Gilbert, *Life, Death, and the Law*, p. 180.

15 Kathryn Tucker, quoted in Harrison and Gilbert, *Life, Death, and the Law*, p. 180.

16 Dennis Vacco, quoted in Harrison and Gilbert, *Life, Death, and the Law*, p. 202.

17 Lawrence Tribe, quoted in Harrison and Gilbert, *Life, Death, and the Law*, p. 202.

18 Humphry and Clement, *Freedom to Die*, pp. 303–304.

19 Stuart Taylor, quoted in Humphry and Clement, *Freedom to Die*, p. 302.

20 Humphry and Clement, *Freedom to Die*, p. 301.

21 Bill Clinton, quoted in Humphry and Clement, *Freedom to Die*, p. 306.

22 Mark Tushnet, quoted in Humphry and Clement, *Freedom to Die*, p. 300.

23 Linda Greenhouse, quoted in Humphry and Clement, *Freedom to Die*, p. 300.

24 Edward Walsh, "Kevorkian Stumbling Through Trial," *Washington Post*, reprinted in *San Francisco Chronicle*, March 24, 1999, p. A5.

25 Norman L. Cantor, "Twenty-five Years after Quinlan: A Review of the Jurisprudence of Death and Dying," *Journal of Law, Medicine and Ethics*, vol. 29, Summer 2001, pp. 182ff.

26 Rebecca Dresser, "The Conscious Incompetent Patient," *Hastings Center Report*, vol. 32, May–June 2002, p. 11.

27 Tom DeLay, quoted in Edward Epstein, "DeLay Blames Judicial System, Promises New Legislation," *San Francisco Chronicle*, April 1, 2005, p. A15.

28 Michele Mathes, "Terri Schiavo and End-of-Life Decisions: Can Law Help Us Out?" *MedSurg Nursing*, vol. 14, June 2005, p. 200.

29 Alan Lichtman, quoted in Marc Sandalow, "Case Reflects How Much Nation Is Split over Religion, Ethics," *San Francisco Chronicle*, March 22, 2005, p. A11.

30 Mathes, "Terri Schiavo and End-of-Life Decisions," *MedSurg Nursing*, vol. 14, June 2005, p. 200.

31 Jonathan Adler, quoted in Liz Halloran, "Of Life and Death," *U.S. News & World Report*, vol. 139, October 10, 2005, p. 31.

CHAPTER 3

CHRONOLOGY

This chapter presents a chronology of important events in the development of the right-to-die movement and changes in the legal status of physician-assisted suicide and euthanasia. It focuses primarily on events that occurred after 1970.

Fourth Century B.C.

- A Greek physician named Hippocrates establishes a school of medicine with standards based on the philosophy of Pythagoras and writes an oath that most physicians still take when graduating from medical school. This oath, traditionally considered the cornerstone of medical ethics, includes the statement, "I will [not] give a deadly drug to anybody if asked for it, nor will I make a suggestion to that effect."[1]
- Aristotle writes in Book III of *Nicomachean Ethics* that suicide to escape evil or misfortune, including pain, is a cowardly act.

399 B.C.

- Convicted of having corrupted the city's youth with his teachings, the philosopher Socrates is ordered by the government of Athens to kill himself by drinking poison hemlock. Socrates, who has maintained that "true philosophers make dying their profession," remains calm and continues discussing philosophy with his students as the poison takes effect.[2]

ca. A.D. 410

- Saint Augustine, Bishop of Hippo, defines the prevailing Christian view when he writes that suicide for any reason (except a direct command from God) is a "detestable and damnable wickedness" because it violates the Sixth Commandment, "Thou shalt not kill."[3]

Chronology

13th Century

- Saint Thomas Aquinas expands the Christian argument against suicide by saying that suicide infringes on God's right to be the sole controller of life and also violates a person's duty to community and family. Indeed, Aquinas maintains, suicide is the worst of sins because it allows no time for repentance.

1516

- English statesman Sir Thomas More writes *Utopia*, a portrait of an ideal society based on reason. The Utopian government offers to assist terminally or incurably ill people to commit suicide. However, it is unclear whether More, a devout Catholic, personally approves of such behavior or is being satirical when he describes it.

17th Century

- British philosopher and statesman Sir Francis Bacon coins the term *euthanasia* (from two Greek words meaning "good death") to describe the "fair and easy passage from life" that people hope to have. Bacon uses the word to refer to a natural death, not a death caused by another to end suffering, the meaning it will acquire in the 20th century.
- In *Biathanatos*, written during a turbulent time in his life, famed English poet John Donne explicitly defends suicide under some conditions and offers arguments refuting the Christian position against it.

1777

- "On Suicide," an essay by renowned Scottish philosopher David Hume, is published a year after Hume's death. In this writing, Hume maintains that suicide to end suffering from a painful, incurable, or terminal illness or disability is not a violation of a person's duty to either God or society. Indeed, it might even confer a net benefit to society.

1828

- New York passes the first state law in the United States that expressly makes assisting suicide a criminal act.

1906

- A bill is introduced into the Ohio legislature to legalize voluntary euthanasia performed by physicians on the incurably and painfully ill. This measure, the first attempt to legalize euthanasia in the United States, fails in a committee vote, 78 to 22.

1931

- C. Killick Millard, health officer for the city of Leicester in Great Britain, drafts the first bill attempting to legalize voluntary euthanasia in that country.

1935

- The British Voluntary Euthanasia Society, the first organization of its kind in the world, is formed in Britain to promote Millard's bill. Prominent members include H. G. Wells, George Bernard Shaw, and Bertrand Russell.

1936

- Millard's euthanasia bill is introduced into Parliament, but the House of Lords votes it down, 35 to 14.

1938

- Charles Potter, a Unitarian minister, forms the Euthanasia Society of America to work for legalization of voluntary and, in some cases, involuntary euthanasia.
- A New York grand jury refuses to indict Harry C. Johnson for gassing his cancer-stricken wife (at her request, he says) after three psychiatrists testify that he had committed the act while temporarily insane. This treatment is typical of that given to "mercy killings" in the period, including killings of children with severe mental retardation.

1939

- The Euthanasia Society of America tries to introduce a bill legalizing voluntary euthanasia for terminally ill adults into the New York legislature but cannot find a sponsor. This is the first of many such attempts by the group, lasting until about 1960. All are unsuccessful.
- Adolf Hitler writes an official letter (dated September 1) to Franz Gartner, German minister of justice, authorizing "mercy death" for "incurable" patients. This directive begins a program that, over a period of three years, "euthanizes" by force some 100,000 Germans with physical or mental defects, claiming that their "life [is] unworthy of life."[4]

Chronology

1950s, 1960s

■ Medical science becomes able to preserve the lives of dying people through new technology such as respirators and feeding tubes.

1957

■ Pope Pius XII tells a conference of anesthesiologists that, although euthanasia and assisted suicide are still forbidden, Catholics are not required to use "extraordinary" medical technology such as respirators to prolong the lives of the terminally ill. Giving large doses of narcotics to such people to control pain is also acceptable, the pope says, even if it shortens the patients' lives.

1961

■ Britain passes the Suicide Act, which decriminalizes attempted suicide but states that aiding, abetting, counseling, or procuring a suicide or attempted suicide is a statutory crime carrying a penalty of up to 14 years in prison.

1962

■ The High Court of Central Japan rules that euthanasia is lawful in that country under certain conditions. Kaoru Narita, one of the three judges making the decision, claims later that this "was the first case in the world where the court actually enunciated the legality or legal acceptability of euthanasia."[5]

1967

■ British physician Dame Cicely Saunders establishes St. Christopher's, the world's first modern hospice, in London. It provides physical, psychological, and spiritual comfort to dying people and their families rather than attempting to cure them or prolong their lives.

1969

■ Swiss-born psychiatrist Elisabeth Kübler-Ross's book *On Death and Dying* becomes a best-seller, helping to erode the modern Western taboo about discussing death.
■ Louis Kutner coins the term *living will* in an article in the Summer issue of the *Indiana Law Journal*. The living will, the first form of advance health care directive to be introduced, allows a competent adult to specify

115

medical treatments to be accepted or refused if he or she should become incompetent.

1973

- Physician Geertruida Postma is put on trial in the Netherlands for giving her terminally ill mother a fatal injection at the mother's request. Postma is found guilty but given only a one-month suspended sentence and a year's probation. Her trial marks the beginning of decriminalization of physician-assisted suicide and euthanasia in the Netherlands.
- The American Hospital Association issues the Patient's Bill of Rights, which includes the right to refuse medical treatment.

1974

- The first American hospice is established in New Haven, Connecticut.
- Barry Keene, California assemblyman from Eureka, introduces a state bill to make living wills legally binding. Similar bills are also introduced in four other states. All fail.

1975

- *March:* British journalist Derek Humphry helps his wife, Jean, terminally ill with cancer, commit suicide with drugs obtained from a doctor for the purpose.
- *April 14:* Karen Ann Quinlan, a 21-year-old New Jersey woman, consumes a mixture of alcohol and drugs at a party and enters what proves to be a persistent vegetative state.
- *July 31:* Joseph and Julia Quinlan, Karen Quinlan's parents, sign a form requesting Robert Morse, her physician, and St. Clare's Hospital to turn off her respirator. Morse and the hospital refuse to comply.
- *October 20:* A hearing begins during which Joseph and Julia Quinlan, represented by lawyer Paul W. Armstrong, appeal to New Jersey probate court judge Robert Muir, Jr., for legal guardianship of Karen and the right to refuse life-sustaining medical treatment (the respirator) on her behalf.
- *November 10:* Muir rules against the Quinlans, maintaining that the state's interest in preserving life outweighs the family's right to privacy in making medical decisions. "There is no constitutional right to die that can be asserted by a parent for his incompetent adult child," he states.[6]

1976

- *January 26:* Following an appeal by the Quinlans, the New Jersey Supreme Court begins a hearing on the Quinlan case.

Chronology

- **March 31:** The New Jersey Supreme Court unanimously reverses Judge Muir's decision, granting Joseph Quinlan guardianship of Karen and permission to order her respirator turned off. The court states that the constitutional right to privacy covers this case. This is the first time a state court has applied the right of privacy to a case of "letting die."
- **June 9:** The Quinlans move Karen to a nursing home and turn her respirator off, but she can now breathe on her own and, therefore, does not die.
- **September 30:** California governor Jerry Brown signs the Natural Death Act into law. The law, a reintroduced form of Assemblyman Barry Keene's 1974 bill to make living wills legally binding, is the first state law to give legal force to advance health care directives.

1977

- A Massachusetts court rules that a court-appointed guardian may refuse life-prolonging chemotherapy on behalf of Joseph Saikewicz, a severely retarded 67-year-old man suffering from leukemia. This extends the range of incompetent people for whom surrogates may refuse life-sustaining treatment to include those who have never been competent to make health care decisions.

1978

- Derek Humphry publishes an account of his first wife's death in a book called *Jean's Way*. Despite his admission of assisting Jean's suicide, British authorities decline to prosecute him.

1980

- In *Declaration on Euthanasia*, Pope John Paul II states that patients may refuse any type of medical treatment without violating Catholic doctrine, provided that death is imminent and treatment is futile; the Church no longer distinguishes between "extraordinary" and "ordinary" treatment in this context. Use of pain-controlling drugs that may shorten life is also permissible, the pope says, but deliberate euthanasia is not.
- **August:** Derek Humphry and his second wife, Ann Wickett, now living in southern California, found the Hemlock Society, an organization dedicated to the legalization of physician-assisted suicide and voluntary euthanasia for competent, terminally ill adults.

1981

- Derek Humphry publishes *Let Me Die Before I Wake*, a book of true stories about people who have helped terminally ill loved ones die. It includes some specific information about assisted suicide, such as doses of drugs expected to cause death.

1982

- *April 9:* A boy, who will be known to the public only as Baby Doe, is born in Bloomington, Indiana, with Down's syndrome (trisomy 21, which produces moderate to severe mental retardation) and a surgically correctable digestive malformation. On their doctor's recommendation, the baby's parents decide not to consent to surgery or intravenous feeding because they believe the child's quality of life will always be extremely poor. The baby dies of starvation shortly afterward.
- *April 30:* As a response to Baby Doe's death, President Ronald Reagan directs the Justice Department and the Department of Health and Human Services to require life-sustaining treatment for all defective newborns. They claim as their legal justification Section 504 of the Rehabilitation Act of 1973, which forbids discrimination on the basis of disability.

1983

- Medicare begins covering hospice care.
- *March:* In the wake of the "Baby Doe" case, the Department of Health and Human Services sends a notice to all hospitals, requiring them to post large signs in every infant-care facility reading "Discriminatory failure to feed and care for handicapped infants in this facility is prohibited by federal law."[7] The signs include a toll-free "Baby Doe Hotline" phone number via which people can report instances of discrimination for immediate federal investigation.
- *April:* Federal district judge Gerhard Gesell blocks the "interim final" Baby Doe rules. He says he has made his decision partly on procedural grounds, but he also calls the rules "arbitrary and capricious" and says that the Baby Doe hotline is "ill-considered."[8]
- *September:* Elizabeth Bouvia, a young woman severely disabled by cerebral palsy and arthritis but not terminally ill, enters Riverside General Hospital in California and asks for help in starving herself to death. The hospital admits her as a psychiatric patient but refuses to help her carry out her plan. She then petitions the courts to force the hospital to honor her refusal of medical treatment—that is, her feeding tube.
- *December:* Probate court judge John Hews rules that Donald Fisher and Riverside General Hospital can force-feed Elizabeth Bouvia if necessary to keep her alive. Hews agrees that Bouvia is mentally competent, rational, and sincere in her request for death but does not grant it because of

the negative effects on the hospital staff and on other disabled people her death might cause.

1984

- A Supreme Court decision in the Netherlands results in an informal agreement that, although euthanasia and assisted suicide remain illegal, doctors taking these actions will not be prosecuted if they follow guidelines established by the Royal Dutch Medical Society.
- *February 12:* Revised (final) Baby Doe rules take effect.
- *February 23:* In a second Baby Doe case ("Baby Jane Doe"), the federal Court of Appeals for the Second Circuit upholds a lower court ruling stating that a hospital is not obliged to turn over such a child's medical records to the government. This ruling renders the Baby Doe rules useless because it denies the government access to the evidence it would need in order to prove discrimination.

1985

- The federal government establishes new Baby Doe rules, based on classifying of refusal of treatment for defective babies as child abuse or neglect. The regulations require any state receiving federal funds for prevention of child abuse to ensure that all infants receive life-supporting treatment unless they are clearly terminally ill, irreversibly comatose, or suffering from conditions that make life support both futile and inhumane. Even in those cases, basic nutrition and liquids must be provided.
- *January:* In the case of Claire Conroy, an elderly, semicomatose woman whose guardian (a nephew) had petitioned for removal of her feeding tube, the New Jersey Supreme Court rules that Conroy would have had the right to refuse medical treatment, including nutrition, if she had been competent, and that she did not lose that right when she became incompetent. However, the court adds that because Conroy left no advance directive or other clear indication of her wishes, the tube could not have been removed in her particular case. (Conroy had already died by the time this ruling was handed down.) This case foreshadows the more famous *Cruzan* case in 1990.

1986

- The American Medical Association (AMA) states that it considers removing both respirator and feeding tubes from someone in a persistent vegetative state to be ethical if the person has left an advance directive requesting such an action or the person's surrogate requests it. This statement is a reversal of an earlier position forbidding such actions.

- The "Humane and Dignified Death Act," a model law prepared by Derek Humphry and several legal experts in the Hemlock Society, is published. It would have legalized not only physician-assisted suicide but voluntary euthanasia for terminally ill, competent adults. It would also have allowed competent adults who were irreversibly but not terminally ill to choose these same options, and it would have allowed competent people with early Alzheimer's disease to nominate a surrogate to end their lives when they became incompetent.
- The California Court of Appeal grants Elizabeth Bouvia the right to have a hospital remove her feeding tube, but she decides not to take advantage of the decision.
- *June 13:* A decade after her respirator was disconnected, Karen Ann Quinlan finally dies (of pneumonia).

1988

- Charles E. Teel, a probate court judge in Jasper County, Missouri, grants Joe and Joyce Cruzan permission to remove the feeding tube from their daughter, Nancy, who has been in a persistent vegetative state since being injured in an automobile accident in 1983. The state appeals the decision.
- Americans Against Human Suffering, the political action arm of the Hemlock Society, attempts to put a proposition legalizing euthanasia on the California ballot but fails to gather enough signatures to qualify.
- The Unitarian Universalist Association of Congregations issues a position paper that makes it the first religious organization to support a right to die for terminally ill people.
- *November:* The Missouri Supreme Court reverses the probate court's decision in the case of Nancy Cruzan because, the justices say, "the state's interest is an unqualified interest in life" and the Cruzans have not presented "clear and convincing" evidence that Nancy would have wanted her care discontinued.[9]

1989

- *December 6:* The U.S. Supreme Court hears the case of Nancy Cruzan, its first right-to-die case.

1990

- The Ministry of Justice in the Netherlands makes a formal agreement not to prosecute physicians who commit euthanasia or assist in suicide while following the guidelines established by the Royal Dutch Medical Society.

Chronology

- The Hemlock Society and other supporters obtain enough signatures to qualify the Death with Dignity Act (Measure 119) for the ballot in the state of Washington.
- Jack Kevorkian, a retired Michigan pathologist, appears on the *Phil Donohue Show* describing his "Mercitron," a device he has invented for physician-assisted suicide.
- *February 25:* Terri Schindler Schiavo, a Florida woman, suffers brain damage during a cardiac arrest of unknown cause, possibly due to an eating disorder; she emerges from a coma and enters a persistent vegetative state.
- *June 4:* Janet Adkins, a 54-year-old Oregon woman suffering from the early stages of Alzheimer's disease, becomes the first person to be assisted in committing suicide by Kevorkian and his machine.
- *June 25:* The U.S. Supreme Court hands down its ruling in the case of *Cruzan v. Director, Missouri Department of Health*, its first decision in a right-to-die case. In somewhat tentative language it agrees that competent adults most likely have a constitutionally protected liberty interest in refusing life-sustaining medical treatment, including nutrition, and that they may also make legally binding advance decisions about refusing treatment if they should become incompetent. However, the high court also rules that states may protect incompetent patients' interest in life by setting up requirements for establishing the patients' previous wishes. The justices agree with the Missouri Supreme Court that clear and convincing evidence of Nancy Cruzan's wishes has not been provided and that her feeding tube, therefore, cannot be removed.
- *November:* At a new hearing of the Nancy Cruzan case in Missouri, friends of Cruzan's offer new testimony about her wishes that Judge Teel accepts as "clear and convincing." Cruzan's physician and the state drop their opposition to the removal of her feeding tube.
- *November 5:* The Patient Self-Determination Act, introduced by Missouri Republican Senator John Danforth in the wake of the Cruzan case, is signed into law. The act requires all hospitals and other health care institutions receiving federal funds to explain state laws and institutional policies concerning advance directives, as well as the patients' right to refuse medical treatment, to all patients they admit.
- *December 14:* Nancy Cruzan's feeding tube is removed.
- *December 26:* Cruzan dies.

1991

- *Final Exit*, Derek Humphry's explicit "how-to" book on assisted suicide for the terminally ill, is published and remains on the *New York Times* bestseller list for 18 weeks.

- The Remmelink Report, a Dutch government report that provides statistics about the practice of physician-assisted suicide and euthanasia in the Netherlands in 1990, is published.
- *March 7:* An article by Timothy Quill, a physician in Rochester, New York, appears in the *New England Journal of Medicine.* In this article, Quill describes how he prescribed barbiturates for "Diane" (Diane Trumbull), a 45-year-old woman with terminal leukemia, knowing that she would use the drugs to kill herself.
- *July 26:* A grand jury in Rochester, New York, refuses to indict Quill for assisting Diane Trumbull's suicide.
- *November 4:* Measure 119 (the Death with Dignity Act), the first state referendum on physician-assisted suicide and euthanasia, fails at the polls in Washington state, with 46 percent voting in favor and 54 percent against.
- *November 20:* The Michigan Board of Medicine suspends Jack Kevorkian's medical license indefinitely.

1992

- *June 30:* The U.S. Supreme Court delivers a decision in *Planned Parenthood v. Casey* that reaffirms the right to choose abortion first enunciated in *Roe v. Wade* (1973). The justices rule that this right can be considered part of the liberty interests protected by the Due Process Clause of the Fourteenth Amendment. Their decision includes language about a general liberty interest in making important personal choices about one's body that right-to-die advocates and judges who support them will quote frequently.
- *November:* A California initiative proposition to legalize physician-assisted suicide and euthanasia for terminally ill, competent adults is defeated at the polls, 54 percent opposed to 46 percent in favor.

1993

- The Dutch Parliament approves a reporting system to be used by physicians who carry out assisted suicide or euthanasia.
- Sue Rodriguez, a British Columbia woman suffering from amyotrophic lateral sclerosis (ALS), petitions Canadian courts for the legal right to have a physician's help in killing herself. Her widely publicized case, which goes all the way to the Supreme Court but ultimately fails, draws Canada's attention to the issue of physician-assisted suicide.
- The National Conference of Commissioners on Uniform State Laws designs the Uniform Health Care Decisions Act, which would legalize a new form of advance directive that combines a living will, durable power of attorney, and instructions about organ donation.

Chronology

- **February 14:** Robert and Mary Schindler, Terri Schiavo's parents, begin arguing with her husband, Michael Schiavo, about control of Terri's care. Michael Schiavo had come to believe that his wife's condition would never improve, but the Schindlers still thought that aggressive treatment could restore Terri to some degree of function.

1994

- Saskatchewan (Canada) farmer Robert Latimer is convicted of second-degree murder and sentenced to 10 years in prison for killing his severely retarded and disabled daughter, Tracy.
- The Supreme Court of the Netherlands acquits Boudewijn Chabot, a psychiatrist who in 1991 prescribed lethal drugs for suicide to Hilly Bosscher. Bosscher was physically healthy but severely depressed and unresponsive to treatment. Chabot's acquittal establishes that euthanasia or assisted suicide on the grounds of mental suffering alone is acceptable in the Netherlands.
- In an influential report, the New York State Task Force on Life and the Law unanimously rejects the idea of legalizing physician-assisted suicide. The group claims that legalization would pose unacceptable risks to vulnerable members of the population.
- Robert and Mary Schindler file the first of many legal actions against Michael Schiavo in an attempt to take control of daughter Terri's care.
- **January 29:** Compassion in Dying (a Seattle-based right-to-die organization), five physicians, and three terminally ill patients file suit against the state of Washington in the U.S. District Court for Western Washington, claiming that the state's law against assisted suicide is unconstitutional because it violates rights guaranteed under both the Due Process Clause and the Equal Protection Clause of the Fourteenth Amendment.
- **May 3:** In Seattle, Barbara Rothstein, chief judge of the federal district court for western Washington, finds the state's law against assisted suicide unconstitutional because it violates rights protected by both clauses of the Fourteenth Amendment.
- **July 29:** Timothy Quill and other physician and patient plaintiffs file suit in a New York federal court, claiming that the state's law against assisted suicide violates rights protected by the Fourteenth Amendment.
- **November 8:** Oregon initiative Measure 16, the Death with Dignity Act, passes at the polls by a narrow margin, 52 percent in favor to 48 percent against. Oregon thus become the first state in the United States to legalize actively assisted dying.

123

- **December 5:** Just hours before the Death with Dignity Act is scheduled to take effect, right-to-life attorneys persuade a federal district court judge, Michael Hogan, to pass a temporary restraining order against it.
- **December 15:** Thomas Griesa, chief judge of the federal court for the southern district of New York, rules in *Quill v. Vacco* that New York's state laws against assisted suicide do not violate either the liberty interest or the right to equal protection guaranteed by the Fourteenth Amendment.

1995

- Pope John Paul II issues *Evangelium Vitae*, an encyclical opposing euthanasia.
- The Netherlands issues an update of its controversial Remmelink Report.
- **March 9:** John T. Noonan, Jr., writes ruling for a three-judge panel of the federal Ninth Circuit Court of Appeals that upholds the constitutionality of the Washington state law against assisted suicide.
- **May 25:** The legislature of Australia's Northern Territory passes the Rights of the Terminally Ill Act, which allows terminally ill people to request a physician's assistance in suicide under certain conditions.
- **June:** A special committee of the Canadian Senate, after reviewing the country's law against assisted suicide, decides by a 4-3 vote that the law does not need to be changed.
- **August 4:** Oregon judge Michael Hogan rules the state's Death with Dignity Act unconstitutional. His ruling is appealed.

1996

- **March 6:** The full 11-judge panel of the federal Ninth Circuit Court of Appeals rules 8-3 to overturn John Noonan's 1995 ruling that the Washington state law against assisted suicide is constitutional. Writing the court's majority opinion, Stephen Reinhardt asserts that there is "constitutionally protected liberty interest in determining the time and manner of one's own death."
- **April 2:** Three judges of the U.S. Second Circuit Court of Appeals, ruling unanimously on *Quill v. Vacco*, strike down New York's laws against assisted suicide. Roger Miner, writing the court's opinion, claims that the laws discriminate against terminally ill people who are not on life support and therefore violate the Equal Protection Clause of the Fourteenth Amendment.
- **May:** Not Dead Yet, a militant disabled group, forms to resist legalization of assisted suicide. A month later it holds its first demonstration, in front of Jack Kevorkian's home.

Chronology

- *July 1:* The Rights of the Terminally Ill Act goes into effect in Australia's Northern Territory.
- *September 9:* Kevin Andrews, a Liberal member of Australia's Parliament from Victoria, introduces a bill to repeal the Rights of the Terminally Ill Act.
- *September 22:* Bob Dent, a 66-year-old man with terminal cancer, becomes the first man anywhere in the world to legally kill himself with the help of a physician. He dies with the help of Philip Nitschke in Australia's Northern Territory.

1997

- A Canadian judge invokes a constitutional amendment to reduce farmer Robert Latimer's prison sentence for the mercy killing of his severely retarded and disabled daughter, Tracy, from 10 years to two years. Later in the year, however, the Saskatchewan Court of Appeal reinstates the 10-year sentence.
- *January 8:* The U.S. Supreme Court hears oral arguments in *Washington v. Glucksberg* and *New York v. Quill,* two cases questioning the constitutionality of state laws against assisted suicide.
- *February 28:* The U.S. Ninth Circuit Court of Appeals votes 3-0 to reverse Michael Hogan's ruling against Oregon's Death with Dignity Act, stating that the plaintiffs in the suit against the act had failed to prove that they would be harmed by it.
- *March 24:* The Australian Parliament strikes down the Northern Territory's Rights of the Terminally Ill Act.
- *April:* Congress passes the Assisted Suicide Funding Restriction Act, which prohibits federally funded health programs from participating in assisted suicide.
- *June:* A ruling by Colombia's Supreme Court makes that country the only one in the Americas in which euthanasia is legal.
- *June 26:* The U.S. Supreme Court rules in *Washington v. Glucksberg* and *New York v. Quill* that state laws forbidding assisted suicide are constitutional and that there is no general constitutionally protected "right to die." Some of the justices, however, suggest that they might grant such a right in particular cases. The court's decision returns the assisted suicide debate to the states.
- *October 14:* The Supreme Court refuses to hear a case challenging Oregon's Death with Dignity Act.
- *October 27:* The Death with Dignity Act goes into effect in Oregon.
- *November 4:* Oregonians vote by 60 percent to 40 percent to defeat Measure 51, which would have repealed the Death with Dignity Act.

- **November 5:** Federal Drug Enforcement Administrator Thomas Constantine writes to the Senate and House Judiciary Committees, reminding them that the Controlled Substances Act authorizes the DEA to revoke the registration (allowing prescription of controlled substances such as narcotics) of any physician who dispenses controlled substances without a legitimate medical purpose. Constantine says the DEA considers a prescription for drugs to be used in suicide to be a violation of the act, even when it is permitted by a state law, and that physicians who make such prescriptions under the Oregon law risk losing their registration.

1998

- Michael Schiavo petitions a Florida court to allow him to have Terri Schiavo's feeding tube removed. Terri left no advance directives, but Schiavo claims that she had said she would not want to be kept alive "on anything artificial." The Schindlers bitterly oppose Schiavo's proposal, saying that Terri's religious beliefs (she and the Schindler's are devout Catholics) would keep her from accepting hastened death. They also produce videotapes that, in their opinion, prove that Terri is at least dimly conscious of her environment and therefore is not in a persistent vegetative state.
- **February 26:** The Oregon Health Services Commission votes 10-1 to include assisted suicide on the list of services for which state-funded Medicaid will pay.
- **March:** A court in the Canadian province of Nova Scotia refuses to try physician Nancy Morrison on murder charges for injecting potassium chloride into the heart of a cancer patient who was dying in agony and did not respond to narcotics. Morrison's treatment could not be justified as pain relief, but there were questions about whether the drug actually entered the patient's body.
- **June 5:** U.S. Attorney General Janet Reno overrules the ruling by Drug Enforcement Agency administrator Thomas Constantine. Reno states that physicians who prescribe controlled substances for suicide in accordance with Oregon's Death with Dignity Act will not have their permission to prescribe controlled substances rescinded.
- **July:** In response to Reno's statement, two Republican legislators introduce the Lethal Drug Abuse Prevention Act into Congress. If passed, the act would require federal prosecution of doctors who prescribe a controlled substance with the knowledge that it will be used for suicide, even if the doctors live in a state where such an act is legal.
- **September 1:** A law making assisted suicide a felony punishable by up to five years in prison and a $10,000 fine takes effect in Michigan.

Chronology

- *September 17:* Jack Kevorkian injects lethal drugs into Thomas Youk, a 52-year-old man suffering from amyotrophic lateral sclerosis (ALS), at Youk's request. Kevorkian videotapes the process.
- *October 14:* The Lethal Drug Abuse Prevention Act is withdrawn from Congress after a coalition of influential medical and palliative care groups protests that it would prevent doctors from relieving severe pain.
- *November:* A measure designed to repeal Michigan's new law against assisted suicide fails spectacularly at the polls, 2,103,697 opposed to 857,707 in favor.
- *November 22:* Kevorkian's videotape showing him committing euthanasia on Thomas Youk is broadcast on the CBS television news program *60 Minutes.*
- *November 25:* Kevorkian is charged with first-degree murder in Youk's death.

1999

- Ludwig Minelli, founder of Dignitas, a pro-euthanasia group in Switzerland (where assisted suicide is legal but euthanasia is not), announces that the group will help foreigners who come to Switzerland to obtain assistance in dying, whether or not the people are terminally ill. People seeking death are screened by a local physician, then (if accepted) given a lethal dose of barbituates. The people must take the drug (by mouth or intravenous injection) on their own, although a member of the Dignitas staff and a relative or friend will be with them as witnesses. Digitas does not require repeated requests for death issued over a period of time, nor does it test fot depression or other mental illness.
- The Senate of Colombia refuses to pass legislation supporting the Colombian Constitutional Court's 1997 acceptance of euthanasia, thereby keeping euthanasia a punishable offense in that country.
- The American Medical Association announces a major new program to educate physicians about end-of-life care.
- *February 18:* The Oregon Health Department publishes a report describing the suicides committed under the state's Death with Dignity Act during the law's first year of operation. The report states that during that time, 23 people received lethal prescriptions and 15 used them to commit suicide.
- *March:* The Advance Planning and Compassionate Care Act is introduced into Congress. If passed, it would strengthen the Patient Self-Determination Act by expanding the availability and portability of advance directives and making other improvements in end-of-life care.
- *March 22:* Jack Kevorkian goes on trial for murder for injecting lethal drugs into ALS sufferer Thomas Youk in September 1998.

- **March 26:** Kevorkian is convicted of second-degree murder and delivery of a controlled substance.
- **April 13:** Kevorkian is sentenced to 10 to 25 years in prison.
- **June 17:** The Pain Relief Promotion Act, a version of the Lethal Drug Abuse Prevention Act revised to make it acceptable to hospice and pain management groups, is introduced into Congress.
- **August:** The South African Parliament opens debate on a bill that would legalize voluntary euthanasia for terminally ill adults. It would also allow courts to order euthanasia for incompetent people, possibly even against the wishes of the people's families.
- **October 27:** The House of Representatives passes the Pain Relief Promotion Act by a vote of 271 to 156.

2000

- **February 11:** Circuit court judge George Greer approves Michael Schiavo's request to have his wife's feeding tube removed.
- **fall:** Senator Ron Wyden of Oregon stalls the Pain Relief Promotion Act in the Senate, leading to the bill's defeat.
- **November 28:** The lower house of the Netherlands parliament votes 104 to 40 to legalize voluntary euthanasia and physician-assisted suicide.

2001

- The Florida Supreme Court denies Robert and Mary Schindler's appeal to prevent Michael Schiavo from having Terri Schiavo's feeding tube removed; the U.S. Supreme Court refuses to hear the case.
- Diane Pretty, a British woman with motor neuron disease (amyotrophic lateral sclerosis), petitions the Department of Public Prosecutions (DPP), asking for assurance that her husband will not be prosecuted if he helps her kill herself. The DPP refuses her request, and its decision is upheld through several appeals. Pretty then takes her case to the European Court of Human Rights, claiming that Britain's law against assisted suicide violates the European Convention on Human Rights.
- **January 18:** The Supreme Court of Canada rules unanimously that Robert Latimer must serve at least 10 years in prison for killing his severely disabled daughter in 1993.
- **April 11:** The Netherlands legalizes euthanasia and physician-assisted suicide.
- **August 9:** The California Supreme Court rules that Rose Wendland, wife of minimally conscious patient Robert Wendland, has not provided

"clear and convincing evidence" that he would have wished to have his feeding tube removed. The court therefore forbids her to order the tube removed. Robert Wendland has already died of pneumonia by the time of the ruling, but the court's decision provides a standard for future cases.

- *November 6:* Attorney General John Ashcroft prohibits physicians from intentionally prescribing lethal doses of federally controlled drugs, thus potentially negating the Oregon assisted-suicide law. His ruling essentially reinstates the 1997 ruling of Drug Enforcement Administrator Thomas Constantine, which had been negated by then-Attorney General Janet Reno in June 1998.
- *November 8:* Following a legal challenge by Oregon state officials, U.S. District Judge Robert Jones in Portland, Oregon, issues a temporary restraining order blocking Ashcroft's order.

2002

- *March:* The British High Court grants Ms. B, a 43-year-old quadriplegic, permission to have her ventilator turned off.
- *April 1:* The Netherlands law permitting voluntary euthanasia and physician-assisted suicide goes into effect, making that country the only one in the world in which euthanasia is legal.
- *April 17:* District judge Robert Jones issues a permanent injunction against Attorney General Ashcroft's order from November 6, 2001.
- *April 29:* The European Court of Human Rights rejects Diane Pretty's application.
- After having her ventilator turned off, Ms. B dies.
- *May 11:* Diane Pretty dies of natural causes.
- *May 16:* Belgium legalizes voluntary euthanasia for people with "hopeless" illnesses, becoming the second country to decriminalize euthanasia.
- *October 1:* The Belgian law permitting euthanasia goes into effect.

2003

- *September 26–27:* Vincent Humbert, a French man left severely disabled by an automobile accident in 2000, is killed by his mother and doctor after repeated, highly publicized requests to die (he had even dictated a book on the subject with movements of one thumb).
- *October 21:* Six days after another removal of Terri Schiavo's feeding tube, the Florida legislature passes "Terri's Law," a special law authorizing Governor Jeb Bush to order the tube to be reinserted.

2004

- *March 20:* In a papal allocution, "Care for Patients in a 'Permanent' Vegetative State," Pope John Paul II states that providing food and water to such people is "ordinary care," not a medical treatment, and thus may not be discontinued. Catholics following the moral tenets of their religion thus may not discontinue such provision.
- *May 26:* Ruling on *Oregon v. Ashcroft*, a three-judge panel of the Ninth Circuit Court of Appeals votes 2 to 1 to reject Ashcroft's attempt to use the federal Controlled Substances Act to punish doctors who comply with Oregon's assisted-suicide law.
- *August:* The Ninth Circuit Court of Appeals rejects the George W. Bush administration's request for a new hearing on *Oregon v. Ashcroft*.
- *September 23:* The Florida Supreme Court rules that "Terri's Law" is unconstitutional.
- *November:* Attorney General Ashcroft appeals *Oregon v. Ashcroft* to the U.S. Supreme Court.
- *November 30:* France's National Assembly overwhelmingly legalizes "passive euthanasia," that is, withholding of life-sustaining care.
- *December:* The movie *Million-Dollar Baby* is released (it later wins four Oscars, including one for Best Picture); in the film's controversial ending, the heroine, a young boxer rendered quadriplegic by an accident, asks for and receives assistance in ending her life.

2005

- *January:* Patty Berg (D.-Eureka) and Lloyd Levine (D.-San Fernando Valley) introduce an assisted suicide bill, modeled on the Oregon law, into the California legislature.
- *January 24:* The U.S. Supreme Court declines to hear Governor Jeb Bush's challenge to the Florida Supreme Court ruling against him in the Terri Schiavo case.
- *February 22:* The Supreme Court agrees to review *Gonzales v. Oregon* (formerly *Oregon v. Ashcroft*) in late 2005 or early 2006.
- *February 25:* Florida circuit court judge George Greer orders removal of Terri Schiavo's feeding tube within three months.
- *March:* Groningen Hospital in the Netherlands proposes guidelines for euthanasia of terminally or incurably ill newborns.
- *March 18:* Doctors remove Terri Schiavo's feeding tube.
- *Late March:* Protesters, including both right-to-life and pro-disabled groups, hold vigils outside the hospice in which Terri Schiavo lies and make impassioned requests to have her feeding tube reinserted. As Easter nears, some of the protesters compare Terri to Christ.

Chronology

- **March 21:** In an emergency night session, Congress passes a bill giving the federal courts jurisdiction over the Terri Schiavo case; President George W. Bush signs the bill.
- **March 23:** A three-judge panel of the 11th Curcuit Court of Appeals rejects the request of Terri Schiavo's parents to have her feeding tube reinserted.
- **March 24:** The U.S. Supreme Court declines to review the appeals court's decision in the Schiavo case, as Schiavo's parents had requested.
- **March 31:** Terri Schiavo dies.
- **June 15:** Private Member's Bill C-407, which would legalize assisted suicide under a wide variety of circumstances, is presented to the Canadian House of Commons.
- The report of an exhaustive autopsy on Terri Schiavo is released; the autopsy shows that centers of consciousness in Schiavo's brain had been completely destroyed.
- **July:** The California assisted suicide bill is defeated for the 2005 legislative term.
- **October 5:** The Supreme Court hears oral arguments on *Gonzales v. Oregon*.
- **October 10:** Britain's House of Lords begins debating the Assisted Dying for the Terminally Ill Bill.

2006

- **January:** Francine Lalonde is reelected to the Canadian House of Commons and promises to reintroduce her bill to legalize assisted suicide, which failed to pass in 2005.
- **January 17:** The Supreme Court rules 6-3 in *Gonzales v. Oregon* that federal officials may not prosecute physicians prescribing lethal drugs in accordance with Oregon's assisted suicide law.
- **February 26:** Following the advice of prosecutors, a judge in France drops all charges against the mother and doctor of Vincent Humbert for euthanizing him in 2003 after Humbert, left deaf, paralyzed, and mute after an automobile accident, repeatedly asked to die.
- **May:** The Dutch Pediatric Society adopts the Groningen Protocol, which permits euthanasia of suffering, incurably sick newborn babies if both parents consent.
- **May 12:** After a seven-hour debate, members of Britain's House of Lords vote 148 to 100 to delay a second reading of Lord Joffe's Assisted Dying for the Terminally Ill Bill, guaranteeing that the bill will not become law during the current session of Parliament.

Right to Die and Euthanasia

- *June:* The Michigan Parole Board rejects Jack Kevorkian's fourth request to commute his prison sentence on the grounds that he is dying of liver disease.
- *June 27:* A bill to legalize assisted suicide, reintroduced into the California legislature, fails in its first legislative hearing when the senator chairing the committee votes against it.
- *July 17:* A doctor and two nurses are arrested on charges of second-degree murder for allegedly euthanizing several patients at Memorial Medical Center in New Orleans on September 1, 2005, in the chaotic days following Hurricane Katrina.
- *November:* Britain's Royal College of Obstetricians and Gynecologists recommends consideration of the ethics of actively euthanizing newborn babies with severe and untreatable disabilities or uncontrollable pain if the parents consent.

---

[1] Hippocratic Oath, quoted in Gregory E. Pence, *Classic Cases in Medical Ethics.* New York: McGraw-Hill, p. 63.

[2] Socrates, in Plato, *Phaedo,* quoted in Pence, *Classic Cases in Medical Ethics,* p. 34.

[3] Augustine, quoted in Derek Humphry and Ann Wickett, *The Right to Die: An Historical and Legal Perspective of Euthanasia.* Eugene, Ore.: Hemlock Society, 1990, p. 6.

[4] Quoted in Humphry and Wickett, *The Right to Die,* p. 19.

[5] Kaoru Narita, quoted in Derek Humphry and Mary Clement, *Freedom to Die: People, Politics, and the Right-to-Die Movement.* New York: St. Martin's Press, 1988, p. 153.

[6] Robert Muir, quoted in Humphry and Clement, *Freedom to Die,* p. 88.

[7] Health and Human Services Notice to Health Care Providers, quoted in Pence, *Classic Cases in Medical Ethics,* p. 179.

[8] Gerhard Gesell, *American Academy of Pediatrics v. Heckler,* U.S. District Court, D.C., No. 83-0774, quoted in Peter G. Filene, *In the Arms of Others: A Cultural History of the Right-to-Die in America.* Chicago: Ivan R. Dee, 1998, p. 117.

[9] *Cruzan v. Harmon,* 760 S.W. 2d 408 (Mo. banc 1988), quoted in Filene, *In the Arms of Others,* p. 171.

CHAPTER 4

BIOGRAPHICAL LISTING

This chapter offers brief biographical information on people who have played major roles in the right-to-die movement, its opposition, or the development of current feelings about physician-assisted suicide and euthanasia.

Janet Adkins, a 54-year-old Oregon woman, became the first person to die by Jack Kevorkian's suicide device. She had recently been diagnosed as being in the early stages of Alzheimer's disease when she sought out Kevorkian's services in 1990 after hearing about his suicide machine on television. Accompanied by her husband and three grown sons, she went to Michigan to meet Kevorkian and died there on June 4, 1990.

Kevin Andrews, a Liberal member of Australia's Parliament, introduced a bill on September 9, 1996, to repeal the Northern Territory's Rights of the Terminally Ill Act, which legalized physician-assisted suicide. Andrews's bill passed in March 1997.

Aristotle, Greek philosopher of the fourth century B.C., wrote in his Ethics that suicide to escape from pain or other evils was an act of cowardice.

John Ashcroft, U.S. attorney general, issued an order on November 6, 2001, stating that physicians who prescribe narcotics in accordance with Oregon's assisted suicide law are violating the Controlled Substances Act and therefore can be deprived of their federal prescription licenses. Supporters of the Oregon law challenged the order in court, resulting in a case (*Oregon v. Ashcroft*, later *Gonzales v. Oregon*) that eventually reached the U.S. Supreme Court.

Saint Augustine, Bishop of Hippo in the early fifth century A.D., wrote around 410 that suicide for any reason except a direct command from God was a "detestable and damnable wickedness" because it violated the Sixth Commandment, "Thou shalt not kill."[1] His view has been the predominant Christian one, and many Christians still hold it.

133

Ms. B, a 43-year-old quadriplegic, became the first Briton to ask a court for permission to have a ventilator turned off. The British High Court granted the permission in March 2002, and Ms. B died on April 29.

Sir Francis Bacon, British philosopher and statesman, coined the term *euthanasia* (from Greek words meaning "good death") in the early 17th century. In Bacon's usage, the word referred to the peaceful, painless natural death that people desired. Only in the 20th century has it come to mean death caused by a person to end another's suffering.

Joseph Cardinal Bernardin, archbishop of Chicago, was a particularly forceful spokesperson against physician-assisted suicide because he made his statements while he himself was dying of cancer in 1996. "As one who is dying, I have especially come to appreciate the gift of life," he wrote in a letter to the Supreme Court a few days before his death. He urged the Court not to legalize assisted suicide, saying, "Creating a new right to assisted suicide will endanger society and send a false signal that a less than 'perfect' life is not worth living."[2]

James Bopp, attorney for the National Right to Life Committee, sued to have implementation of the Oregon Death with Dignity Act blocked after its first passage by voters in 1994. He claimed that the law violated the Americans with Disabilities Act as well as constitutional guarantees of due process and equal protection. He argued that its safeguards were inadequate to protect dying patients from undue influence of third parties.

Els Borst, health minister in the Netherlands, spearheaded the drive to legalize euthanasia in that country. In the early 2000s he also supported making a "suicide pill" available to elderly people who wish to end their lives, regardless of their state of health.

Hilly Bosscher, a physically healthy 50-year-old Dutch woman, was severely depressed after enduring an abusive marriage and losing two sons. She asked for help in killing herself and, after her depression failed to respond to treatment, her psychiatrist, Boudewijn Chabot, granted her request in 1991. Subsequent court proceedings, in which the Dutch Supreme Court ultimately acquitted Chabot in 1994, established that assisted suicide or euthanasia on grounds of mental suffering alone was acceptable in the Netherlands.

Elizabeth Bouvia, a young woman severely disabled by cerebral palsy and arthritis, petitioned a California court in 1983 for the right to force doctors to remove her nutrition tubes and let her die, even though she was not terminally ill. The California Court of Appeals finally granted her permission in 1986, but she decided not to kill herself after all.

Jeb Bush, governor of Florida and brother of President George W. Bush, attempted several times to intervene in the Terri Schiavo case on behalf of Schiavo's parents. On October 21, 2003, the Florida legislature passed

"Terri's Law," authorizing Governor Bush to order Schiavo's feeding tube reinserted, but the Florida Supreme Court ruled the law unconstitutional on September 23, 2004. Bush challenged the ruling, but on January 24, 2005, the U.S. Supreme Court declined to hear his appeal.

Boudewijn Chabot, a Dutch psychiatrist, gave lethal drugs for the purpose of suicide to Hilly Bosscher, a physically healthy but depressed woman whose mental suffering had not responded to treatment, in 1991. In 1994 the Dutch Supreme Court acquitted him of charges stemming from this action, affirming that granting physician-assisted suicide or euthanasia on the grounds of mental suffering alone was acceptable in the Netherlands.

Diane Coleman, a leader of Not Dead Yet, a militant disabled group formed in May 1996, fights against the legalization of assisted suicide. "We don't want to die," Coleman says. "We want health care and community-based services so we can live."[3]

Claire Conroy, an 82-year-old woman, was suffering from a variety of physical ailments and semi-comatose in January 1983, when her nephew petitioned to have her nutrition tubes removed because he believed that she would not want to continue living in her present condition. The New Jersey Supreme Court ruled two years later that, although Conroy would have had the right to refuse treatment, including nutrition, if competent or to have a previous refusal honored after she became incompetent, there was not enough evidence concerning her wishes to authorize the tube removal. By then, however, Conroy had died.

Thomas Constantine, federal Drug Enforcement Administrator, wrote to the House and Senate Judiciary Committees on November 5, 1997, the day after the Death with Dignity Act passed for the second time in Oregon, warning that assisted suicide was not a legitimate medical purpose for prescribing controlled substances (narcotics). Doctors who made such prescriptions would therefore be liable to lose their registration (permission to prescribe controlled substances), he said, even if their actions were legal in a particular state. Attorney General Janet Reno overruled him in June 1998.

Nancy Crick, a 69-year-old Australian woman, killed herself on May 22, 2002, with the advice of euthanasia supporter Philip Nitschke. Crick had had bowel cancer, but it was in remission.

Lester (Joe) and Joyce Cruzan, parents of Nancy Cruzan, petitioned a Missouri probate court for the right to remove the feeding tube from their comatose daughter early in 1988. The probate court granted their request, but the Missouri Supreme Court reversed the decision in November, saying that the Cruzans had not presented "clear and convincing evidence" of Nancy's wishes about medical care. In a decision on June 25,

1990, the U.S. Supreme Court affirmed that Nancy would have had the right to refuse medical treatment, including nutrition, had she been competent. However, the justices also agreed with the Missouri court that sufficient evidence of Nancy's wishes had not been provided. The Cruzans returned to the Missouri courts and provided additional testimony, after which the probate court's decision was reinstated and they were allowed to remove Nancy's feeding tube, causing her death. Joe Cruzan, still suffering from the effects of these events, killed himself in August 1996.

Nancy Beth Cruzan, a Missouri woman, entered a persistent vegetative state as a result of injuries sustained when her car crashed on January 11, 1983. She could breathe on her own but had to receive nutrition through a feeding tube. After a battle that went all the way to the U.S. Supreme Court, Cruzan's parents were finally granted their request to remove her feeding tube. The tube was removed on December 14, 1990, and Cruzan died two weeks later.

John Danforth, a Republican senator from Missouri, was inspired by the Nancy Cruzan case to draft the Patient Self-Determination Act, which requires all hospitals and other health care delivery institutions receiving federal funds (primarily Medicare and Medicaid) to explain advance directives to patients upon admission. Danforth's bill became law on December 1, 1991.

Bob Dent, a 66-year-old cancer patient, became the first man in the world to legally avail himself of physician-assisted suicide. He died on September 22, 1996, with the help of Philip Nitschke in Australia's Northern Territory, where physician-assisted suicide for terminally ill people became legal in July 1996.

Baby Doe, a male child born in Bloomington, Indiana, on April 9, 1982, had Down's syndrome (trisomy 21), which causes moderate to severe mental retardation, and a surgically correctable digestive defect. Following their doctor's recommendation, his parents refused permission for surgery or intravenous feeding because they believed that the child's quality of life would always be extremely poor. Baby Doe died of starvation shortly afterward. His case touched off a public outcry and a government attempt to prevent hospitals from denying treatment to such infants.

John Donne, famed 17th-century English poet, wrote an essay called *Biathanatos,* in which he explicitly defended the morality of suicide under some circumstances and offered arguments against the traditional Christian opposition to the act.

Geoffrey Fieger, Jack Kevorkian's lawyer, played a large part in helping the controversial physician escape conviction in several murder trials.

Biographical Listing

Harold Glucksberg, a Washington oncologist (cancer specialist), was one of five physicians who agreed to be plaintiffs in a 1994 suit filed by Compassion in Dying to challenge the constitutionality of the Washington state law against assisted suicide. His name replaced that of Compassion in Dying in later versions of the suit, which reached the Supreme Court in 1997.

Alberto Gonzales, U.S. attorney general, succeeded John Ashcroft in this post in October 2004, and Gonzales's name replaced Ashcroft's in the suit concerning the Oregon assisted-suicide law. The U.S. Supreme Court heard oral arguments in the case, *Gonzales v. Oregon* (04-623), on October 5, 2005. On January 17, 2006, the Court voted 6 to 3 to uphold the blocking of Ashcroft's order, thereby protecting the Oregon law.

George Greer, a circuit court judge in Florida, repeatedly ruled in Michael Schiavo's favor during legal contests between Schiavo and the parents of his wife, Terri Schiavo, over Terri's care. Greer's rulings allowed Michael Schiavo to order the removal of the feeding tube that sustained Terri, who was in a persistent vegetative state.

Thomas Griesa, chief judge of the federal court for the southern district of New York, ruled in *Quill v. Vacco* in December 1994 that there was no constitutional right to assisted suicide and that the New York state laws forbidding this activity, therefore, should stand.

Herbert Hendin, executive director of the American Foundation for Suicide Prevention in New York City, is a vocal critic of euthanasia and physician-assisted suicide, particularly as they are practiced in the Netherlands. He claims that euthanasia in that country is too often performed without patients' explicit requests and that similar, if not worse, abuses will occur in the United States if these practices are widely legalized.

Hippocrates, a Greek physician who lived in the fourth century B.C., is credited with the oath that most doctors still take when graduating from medical school. Part of the oath states, "I will [not] give a deadly drug to anybody if asked for it, nor will I make a suggestion to that effect."[4]

John Hofsess, a journalist and filmmaker, is founder and executive director of the Right to Die Society of Canada. He is a leader of the right-to-die movement in that country, equivalent in standing to Derek Humphry in the United States.

Michael Hogan, a Salem, Oregon, federal district court judge who was sympathetic to the right-to-life movement, passed a temporary restraining order that blocked the state's newly passed Death with Dignity Act just six hours before it was scheduled to go into effect on December 5, 1994. On August 4, 1995, he ruled the law unconstitutional. The ruling was appealed.

Right to Die and Euthanasia

Vincent Humbert, a 22-year-old French man, was severely disabled by an automobile accident in September 2000. He used movements of one thumb to dictate a book, *I Ask the Right to Die,* and he wrote a letter to French president Jacques Chirac, making the same request. His mother and doctor killed him with a drug overdose on September 26, 2003, just after the book was published. They were charged with murder, but, following the advice of prosecutors, a French judge dropped all charges against them in February 2006.

David Hume, Scottish philosopher. In an essay published in 1777 (a year after his death), Hume wrote that suicide to end suffering from a painful, incurable, or terminal illness or disability was not a violation of one's duty to either God or society. Indeed, he asserted that such an act might even provide a net benefit to society.

Derek Humphry, British-born journalist, founded the Hemlock Society, an organization dedicated to legalizing physician-assisted suicide and voluntary euthanasia for terminally ill adults. He became interested in the issue in 1975, when he helped his first wife, Jean, who was dying of cancer, kill herself with drugs he had obtained from a doctor. He was not prosecuted for the act, even though he described it publicly in a book called *Jean's Way* (1978). He moved to the United States, married again, and, with his second wife, Ann Wickett, founded the Hemlock Society in 1980. Humphry wrote several additional books about assisted suicide, some of them (especially *Final Exit,* published in 1991) providing specific "how-to" details. Humphry and the Hemlock Society were also active in the attempts to legalize physician-assisted suicide in the states of Washington, California, and Oregon in the early 1990s. Humphry retired from his post as executive director of the Hemlock Society in 1992 but has remained active in the right-to-die movement.

Henry Hyde, Republican representative from Illinois. In July 1998 he introduced a bill called the Lethal Drug Abuse Prevention Act (H.R. 4006) into the House of Representatives. The bill was essentially an attempt to nullify the Oregon law permitting physician-assisted suicide by amending the Controlled Substances Act to require federal prosecution of doctors who prescribed a controlled substance knowing that it would be used for suicide. It was withdrawn in October 1998 and modified to meet the objections of medical and hospice organizations, which had protested its likely dampening effect on treatment of severe pain. Hyde reintroduced the modified bill as the Pain Relief Promotion Act (H.R. 2260) in June 1999, and the House passed it by a vote of 271 to 156 on October 27, 1999. The bill was defeated in the Senate in late 2000.

Joel Goodman Joffe (Baron Joffe), a member of the British parliament's House of Lords, worked as a human rights attorney in the 1950s and 1960s.

He introduced the Assisted Dying for the Terminally Ill Bill into Parliament in 2003 and again in 2005. The bill was debated in October 2005. On May 12, 2006, the House of Lords voted 148 to 100 to delay a second reading of the bill, effectively killing it for that session of Parliament.

John Paul II, formerly known as Karol Wojtyla, became pope of the Catholic Church on October 16, 1978. He issued an encyclical opposing euthanasia in 1995 and stated in a papal allocution on March 20, 2004, that providing food and water to people in a persistent vegetative state is "ordinary care," not a medical treatment, and thus may not be discontinued. Pope John Paul II died on February 4, 2005.

Immanuel Kant, 18th-century German philosopher, wrote that suicide was never justified because it was a self-interested act. Kant maintained that committing suicide showed a disrespect for life and violated people's duty to be "sentinels on earth [who] may not leave their posts" until relieved by God.[5]

Barry Keene, a California assemblyman from Eureka, introduced a state bill to make living wills legally binding in 1974 after witnessing the deaths of two acquaintances. In both cases, the deaths were made more protracted and painful by hospitals' disregard of the patients' wishes concerning end-of-life treatment. Keene's bill failed, but when it was reintroduced as the Natural Death Act in 1976, in the wake of the widely publicized Karen Ann Quinlan case, it passed (albeit narrowly and after much debate). The result was the first state law to give legal force to advance health care directives.

Jack Kevorkian, a retired Michigan pathologist, did more than anyone else to make physician-assisted suicide a hot public issue in the 1990s. He claims that, beginning with Janet Adkins on June 4, 1990, he helped some 150 people take their own lives. All left explicit evidence of their wish to die, and all believed that they were incurably (though not necessarily terminally) ill, although autopsies on some revealed no sign of disease. Kevorkian was acquitted three times in assisted suicide trials (a fourth trial was declared a mistrial), partly because juries sympathized with his work and partly because Michigan law against assisted suicide was either nonexistent or unclear until September 1998. Finally, it became clear that he had turned from assisted suicide to unquestionable euthanasia. He allowed a videotape showing him injecting fatal drugs into ALS sufferer Thomas Youk to be shown on national television in November 1998, and as a result he was convicted of second-degree murder on April 13, 1999, and sentenced to 10 to 25 years in prison. Kevorkian has repeatedly asked for early release from prison on grounds of extreme ill health, but the state parole board denied his request for the fourth time in June 2006.

Elisabeth Kübler-Ross, Swiss-born psychiatrist, helped to break the modern Western taboo against discussing death with best-selling books such as *On Death and Dying* (1969), which described five stages of reaction to death.

Louis Kutner, a lawyer, introduced the concept of the "living will" in an article in the Summer 1969 *Indiana Law Review*. This document, one form of advance health care directive, is made by a competent adult and states what medical treatments should be given or refused if he or she becomes incompetent.

Francine Lalonde, a member of the Canadian Parliament, introduced C-407, a private member's bill, into Parliament on June 15, 2005. If passed, the bill would legalize assisted suicide for terminally ill adults. It received a second reading in October 2005 but, as of mid 2006, had not passed. Lalonde is a member of the Bloc Québécois, a separatist party in Quebec. She was re-elected in January 2006 and promised to reintroduce her bill.

Robert Latimer, a farmer in Saskatchewan, Canada, was convicted in 1994 of second-degree murder for killing his severely retarded and disabled 12-year-old daughter, Tracy. The case was widely publicized. He was initially sentenced to 10 years in prison, but in 1997 a judge invoked a constitutional exemption to reduce the sentence to two years. In 1998 the Saskatchewan Court of Appeal reinstated the mandatory 10-year minimum sentence. The Supreme Court of Canada upheld the sentence in a unanimous ruling on January 18, 2001.

Barbara Coombs Lee, was director of Oregon Right to Die, was the coauthor of Oregon's Death with Dignity Act. Formerly the executive director of Compassion in Dying, she is now co-CEO of Compassion and Choices, the group formed when Compassion in Dying and End-of-Life Choices (formerly the Hemlock Society) merged in January 2005.

C. Killick Millard, health officer for the city of Leicester in Britain, in 1931 drafted the first bill that attempted to legalize voluntary euthanasia in that country. The British Voluntary Euthanasia Society was formed in 1935 to work for passage of this bill, but when the bill was presented to Parliament in 1936, the House of Lords voted it down, 35 to 14.

Ludwig Minelli, a Swiss lawyer, founded Dignitas, an assisted-suicide support group, in Zurich, Switzerland, in 1998 and currently heads the group. Dignitas arranges suicides for members with untreatable illnesses, including those who come from outside Switzerland. Assisting in suicide is legal, or at least not prosecuted, in Switzerland as long as the assister has no selfish motives.

Roger J. Miner, judge in the federal Second Circuit Court of Appeals, wrote the opinion in the case of *Quill v. Vacco,* in which the court ruled in

April 1996 that the New York state laws against assisting in suicide are unconstitutional because they violate the Equal Protection Clause of the Fourteenth Amendment. The Supreme Court reversed this ruling in June 1997.

Sir Thomas More, English statesman, included state-assisted suicide for the terminally or incurably ill in *Utopia,* the portrait of an ideal society that he wrote in 1516. It is unclear whether More, a devout Catholic, really approved of such acts or described them satirically.

Nancy Morrison, a Nova Scotia physician, was freed by a court in March 1998 after being accused of murder. She had injected potassium chloride into the heart of a dying cancer patient, who was in agony and did not respond to narcotics. The court held that there was not enough evidence to charge Morrison because it was not clear whether the drug (injected through a faulty intravenous line) had entered the man's body.

Robert Morse, a neurologist, was the physician assigned to Karen Ann Quinlan after she entered a persistent vegetative state in 1975. For ethical reasons he opposed her parents' desire to turn off her respirator, even though he agreed that her condition was irreversible.

Robert Muir, Jr., probate court judge in Morristown, New Jersey, gave the first ruling for the Karen Ann Quinlan case. He ruled on November 10, 1975, that the state's interest in preserving life required him to deny Joseph and Julia Quinlan's request to turn off the respirator sustaining the life of their comatose daughter, Karen. The Quinlans appealed Muir's ruling, and the New Jersey Supreme Court overturned it the following year.

Don Nickles, Republican senator from Oklahoma, introduced a bill called the Lethal Drug Abuse Prevention Act (S. 2151) into the Senate in July 1998. The bill was essentially an attempt to nullify the Oregon law permitting physician-assisted suicide by amending the Controlled Substances Act to require federal prosecution of doctors who prescribed a controlled substance knowing that it would be used for suicide. It was withdrawn in October 1998 and modified to meet the objections of medical and hospice organizations, which had protested its likely dampening effect on treatment of severe pain. Nickles reintroduced the modified bill as the Pain Relief Promotion Act (S. 1272) in June 1999. The bill was defeated in the Senate in late 2000.

Philip Nitschke, the only physician willing to help terminally ill people commit suicide under Australia's Northern Territory's Rights of the Terminally Ill Act (in effect from July 1996 to March 1997), is often considered the Australian equivalent of Jack Kevorkian. Using a machine that injected lethal drugs at the command of a computer program triggered by the patient, Nitschke helped four people die while the law was in effect. He gave advice that Nancy Crick used in her highly publicized suicide in 2002. He still offers workshops in Australia on how to commit suicide, but because of a new law that went into effect on January 6, 2006, which makes it a crime to use telephone, e-mail, fax, or the Internet to discuss assisted suicide or euthanasia, most of the web site of Nitschke's organization, Exit International, is now hosted by the Voluntary Euthanasia Society of New Zealand.

John T. Noonan, Jr., Ninth Circuit Court of Appeals judge, wrote the March 9, 1995, decision of a three-judge panel from the court that upheld the constitutionality of the Washington state law against assisted suicide. Noonan maintained that claims to a constitutional right to assisted suicide were ridiculous and that the state had five compelling interests in forbidding such actions. Opponents claimed that his Catholic religion may have biased his decision.

Marshall Perron, at the time chief minister of Australia's Northern Territory, introduced legislation that would permit terminally ill people to request physician-assisted suicide under certain conditions. The law was passed in May 1995, went into effect in July 1996, and was repealed by the Australian Parliament in March 1997.

Plato, Greek philosopher of the fifth century B.C., said that suicide in the face of "intolerable misfortune" such as a painful, incurable illness could be forgiven as an act of temporary insanity and that ending medical treatment of a hopelessly ill person was acceptable. In general, however, he maintained that suicide was a cowardly act.

Geertruida Postma, a Dutch physician, was put on trial in 1973 for giving her terminally ill mother a fatal injection at her mother's request. She was found guilty but given only a one-month suspended sentence and a year's probation. Postma's trial marked the beginning of decriminalization of physician-assisted suicide and euthanasia in the Netherlands.

Charles Potter, a Unitarian minister, formed the Euthanasia Society in 1938 to work for legalization of voluntary and, in some cases, involuntary euthanasia.

Diane Pretty, a British woman with motor neuron disease (amyotrophic lateral sclerosis), in 2001 petitioned the British Department of Public Prosecutions and, later, the European Court of Human Rights to exempt her husband from prosecution if he helped her kill herself. Both denied her request. She died naturally on May 11, 2002, less than two weeks after the ruling from the European court.

Timothy E. Quill, an internist and professor of medicine and psychiatry at the University of Rochester School of Medicine in New York as well as associate director of medicine at Genesee Hospital, has become a well-known advocate of physician-assisted suicide; however, he sees this action as a last resort to be used only when all other attempts to relieve suffering have failed. His temperate manner has made him a much more widely acceptable spokesperson for the right-to-die movement than Jack Kevorkian. Quill first came to public attention when he published an article in the March 7, 1991, issue of the *New England Journal of Medicine* describing how he had prescribed barbiturates for "Diane" (Diane Trumbull), a 45-year-old woman with terminal leukemia, knowing she would use them to kill herself. Quill was the chief plaintiff in *Quill v. Vacco*, a legal case that attempted to have New York's laws against assisted suicide declared unconstitutional. This became one of the two right-to-die cases that the U.S. Supreme Court ruled on in June 1997.

Joseph and **Julia Quinlan,** parents of Karen Ann Quinlan, sought the legal right to force doctors to turn off the respirator that was keeping their comatose daughter alive. The granting of that right by the New Jersey Supreme Court on March 31, 1976, set a landmark precedent in establishing that family members could refuse life-sustaining medical treatment on behalf of an incompetent adult who has previously expressed a wish not to have such treatment. Feelings aroused by the Quinlan family's highly publicized plight helped to establish the right-to-die movement.

Karen Ann Quinlan, a young New Jersey woman, entered a persistent vegetative state, after consuming a mixture of alcohol and drugs at a party in April 1975. After she had remained in this condition for three months, her breathing maintained by a respirator, her parents petitioned the courts for permission to have the respirator turned off. The New Jersey Supreme Court granted that permission on March 31, 1976. By then, however, Quinlan had become able to breathe without it. She remained alive, though still unconscious, until June 13, 1986.

William Rehnquist, former chief justice of the U.S. Supreme Court, wrote the majority opinion in two of the Court's right-to-die cases, *Cruzan v. Director, Missouri Department of Health* (1990) and *Washington v. Glucksberg/New York v. Quill* (1997).

Stephen Reinhardt, a judge on the federal Ninth Circuit Court of Appeals, has became famous for offering liberal opinions, many of which the U.S. Supreme Court has later reversed. On March 6, 1996, he wrote the majority opinion for the full court's ruling on the case of *Compassion in Dying v. Washington,* stating that liberty and privacy interests protected by the Due Process Clause of the Fourteenth Amendment included the right to choose the time and manner of one's death. Therefore, the court held, the Washington state law prohibiting physician-assisted suicide was unconstitutional. The June 1997 U.S. Supreme Court ruling on the case reversed the appeals court's decision.

Right to Die and Euthanasia

Janet Reno, U.S. Attorney General, in June 1998 overruled a November 1997 statement by Thomas Constantine, administrator of the Drug Enforcement Administration. Constantine stated that doctors who prescribed controlled substances for suicide under Oregon's Death with Dignity Act risked having their permission to prescribe controlled substances rescinded. Reno, on the contrary, said that doctors who acted in accordance with the law would not be punished or sanctioned. Her statement angered right-to-life groups and other opponents of physician-assisted suicide, who felt that she had overstepped her authority.

Sue Rodriguez, a British Columbia woman who suffered from ALS, challenged the Canadian law forbidding assisted suicide in 1992–93. The country's Supreme Court ruled against her. Her case drew public and legislative attention to the question of assisted suicide for the terminally or incurably ill in Canada. Rodriguez killed herself in February 1994 with the help of an anonymous physician.

Barbara Rothstein, chief judge of the federal district court for western Washington, declared Washington's law against assisted suicide unconstitutional on May 3, 1994. She said it violated rights guaranteed under both the Due Process Clause and the Equal Protection Clause of the Fourteenth Amendment.

Joseph Saikewicz, a severely retarded 67-year-old man, was diagnosed with leukemia in 1976. In 1977 a Massachusetts court ruled that Saikewicz's court-appointed guardian could decline chemotherapy on his behalf because the treatment would cause Saikewicz great distress and offer only a moderate chance of prolonging his life for about a year. This ruling set a precedent for allowing surrogates to refuse life-extending medical treatment on behalf of never-competent people. Saikewicz died before his case was decided.

Dame Cicely Saunders, a British physician, established the world's first hospice, St. Christopher's, in London in 1967 to provide physical, psychological, and spiritual comfort to dying people and their families.

Michael Schiavo, husband of Terri Schindler Schiavo, became her legal guardian after she collapsed and entered a persistent vegetative state in 1990. Beginning in 1998, he petitioned Florida courts to allow him to remove his wife's feeding tube, claiming that she would not have wanted to live in her present condition. Terri Schiavo's parents, Robert and Mary Schindler, bitterly opposed this move. The conflict between Michael Schiavo and the Schindlers resulted in court battles that gained nationwide publicity and the eventual attention of Florida's governor, Jeb Bush, and the U.S. Congress. The courts usually and ultimately sided with Michael Schiavo.

Terri Schindler Schiavo, a Florida woman, suffered a cardiac arrest from unknown causes (possibly related to an eating disorder) on February 25, 1990. She was revived, but brain damage from lack of oxygen left her in a persistent vegetative state that most of the doctors who saw her classified as permanent and incurable. Schiavo had not signed an advance directive, so there was no clear evidence of her wishes. Beginning in 1998, Michael Schiavo, Terri Schiavo's husband and legal guardian, petitioned Florida courts to allow him to remove her feeding tube, claiming that she would not have wanted to live in her present condition. Her parents, Robert and Mary Schindler, who had disagreed increasingly with Michael Schiavo about the type of care Terri should receive, strongly opposed this move. Terri Schiavo's case became a cause célèbre and resulted in special laws being passed at both the state and the federal level. Ultimately, however, the courts supported Michael Schiavo's position. Terri Schiavo's feeding tube was removed for the final time on March 18, 2005, and she died on March 31. An autopsy revealed that the centers of consciousness in her brain had long been completely destroyed.

Robert and Mary Schindler, Terri Schiavo's parents, believed that their daughter could recover from her persistent vegetative state with proper treatment. They therefore opposed the attempts of Terri's husband, Michael Schiavo, to have Terri's feeding tube removed. Supported by right-to-life and disability-rights groups, the Schindlers waged a highly publicized court battle against Michael Schiavo that ended only with Terri's death on March 31, 2005.

Seneca, first-century Roman Stoic philosopher, wrote that suicide was a justifiable response to incurable illness or bodily degeneration. He later killed himself, but he did so at the order of the Emperor Nero, not because of illness.

Socrates, Athenian (Greek) philosopher, committed suicide by drinking hemlock at the city's order in 399 B.C., after being convicted of corrupting the city's youth with his teachings. Although Socrates did not approve of suicide under most circumstances, his student, Plato, wrote that the older philosopher was not afraid of death and had said that philosophers should "make dying their profession."[6]

John Paul Stevens, justice of the U.S. Supreme Court, was considered to be the Court's most liberal member in the late 1990s. Stevens gave hope to the right-to-die movement with his concurring opinion in *Washington v. Glucksberg* in June 1997, in which he suggested that, although there was no general constitutional right to assistance in suicide for the terminally ill, the Court might in the future find such a right in particular cases.

Charles E. Teel, probate court judge in Jasper County, Missouri, granted Joe and Joyce Cruzan permission to remove the feeding tube from their comatose daughter, Nancy, early in 1988. Teel's decision was reversed on appeal because Nancy had not left "clear and convincing evidence" of her wishes, but he was able to reinstate it in 1990 after additional testimony was provided.

Saint Thomas Aquinas, 13th-century theologian, expanded the Christian argument against suicide by saying that suicide infringed on God's right to be the sole controller of life and also violated a person's duty to community and family. Aquinas wrote that suicide was the worst of sins because it allowed no time for repentance.

Richard Thompson, public prosecutor in Oakland County, Michigan, became famous for his determination to see controversial physician Jack Kevorkian go to prison for assisting in suicides. Comparing Kevorkian to a well-known serial killer, Thompson called Kevorkian "Jeffrey Dahmer in a lab coat."[7]

Laurence H. Tribe, professor at Harvard Law School, presented arguments to the U.S. Supreme Court in January 1997 in the case of *New York State v. Quill,* claiming that laws banning assisted suicide were unconstitutional.

Diane Trumbull, a 45-year-old woman with acute leukemia, asked her physician, Timothy E. Quill, for help in killing herself near the end of her terminal illness. He provided a barbiturate prescription and published what would become a famous account of Trumbull's death in the March 7, 1991, issue of the *New England Journal of Medicine.*

Kathryn Tucker, a Seattle attorney, played a major role in the unsuccessful 1991 attempt to legalize physician-assisted suicide in Washington state. She filed both of the right-to-die cases eventually heard by the U.S. Supreme Court in January 1997 and argued before the Court in the case of *Washington v. Glucksberg* that laws banning assisted suicide were unconstitutional. She was the legal affairs director of the right-to-die counseling organization Compassion in Dying.

Dennis C. Vacco, New York state attorney general, was the defendant in *Quill v. Vacco,* the suit filed by physician and assisted suicide supporter Timothy E. Quill and others to try to have the New York laws prohibiting assisted suicide declared unconstitutional. Vacco argued the state's position before the U.S. Supreme Court when the case reached the Court as *New York v. Quill* in January 1997.

Robert Wendland, a California man, was left in a minimally conscious state after an automobile accident. He had made no written directives concerning his health care. His wife, Rose, requested the removal of his feeding tube in compliance with what she claimed were his wishes, but his mother and sister opposed the action. Wendland died of pneumonia on July 17, 2001. On August 9 of that year, the California Supreme Court ruled that Rose Wendland had not provided "clear and convincing evidence" of Wendland's wishes and therefore would not have had the legal right to remove his feeding tube.

William Williams, assistant attorney general of the state of Washington in 1997, argued the state's position in *Washington v. Glucksberg* before the U.S. Supreme Court on January 8, 1997.

Ron Wyden, a Democratic senator from Oregon, blocked the Pain Relief Promotion Act in the Senate in late 2000, leading to the bill's defeat for that term. The bill was not reintroduced.

Thomas Youk, 52, suffered from amyotrophic lateral sclerosis (ALS) when, with the support of his wife, he asked Jack Kevorkian for help in dying. Kevorkian obliged on September 17, 1998, and for the first time in his career Kevorkian injected the lethal drugs himself rather than having the client do so. Kevorkian (with Youk's consent) videotaped the process, and the tape was broadcast on CBS's news program *60 Minutes* on November 22. The state of Michigan charged Kevorkian with murder in Youk's death. After a trial in which the testimony of Youk (on the tape) and his family were not allowed as evidence, Kevorkian was convicted and sentenced to prison.

---

[1] Augustine, quoted in Derek Humphry and Ann Wickett, *The Right to Die: An Historical and Legal Perspective of Euthanasia.* Eugene, Ore.: Hemlock Society, 1990, p. 6.

[2] Joseph Cardinal Bernardin, quoted in Sue Woodman, *Last Rights: The Struggle over the Right to Die.* New York: Plenum, 1998, p. 217.

[3] Diane Coleman, quoted in Kathi Wolfe, "Disabled Activists Fight Assisted Suicide," *Progressive,* September 1996, p. 16.

[4] Hippocratic Oath, quoted in Gregory E. Pence, *Classic Cases in Medical Ethics.* New York: McGraw-Hill, 1995, p. 63.

[5] Immanuel Kant, quoted in Pence, *Classic Cases in Medical Ethics,* p. 39.

[6] Socrates, in Plato, *Phaedo,* quoted in Pence, *Classic Cases in Medical Ethics,* p. 34.

[7] Richard Thompson, quoted in Pence, *Classic Cases in Medical Ethics,* p. 85.

CHAPTER 5

GLOSSARY

Terms used in discussions about euthanasia, including such distinctions as active and passive euthanasia, have played an important part in shaping people's opinions about the subject. This chapter presents some of the terms that the general reader is most likely to encounter while researching euthanasia and its ethical, legal, and social implications.

ableism The prejudicial belief that the lives of disabled people are less valuable than those of nondisabled people.

active euthanasia Taking specific steps (such as injecting a legal drug or smothering) to end someone's life for the purpose of relieving the person's suffering. Compare with **passive euthanasia.**

advance directive (health care directive) One of several types of legal document that competent adults may use to influence health care decisions, including end-of-life decisions, made on their behalf if they should become incompetent. All states in the United States now recognize the legality of some form of advance directive. See also **do-not-resuscitate (DNR) order, durable power of attorney for health care, living will.**

aid in dying Often used as a synonym for physician-assisted suicide, but may also cover discontinuation of life-sustaining medical treatment and/ or voluntary euthanasia carried out by a physician.

amyotrophic lateral sclerosis (ALS, "Lou Gehrig's disease") An incurable neurodegenerative disease that eventually leads to wasting of most muscles and increasing paralysis. It is called motor neurone disease in Britain. Some people with this condition have asked for assisted suicide or euthanasia.

Assisted Dying for the Terminally Ill Bill A proposed law, debated in Britain's House of Lords beginning on October 10, 2005, that would allow medical assistance to be provided to terminally ill adults who are suffering unbearably and wish to die. On May 12, 2006, the House of

Lords voted 148 to 100 to delay the second reading of the bill, effectively killing it for the current session of parliament.

autonomy The principle of independence or self-determination; the right to make decisions regarding one's own life.

battery A tort law term meaning unlawful touching or invasion of the body. The U.S. Supreme Court ruled in 1905 that unwanted medical treatment can be classified as battery.

brain death Death defined as the permanent cessation of brain activity rather than the cessation of breathing and heartbeat; this new criterion of death began to be used in the late 1960s and came to be widely accepted in the 1970s. There are several definitions of brain death, some requiring cessation of all brain activity and others requiring cessation of activity only in certain parts of the brain, such as those that control consciousness. This new concept of death is an example of the way the meaning and process of death have been changed by technology. It also has played a role in deciding when life-sustaining medical treatment, such as a respirator, should be stopped.

brain stem The part of the brain, located at the back of the neck, that maintains automatic processes such as breathing and heartbeat; it may function in people in a persistent vegetative state, even though their consciousness has been permanently destroyed.

clear and convincing evidence The highest standard of legal certainty applicable to civil cases.

coma A condition, caused by brain injury, in which a person is deeply unconscious and cannot be awakened. Compare with **minimally conscious state, persistent vegetative state.**

comfort care See **palliative care.**

competent Capable of understanding a subject such as health care, including consequences and implications of particular actions, and of making and communicating rational decisions about the subject.

Controlled Substances Act A law, passed in 1970, that gives the federal government the right to regulate the use of certain drugs deemed likely to be abused. Among other things, it requires physicians to distribute federally controlled drugs strictly within the scope of "accepted medical practice." On November 6, 2001, then-Attorney General John Ashcroft stated that doctors prescribing barbiturates in accordance with Oregon's assisted-suicide law violated this provision of the act and therefore were liable to federal prosecution.

death tourism A derogatory term for actions of non-Swiss who come to Switzerland in order to commit suicide with the help of the Swiss organization Dignitas.

Death with Dignity Act The law in Oregon that legalizes physician-assisted suicide for terminally ill people under certain conditions. First passed as an initiative (Measure 16) in 1994, the law was blocked by court challenges until October 1997. A month later, voters soundly defeated a measure that would have repealed it. In the law's first year of operation, 15 terminally ill people committed suicide under its provisions.

do-not-resuscitate order (DNR order)   An order on a patient's medical chart (signed by a physician, usually after consultation with a patient and/or the patient's family), requiring health care personnel not to attempt to revive the person if the person's breathing or heartbeat stops. A DNR order is one form of advance health care directive. Some states, but not all, allow DNR orders to be honored in nonhospital settings.

double effect   Refers to an action having both a desirable effect that is intended and an undesirable effect that is foreseen but not specifically intended. In the right-to-die context, this term most often refers to giving high doses of narcotics to terminally ill people for the purpose of controlling pain, knowing that such doses may also shorten the people's lives. Such a practice is generally considered legal, and most ethicists and religious groups also accept it. It is sometimes called terminal sedation.

Down's syndrome (trisomy 21)   A group of birth defects caused by the presence of an extra chromosome 21. It results in moderate to severe mental retardation, a characteristic physical appearance, and sometimes other physical defects. Parents of babies and children with Down's syndrome have sometimes refused medical treatment for them or even euthanized them because they expected the children's quality of life to be extremely poor. Today, however, experts say that most people with Down's syndrome can lead meaningful lives if placed in a supportive environment.

due process clause   Part of the Fourteenth Amendment to the U.S. Constitution that reads, "No State shall deprive any person of life, liberty, or property without due process of law." The Supreme Court has identified "liberty interests" protected by this clause as including an interest in making certain personal decisions about one's body, chiefly about reproduction (including abortions) but possibly including refusal of life-sustaining medical treatment. Right-to-die supporters have claimed that a right to ask for active hastening of death is also covered under this clause, but in its 1997 decisions on *Washington v. Glucksberg* and *New York v. Quill*, the high court disagreed.

durable power of attorney for health care (health care proxy)   Form of advance health care directive in which a competent adult appoints someone to act as a proxy in making health care decisions if he or she should become incompetent.

equal protection clause   Part of the Fourteenth Amendment to the U.S. Constitution that states, "No State shall deny to any person within its jurisdiction the equal protection of the laws." This has been interpreted to mean that similarly situated groups must be treated equally under the law. Right-to-die advocates have maintained that terminally ill people who ask for medication to end their lives are similarly situated to terminally ill people who ask for discontinuation of life-sustaining treatment, such as a respirator or feeding tube, and that laws that permit one of these actions but not the other, therefore, are unconstitutional.

ethics committee A multidisciplinary body, made up of such people as physicians, lawyers, ethicists, social workers, and clergy, that helps health care professionals make decisions involving medical ethics; most hospitals now have such committees.

eugenics A belief, popular from the late 19th through the mid-20th century, that only healthy people with socially desirable characteristics should reproduce. Supporters of eugenics also often approved of euthanasia—not necessarily voluntary—for the physically or mentally disabled.

euthanasia Ending another person's life to relieve otherwise uncontrollable suffering. Sir Francis Bacon coined the term in the 17th century from Greek words meaning "good death" and used it to mean a peaceful, painless natural death. Its meaning changed in the 20th century. Today, *euthanasia* is sometimes used as an umbrella term for any type of assisted dying, but most often it means taking direct action to end another's life; for instance, giving a lethal injection. See also **active euthanasia, passive euthanasia, voluntary euthanasia, involuntary euthanasia, physician-assisted suicide.**

Groningen Protocol Guidelines for euthanasia of terminally or incurably ill newborns, issued by a hospital in the Netherlands in March 2005. The Dutch Pediatric Society adopted the guidelines in May 2006.

health care proxy See **durable power of attorney for health care.**

Hippocratic Oath An oath credited to the Greek physician Hippocrates, who lived in the fourth century b.c. Traditionally considered the cornerstone of medical ethics, this oath includes a promise to give no deadly drug, even if asked for it. It is frequently cited by those who oppose physician-assisted suicide.

hospice An institution or program that provides physical, psychological, and spiritual comfort to dying people and their families.

incompetent Opposite of **competent.**

informed consent Consent to receive a medical procedure after having been told about the treatment's risks, benefits, and alternatives.

Intensive Care Unit (ICU) Part of a hospital in which critically ill and, sometimes, dying patients are treated by high technology.

involuntary euthanasia Killing a person for the stated reason of relieving suffering but without obtaining the person's permission. Some people use this term to refer only to euthanasia of competent adults done against their will or without consulting them; others also include euthanasia of incompetent people. Compare with **nonvoluntary euthanasia, voluntary euthanasia.**

Lethal Drug Abuse Prevention Act   A pair of bills (S. 2151 and H.R. 4006) introduced into Congress in July 1997. If passed, the act would have amended the Controlled Substances Act to require federal prosecution of doctors who prescribed a controlled substance with the knowledge that it would be used for suicide, even if the doctors lived in a state where such an act was legal. The bills were withdrawn in October 1998 after medical and hospice groups complained that the proposed law would greatly hamper treatment of severe pain. It was later replaced by a modified version, the **Pain Relief Promotion Act.**

letting die   See **passive euthanasia.**

living will   The first form of advance health care directive to be introduced. Made by a competent adult, it specifies which medical treatments should be given or withheld if he or she becomes incompetent. It may also specify the conditions under which the person wants all medical treatment stopped. A living will can be revoked at any time, and some states require that it be renewed periodically. Compare with **advance (health care) directive, do-not-resuscitate (DNR) order, durable power of attorney for health care.**

"locked-in" syndrome   A condition, caused by a stroke or some other brain-damaging event, in which a person is aware of the environment, sometimes even fully conscious, but cannot communicate; this condition is sometimes difficult to tell from a persistent vegetative state, but recovery from it is possible. Compare with **minimally conscious state, persistent vegetative state.**

Lou Gehrig's disease   See **amyotrophic lateral sclerosis.**

Medicaid   A combined state and federal program that pays for medical care for the poor.

Medicare   A federal program that helps to pay for medical care for the elderly.

medicide   A term coined by Jack Kevorkian, who defines it as "the termination of life performed by . . . professional medical personnel (such as a doctor, nurse, paramedic, physician's assistant, or medical technologist)."[1]

Mercitron   Jack Kevorkian's first suicide machine, which allowed a patient to commit suicide by pressing a button that triggered injection of a sedative followed by fast-acting poisons.

mercy killing   See **euthanasia.** Sometimes used to refer only to **involuntary euthanasia.**

minimally conscious state   A condition in which a person is essentially unconscious but can respond to the environment to a limited extent, for example by visually tracking objects. Compare with **coma, "locked-in" syndrome, persistent vegetative state.**

motor neurone disease   See **amyotrophic lateral sclerosis (ALS, "Lou Gehrig's disease").**

multiple sclerosis   An incurable degenerative nerve disease that produces progressive loss of physical and, sometimes, mental function. Some people with this disease have asked for assisted suicide or euthanasia.

Natural Death Act   A California law, passed in 1976, that makes living wills legally binding. It was the first state law to give legal force to advance directives.

nonvoluntary euthanasia   Euthanasia of an incompetent person at the request of a third party.

Pain Relief Promotion Act   A pair of bills (S. 1272 and H.R. 2260) introduced into Congress in June 1999. The act was a form of the Lethal Drug Abuse Prevention Act, modified to make it more acceptable to the medical and hospice communities. The House of Representatives passed its bill on October 27, 1999, but the Senate's bill was defeated in fall 2000. See also **Lethal Drug Abuse Prevention Act.**

palliative care   Care that provides comfort to dying or incurably ill people by relieving unpleasant symptoms, such as pain and nausea, but does not attempt to cure an illness. It may also include psychological and spiritual counseling for the people and their families.

passive euthanasia   Causing a person's death by withdrawing or not beginning life-sustaining medical treatment, such as a respirator or feeding tube; sometimes called "letting die." Compare with **active euthanasia.**

Patient Self-Determination Act   An act passed by Congress in November 1990. It modifies Title 42, the part of the U.S. Code that deals with health and welfare, to require that all hospitals and other health care facilities that receive federal funding inform patients of their right to fill out advance directives and refuse medical treatment.

persistent vegetative state (PVS)   A deep and usually permanent state of unawareness, caused by damage to the higher brain. People in PVS can maintain such automatic activities as heartbeat and (sometimes) breathing because their brain stem still functions. They may go through cycles of sleeping and waking and can make random movements and sounds, but they are not conscious of their surroundings. Compare with **coma, "locked-in" syndrome, minimally conscious state.**

physician-assisted dying   Some right-to-die groups prefer this term to **physician-assisted suicide** because it avoids the negative connotations of *suicide*. See also **aid in dying.**

physician-assisted suicide   An act in which a physician provides the means for suicide, usually a prescription for a lethal dose of medication, to someone who is terminally or incurably ill. The patient, not the doctor, takes the final action that results in his or her death, such as swallowing the medication. Compare with **euthanasia.**

Remmelink Report   An influential report, published in the Netherlands in 1991, that offered statistics about the practice of physician-assisted suicide and euthanasia in that country. The report was updated in 1995 and 2003.

Rights of the Terminally Ill Act   A law that became effective in Australia's Northern Territory in July 1996, legalizing physician-assisted suicide for terminally ill people under certain conditions. The Australian Parliament repealed it in March 1997.

right-to-die movement   A social and political movement dedicated to guaranteeing the legal right to have some degree of control over the time and manner of one's death, which may include the right to request a physician's aid in dying.

right-to-life movement   A social and political movement based on the belief, usually arising from religious doctrine, that human life should be preserved under all circumstances. The movement strongly opposes abortion and all forms of aid in dying.

self-deliverance   Term preferred by some right-to-die groups for terminally or incurably ill people's ending their own lives. Such groups do not consider this act to be suicide.

"slippery slope" argument   Argument based on the idea that certain acts, although not morally wrong in themselves, lead inevitably to other acts that are wrong. For some right-to-die opponents, this argument means that social or legal acceptance of each stage of aid in dying (refusal of life-sustaining treatment, physician-assisted suicide, voluntary euthanasia) leads unavoidably to the next stage, eventually resulting in euthanasia of people against their will. The argument can also refer to broadening the categories of people for whom aid in dying is acceptable, beginning with terminally ill, competent adults and ending with competent elderly or disabled people who have not given their consent.

Stoics   School of ancient Greek and Roman philosophers, including Seneca, who maintained that suicide was justifiable or even honorable in certain circumstances. They saw suicide to escape painful or terminal illness as acceptable but not honorable.

substituted judgment   A legal standard that requires the guardian of an incompetent person to do what that person is thought to have wished when competent.

surrogate A person designated to make decisions, such as health care decisions, on behalf of an incompetent person. Competent adults may choose surrogates to act for them if they should become incompetent, and courts may appoint surrogates to act for never-competent people or formerly competent people whose previous wishes are not known. See also **durable power of attorney for health care.**

terminal illness An illness that is expected to cause death soon, usually within approximately six months.

terminal sedation See **double effect.**

Terri's Law A special law passed by the Florida legislature in October 2003, allowing Governor Jeb Bush to order the reinsertion of a feeding tube into Terri Schiavo, a woman in a permanent vegetative state; the Florida Supreme Court declared the law unconstitutional on September 23, 2004.

trisomy 21 See **Down's syndrome.**

voluntary euthanasia Killing a person, at the person's request, to relieve otherwise uncontrollable suffering from a terminal or incurable illness or injury. Compare with **involuntary euthanasia.**

---

[1] Jack Kevorkian, *Prescription: Medicide.* Buffalo, N.Y.: Prometheus Books, 1991, p. 202.

PART II

GUIDE TO FURTHER RESEARCH

CHAPTER 6

HOW TO RESEARCH
RIGHT-TO-DIE ISSUES

The tremendous growth in the resources and services available through the Internet (and particularly the World Wide Web) is providing powerful new tools for researchers. Mastery of a few basic online techniques enables today's researcher to accomplish in a few minutes what used to require hours in the library poring through card catalogs, bound indexes, and printed or microfilmed periodicals.

Not everything is to be found on the Internet, of course. While a few books are available in electronic versions, most must still be obtained as printed text. Many periodical articles, particularly those more than ten years old, must still be obtained in "hard copy" form from libraries. Knowing one's way around library catalogs thus remains a useful skill.

ONLINE RESOURCES

Today it makes sense to use the Internet and its overlapping cousin the World Wide Web as the starting point for most research projects. This is particularly true regarding recent events affecting euthanasia and physician-assisted suicide. Web/Internet links can lead the researcher not only to organizations supporting or opposing these activities but also to groups and information related to hospice/palliative care, advance directives, the grieving process, health care in general, specific illnesses, disability rights, and much more.

THINKING LIKE A SPIDER: A PHILOSOPHY
OF WEB SEARCHING

For someone who is not used to it, searching the Internet and the World Wide Web can feel like spending hours trapped inside a pinball machine.

159

The shortest distance between a researcher and what he or she wants to know is seldom a straight line, at least not a single straight line. These things are called nets and webs for good reason: Everything is connected by links, and often a researcher must travel through a number of such links to find the desired information.

Net/web searching is best approached with a combination of patience, alertness, and, preferably, humor. A given search often will not reveal the desired information but will unearth at least three things, or groups of things, that are even more interesting. The information sought on the initial search, meanwhile, will be uncovered by chance at a later time when the researcher is looking for something else entirely. The sooner one accepts this, the sooner searching is likely to become rewarding rather than painful. In addition to specific files related to particular areas of research, it is a good idea to maintain a general file into which promising URLs (web addresses) or pieces of web sites can be copied as they are encountered.

It is easy to feel lost on the web, but it is also easy to find one's way back. During any given search, the Back button is the Ariadne's thread that can guide the researcher back through the labyrinth to the beginning of the adventure on the browser's home page, passing en route through all the sites visited (so that one can stop for another look or, if desired, jump off to somewhere else). The History button provides a list of all the sites visited on recent previous sessions.

Finally, a word of caution about the Internet. It is important to critically evaluate all materials found on the Net. Many sites have been established by well-known, reputable organizations or individuals. Others may come from unknown individuals or groups. Their material may be equally valuable, but it should be checked against reliable sources. Gradually, each researcher will develop a feel for the quality of information sources as well as a trusty tool kit of techniques for dealing with them.

TOOLS FOR ORGANIZING RESEARCH

Several techniques and tools can help the researcher keep materials organized and accessible:

Use the web browser's "Favorites" or "Bookmarks" menu to create a folder for each major research topic (and, optionally, sub-folders). For example, folders used in researching this book included organizations, laws, cases, current news, reference materials, and bibliographic sources.

Use favorites or bookmark links rather than downloading a copy of the actual web page or site, which can take up a large amount of both time and disk space. Exception: if the site has material that will definitely be needed in the future, download it to guard against it disappearing from the web.

If a whole site needs to be archived, obtain one of a variety of free or low-cost utility programs such as WebWhacker, which make it easier to download a whole site automatically, including all levels of links. But use the program judiciously: a site such as Euthanasia.com has hundreds of megabytes worth of material.

Where applicable, "subscribe" to a site so it will automatically notify you when new material is available.

Use a simple database program (such as Microsoft Works) or, perhaps better, a free-form note-taking program (such as the shareware program WhizFolders, available at http://www.whizfolders.com). This makes it easy to take notes (or paste in text from web sites) and organize them for later retrieval.

WEB INDEXES

A web guide or index is a site that offers what amounts to a structured, hierarchical outline of subject areas. This enables the researcher to zero in on a particular aspect of a subject and find links to web sites for further exploration.

The best known (and largest) web index is Yahoo! (http://www.yahoo. com). The directory on the Yahoo! home page can be searched for such topics as death and dying, advance directives, palliative care, suicide, and euthanasia. News stories and additional links can be found at http://headlines. yahoo.com/Full_Coverage/US/Assisted_Suicide.

Yahoo!'s Government topic provides listings including documents, ethics, and law. Categories under the Law subhead that are likely to be useful include cases, disability, constitutional law, elder law, health, and legal research.

In addition to following Yahoo!'s outlinelike structure, there is also a search box into which the researcher can type one or more keywords and receive a list of matching categories and sites.

Web indexes such as Yahoo! have two major advantages over undirected surfing. First, the structured hierarchy of topics makes it easy to find a particular topic or subtopic and then explore its links. Second, Yahoo! does not make an attempt to compile every possible link on the Internet (a task that is virtually impossible, given the size of the Web). Rather, sites are evaluated for usefulness and quality by Yahoo!'s indexers. This means that the researcher has a better chance of finding more substantial and accurate information. The disadvantage of web indexes is the flip side of their selectivity:

the researcher is dependent on the indexer's judgment for determining what sites are worth exploring.

Two other Web indexes are LookSmart (http://www.looksmart.com) and About.com (http://home.about.com).

SEARCH ENGINES

Search engines take a very different approach to finding materials on the Web. Instead of organizing topically in a "top down" fashion, search engines work their way "from the bottom up." Basically, a search engine consists of two pieces of software. The first is a "web crawler" that systematically and automatically surfs the net, following links and compiling them into an index with keywords (drawn either from the text of the sites themselves or from lists of words that have been flagged in a special way by the site's creators). The second program is the search engine's "front end": it provides a way to match user-specified keywords or phrases with the index and display a list of matching sites.

There are hundreds of search engines, but some of the most widely used include:

AltaVista (http://www.altavista.com)
Excite (http://www.excite.com)
Go.com (http://go.com)
Google (http://www.google.com)
Lycos (http://www.lycos.com)
Northern Light (http://www.northernlight.com)
WebCrawler (http://www.WebCrawler.com)

Search engines are generally easy to use by employing the same sorts of keywords that work in library catalogs. There are a variety of Web search tutorials available online (try "web search tutorial" in a search engine). A good one is published by Bright Planet at http://www.brightplanet.com/resources/details/searching.html.

Here are a few basic rules for using search engines:

When looking for something specific, use the most specific term or phrase. For example, when looking for information about physician-assisted suicide, use *"physician-assisted suicide"*, not *suicide*. (When using phrases as search specifications, enclose them in quotation marks.)

When looking for a more general topic, use several descriptive words (nouns are more reliable than verbs), such as *euthanasia laws*. (Most engines will automatically put pages that match both terms first on the results list).

Use "wildcards" when a desired word may have more than one ending. For example, *hospice** matches hospices, hospice care, and so on.

Most search engines support Boolean (*and, or, not*) operators that can be used to broaden or narrow a search.

Use AND to narrow a search. For example, *physician-assisted suicide AND euthanasia* will match only pages that have both terms.

Use OR to broaden a search: *physician-assisted suicide OR euthanasia* will match any page that has *either* term.

Use NOT to exclude unwanted results: *physician-assisted suicide NOT euthanasia* finds articles that discuss physician-assisted suicide but do not discuss euthanasia.

Since each search engine indexes somewhat differently and offers somewhat different ways of searching, it is a good idea to use several search engines, especially for a general query. Several "metasearch" programs automate the process of submitting a query to multiple search engines. These include the following:

Dogpile (http://www.dogpile.com)
Metacrawler (http://www.metacrawler.com)
Search (http://www.search.com)
SurfWax (http://www.surfwax.com)

There are also search utilities that can be run from the researcher's own PC rather than through a web site. A good example is Copernic, available at http://www.copernic.com.

MEGASITES: EVERYTHING ABOUT DEATH AND THEN SOME

One basic principle of research is to take advantage of the possibility that other people may have already found and organized much of the most useful information about a particular topic. For issues related to death and end-of-life decisions in general, several web sites can serve as excellent starting points for research because they provide links to vast numbers of other resources. These sites often contain specific pages on physician-assisted suicide and euthanasia.

- About.com's Death and Dying site, http://dying.about.com, provides links for a variety of death-related topics, including end-of-life care and death, dying, and culture.

- Ethics Updates from the University of San Diego has an extensive list of links related to euthanasia and end-of-life decisions at http://ethics. sandiego.edu/Applied/Euthanasia/index.asp.
- Growth House has a searchable end-of-life database accessible through http://www.hospicefoundation.org/searchEOL.asp.
- MedLinePlus, part of the National Library of Medicine, has links on end-of-life issues at http://www.nlm.nih.gov/medlineplus/endoflifeissues. html. Subjects covered include end-of-life decision-making and financial issues. Related pages, accessible from this one, cover topics such as suicide, hospice care, and advance directives.
- Michael Kearl of Trinity University in San Antonio, Texas, has an idiosyncratic but very interesting site devoted to the sociology of death and dying at http://www.trinity.edu/~mkearl/death.html. It covers not only euthanasia and related right-to-die issues (at http://www.trinity. edu/~mkearl/dtheuth.html) but also such topics as death across cultures and time, death in the arts, "immortality capitalism style," experiences of being in contact with the dead, death-related urban legends, death and political economies, personal impacts of death, and funeral planning. Something for everyone!
- Death Education, http://www.fidnet.com/~weid/deathed.htm#top, has links to information about death, grief, hospice, and many related topics. It has a subsite devoted to euthanasia and assisted suicide at http://www. fidnet.com/~weid/deathed.htm#euthanasia. This includes a glossary of terms, essays on euthanasia by Derek Humphry (founder of the Hemlock Society), pro and con information about Jack Kevorkian, a FAQ (Frequently Asked Questions) sheet about "death with dignity," and a fact sheet about euthanasia in the Netherlands.

EUTHANASIA-SPECIFIC SITES

In addition to the general death-related sites listed above and the sites specific to euthanasia within some of them, there are a number of sites that focus specifically on euthanasia and/or physician-assisted suicide. These sites are often sponsored by organizations with a strong bias for or against these actions. Researchers should not reject sites because the views expressed there disagree with their own; such sites often contain useful text (such as court opinions), bibliographies, or links.

Neutral:
- Ethics Update has a site on euthanasia and end-of-life decisions at http://ethics.acusd.edu/Appliedeuthanasia/index.asp. It includes discus-

164

sion forums and questions, Internet resources, a bibliography, legal decisions, and web links.

- Yahoo! has a site devoted to assisted suicide at http://headlines.yahoo. com/Full_Coverage/US/Assisted_Suicide. It includes current newspaper articles and links to other web sites and chat rooms.
- Valerie J. Vollmar, a professor at the Willamette College of Law in Salem, Oregon, provides quarterly updates on legal and other events related to physician-assisted suicide at http://www.willamette.edu/ wucl/pas.

In favor of euthanasia/physician-assisted suicide:

- Dignity in Dying, http://www.dignityindying.org.uk, is a British group formerly called the Voluntary Euthanasia Society. Their site includes news, people's stories, campaigns, and information on end-of-life rights and living wills.
- Euthanasia Research and Guidance Organization (ERGO), http://www. FinalExit.org, has a chronology, glossary, FAQ sheet, laws and court opinions from the United States and elsewhere, links to other right-to-die organizations, and newsbreaks.
- Death with Dignity National Center has a resources site at http://www. deathwithdignity.org. It includes news updates, surveys and opinions, a legal corner, glossaries, links, and other resources. The site features information about the Oregon assisted suicide law.

Opposed to euthanasia/physician-assisted suicide:

- International Task Force on Euthanasia and Assisted Suicide, http:// www.internationaltaskforce.org, has a glossary, library, links, court cases, and fact sheets on euthanasia and specific topics such as the *Gonzales v. Oregon* decision, euthanasia in the Netherlands, and assisted suicide in Oregon.
- Ohio Right to Life's web page on euthanasia, http://www.ohiolife.org/ euthanasia/index.asp, has the group's position statement on euthanasia and a variety of articles on euthanasia and related topics, including Jack Kevorkian, euthanasia in the Netherlands, and pain management as an alternative to euthanasia.
- The Pro-Life Council's web page on euthanasia is at http://www. euthanasia.com. It has articles and statements on medical, legal, religious, personal, and other aspects of euthanasia as well as fact sheets and links to other groups.

SPECIFIC ORGANIZATIONS AND PEOPLE

All the death-related and euthanasia-related megasites, as well as the web sites of most of the specific organizations listed in Chapter 8, have links to other organizations dealing with their particular topic or subtopic. Index sites such as Yahoo! also have links. If such sites do not yield the name of a specific organization, the name can be given to a search engine. Put the name of the organization in quotation marks.

Another approach is to take a guess at the organization's likely web address. For example, the American Civil Liberties Union (which includes choice in dying among its concerns) is commonly known by the acronym ACLU, so it is not a surprise that the organization's web site is at http://www.aclu.org. (Note that noncommercial organization sites normally use the *.org* suffix, government agencies use *.gov*, educational institutions use *.edu*, and businesses use *.com*.) This technique can save time, but it doesn't always work.

There are several ways to find a person on the Internet:

Put the person's name (in quotes) in a search engine and possibly find that person's home page on the Internet.

Contact the person's employer (such as a university for an academic, or a corporation for a technical professional). Most such organizations have web pages that include a searchable faculty or employee directory.

Try one of the people-finder services such as Yahoo! People Search (http://people.yahoo.com) or BigFoot (http://www.bigfoot.com/). This may yield contact information such as e-mail address, regular address, and phone number.

BIBLIOGRAPHIC RESOURCES

Bibliographic resources is a general term for catalogs, indexes, bibliographies, and other guides that identify the books, periodical articles, and other printed resources that deal with a particular subject. They are essential tools for the researcher.

LIBRARY CATALOGS

Most public and academic libraries have replaced their card catalogs with online catalogs, and many institutions now offer remote access to their catalog, either through dialing a phone number via software from a terminal or connecting via the Internet.

Access to the largest library catalog, that of the Library of Congress, is available at http://catalog.loc.gov. This page explains the different kinds of catalogs and searching techniques available. A subject search for *euthanasia* produces almost 200 listings and sublistings, including:

- names of different countries
- case studies
- fiction
- government policy
- history
- law and legislation
- moral and ethical aspects
- periodicals
- political aspects
- religious aspects
- social aspects

Physician-assisted suicide refers one to *assisted suicide*, which produces a shorter list (about 35 subheads) similar to that for euthanasia.

Yahoo! offers a categorized listing of libraries at http://dir.yahoo.com/Reference/Libraries/. Of course one's local public library (and for students, the high school or college library) is also a good source for help in using online catalogs.

With traditional catalogs, lack of knowledge of appropriate subject headings can make it difficult to make sure the researcher finds all relevant materials. Online catalogs, however, can be searched not only by author, title, and subject, but also by matching keywords in the title. Thus a title search for "euthanasia" will retrieve all books that have that word somewhere in their title. (Of course a book about euthanasia may not have the word *euthanasia* in the title, so it is still necessary to use subject headings to get the most comprehensive results.)

The Library of Congress catalog online can be searched with subject keywords such as *euthanasia, assisted suicide,* and *right to die.* Such searches produce lists of titles, with the most recent being listed first. The lists can be potentially overwhelming: searches for *physician-assisted suicide* and *right to die* produced over 10,000 titles apiece! (*Euthanasia* produced a mere 700 or so.) Consulting a list of Library of Congress subject headings, which is available as a reference in many public libraries, can help a researcher narrow or expand a search. The heading *euthanasia,* for instance, contains subdivisions on law and legislation and on religious aspects. It also gives "see also" references to such subjects as "aged, killing of the" and "trials (euthanasia)."

Once the record for a book or other item is found, it is a good idea to see what additional subject headings and name headings have been assigned to it. These headings in turn can be used for further searching for other items.

BOOKSTORE CATALOGS

Many people know that online bookstores such as Amazon.com at http://www.amazon.com and Barnes & Noble at http://www.barnesandnoble.com are convenient ways to shop for books. A lesser-known benefit of online bookstore catalogs is their inclusion of publisher's information, book reviews, and readers' comments about a given title. They can thus serve as a form of annotated bibliography.

Amazon has recently added a feature called "search inside the book" that applies to an increasing proportion of available titles. By default, this means that a standard search will also retrieve books that contain the keyword or phrase somewhere in the text. This can be a mixed blessing—it can help one find obscure topics that might not otherwise be indexed, but it can also retrieve irrelevant titles. If that happens, one can try the "advanced search" with more specific criteria or try Barnes & Noble instead.

In future years, the popular search engine Google may also offer a book search feature through its Library Project.

PERIODICAL DATABASES

Most public libraries subscribe to database services such as InfoTrac, which index articles from hundreds of general-interest periodicals (and many specialized ones). The database can be searched by author or by words in the title, subject headings, and sometimes words found anywhere in the article text. Depending on the database and periodical, "hits" in the database can result in just a bibliographical description (author, title, pages, periodical name, issue date, etc.), a description plus an abstract (a paragraph summarizing the contents of the article), or the full text of the article.

Many libraries provide dial-in, Internet, or telnet access to their periodical databases as an option in their catalog menu. However, licensing restrictions usually mean that only researchers who have a library card for that particular library can access the database (by typing in their name and card number). Check with local public or school libraries to see what databases are available.

A good general periodical index with unrestricted search access is IngentaConnect, http://www.ingentaconnect.com, which contains brief descriptions of about 13 million documents from about 26,000 journals in just about every subject area. Copies of complete documents can be ordered with a credit card, or they may be obtainable for free at a local library.

A somewhat more time-consuming alternative is to find the web sites for magazines likely to cover a topic of interest. Some scholarly publications are putting all or most of their articles online. Popular publications tend to offer only a limited selection. Some publications of both types offer archives of several years' back issues that can be searched by author or keyword.

LEGAL RESEARCH

As issues related to physician-assisted suicide, euthanasia, and various aspects of end-of-life care and decision-making continue to capture the attention of legislators and the public, a growing body of legislation and court cases is emerging. Because of the specialized terminology of the law, legal research can be more difficult to master than bibliographic or general research tools. Fortunately, the Internet has also come to the rescue in this area, offering a variety of ways to look up laws and court cases without having to pore through huge bound volumes in law libraries (which may not be accessible to the general public, anyway).

Finding Laws

When federal legislation passes, it becomes part of the United States Code, a massive legal compendium. Laws can be referred to either by their popular name or by a formal citation. The U.S. Code can be searched online in several locations, but the easiest site to use is probably the U.S. Code database at http://uscode.house.gov/search/criteria.shtml. The U.S. Code may also be found at Cornell Law School (a major provider of free online legal reference material) at http://www4.law.cornell.edu/uscode/. The fastest way to retrieve a law is by its title and section citation, but phrases and keywords can also be used. Finding a law by searching the U.S. Code can sometimes be difficult because a single law may modify a number of related paragraphs in the code.

Many states also have their codes of laws online. The Internet Law Library has a page of links to state laws. This library can be accessed through a number of sites, including http://www.lawguru.com/ilawlib and http://www.lectlaw.com/inll/1.htm.

Keeping Up with Legislative Developments

Bills related to physician-assisted suicide and related subjects such as end-of-life care and advance directives are proposed in Congress and state legislatures each year. The Library of Congress catalog site includes files summarizing legislation by the number of the Congress (each two-year session of Congress has a consecutive number: for example, the 110th Congress was in session in 2007 and 2008). Legislation can be searched for by the name of its sponsor(s), the bill number, or topical keywords.

The Library of Congress THOMAS site (http://thomas.loc.gov) provides a web-based interface that may be easier to use for many purposes. Summaries of legislation considered by each Congress can be searched by name, bill number, or keyword. Clicking on the bill number of a particular listing gives a screen with links to summary, text of legislation, current status, floor actions, and so on.

FINDING COURT DECISIONS

Like laws, legal decisions are organized using a system of citations. The general form is: *Party1 v. Party2 volume reporter (court, year).*

Here are two examples from Chapter 2:

Washington State v. Glucksberg, 117 U.S. 2258 (1997)

Here the parties are the state of Washington (plaintiff) and Glucksberg (defendant), the case is in volume 117 of the U.S. *Supreme Court Reports*, and the case was decided in 1997. (For the Supreme Court, the name of the court may be omitted).

Compassion in Dying et al. v. State of Washington, 850 F. Supp. 1454 (1994)

Here the parties are Compassion in Dying (plaintiff) and the state of Washington (defendant), the decision is in volume 850 of the Washington federal district court records, and the case was decided in 1994.

To find a federal court decision, first ascertain the level of court involved: district (the lowest level, where trials are normally held), circuit (the main court of appeals), or the Supreme Court. The researcher can then go to a number of places on the Internet to find cases by citation and often, the names of the parties. Two of the most useful sites are:

- The Legal Information Institute (http://supct.law.cornell.edu/supct/index.html) has all Supreme Court decisions since 1990 plus 610 of the most important earlier decisions. It also links to other databases with early court decisions.

- Washlaw Web (http://www.washlaw.edu) has a variety of courts (including states) and legal topics listed, making it a good jumping-off place for many sorts of legal research.

For more information on conducting legal research, "The Virtual Chase," http://www.virtualchase.com/resources/index.shtml, provides instructions and resources for law-related and general Internet research. After a certain point, however, the researcher who lacks formal legal training may need to consult with or rely on the efforts of professional researchers or academics in the field.

CHAPTER 7

ANNOTATED BIBLIOGRAPHY

Hundreds of books, articles, and Internet documents relating to various types of aid in dying have appeared, especially as the subject has gained in prominence during the 1990s and early 2000s. They range from histories of the right-to-die movement to impassioned arguments for or against legalizing some or all forms of assisted dying. This bibliography lists a representative sample of serious nonfiction sources dealing with assisted suicide, euthanasia, and the right to die, primarily those published after 2000. It also includes some earlier materials that are important for understanding the development of the right-to-die movement. Sources have been selected for clarity and usefulness to the general reader and for variety of points of view.

Listings in this bibliography are divided into books, magazine articles, and Internet/web documents. Magazine articles available on the Internet are listed under Articles rather than under Internet documents if the magazine is easily available. For the most part, newspaper articles have been omitted because most major events in the right-to-die movement have also been covered in magazines, and back issues of magazines are usually easier to obtain than back issues of newspapers.

BOOKS

Adamson, Kate. *Kate's Journey: Triumph over Adversity.* Redondo Beach, Calif.: Nosmada Press, 2004. This book describes the author's recovery after a severe stroke. Adamson opposes euthanasia for people in apparent persistent vegetative states because, like herself, they may sometimes recover consciousness.

Amarasekara, Kumar, and Mirko Bagaric. *Euthanasia, Morality and the Law.* New York: Peter Lang Publishing, 2003. Volume 19 of the Teaching Texts in Law and Politics series.

Annotated Bibliography

Anderson, Patricia, ed. *All of Us: Americans Talk about the Meaning of Death*. New York: Delacorte, 1996. This book presents more than 60 interviews with famous and not-so-famous individuals, ranging from teenage gang members to biogenetic engineers, on the subject of death.

Balkin, Karen F., ed. *Current Controversies: Assisted Suicide*. San Diego, Calif.: Greenhaven Press, 2005. An anthology of essays exploring the social, medical, and ethical dilemmas of assisted suicide, this book includes international as well as domestic viewpoints.

Basta, Lofty L. *A Graceful Exit: Life and Death on Your Own Terms*. Philadelphia, Pa: Xlibris Corp., 2000. This book explores complex ethical, economic, legal, moral, and social issues surrounding death. Basta emphasizes the inability of current forms of living wills to express patient wishes and offers alternative ways to control one's death.

Battin, Margaret Pabst. *The Death Debate: Ethical Issues in Suicide*. Upper Saddle River, N.J.: Prentice Hall, 1996. This book includes a chapter on physician-assisted suicide as well as a history of attitudes toward suicide and chapters on the concept of rational suicide and on suicide and rights.

———. *Ending Life: Ethics and the Way We Die*. New York: Oxford University Press, 2005. A collection of essays, a sequel to *The Least Worst Death* (1994), which covers a wide range of end-of-life topics, including suicide prevention, suicide in old age, and the "duty to die." Battin examines physician-assisted suicide and euthanasia in both United States and international contexts.

Battin, Margaret Pabst, Rosamond Rhodes, and Anita Silvers, eds. *Physician Assisted Suicide: Expanding the Debate*. New York: Routledge, 1998. This essay collection provides discussions and background material to enlarge the debate about whether physician-assisted suicide should be legalized. Many of the essays are by philosophers.

Beauchamp, Tom L., ed. *Intending Death: The Ethics of Assisted Suicide and Euthanasia*. Upper Saddle River, N.J.: Prentice Hall, 1996. This book presents clinical, political, legal, economic, and philosophical perspectives in papers from a conference sponsored by the Kennedy Institute of Ethics at Georgetown University and the Schools of Medicine and Public Health at Johns Hopkins University.

Beauchamp, Tom L., and Robert M. Veatch, ed. *Ethical Issues in Death and Dying*. Upper Saddle River, N.J.: Prentice Hall, 1995. This essay collection covers topics including suicide, euthanasia, limiting of care for terminal patients, and physician-assisted suicide. Points of view include those of presidential commissions, courts, and the American Medical Association.

173

Right to Die and Euthanasia

Beauchamp, Tom L., and Leroy Walters, eds. *Contemporary Issues in Bioethics,* 5th ed. Belmont, Calif.: Wadsworth, 1999. This book provides essays and documents, including court decisions and news articles, relating to the right to die, euthanasia, and assisted suicide as well as other bioethical issues.

Behuniak, Susan M., and Arthur G. Svenson. *Physician-Assisted Suicide: The Anatomy of a Constitutional Law Issue.* Lanham, Md.: Rowman & Littlefield, 2002. This book revolves around the questions of whether competent, terminally ill patients have a right to die with the assistance of their physicians and whether state and national governments have legitimate interests in interfering with the exercise of this right.

Betzold, Michael. *Appointment with Doctor Death.* Troy, Mich.: Momentum Books, 1993. Critical biography of Jack Kevorkian.

Biggs, Hazel. *Euthanasia, Death with Dignity, and the Law.* Oxford, England: Hart Publishing, 2000. This book examines the legal response to euthanasia and end-of-life decisions. Biggs considers whether legal reform is the best way to make euthanasia more readily available.

Brogden, Mike. *Geronticide: Killing the Elderly.* Washington, D.C.: Taylor & Francis, 2001. The author places ethical issues surrounding the voluntary or involuntary killing of the elderly in a social and historical context, pointing out that many societies have carried out this practice. Brogden claims that killing of the elderly today is commonly concealed in homes or care institutions.

Bryant, Michael S. *Confronting the "Good Death": Nazi Euthanasia on Trial, 1945–1953.* Boulder: University Press of Colorado, 2005. This book describes the postwar trials of people involved in the Nazi euthanasia program of the early 1940s, claiming that international power relationships hindered the prosecutions.

Burleigh, Michael. *Death and Deliverance: "Euthanasia" in Germany, c. 1900–1945.* New York: Cambridge University Press, 1995. The author describes how a program that began as "mercy killing" of mentally and physically disabled children broadened to include many other groups considered to possess "life unworthy of life" as the Nazis consolidated their power in Germany. The Nazis may have killed as many as 200,000 mentally and physically disabled people between 1939 and 1945.

Byock, Ira. *Dying Well: The Prospect for Growth at the End of Life.* New York: Riverhead Books, 1997. The author, a hospice physician, provides guidance to relieve fears about death and dying and to help people enjoy their lives until their final moments.

Clark, Nina. *The Politics of Physician-Assisted Suicide.* New York: Garland Publishing, 1997. The author considers the influence of a variety of groups, including the general public, the elderly, special-interest groups, and the courts, on making policy in this area. The book includes an extensive survey of seniors' attitudes toward physician-assisted suicide.

Cohen-Almagor, Raphael. *Euthanasia in the Netherlands: The Policy and Practice of Mercy Killing.* New York: Springer, 2004. Based on interviews that the author conducted in research centers, universities, and hospitals in the Netherlands, this book covers a wide range of theoretical and practical issues. It points out the pitfalls of policy-making concerning euthanasia and physician-assisted suicide.

————. *The Right to Die with Dignity: An Argument in Ethics, Medicine, and the Law.* Piscataway, N.J.: Rutgers University Press, 2001. The author views the debate on euthanasia and assisted suicide from public policy and international perspectives. The book includes a critical analysis of euthanasia policy in the Netherlands and the results of legalization of physician-assisted suicide in Oregon.

Colby, William H. *Long Goodbye: The Deaths of Nancy Cruzan.* Carlsbad, Calif.: Hay House, 2003. This is a memoir by the lawyer who handled the famous Nancy Cruzan case (which eventually reached the U.S. Supreme Court) for the Cruzan family.

Davies, Jean. *Choice in Dying.* London: Ward Lock, 1999. The author, a member of the British Voluntary Euthanasia Society, presents a wide-ranging set of arguments in support of physician-assisted suicide and euthanasia.

De Leo, Diego, ed. *Suicide and Euthanasia in Older Adults.* Seattle, Wash.: Hogrefe & Huber, 2001. Contributors in medical ethics, psychiatry, and suicide research address cultural aspects of aging, euthanasia, and suicide among the elderly in nine countries. They consider the effects of psychological, family, and socioeconomic factors on these end-of-life decisions.

Donnellan, Craig. *The Euthanasia Issue.* Cambridge, England: Independence Educational Publishers, 2001. Part of a comprehensive reference series on controversial topics, this volume presents information and opposing views on a wide range of medical, ethical, and legal aspects of euthanasia.

Dowbiggin, Ian. *A Concise History of Euthanasia: Life, Death, God, and Medicine.* Lanham, Md.: Rowman & Littlefield, 2005. This volume examines the evolution of opinions on what constitutes a "good death" and traces the controversial record of so-called mercy killing.

————. *A Merciful End: The Euthanasia Movement in Modern America.* New York: Oxford University Press, 2002. Drawing on archives of the Euthanasia Society of America, the author presents a full-scale historical account of the modern euthanasia movement, including its interaction with other progressive social causes and its uneasy alliance with eugenics in the early 20th century.

Downie, Jocelyn. *Dying Justice: A Case for Decriminalizing Euthanasia and Assisted Suicide in Canada.* Toronto, Ontario: University of Toronto Press, 2004. This work focuses on the Canadian Supreme Court's 1993 ruling that the country's constitution does not guarantee a right to physician-assisted suicide. The author stresses the importance of individual autonomy and claims that any mentally competent adult should be permitted to request euthanasia or assisted suicide, but she believes that more effective tests of decision-making competency are needed.

Drahos, Mary. *The Healing Power of Hope: Down-to-Earth Alternatives to Euthanasia and Assisted Suicide.* Ann Arbor, Mich.: Servant Publications, 1997. This book provides uplifting true stories that suggest ways to face chronic illness and overcome physical limitations in a Christian context rather than accepting the "culture of death."

Dudley, William, ed. *Examining Issues Through Political Cartoons: Euthanasia.* San Diego, Calif.: Greenhaven Press, 2002. In this work, cartoons are accompanied by detailed, serious commentary.

Dworkin, Gerald, R. G. Frey, and Sissela Bok. *Euthanasia and Physician-Assisted Suicide (For and Against).* New York, N.Y.: Cambridge University Press, 1998. Philosophers Dworkin and Frey argue the case for legalization of physician-assisted suicide, and ethicist Bok presents the opposing argument.

Dworkin, Ronald D. *Life's Dominion: An Argument about Abortion, Euthanasia, and Individual Freedom.* New York: Vintage Books, 1994. An internationally known philosopher offers an original and persuasive view of these two divisive issues and discusses the assumptions underlying different positions on them.

Eisenberg, Jon. *Using Terri: The Religious Right's Conspiracy to Take Away Our Rights.* San Francisco, Calif.: HarperSanFrancisco, 2005. The author is a lawyer who filed briefs on behalf of Michael Schiavo during Schiavo's long legal battle to have his wife, Terri, disconnected from her feeding tube after she entered a persistent vegetative state. Eisenberg provides a combination of memoir, reportage, analysis, and declaration, supporting the right to make end-of-life decisions without outside interference.

Emanuel, Linda L., ed. *Regulating How We Die: The Ethical, Medical, and Legal Issues Surrounding Physician-Assisted Suicide.* Cambridge, Mass.: Harvard University Press, 1998. Essays from experts provide historical, legal, and practical perspectives on euthanasia and physician-assisted suicide and arguments for and against these practices.

Enns, Ruth. *A Voice Unheard: The Latimer Case and People with Disabilities.* Black Point, Nova Scotia: Fernwood Publishing Co., Ltd., 2000. The author uses the highly publicized case of Robert Latimer, who killed his severely disabled daughter, Tracy, to reveal the stigma attached to disability in Canada.

Ewin, R. E. *Reasons and the Fear of Death*. Lanham, Md.: Rowman & Littlefield, 2002. The author claims that fear of death is not something that follows or fails to follow from reason, but rather forms the basis of reasoning. Ewin provides a new understanding of brain death and of physician-assisted suicide.

Field, Marilyn, and Christine K. Cassel, eds. *Approaching Death: Improving Care at the End of Life*. Washington, D.C.: National Academy Press, 1997. This is a comprehensive report on the care of dying people in the United States, prepared by the Institute of Medicine's Committee on Care at the End of Life. The book includes recommendations for improving care.

Filene, Peter G. *In the Arms of Others: A Cultural History of the Right-to-Die in America*. Chicago, Ill.: Ivan R. Dee, 1998. This work focuses on the Karen Ann Quinlan case and on the idea that dying is not a solitary activity but rather involves a "tapestry of relatedness" and is affected by culture.

Foley, Kathleen, and Herbert Hendin, eds. *The Case against Assisted Suicide: For the Right to End-of-Life Care*. Baltimore, Md.: Johns Hopkins University Press, 2004. This volume introduces 14 arguments against legalization of physician-assisted suicide, including the fear that legalization will put marginalized populations at risk and the claim that better end-of-life care will make assisted suicide unnecessary.

Fuhrman, Mark. *Silent Witness: The Untold Story of Terri Schiavo's Death*. New York: William Morrow, 2005. This author, a detective who independently investigated the case of Terri Schiavo, tells the Schiavo story from the viewpoint of Terri Schindler Schiavo's parents, who opposed the attempts of Michael Schiavo, Terri's husband, to remove Terri's feeding tube. Fuhrman provides background on the Schiavos' marriage and what happened on the day Terri collapsed.

Gailey, Elizabeth Atwood. *Write to Death: News Framing of the Right to Die Conflict, from Quinlan's Coma to Kevorkian's Conviction*. New York: Praeger, 2003. This book looks at the way the media in the United States have framed issues related to euthanasia and physician-assisted suicide. The author claims that media accounts tend to favor pro-euthanasia over pro-life views.

Galli, Richard. *Rescuing Jeffrey: A True Story*. Chapel Hill, N.C.: Algonquin Books of Chapel Hill, 2000. This is an account by the father of a teenaged boy left paralyzed from the neck down after a diving accident. At first, both parents and son wanted to discontinue his life support, but Jeffrey soon changed his own mind in favor of life and persuaded his parents to do so as well.

Geis, Sally B., and Donald E. Messer, eds. *How Shall We Die? Helping Christians Debate Assisted Suicide.* Nashville, Tenn.: Abingdon Press, 1997. The editors include case studies on refusal and withdrawal of medical treatment, assisted suicide, and euthanasia as well as essays by Roman Catholic and Protestant authors.

Gentles, Ian, ed. *Euthanasia and Assisted Suicide: The Current Debate.* Toronto, Ontario: Stoddart, 1995. This volume considers these issues from a Canadian point of view. The book includes analysis of famous Canadian right-to-die cases such as those of Sue Rodriguez and Robert Latimer.

Greenberg, Samuel. *Euthanasia and Assisted Suicide: Psychosocial Issues.* Springfield, Ill.: Charles C. Thomas, 1997. Greenberg considers court cases, experience in other countries, physicians' attitudes, legal aspects, religious/moral/ethical issues, the hospice movement, and right-to-die societies.

Haley, James, ed. *Opposing Viewpoints: Death and Dying.* San Diego: Calif.: Greenhaven Press, 2003. This is an anthology of pro-and-con articles on various aspects of death and dying, including euthanasia and physician-assisted suicide.

Harris, Nancy, ed. *At Issue: The Ethics of Euthanasia.* San Diego, Calif.: Greenhaven Press, 2004. This is a short anthology of opinion pieces on different aspects of the ethics of euthanasia.

Harrison, Maureen, and Steve Gilbert, eds. *Life, Death, and the Law: Landmark Right-to-Die Decisions.* San Diego, Calif.: Excellent Books, 1997. This book provides the text of judicial decisions in the cases of Karen Ann Quinlan and Nancy Cruzan, in the New York and Washington cases that led to the June 1997 Supreme Court review of the issue, and in the resultant Supreme Court ruling.

Hendin, Herbert. *Seduced by Death: Doctors, Patients, and Assisted Suicide.* New York: Norton, 1998. A world-famous authority on suicide prevention offers arguments against legalizing assisted suicide, based on experience in the United States and the Netherlands.

Hillyard, Daniel, and John Dombrink. *Dying Right: The Death with Dignity Movement.* New York: Routledge, 2001. This work provides a history of the death with dignity movement and the legalization of physician-assisted suicide in Oregon. This book analyzes the future of physician-assisted suicide, considering the legal, ethical, medical, and moral complexities of the issue.

Hoefler, James M., and Brian E. Kamoie. *Deathright: Culture, Medicine, Politics, and the Right to Die.* Boulder, Colo.: Westview Press, 1994. This book covers every aspect of the right-to-die debate.

———. *Managing Death: The First Guide for Patients, Family Members, and Care Providers on Forgoing Treatment at the End of Life.* Boulder, Colo.:

Westview Press, 1999. This work discusses medical, legal, and ethical aspects of deciding whether to continue life-sustaining treatment of incompetent patients whose death is imminent or inevitable.

Horn, Robert C., III. *How Will They Know If I'm Dead? Transcending Disability and Terminal Illness.* Boca Raton, Fla.: Saint Lucie Press, 1996. The author provides a firsthand description of what it is like to have amyotrophic lateral sclerosis. Some ALS sufferers have sought assisted suicide or euthanasia, but Horn finds wisdom and even humor in his experience.

Howell, R. Patton, and James Hall. *Locked in to Life.* Boise, Id.: unknown publisher, 2002. Hall, a Jungian analyst, suffered a severe stroke that, in effect, separated his mind from his body. At first he could not communicate and was assumed to have no consciousness, but with the help of his wife and a friend, he revealed that his intelligence was intact. The book describes his spiritual experience as well as psychological and medical experiences.

Humphry, Derek. *Final Exit: The Practicalities of Self-Deliverance and Assisted Suicide for the Dying.* 3rd edition. New York: Delta, 2002. This book describes methods of assisted suicide for the terminally ill.

————. *Jean's Way.* London, England: Quartet Books, 1978. This book describes the decision of Humphry's first wife, Jean, to commit suicide in order to end the pain of terminal breast cancer, as well as Humphry's role in assisting her to die.

Humphry, Derek, and Mary Clement. *Freedom to Die: People, Politics, and the Right-to-Die Movement.* New York: St. Martin's Press, 2000. This work presents a history of the movement from the standpoint of one of its founders. The book explains why the movement arose, who opposes it and for what reasons, and how the right to die was defended in Oregon and before the Supreme Court.

Jaffe, Carolyn, and Carol H. Ehrich. *All Kinds of Love: Experiencing Hospice.* Amityville, N.Y.: Baywood Publishing, 1997. The authors describe the experience of hospice through case studies, showing how good hospice "comfort care" can relieve the physical and psychological pain of dying patients and their families. The book includes discussions of assisted suicide and advance directives.

Jamison, Stephen. *Assisted Suicide: A Decision-Making Guide for Health Professionals.* San Francisco, Calif.: Jossey-Bass, 1997. This book offers step-by-step guidelines for counseling and helping patients who are thinking about suicide, based on the author's extensive experience.

————. *Final Acts of Love: Family, Friends, and Assisted Dying.* New York: Putnam, 1995. This book considers the questions of when it is appropriate for the dying to end their lives and when it is appropriate for family, friends, or health care professionals to help them do so. It points out pitfalls to avoid and provides inspiring examples of death accompanied by loving rituals.

Jennings, Bruce, and True Ryndes. *Access to Hospice Care: Expanding Boundaries, Overcoming Barriers*. Garrison, N.Y.: Hastings Center, 2003. Presents the result of a three-year research project that looked at issues of social justice, access, and public policy in hospice and palliative care. The site recommends ways to expand the definition of hospice to include more U.S. citizens for a longer period of time.

Johnston, Brian P. *Death as a Salesman: What's Wrong with Assisted Suicide*. Sacramento, Calif.: New Regency Publishers, 1998. This volume provides evidence that assisted suicide is a bad idea for the vulnerable and depressed. Johnston attacks arguments and personalities of euthanasia proponents.

Kaplan, Kalman J., and Matthew B. Schwartz, eds. *Jewish Approaches to Suicide, Martyrdom, and Euthanasia*. Northvale, N.J.: Jason Aronson, 1998. This work discusses suicide in Jewish, Greek, and Christian thought; suicide and euthanasia in Jewish and American law; and suicide and suicide prevention in biblical and Greco-Western narratives.

Keizer, Bert. *Dancing with Mister D.: Notes on Life and Death*. New York: Doubleday, 1997. A Dutch doctor trained in philosophy and medicine shares his experiences among the terminally ill and discusses issues surrounding the end of life, including physician-assisted suicide.

Kemp, N. D. A. *Merciful Release: A History of the British Euthanasia Movement*. Manchester, England: Manchester University Press, 2002. This book uses previously unexplored archival and periodical material to examine the origins of the euthanasia debate in Britain in the 1870s and trace its development through the 1960s. Kemp ties changes in the euthanasia debate to broader changes in society.

Keown, John. *Euthanasia, Ethics, and Public Policy: An Argument against Legalisation*. New York: Cambridge University Press, 2002. The author draws on the Netherlands' experience with legal euthanasia and the views of specialists in Britain, Canada, and the United States to investigate the fear that voluntary active euthanasia and physician-assisted suicide, if legalized, would not remain voluntary for long.

Keown, John, ed. *Euthanasia Examined: Ethical, Clinical, and Legal Perspectives*. New York, N.Y.: Cambridge University Press, 1995. These essays by several authors present arguments for and against euthanasia and physician-assisted suicide.

Kevorkian, Jack. *Prescription Medicide: The Goodness of Planned Death*. Buffalo, N.Y.: Prometheus, 1991. The author explains why he feels that physicians can be justified in helping terminally or incurably ill people end their lives. He also proposes harvesting organs from those who wish to be euthanized or using such people for medical experiments.

Annotated Bibliography

Kilner, John F., Arlene B. Miller, and Edmund D. Pellegrino, eds. *Dignity and Dying: A Christian Appraisal.* Grand Rapids, Mich.: William B. Eerdmans, 1996. This book of essays considers moral/ethical, legal, medical, and other aspects of end-of-life decisions, including those related to physician-assisted suicide and euthanasia, from a Christian point of view.

Kopelman, Loretta M., and Kenneth A. De Ville, eds. *Physician-Assisted Suicide: What Are the Issues?* New York: Kluwer Academic Press, 2001. This book provides a detailed discussion of the landmark 1997 Supreme Court rulings on assisted suicide, as well as ethical/moral stances on physician-assisted suicide and the assumptions underlying them. Some authors conclude that, as with abortion, a powerful culture gap exists around the issue of assisted suicide and euthanasia.

Kübler-Ross, Elisabeth. *On Death and Dying.* New York: Macmillan, 1969. This is the classic book that helped to bring discussion of death into the open in the early 1970s.

Kuhse, Helga, and Peter Singer, eds. *A Companion to Bioethics.* Malden, Mass.: Blackwell, 1998. This book includes discussion of advance directives, voluntary euthanasia, physician-assisted suicide, and treatment of severely disabled newborns and people in persistent vegetative states.

Kuntz, Dieter, and Susan D. Bachrach, eds. *Deadly Medicine: Creating the Master Race.* Chapel Hill, N.C.: University of North Carolina Press, 2004. This work showcases material from an exhibit at the U.S. Holocaust Memorial Museum, along with essays by distinguished scholars. The book shows how physicians regularly cooperated with the Nazis to create a medicalization of mass murder and to develop the technology to carry it out.

Landes, Alison, ed. *Death and Dying: Who Decides?* Wylie, Tex.: Information Plus, 1996. This book includes a historical survey of attitudes toward dying, considerations related to the right to die, euthanasia and assisted suicide, and alternatives to them.

Larue, Gerald. *Playing God: Fifty Religious Views on Your Right to Die.* Wakefield, R.I.: Moyer Bell, 1996. Larue describes a range of religious views on cessation of life-sustaining medical treatment, physician-assisted suicide, and euthanasia.

Lattanzi-Licht, Marcia, et al. *The Hospice Choice: In Pursuit of a Peaceful Death.* New York: Simon & Schuster, 1998. This volume uses case studies to answer questions about hospice care and presents hospice as an alternative to physician-assisted suicide and euthanasia.

Lavi, Shai J. *The Modern Art of Dying: A History of Euthanasia in the United States.* Princeton, N.J.: Princeton University Press, 2005. The author uses primary sources to show the development of the practice and the movement. Lavi discusses how the issue relates to cultural interpretations of death and considers why law and medical technique have come to play such a central role in the way modern U.S. citizens die.

Lee, Barbara Coombs, ed. *Compassion in Dying: Stories of Dignity and Choice.* Troutdale, Ore.: NewSage Press, 2003. This book provides accounts of individuals who chose assisted dying, and their family members, drawn from the files of the Oregon organization Compassion in Dying, which favors assisted dying.

Loewy, Erich H., and Roberta Springer Loewy. *The Ethics of Terminal Care: Orchestrating the End of Life.* New York: Kluwer Academic Publishers, 2000. The authors discuss such topics as attitudes toward death; suicide, assisted suicide, and euthanasia; hospice; and pain management.

Lynn, Joanne, and Joan Harrold. *Handbook for Mortals: Guidance for People Facing Serious Illness.* New York: Oxford University Press, 1999. This work helps individuals and their families use personal feelings and values to live with serious illness, manage loss and pain, make important decisions about health care and other matters, and prepare for death. The book includes discussion of forgoing medical treatment and asking for assistance in suicide.

Magnusson, Roger. *Angels of Death: Exploring the Euthanasia Underground.* New Haven, Conn.: Yale University Press, 2002. The author interviews doctors, nurses, and therapists who work in the HIV/AIDS communities in the United States and Australia to obtain information on the "euthanasia underground." Magnusson reveals disturbing aspects such as botched attempts and euthanasia without consent.

McKhann, Charles F. *A Time to Die: The Place for Physician Assistance.* New Haven, Conn.: Yale University Press, 1999. This book explains why the author believes that "rational suicide" and physician-assisted dying should be made legally available under some circumstances.

McLean, Sheila, and Alison Britton. *The Case for Physician Assisted Suicide.* San Francisco, Calif.: Pandora Books, 1997. The authors present arguments for the legalization of physician-assisted suicide, based on honoring patients' autonomy and their wish not to be kept alive uselessly by medical technology.

Medina, Loreta M., ed. *History of Issues: Euthanasia.* San Diego, Calif.: Greenhaven Press, 2004. These essays describe the development of attitudes, themes, and rhetoric about euthanasia from the 18th century to the present day.

Meisel, Alan, and Kathy L. Cerminara. *The Right to Die.* 3rd edition. New York: Aspen Publishers, 2004. This volume surveys the statutes involved and analyzes the legal issues raised when surrogates decide to withhold or withdraw medical treatment from noncompetent patients.

Moreno, Jonathan D., ed. *Arguing Euthanasia: The Controversy over Mercy Killing, Assisted Suicide, and the "Right to Die."* New York: Simon &

Schuster/Touchstone, 1995. These essays present different viewpoints on these hotly debated subjects.

Muelenbergs, Tom, and Paul Schotsmans, eds. *Euthanasia and Palliative Care in the Low Countries.* Leuven, Belgium: Peeters, 2005. This book provides an overview and comparison of the laws in the Netherlands and Belgium that permit euthanasia and assisted suicide, as well as discussions of palliative care initiatives and the ethics of the new legislation.

Nayaka, Andrea C. *Opposing Viewpoints: Terminal Illness.* San Diego, Calif.: Greenhaven Press, 2005. This book includes articles supporting and opposing euthanasia.

Neils, Rob. *Death with Dignity FAQs—Frequently Asked Questions.* Dubuque, Ia.: Kendal/Hunt Publishing Co., 1997. The author provides a rationale for the right to die and clear, data-based answers to questions about assisted suicide and death with dignity.

New York Times. The Philosophy of Euthanasia: A New York Times *Reader.* Upper Saddle River, N.J.: Pearson Higher Education, 2000. This is an anthology of articles from the *New York Times* and elsewhere, offering an introduction to the philosophical questions surrounding euthanasia.

Nitschke, Philip, and Fiona Stewart. *Killing Me Softly: Voluntary Euthanasia and the Road to the Peaceful Pill.* New York: Penguin, 2005. Written by Australia's best-known activist for assisted suicide, this book describes Nitschke's work and the organization he founded, Exit International. Nitschke explains his attempt to develop a "peaceful pill" for suicide.

Nuland, Sherwin B. *How We Die: Reflections on Life's Final Chapter.* New York: Knopf, 1994. Nuland shows that most people are no longer able to achieve a classic "good death," but instead die in hospitals or nursing homes, surrounded and often painfully maintained by machines.

Ogden, Russel. *Euthanasia, Assisted Suicide, and AIDS.* New Westminster, B.C.: Peroglyphics Publishing, 1994. This book presents a sociological study of the "assisted suicide underground" of gay men with AIDS in Vancouver, British Columbia.

Olevitch, Barbara A. *Protecting Psychiatric Patients from the Assisted-Suicide Movement: Insights and Strategies.* New York: Praeger, 2002. The author believes that surrogate medical decisions to end life are a growing threat to incompetent patients. She encourages therapists to demonstrate that the mental problems of even seriously ill and disabled people can be treated.

Orr, Robert D., David L. Schiedermayer, and David B. Biebel. *More Life and Death Decisions: Help in Making Tough Choices About Care for the Elderly, Euthanasia, and Medical Treatment Options.* Grand Rapids, Mich.: Baker Book House, 1997. This book provides guidelines for making wise, moral choices on these subjects for oneself or loved ones within a Christian context.

Ost, Suzanne. *An Analytical Study of the Legal, Moral, and Ethical Aspects of the Living Phenomenon of Euthanasia.* Lewiston, N.Y.: Edwin Mellen Press, 2003. This is a scholarly study of euthanasia.

Otlowski, Margaret. *Voluntary Euthanasia and the Common Law.* Revised edition. New York, N.Y.: Oxford University Press, 2000. The author investigates active voluntary euthanasia from a legal standpoint. Otlowski argues, based on results of legalization in the Netherlands, that laws elsewhere should be changed.

Palmer, Larry I. *Endings and Beginnings: Law, Medicine, and Society in Assisted Life and Death.* New York: Praeger, 2000. Palmer claims that legislative analysis is more important than judicial analysis for understanding issues related to medical technologies that affect the beginning and end of life. The author believes that claims of individual rights are not sufficient to deal with these complex ethical matters.

Peck, M. Scott. *Denial of the Soul.* New York: Random House, 1997. The author, a physician, psychiatrist, and theologian, discusses the spiritual lessons of dying and what the euthanasia debate reveals about the status of the soul in the modern age.

Pence, Gregory E. *Classic Cases in Medical Ethics: Accounts of Cases that Have Shaped Medical Ethics, with Philosophical, Legal, and Historical Backgrounds.* New York: McGraw-Hill, 1995. This book includes cases involving ending medical treatment for people in persistent vegetative states, disabled people's requests for help in committing suicide, and withholding medical treatment from severely impaired newborns.

Pool, Robert. *Negotiating a Good Death: Euthanasia in the Netherlands.* Binghamton, N.Y.: Haworth Press, 2000. The author, a British medical anthropologist, provides a firsthand description of euthanasia in the Netherlands, based on observations made during two years in a Dutch hospital.

Prado, C. G., ed. *Assisted Suicide: Canadian Perspectives.* Ottawa, Ontario: University of Ottawa Press, 2000. This volume analyzes laws, famous cases, and feelings of the Canadian public related to assisted suicide.

Quill, Timothy E. *A Midwife through the Dying Process: Stories of Healing and Hard Choices at the End of Life.* Baltimore, Md.: Johns Hopkins University Press, 1997. A physician advocate for the right to die uses stories of nine deaths to examine the relationship of doctors, dying patients, and the patients' families. He describes the difficult choices these groups often must make, including those related to physician-assisted suicide.

Quill, Timothy E., and Margaret P. Battin, eds. *Physician-Assisted Dying: The Case for Palliative Care and Patient Choice.* Baltimore, Md.: Johns Hopkins University Press, 2004. This book explains why both improved end-of-life care and legally regulated assisted dying should be available to terminally ill people.

Quinlan, Joseph, and Julia Quinlan, with Phyllis Battelle. *Karen Ann: The Quinlans Tell Their Story*. Garden City, N.Y.: Doubleday, 1977. The parents of Karen Ann Quinlan describe the tragedy of seeing their young daughter in a steadily worsening vegetative state, their painful decision to allow her to die by removing her respirator, and their landmark court battle to win permission to do so.

Quinlan, Julia Duane. *My Joy, My Sorrow: Karen Ann's Mother Remembers*. Cincinnati, Ohio: Saint Anthony Messenger Press, 2005. Karen Ann Quinlan's mother describes her experiences during the long ordeal that led to Quinlan's death.

Rollin, Betty. *Last Wish*. Revised edition. New York: Public Affairs, 1998. First published in 1985, when it became a best-seller and drew attention to the right-to-die movement, this book describes Rollin's mother's battle with cancer and her suicide by drug overdose, committed with her daughter's help. The revised edition includes information about the physician-assisted suicide debate, the Oregon Death with Dignity Act, and end-of-life resources.

Rosenfeld, Barry. *Assisted Suicide and the Right to Die: The Interface of Social Science, Public Policy, and Medical Ethics*. Washington, D.C.: American Psychological Association, 2004. The author shows how social science can inform policy and practice connected with this controversial issue. Rosenfeld discusses experience with legalized assisted suicide in the Netherlands and Oregon.

Rothman, Juliet Cassuto. *Saying Goodbye to Daniel: When Death Is the Best Choice*. New York: Continuum, 1995. Almost completely paralyzed after a diving accident, a young man decides to discontinue life-sustaining treatment. This memoir is written by his mother, who supported his decision.

Rubin, Susan B. *When Doctors Say No: The Battleground of Medical Futility*. Bloomington, Ind.: Indiana University Press, 1998. Rubin critiques the concept of medical futility, which some doctors and hospitals use to deny life-sustaining treatment when patients or families wish it to continue.

Schneider, Carl E., ed. *Law at the End of Life: The Supreme Court and Assisted Suicide*. Ann Arbor, Mich.: University of Michigan Press, 2000. Distinguished scholars examine the key 1997 Supreme Court decision from a variety of viewpoints, considering such questions as whether constitutional adjudication is a good way to make public policy and what policy the law should take in regard to the end of life.

Schneiderman, L. J., and N. S. Jecker. *Wrong Medicine: Doctors, Patients, and Futile Treatment*. Baltimore, Md.: Johns Hopkins University Press, 1995. This book describes the concept of medical futility and considers whether doctors and hospitals have (or should have) the right to stop life-sustaining treatment if patients or their families wish it to be continued.

Shannon, Thomas A., ed. *Death and Dying: A Reader.* Lanham, Md.: Rowman & Littlefield, 2004. This anthology discusses bioethical issues related to death and dying, including assisted suicide.

Shavelson, Lonny. *A Chosen Death: The Dying Confront Assisted Suicide.* Berkeley, Calif.: University of California Press, 1998. The author describes five terminally ill people who are trying to decide whether to end their lives.

Smith, J. Donald. *Right-to-Die Policies in the American States: Judicial and Legislative Innovation.* New York: LFB Scholarly Publishing, 2002. This book discusses policies in different states in light of a general theory of "permissive" or "morality-based" policy adoption. Smith analyzes the interplay between judicial and legislative branches of state governments during policy making.

Smith, Wesley J. *Forced Exit: Euthanasia, Assisted Suicide and the New Duty to Die.* New York: Encounter Books, 2006. A leading pro-life writer explains his belief that if euthanasia and assisted suicide are legalized, the health care system will pressure chronically ill and disabled people to kill themselves or even forcibly kill them.

Snyder, Lois, and Arthur L. Caplan, eds. *Assisted Suicide: Finding Common Ground.* Bloomington, Ind.: Indiana University Press, 2001. Rather than arguing for or against the legalization of assisted suicide, these essays provide a framework for possible regulation of the practice if legalization should occur.

Somerville, Margaret A. *Death Talk: The Case against Euthanasia and Physician-Assisted Suicide.* Montreal, Quebec: McGill-Queen's University Press, 2001. Somerville describes dangerous consequences for individuals and society if euthanasia and physician-assisted suicide are legalized.

Spiers, John. *Who Owns Our Bodies: Making Moral Choices in Health Care.* Cambridge, Mass.: Radcliffe Medical Press, 1997. The author discusses patients' rights and moral issues in health care, including those involved in end-of-life decisions, from the patient's point of view. Spiers encourages patients to take control of health care decisions that affect them.

Tännsjö, Torbjörn. *Coercive Care: Ethics of Choice in Health and Medicine.* New York: Routledge, 1999. The author compares social policy and law concerning coercion in medical care in a number of different countries.

Tännsjö, Torbjörn, ed. *Terminal Sedation: Euthanasia in Disguise?* New York: Kluwer Academic Publishers, 2004. This book examines the debate between those for and against terminal sedation as a form of palliative care.

Ten Have, Henk, and David Clark, eds. *The Ethics of Palliative Care: European Perspectives.* Maidenhead, Berkshire, U.K.: Open University Press,

2002. This work discusses the ethics of palliative care in Europe, which the authors say are changing.

Tobin, Daniel R., and Karen Lindsey. *Peaceful Dying*. Reading, Mass.: Perseus Books, 1998. This volume presents a 26-step system to help dying people take control of the remainder of their life and death, communicate with doctors and family, and preserve dignity and inner peace.

Uhlmann, Michael M., ed. *Last Rights?: Assisted Suicide and Euthanasia Debated*. Grand Rapids, Mich.: William B. Eerdmans, 1998. These essays discuss theological, moral, medical, and legal perspectives on assisted suicide and euthanasia.

Urofsky, Melvin I. *Lethal Judgments: Assisted Suicide and American Law*. Lawrence, Kans.: University Press of Kansas, 2000. Urofsky examines the tangled historical, legal, medical, and ethical issues affecting the famous 1997 Supreme Court decision in the cases of *Washington v. Glucksberg* and *New York v. Quill*, which gave the high court's opinion on assisted suicide and the right to die.

————. *Letting Go: Death, Dying, and the Law*. Norman, Okla.: University of Oklahoma Press, 1994. This work provides thoughtful appraisal of courts' responses to right-to-die issues, including the difficulty of balancing the needs of patients and their families for autonomy and states' interest in protecting and preserving life. Urofsky also considers theologians' and health care professionals' perspectives.

Urofsky, Melvin I., and Philip E. Urofsky, eds. *The Right to Die*. New York: Garland Publishing, 1996. These are two volumes of scholarly articles on the subject.

Van Zyl, Liezl L. *Death and Compassion*. Aldershot, Hampshire, U.K.: Ashgate Publishing, 2000. The author draws on Aristotle to present a philosophical decision-making framework based on the virtues of compassion, benevolence, and respectfulness rather than benificence, non-maleficence and respect for patient autonomy.

Vitez, Michael. *Final Choices: Seeking the Good Death*. Philadelphia: Camino Books, 1998. This book, based on a series of Pulitzer Prize–winning articles published in the *Philadelphia Inquirer* in 1996, covers deciding when to quit, living, hospice care, home care, an account of a right-to-die crusader (Janet Good) who herself suffered from a terminal illness, and an account of and a 99-year-old woman who had lived the long and healthy life for which most people hope.

Walters, James W., ed. *Choosing Who's to Live: Ethics and Aging*. Champaign, Ill.: University of Illinois Press, 1996. Walters discusses the position of the elderly in an age of increasing health care rationing. The book includes a chapter on whether there is a place for euthanasia in the care of the elderly.

Webb, Marilyn. *The Good Death: The New American Search to Reshape the End of Life.* New York: Bantam, 1997. The author, a former editor-in-chief of *Psychology Today*, presents interviews with health care workers, supporters of organizations working for and against physician-assisted suicide and euthanasia, and patients and families struggling with these issues. She suggests 10 reforms that will help to ensure a "good death" for everyone.

Weir, Robert F., ed. *Physician-Assisted Suicide.* Bloomington, Ind.: Indiana University Press, 1997. These essays offer a history of the practice and opposing points of view on its appropriateness. The book includes judicial opinions from key court cases.

Werth, James, ed. *Contemporary Perspectives on Rational Suicide.* Philadelphia, Pa.: Brunner/Mazel, 1999. These essays discuss different aspects of the idea that suicide can sometimes be a rational choice rather than a product of mental illness.

Whiting, Raymond L. *A Natural Right to Die: Twenty-three Centuries of Debate.* Westport, Conn.: Greenwood Press, 2001. Whiting shows that the right-to-die controversy extends more than 2,000 years into the past and has been influenced by the legal and cultural development of the western world.

Wood, Robert S., and Tomi Keitlen. *Peaceful Passing: Die When You Choose with Dignity and Ease.* Sedona, Ariz.: In Print Publishing, 2000. This book provides a new paradigm for dying, offering a way to control one's passing and banish the fear of death.

Woodman, Sue. *Last Rights: The Struggle Over the Right to Die.* New York: Perseus, 2001. This work presents an overview of the right-to-die movement in the United States and the legal, ethical, medical, and social issues surrounding euthanasia, including descriptions of affected individuals and families.

Woodward, John, ed. *At Issue: The Right to Die.* San Diego, Calif.: Greenhaven Press, 2005. This is a short anthology of opinion pieces on various aspects of the right-to-die debate.

Yount, Lisa, ed. *Contemporary Issues Companion: Euthanasia.* San Diego, Calif.: Greenhaven Press, 2002. An anthology of articles presents a wide range of views on issues related to euthanasia.

Zucker, Marjorie B., ed. *The Right to Die Debate: A Documentary History.* Westport, Conn.: Greenwood Press, 1999. This book provides excerpts from 138 primary documents to show the evolution of the right-to-die movement.

MAGAZINES AND JOURNALS

Achille, Marie A., and James R. P. Ogloff. "Attitudes toward and Desire for Assisted Suicide among Persons with Amyotrophic Lateral Sclerosis."

Omega, vol. 48, February 2004, pp. 1–21. A survey of 44 people with this incurable, progressive neurological disease revealed that, although 70 percent found assisted suicide morally acceptable and 60 percent said they would consider it under some circumstances, only 7 percent said they would have requested it already if it were legal.

Akabayashi, Akira. "Euthanasia, Assisted Suicide, and Cessation of Life Support." *Social Science and Medicine*, vol. 55, August 15, 2002, pp. 517–528. This piece summarizes the historical and current status of euthanasia and cessation of life support in Japan, then analyzes the legal and ethical aspects of two recent euthanasia cases in that country.

Allmark, Peter. "Death with Dignity." *Journal of Medical Ethics*, vol. 28, August 2002, pp. 255–257. Only a person's own character can confer a death with dignity, but health care professionals can try to ensure a death without indignities.

"Allowing to Die II." *Commonweal*, vol. 131, April 23, 2004, pp. 5–6. This article claims that Pope John Paul II's allocution stating that patients in a persistent vegetative state must always be given food and water goes against earlier Catholic teachings and attempts to use papal fiat to end legitimate debate on the subject.

American Medical Association Council on Ethical and Judicial Affairs. "Decisions near the End of Life." *Journal of the American Medical Association*, vol. 267, April 22 and 29, 1992, pp. 2,229–2,233. This piece reexamines the council's positions on withdrawing or withholding life-prolonging treatment from terminally ill patients, do-not-resuscitate orders, euthanasia, physician-assisted suicide, and withdrawing or withholding life-sustaining treatment from competent patients who are not terminally ill.

Amundson, Ron, and Gayle Taira. "Our Lives and Ideologies." *Journal of Disability Policy Studies*, vol. 16, Summer 2005, pp. 53–57. The authors explain why they changed their opinion on physician-assisted suicide from support to opposition after they became disabled.

Annas, George J. "'Culture of Life' Politics at the Bedside: The Case of Terri Schiavo." *New England Journal of Medicine*, vol. 352, April 21, 2005, pp. 1,710–1,715. Terri Schiavo's case, which made history in the United States by bringing the U.S. Congress to pass legislation specifically involving her medical care, has encouraged supporters of others in situations similar to Terri's to seek protection from the law.

———. "How We Lie." *Hastings Center Report*, vol. 25, November–December 1995 pp. S12–S14. This work criticizes physicians for being reluctant to tell terminally ill patients the truth about their prognosis or, sometimes, to talk with them at all.

Anonymous. "It's Over, Debbie." *Journal of the American Medical Association*, vol. 259, January 8, 1988, p. 272. A short personal essay by an anonymous doctor describes administering a lethal injection to a young woman dying of ovarian cancer who said, "Let's get this over with." The article caused considerable controversy, both because of its confession of euthanasia and because of questions about what the patient's words really meant.

Appel, Jacob M. "A Duty to Kill? A Duty to Die?" *Bulletin of the History of Medicine*, vol. 78, Fall 2004, pp. 10–34. This chronicles and provides historical context for the controversy over euthanasia that came to a head in the United States around 1906, following proposals to legalize the practice in Ohio and Iowa.

Arnold, Elizabeth Mayfield. "Factors that Influence Consideration of Hastening Death among People with Life-Threatening Illnesses." *Health and Social Work*, vol. 29, Feb. 2004, pp. 17–26. A survey suggests that the factors most important in determining whether people with life-threatening illnesses would consider hastening their death are depression, social support, and hope. Pain and anxiety were deemed unimportant.

Asai, Atsushi, et al. "Doctors' and Nurses' Attitudes towards and Experiences of Voluntary Euthanasia." *Journal of Medical Ethics*, vol. 27, October 2001, pp. 324–330. A survey of members of the Japanese Association of Palliative Medicine taken in 1999 showed that a minority of responding doctors and nurses thought that voluntary euthanasia was ethically acceptable. The authors conclude that legalization of this practice and clearly spelling out the circumstances under which it could be used would benefit the Japanese.

Asch, Adrienne. "Recognizing Death while Affirming Life." *Hastings Center Report*, vol. 35, November–December 2005, pp. S31–S35. Disability rights activists can provide valuable insights to the end-of-life movement by revealing social problems that severely disabled people face and showing that many disabled people still find their lives enjoyable and fulfilling.

Ashcroft, John. "Dispensing of Controlled Substances to Assist Suicide." *Issues in Law and Medicine*, vol. 17, Spring 2002, pp. 265–267. This is the text of the memorandum from then-attorney general Ashcroft to the administrator of the Drug Enforcement Administration, issued on November 6, 2001, which began the *Oregon v. Ashcroft/Gonzales v. Oregon* case.

"At Death's Door." *National Issues Forums*, 1997. The entire issue is devoted to the topic of death and dying. Articles provide pro and con viewpoints on subjects including letting patients die with dignity, improving care for the dying, and the morality of sustaining life.

Avila, Daniel. "Assisted Suicide and the Inalienable Right to Life." *Issues in Law and Medicine*, vol. 16, Fall 2000, pp. 111ff. This article contends that the right to the protection of life is inalienable and therefore cannot be given up, even by the persons whose lives are in question. According to this reasoning, assisting in suicide should remain a crime.

Annotated Bibliography

Bachman, Helena. "One-Way Ticket." *Time International*, vol. 160, October 14, 2002, pp. 40ff. The Swiss group Dignitas is attracting increasing criticism for its willingness to help non-Swiss "death tourists" with incurable illnesses commit suicide.

Bannink, Marjolein, et al. "Psychiatric Consultation and Quality of Decision Making in Euthanasia." *Lancet*, vol. 356, December 16, 2000, pp. 2,067ff. On the basis of research conducted in the Netherlands in the late 1990s, the authors conclude that a psychiatrist should be consulted following a euthanasia request if the treatment team has doubts about the patient's state of mind, but such consultations should not be mandatory.

Barry, Robert. "The Papal Allocution on Caring for Persons in a 'Vegetative State.'" *Issues in Law and Medicine*, vol. 20, Fall 2004, pp. 155–164. This piece summarizes Pope John Paul II's statement, issued on March 20, 2004, in which the Pope stated that food and water are "ordinary" care and must be provided to all people, no matter how severe their disability.

Bascom, Paul B., and Susan W. Tolle. "Responding to Requests for Physician-Assisted Suicide." *Journal of the American Medical Association*, vol. 288, July 3, 2002, pp. 91–98. This article holds that many critically ill patients who request physician-assisted suicide will change their minds if they receive adequate pain relief and other forms of palliative care.

Bender, Leslie A. "A Feminist Analysis of Physician-Assisted Dying and Voluntary Active Euthanasia." *Tennessee Law Review*, vol. 59, Spring 1992, pp. 519–546. This article considers ways in which these issues may affect women differently from how they affect men.

Bergman, Brian. "The Final Hours." *Maclean's*, vol. 111, March 9, 1998, pp. 46–49. Bergman describes the trial of Nancy Morrison, a physician alleged to have injected a lethal drug into a cancer patient dying in agony. The court refused to indict Morrison.

Betzold, Michael. "The Selling of Doctor Death: How Jack Kevorkian Became a National Hero." *New Republic*, vol. 216, May 26, 1997, pp. 22ff. Betzold presents a detailed, highly critical portrait of Kevorkian and his lawyer, Geoffrey Fieger.

Bleich, J. David. "The Physician as a Conscientious Objector." *Fordham Urban Law Journal*, vol. 30, November 2002, pp. 245–265. There has been some legal support for the claim that physicians and hospitals have the right to refuse to discontinue artificial feeding and hydration of patients, even when the patients request such discontinuation, because the physicians or facilities believe that the action is morally wrong.

Bradley, Gerard V. "Death and the Law: Why the Government Has an Interest in Preserving Life." *World and I*, vol. 18, May 2003, pp. 255ff. Bradley maintains that physicians must not be allowed to commit murder, even at a patient's request.

191

Braun, Kathryn L., Virginia M. Tanji, and Ronald Heck. "Support for Physician-Assisted Suicide." *Gerontologist*, vol. 41, February 2001, pp. 51ff. A survey of adults in five ethnic groups showed that ethnicity as well as personal attitude factors had a direct effect on individuals' feelings about physician-assisted suicide.

Burdette, Amy M., Terrence D. Hill, and Benjamin E. Moulton. "Religion and Attitudes toward Physician-Assisted Suicide and Terminal Palliative Care." *Journal for Scientific Study of Religion*, vol. 44, March 2005, pp. 79–94. Conservative and moderate Protestants are usually less accepting of physician-assisted suicide and terminal palliative care than nonaffiliates, but their feelings vary according to the strength of their religious affiliation.

Burt, Robert A. "The End of Autonomy." *Hastings Center Report*, vol. 35, November–December 2005, pp. S9–S13. Burt maintains that decisions about end-of-life care should be made by groupwide or systemwide consensus rather than by individuals.

Butler, Robert N. "The Dangers of Physician-Assisted Suicide: Will We Choose to Provide a Right to Euthanasia for the Few or Palliative Care for the Many?" *Geriatrics*, vol. 51, July 1996, pp. 14–15. Butler maintains that legalization of physician-assisted suicide will draw attention and funding away from the need for better palliative care at the end of life.

Callahan, Daniel. "Assisted Suicide Is a Power Too Far." *BioLaw*, vol. 2, July–August 1996, pp. S125–S126. Callaghan states that legalizing physician-assisted suicide would place too much power in the hands of doctors.

———. "When Self-Determination Runs Amok." *Hastings Center Report*, vol. 22, March–April 1992, pp. 52–55. The author states that the debate on euthanasia is emblematic of three important issues in Western thought (the conditions under which one person may legitimately kill another, the meaning and limits of self-determination, and the purposes for which medicine should make itself available to individuals) and that supporters of euthanasia push society in the wrong direction on all of them.

Callahan, Daniel, and Margot White. "The Legalization of Physician-Assisted Suicide: Creating a Potemkin Village." *University of Richmond Law Review*, vol. 30, January 1996, n.p. This article maintains that "it is impossible in principle and in practice to regulate either euthanasia or physician-assisted suicide successfully" and that attempts to do so create a false sense of security.

Campo-Flores, Arian. "Who Has the Right to Die?" *Newsweek*, November 3, 2003, p. 50. Campo-Flores discusses the toxic family conflicts that were in the background of the Terri Schiavo case.

Caneto, Silvia Sara, and Janet D. Hollenshead. "Gender and Physician-Assisted Suicide: An Analysis of the Kevorkian Cases, 1990–1997."

Omega, vol. 40, February 2000, pp. 165ff. In contrast to U.S. suicides in general, a significant majority of the 75 people whom Jack Kevorkian admitted assisting in suicide during this period were women. The authors examine individual, interpersonal, social, economic, and cultural factors encouraging assisted suicide in women.

————. "Older Women and Mercy Killing." *Omega*, vol. 42, February 2001, pp. 83ff. Among U.S. cases of mercy killing recorded by the Hemlock Society between 1960 and 1993, the typical case involved an older woman being killed by a man, often her husband, who cited her poor health as justification for the act.

Cantor, Norman L. "On Kamisar, Killing, and the Future of Physician-Assisted Death." Michigan Law Review, vol. 102, August 2004, pp. 1,793–1,842. Cantor believes that the status quo, in which physician-assisted death is illegal but sometimes (in effect) practiced, should be maintained.

————. "Twenty-five Years after Quinlan: A Review of the Jurisprudence of Death and Dying." *Journal of Law, Medicine and Ethics*, vol. 29, Summer 2001, pp. 182ff. Competent patients have gained a clear right to request cessation of lifesaving medical treatment, but the status of surrogate decision making for dying incompetent patients remains murky.

Caralis, P. V., et al. "The Influence of Ethnicity and Race on Attitudes toward Advance Directives, Life-Prolonging Treatments, and Euthanasia." *Journal of Clinical Ethics*, vol. 4, 1993, pp. 155–165. The author describes important differences among racial and ethnic groups in attitude toward these controversial topics.

"Caring for the Dying." *CQ Researcher*, vol. 7, September 5, 1997. The entire issue is devoted to care of the dying, including consideration of whether better palliative care would reduce the demand for assisted suicide.

Chan, David K. "Active Voluntary Euthanasia and the Problem of Intending Death." *Journal of Philosophical Research*, vol. 30, Annual 2005, pp. S379–S389. Chan examines the issue of physician intention in determining the morality of causing death by discontinuance of medical treatment.

Cheyfitz, Kirk. "Who Decides? The Connecting Thread of Euthanasia, Eugenics, and Doctor-Assisted Suicide." *Omega*, vol. 40, February 2000, pp. 5ff. These three ideas are connected by two troublesome questions: *Which lives are not worth living?* and *Who will decide?*

Chong, Alice Ming-Lin, and Shiu-Yeu Fok. "Attitudes toward Euthanasia in Hong Kong—A Comparison between Physicians and the General Public." *Death Studies*, vol. 29, January–February 2005, pp. 29–54. The general public supported active euthanasia and nonvoluntary euthanasia but was neutral about passive euthanasia, whereas physicians supported passive euthanasia, were neutral about nonvoluntary euthanasia, and opposed active euthanasia.

Chorney, Jeff. "Ninth Circuit Orders Ashcroft to Back Off." *The Legal Intelligencer*, vol. 230, May 28, 2004, n.p. A divided panel of the Ninth U.S. Circuit Court of Appeals blocked Attorney General John Ashcroft's attempt to halt implementation of Oregon's Death with Dignity Act.

Clark, David, et al. "U.K. Geriatricians' Attitudes to Active Voluntary Euthanasia and Physician-Assisted Death." *Age and Ageing*, vol. 30, September 2001, pp. 395–398. Of British geriatricians, 81 percent considered active voluntary euthanasia always to be unethical, and 68 percent felt the same way about physician-assisted death. Many of the specialists felt that better palliative care was the best response to patients' requests for hastened death.

Cohen, Eric. "How Liberalism Failed Terri Schiavo." *Weekly Standard*, vol. 10, April 4, 2005, pp. 19–22. Cohen maintains that we owe care to all people, regardless of their own wishes or the profoundness of their disability.

———. "What Living Wills Won't Do." *Weekly Standard*, vol. 10, April 18, 2005, pp. 18–19. The author argues that at some time in their lives, everyone will probably have to make health care decisions for others without a completely clear understanding of what those others would have wished.

Cohen-Almagor, Raphael. "'Culture of Death' in the Netherlands: Dutch Perspectives." *Issues in Law and Medicine*, vol. 17, Fall 2001, pp. 167–179. When interviewed by the author, a majority of authorities on euthanasia policy in the Netherlands disagreed with Daniel Callahan's statement that a "culture of death" exists in that country.

———. "Dutch Perspectives on Palliative Care in the Netherlands." *Issues in Law and Medicine*, vol. 18, Fall 2002, pp. 111–126. Interviews with Dutch authorities on euthanasia revealed wide differences of opinion on the state of palliative care in the Netherlands.

———. "Non-voluntary and Involuntary Euthanasia in the Netherlands: Dutch Perspectives." *Issues in Law and Medicine*, vol. 18, Spring 2003, pp. 239–257. In interviews conducted in 1999, most authorities on euthanasia policy in the Netherlands were unconcerned about breaches of legal guidelines that resulted in nonvoluntary euthanasia (in which patients could not consent because they were incompetent) or involuntary euthanasia (in which competent patients were euthanized even though they had made no request to die).

———. "An Outsider's View of Dutch Euthanasia Policy and Practice." *Issues in Law and Medicine*, vol. 17, Summer 2001, pp. 35ff. According to the author, interviews conducted in 1999 revealed pressure to conform among authorities on euthanasia in the Netherlands; critics of the country's policy were not welcomed. Cohen-Almagor believes that Dutch euthanasia guidelines do not prevent possible abuse.

———. "Why the Netherlands?" *Journal of Law, Medicine and Ethics,* vol. 30, Spring 2002, pp. 95–105. Interviews revealed that the Netherlands' current policy on euthanasia grew out of a complex combination of historical, cultural, social, religious, and political factors, including the nature of the country's health care system.

Coleman, Carl H. "The 'Disparate Impact' Argument Reconsidered: Making Room for Justice in the Assisted Suicide Debate." *Journal of Law, Medicine and Ethics,* vol. 30, Spring 2002, pp. 17–24. Coleman claims that justice is as important as autonomy in deciding whether to legalize assisted suicide: One needs to consider how benefits and burdens of legalization are likely to be distributed among various social groups.

Coleman, Carl H., and Alan R. Fleischman. "Guidelines for Physician-Assisted Suicide: Can the Challenge Be Met?" *Journal of Law, Medicine, and Ethics,* vol. 24, Fall 1996, pp. 217–224. The authors consider whether guidelines in actual or proposed laws permitting physician-assisted suicide can protect against abuse such as the persuasion or coercion of the sick, disabled, or elderly to kill themselves.

Cooper, Jessica. "Consider Yourself Stopped." *National Right to Life News,* vol. 26, May 11, 1999, p. 12. This is the text of the statement made on April 13, 1999, by Cooper, circuit court judge in Oakland County, Michigan, to Jack Kevorkian while sentencing him to 10 to 25 years in prison for second-degree murder in the euthanasia killing of Thomas Youk.

Cooper, Rand Richards. "The Dignity of Helplessness: What Sort of Society Would Euthanasia Create?" *Commonweal,* vol. 123, October 25, 1996, pp. 12ff. Cooper claims that the widespread practice of assisted suicide would make society callous to humanity's physical weaknesses and remove an opportunity for spiritual growth.

Corry, John. "Who Is Jack Kevorkian, Really?" *Reader's Digest,* vol. 154, April 1999, pp. 87ff. Corry recounts the story of Kevorkian, a retired pathologist who assisted more than 100 people to commit suicide. Kevorkian was charged with murder after a videotape, which was broadcast at his urging on CBS's news program *60 Minutes,* showed him crossing the line into euthanasia by injecting a lethal dose of chemicals into a 52-year-old man.

Cossman, Jeralynn. "The Hemlock Society Membership: Comparisons between 1983 and 1995 Surveys and the General Population." *Omega,* vol. 45, August 2002, pp. 43–55. Cossman concludes that the population of the Hemlock Society (now part of Compassion & Choices) is increasing in religiosity and remains well educated and healthy. The society contains a higher proportion of women, people over 55 years of age, divorcees and widows/widowers, and atheists than the general population.

Cowart, Dax, and Robert Burt. "Confronting Death: Who Chooses, Who Controls?" *Hastings Center Report*, vol. 28, January–February 1998, pp. 14ff. This is a transcript of a debate about the right to die. Cowart asked to die after being severely burned in a gas explosion, and, although he later moved forward with his life, including getting married and starting his own business, he still feels that his request should have been honored.

Cranford, Ronald. "Facts, Lies, and Videotapes." *Journal of Law, Medicine and Ethics*, vol. 33, Summer 2005, pp. 363–371. Cranford maintains that Terri Schiavo's parents attempted to use videotapes of her to mislead the courts and the media, but the tapes nonetheless provided valuable evidence about Schiavo's neurological state.

———. "What Is a Minimally Conscious State?" *Western Journal of Medicine*, vol. 176, March 2002, pp. 129–130. The author offers a medical definition of the minimally conscious state and distinguishes it from a permanent vegetative state.

"Curtains for Dr. Death." *Time*, vol. 153, April 5, 1999, p. 48. This article reports that after assisting at least 130 suicides since 1990 without being found guilty of a crime, retired Michigan pathologist Jack Kevorkian has been found guilty of second-degree murder in the euthanasia killing of ALS victim Thomas Youk.

Cuttini, M., et al. "End-of-Life Decisions in Neonatal Intensive Care: Physicians' Self-Reported Practices in Seven European Countries." *Lancet*, vol. 355, June 17, 2000, pp. 2,112ff. Criteria for withholding or removing treatment from newborns with incurable disorders differ from country to country, but such acts occur often in all the countries surveyed. Cultural and other country-specific factors are more important than characteristics of individual physicians in explaining this variation.

———. "Should Euthanasia Be Legal? An International Survey of Neonatal Intensive Care Unit Staff." *Archives of Disease in Childhood, Fetal and Neonatal Edition*, vol. 89, January 2004, pp. F19–24. Active euthanasia appeared to be both acceptable and practiced in the Netherlands, France, and Lithuania, but it was less acceptable in several other European countries surveyed. Health professionals' opinions about legalization of euthanasia varied widely both between and within countries.

Darr, Kurt. "Terri Schindler Schiavo: End-Game." *Hospital Topics*, vol. 83, Spring 2005, pp. 29–31. Darr offers lessons to be learned from the Schiavo case about court rulings affecting end-of-life decisions.

"Debate over Schiavo and PVS: Will—and Should—Anything Change?" *Medical Ethics Advisor*, May 1, 2005, n.p. This piece concludes that the issues in this case are the same as in earlier right-to-die cases and that Michael Schiavo's actions were appropriate, given his wife's neurological condition.

De Beer, T. C. Gastmans, and B. Dierckx de Casterle. "Involvement of Nurses in Euthanasia: A Review of the Literature." *Journal of Medical Ethics*, vol. 30, October 2004, pp. 494–498. This article concludes that, on occasion, nurses have been involved in all phases of the euthanasia process.

DeCesare, Michael A. "Public Attitudes toward Euthanasia and Suicide for Terminally Ill Persons: 1977 and 1996." *Social Biology*, vol. 47, Fall–Winter 2000, pp. 264–266. The author shows that people in the United States were more supportive of euthanasia and suicide for terminally ill persons in 1996 than they were in 1977.

De Haan, Jurriaan. "The Ethics of Euthanasia: Advocates' Perspectives." *Bioethics*, vol. 16, April 2002, pp. 154–172. The author points out deficiencies of moral arguments advanced in favor of euthanasia in the Netherlands, including the pure autonomy view and the joint view (the claim that euthanasia is supported by the principles of autonomy and beneficence taken together).

Dennehy, Raymond L. "Physician-Assisted Suicide and Democracy." *Journal of Interdisciplinary Studies*, vol. 15, Summer–Autumn 2003, pp. 99–119. Dennehy argues that permitting physician-assisted suicide is anti-democratic because giving a person the right to dispose of his or her own life implies that the person's right to life is also disposable by others.

Derish, Melinda T., and Kathleen Vanden Heuvel. "Mature Minors Should Have the Right to Refuse Life-Sustaining Medical Treatment." *Journal of Law, Medicine and Ethics*, vol. 28, Summer 2000, pp. 109ff. This article argues that mature minors should have the legal right to make their own decisions about treatment at the end of life, even if their choices are different from those of their parents.

Dickinson, George E., et al. "U.K. Physicians' Attitudes toward Active Voluntary Euthanasia and Physician-Assisted Suicide." *Death Studies*, vol. 26, July–August 2002, pp. 479–490. A survey found that 80 percent of British geriatricians, but only 52 percent of intensive care physicians, felt that active voluntary euthanasia was never justified ethically.

Didion, Joan. "The Case of Theresa Schiavo." *New York Review of Books*, vol. 52, June 9, 2005, pp. 60–64. A well-known author comments on the Schiavo case and the legal, political, social, and moral issues it raises.

Diloreto, Stacy. "The Complexities of Assisted Suicide." *Patient Care*, vol. 34, November 30, 2000, pp. 65ff. Physicians will benefit from learning how to evaluate and discuss patients' requests for assistance in suicide.

Dinan, John. "Rights and the Political Process: Physician-Assisted Suicide in the Aftermath of *Washington v. Glucksberg*." *Publius*, vol. 31, Fall 2001, pp. 1–22. Dinam examines developments within states in the two years following the key 1997 Supreme Court decision and concludes that the decision enhanced democratic deliberation, secured representation of relevant interests, and provided opportunities for policy experimentation in the states.

Domino, George. "Community Attitudes toward Physician-Assisted Suicide." *Omega*, vol. 46, May 2003, pp. 199–211. A survey showed significant socioeconomic class differences in attitudes toward physician-assisted suicide, with better educated, upper-class individuals favoring the practice more than less educated, lower-class individuals. Younger people also supported assisted suicide more than older ones.

Dorff, Elliot N. "Assisted Suicide: A Jewish Perspective." *Sh'ma: A Journal of Jewish Responsibility*, vol. 27, September 20, 1996, pp. 6–7. Dorff surveys Jewish teachings that affect judgment about the morality of assisted suicide.

Dowbiggin, Ian. "'A Prey on Normal People': C. Killick Millard and the Euthanasia Movement in Great Britain, 1930–55." *Journal of Contemporary History*, vol. 36, January 2001, pp. 59–85. Dowbiggin examines the founding of the Voluntary Euthanasia Legislation Society by English health activist C. Killick Millard and the relationship between religion and public health ideology in the subsequent euthanasia movement.

Downie, Jocelyn, and Susan Sherwin. "A Feminist Exploration of Issues Around Assisted Death." *Saint Louis University Public Law Review*, vol. 15, 1996, pp. 303–330. This article discusses aspects of assisted death that particularly affect women.

Doyal, Len, and Lesley Doyal. "Why Active Euthanasia and Physician Assisted Suicide Should Be Legalized," *British Medical Journal*, vol. 323, November 10, 2001, pp. 1,079–1,080. This piece claims that the British courts' rejection of Diane Pretty's request for help in killing herself was consistent with legal precedent but morally wrong.

Dresser, Rebecca. "The Conscious Incompetent Patient." *Hastings Center Report*, vol. 32, May–June 2002, pp. 9–11. Dresser analyzes the California Supreme Court's 2001 decision in *Wendland v. Wendland*.

Dworkin, Ronald M., et al. "Assisted Suicide: The Philosophers' Brief." *New York Review of Books*, vol. 44, March 27, 1997, pp. 41ff. This is a reprint of *amicus curiae* brief on the subject of physician-assisted suicide submitted to the Supreme Court in 1997 by six prominent philosophers.

Eisenberg, Daniel. "Lessons of the Schiavo Battle." *Time*, vol. 165, April 4, 2005, pp. 22 ff. Eisenberg shows elements of a political circus in events surrounding Terri Schiavo's last days.

Eisenberg, Jon B., and J. Clark Kelso. "Legal Implications of the Wendland Case for End-of-Life Decision Making." *Western Journal of Medicine*, vol.

176, March 2002, pp. 124–127. This article discusses what evidence of a patient's end-of-life wishes will be required in California in order for a physician to withhold life-sustaining treatment from conscious but incompetent patients. The article encourages physicians to persuade patients to make advance directives.

Ellis, Jane. "Ethical Debate: The Great Divide." *Chemist and Druggist*, December 10, 2005, pp. 38ff. Ellis summarizes debate in the House of Lords on the Assisted Dying for the Terminally Ill Bill, as well as views of the public and medical profession regarding assisted suicide.

———. "Ethical Debate: On the Horns of a Dilemma." *Chemist and Druggist*, December 3, 2005, pp. 30ff. Ellis describes the aspects of assisted suicide and euthanasia in Britain that are likely to concern pharmacists. The article summarizes the legal status of these acts in other countries.

Emanuel, Ezekiel J., Diane L. Fairclough, and Linda L. Emanuel. "Attitudes and Desires Related to Euthanasia and Physician-Assisted Suicide among Terminally Ill Patients and Their Caregivers." *Journal of the American Medical Association*, vol. 284, November 15, 2000, pp. 2,460ff. In a survey of 988 terminally ill patients, only 11 percent were seriously considering euthanasia or physician-assisted suicide. Half of these had changed their minds several months later, but an equal number who had not been considering those options had changed their minds as well.

Emanuel, Ezekiel J., and Linda L. Emanuel. "The Promise of a Good Death." *Lancet*, vol. 351, May 16, 1998, pp. S21–S29. This article provides a framework for evaluating and improving the many dimensions of the dying experience.

Emanuel, Linda L. "Facing Requests for Physician-Assisted Suicide." *Journal of the American Medical Association*, vol. 280, August 19, 1998, pp. 643–657. An eight-step plan is presented to help physicians deal with requests for assisted suicide. The plan emphasizes evaluating a patient's reasons for requesting help in dying and meeting the patient's needs in other ways.

Ersek, Mary. "Assisted Suicide: Unraveling a Complex Issue." *Nursing*, vol. 35, April 2005, pp. 48–52. Ersek summarizes ethical arguments for and against assisted suicide, based on the role and responsibilities of medical authorities toward their terminally ill patients.

European Court of Human Rights. "Case of *Pretty v. the United Kingdom*." *Issues in Law and Medicine*, vol. 18, Summer 2002, pp. 67–89. This article provides text of the court judgment, which denied Diane Pretty's request to exempt her husband from prosecution if he helped her commit suicide.

Faber-Langendoen, Kathy, and Jason H. T. Karlawish. "Should Assisted Suicide Be Only Physician Assisted?" *Annals of Internal Medicine*, vol. 132, March 21, 2000, pp. 482ff. This piece argues that the physician's role in

assisted suicide is necessary but not sufficient; other professionals, including nurses, social workers, and clergy, can participate and may even take
the lead.

Fade, Anne E. "Withdrawing Life Support from the Terminally Ill." *USA
Today*, vol. 124, January 1996, pp. 41ff. Fade argues that dying people
naturally slow or stop eating and drinking and that withholding nutri-
tional life support (especially in the form of feeding tubes), therefore, not
only is morally and legally permissible but may be desirable for easing a
terminally ill patient's death.

Fagerlin, Angela, and Carl E. Schneider. "Enough: The Failure of the Living Will." *Hastings Center Report*, vol. 34, March–April 2004, pp. 30–42.
This article gives reasons for believing that living wills, even when executed, are of little use; it recommends durable power of attorney as an
advance directive instead.

Farsides, Bobby, and Robert J. Dunlop. "Is There Such a Thing as a Life
Not Worth Living?" *British Medical Journal*, vol. 322, June 16, 2001,
pp. 1,481ff. This article concludes that the concept of a life not being
worth living is not very useful in terms of either competent people
evaluating their own lives or incompetent people whose lives are evaluated by others.

Fenigsen, Richard. "Dutch Euthanasia: The New Government Ordered
Study." *Issues in Law and Medicine*, vol. 20, Summer 2004, pp. 73–79.
Fenigsen summarizes a new nationwide survey of euthanasia commissioned in 2001 by the Dutch Ministers of Health and Justice and published in 2003. The study focused on the effectiveness of the review and
verification procedure required by the law that permits euthanasia in the
Netherlands.

Ferry, Carol Bernstein. "A Good Death." *The Nation*, vol. 273, September
17, 2001, p. 8. This is an argument in favor of the right to die, written by
a terminally ill woman who subsequently killed herself in the presence of
family members.

Fickling, David. "A Happy Ending?" *Lancet*, vol. 364, September 4, 2004,
p. 831. This is a description of a workshop on euthanasia offered by
controversial Australian physician Philip Nitschke.

Foley, Kathleen M. "The Past and Future of Palliative Care." *Hastings
Center Report*, vol. 35, November–December 2005, pp. S42–46. Foley
discusses relationships between hospice care and palliative care. The latter is a broader term that covers prevention and treatment of suffering
connected with chronic, incurable diseases, whether or not those diseases are terminal.

Frey, Darcy. "Does Anyone Here Think This Baby Can Live?" *New York
Times Magazine*, July 9, 1995, pp. 22ff. Frey describes factors in the dif-

ficult choices doctors face when an extremely premature and possibly defective infant is delivered and they must decide whether to try to save the infant with expensive efforts that may be futile.

Frileux, Stephanie, et al. "Acceptability for French People of Physician-Assisted Suicide." *Death Studies,* vol. 28, December 2004, pp. 941–953. A survey found that acceptability was based on an additive combination of the number of requests for assisted suicide, the patient's age, the amount of physical suffering, and the degree to which the patient's illness was curable.

————. "When Is Physician Assisted Suicide or Euthanasia Acceptable?" *Journal of Medical Ethics,* vol. 29, December 2003, pp. 330–336. Repetitiveness of patient requests was the most important determinant of acceptability of physician-assisted suicide in the survey. Younger people considered hypothetical patients' age less important than older people did.

Gallagher, Hugh. "What the Nazi 'Euthanasia Program' Can Tell Us about Disability Oppression." *Journal of Disability Policy Studies,* vol. 12, Fall 2001, pp. 96ff. People with physical and mental disabilities killed under the T4 euthanasia program in Nazi Germany were oppressed in every sense of the word. Disabled people in the United States do not suffer similar oppression.

Ganzini, Linda, et al. "Oregon Physicians' Attitudes about and Experiences with End-of-Life Care Since Passage of the Oregon Death with Dignity Act." *Journal of the American Medical Association,* vol. 285, May 9, 2001, pp. 2,363ff. A survey of 2,641 Oregon doctors indicates that they feel they are providing better care to their dying patients since their state passed its controversial assisted-suicide law.

————. "Physicians' Experiences with the Oregon Death with Dignity Act." *New England Journal of Medicine,* vol. 342, February 24, 2000, pp. 557–563. Only 5 percent of the Oregon physicians surveyed had received a request for assisted suicide under the state law. Half of those making the requests changed their minds when offered palliative treatment.

Gardner, Christine J. "Severe Mercy in Oregon." *Christianity Today,* vol. 43, June 14, 1999, p. 66. Gardner contrasts the lives and deaths of two Oregon men with ALS, one of whom opted for assisted suicide and the other of whom did not.

Garrard, E., and S. Wilkinson. "Passive Euthanasia." *Journal of Medical Ethics,* vol. 31, February 2005, pp. 64–68. This article disagrees with a claim by the European Association of Palliative Care that passive euthanasia is not a valid concept.

Gentzler, Jyl. "What Is a Death with Dignity?" *Journal of Medicine and Philosophy,* vol. 28, August 2003, pp. 461–487. After examining and rejecting different notions of "dignity" presented in arguments for legalization of assisted suicide, the author advances an alternative concept based on Aristotle's conception of the conditions of the best life. In this view, assisted suicide should be legal only under very limited circumstances.

George, R. J. D., I. G. Finlay, and David Jeffrey. "Legalized Euthanasia Will Violate the Rights of Vulnerable Patients." *British Medical Journal*, vol. 331, September 24, 2005, pp. 684–685. This article claims that there is a permanent moral conflict between respecting a patient's autonomous wish for death and ensuring that vulnerable or voiceless patients are not killed without their consent.

George, Robert P., and William C. Porth, Jr. "Death, Be Not Proud." *National Review*, vol. 47, June 26, 1995, pp. 49–52. This is a nonreligious critique of arguments in favor of assisted suicide.

Gilgoff, Dan, Kenneth T. Walsh, and Angie C. Marek. "Life and Death Politics." *U.S. News & World Report*, vol. 138, April 4, 2005, pp. 14–18. The religious right sees its support for Terri Schiavo as an extension of its antiabortion stance. Social conservatives hope to use the Schiavo case to rein in what they view as a runaway court system.

Girsh, Faye. "The Case for Physician Aid in Dying." *Journal of the Hippocratic Society*, Fall 1997, n.p. The author presents reasons why physicians should be legally permitted to fulfill the wishes of terminally ill people who request help in committing suicide. Girsh maintains that assisting suicide can be part of a doctor's duty to relieve suffering.

Glass, Nigel. "Survey Finds Most Germans in Support of Assisted Euthanasia." *Lancet*, vol. 355, June 10, 2000, p. 2,057. Although euthanasia and assisted suicide are illegal in Germany, more than 80 percent of Germans surveyed favored assisted euthanasia, and half of those surveyed said they would consider it for themselves under some circumstances.

Gordon, Rick. "Robert Latimer, Catastrophic Rights and the Left." *Canadian Dimension*, vol. 35, November–December 2001, pp. 7–10. Gordon maintains that Robert Latimer's killing of his daughter, Tracy, was justified because she was "beyond disabled." The article includes response by disability-rights activist Ravi Malhotra.

Gorsuch, Neil M. "The Right to Assisted Suicide and Euthanasia." *Harvard Journal of Law and Public Policy*, vol. 23, Summer 2000, pp. 599ff. Gorsuch discusses major court decisions on these subjects and argues that courts and legislatures should consider a new perspective grounded in recognition of the sanctity of human life.

Gostin, Lawrence O. "Deciding Life and Death in the Courtroom: From Quinlan to Cruzan, Glucksberg, and Vacco." *Journal of the American Medical Association*, vol. 278, November 12, 1997, pp. 1,523ff. This is a detailed review and analysis of the Supreme Court's 1997 decision in two right-to-die cases, including descriptions of previous judicial rulings on which the decision was based.

———. "Ethics, the Constitution, and the Dying Process: The Case of Theresa Marie Schiavo." *Journal of the American Medical Association*, vol. 293, May 18, 2005, pp. 2,403–2,407. Gostin concludes that policies encouraging living wills and durable powers of attorney can minimize the kind of bitter disputes displayed in the Schiavo case.

Grayling, A. C. "'If All Else Fail. . .'" *Index on Censorship*, vol. 31, October 2002, pp. 26–34. Grayling concludes that the right to decide how, when, and where to die is conveyed to humans by natural justice.

Groenewoud, Johanna H., et al. "Clinical Problems with the Performance of Euthanasia and Physician-Assisted Suicide in the Netherlands." *New England Journal of Medicine*, vol. 342, February 24, 2000, pp. 551ff. Complications such as seizures, vomiting, and failure to induce coma occurred in 7 percent of physician-assisted suicides and 3 to 6 percent of euthanasias reported in the Netherlands in 1990–91 and 1995–96. In 18 percent of the assisted suicide cases where complications occurred, physicians stepped in and administered lethal medication.

Guedj, M., et al. "The Acceptability of Ending a Patient's Life." *Journal of Medical Ethics*, vol. 31, June 2005, pp. 311–317. A survey conducted in France showed that laypeople were more accepting of life-ending interventions than were health professionals but overall judged the acceptability of such actions in the same way.

Guglielmo, Wayne J. "Assisted Suicide? Pain Control? Where's the Line?" *Medical Economics*, vol. 79, October 11, 2002, pp. 48–52. A survey of U.S. physicians' views of pain management showed that most distinguish assisted suicide from the use of pain-relieving drugs in doses that may hasten death.

Gunderson, Martin, and David J. Mayo. "Restricting Physician-Assisted Death to the Terminally Ill." *Hastings Center Report*, vol. 30, November 2000, pp. 17ff. This article recommends an incremental approach to legalization of assisted suicide, for now limiting the practice to those who are terminally ill because the risks of legalization are much less for terminally ill people than for those who are not terminally ill.

Gutmann, Stephanie. "Death and the Maiden." *New Republic*, vol. 214, June 24, 1996, pp. 20–24, 28. Gutmann points out that a majority of the people Jack Kevorkian helped to die, especially in the early part of his career in assisted suicide, were women. Gutmann claims that Kevorkian and what he represents may be dangerously appealing to some women.

Hall, Alison C. "To Die with Dignity: Comparing Physician-Assisted Suicide in the United States, Japan, and the Netherlands." *Washington*

Right to Die and Euthanasia

University Law Quarterly, vol. 74, Fall 1996, pp. 803–840. Hall compares practice in the United States, where physician-assisted suicide is illegal; Japan, where it is technically legal but very rarely occurs; and the Netherlands, where it was (at the time of this article) technically illegal but condoned by courts and government and relatively common.

Halloran, Liz. "Of Life and Death." *U.S. News & World Report*, vol. 139, October 10, 2005, pp. 31–32. Describes the legal issues in *Gonzales v. Oregon.*

Hamel, Ronald, and Michael Panicola. "Must We Preserve Life? The Narrowing of Traditional Catholic Teaching." *America*, vol. 190, April 19, 2004, pp. 6ff. The recent papal requirement that food and water be provided to sick people under almost all circumstances conflicts with traditional Catholic teaching, which holds that "ordinary" means must be used to preserve life but "extraordinary" means (those that offer little benefit or impose an excessive burden on the patient) need not be, and confuses Catholics. The authors recommend the traditional approach combined with palliative care.

Hanson, Ann Aubrey. "Doctor: Pain Care Refutes Case for Euthanasia." *National Catholic Reporter*, vol. 39, February 7, 2003, p. 4. Palliative care, which goes well beyond pain management, is a preferred alternative to euthanasia.

Hardwig, John. "Is There a Duty to Die?" *Hastings Center Report*, vol. 27, March–April 1997, pp. 34–42. Hardwig maintains that under some circumstances, the incurably ill and elderly may have a duty to die in order to conserve scarce health care resources.

Harrow, Judy. "Neo-Pagan Ethics and Assisted Suicide." *Gnosis*, Winter 1997, n.p. The author maintains that people suffering uncontrollable pain or deterioration from illness, whether terminal or not, should be legally entitled to decide whether they wish to continue their lives. If they decide to die, they should have the right not only to commit suicide but also to obtain help in doing so.

Haverkate, Ilinka, et al. "The Emotional Impact on Physicians of Hastening the Death of a Patient." *Medical Journal of Australia*, vol. 175, November 19, 2001, pp. 519–522. A survey of physicians in the Netherlands who have performed euthanasia or assisted suicide showed that 52 percent felt comfortable after the procedure, while 42 percent did not. Almost all the physicians questioned said that they were willing to perform the act again.

———. "Refused and Granted Requests for Euthanasia and Assisted Suicide in the Netherlands." *British Medical Journal*, vol. 321, October 7, 2000, pp. 865ff. Many doctors in the Netherlands refuse some requests for euthanasia or assisted suicide.

Annotated Bibliography

Hayry, Heta. "Bioethics and Political Ideology: The Case of Active Voluntary Euthanasia." *Bioethics*, no. 11, July 1997, pp. 271ff. Hayry claims that legalizing euthanasia would be dangerous in some countries because of circumstances that presently prevail there, but that the solution to this situation is to change the circumstances, not to block the legalization of euthanasia.

Hendin, Herbert. "The Dutch Experience." *Issues in Law and Medicine*, vol. 17, Spring 2002, pp. 223–246. Studies approved by the Dutch government reveal that guidelines established for regulation of euthanasia in the Netherlands are consistently violated. Some patients are put to death without their consent.

———. "Suicide, Assisted Suicide, and Medical Illness." *Harvard Mental Health Letter*, vol. 16, January 2000, n.p. Hendin claims that many terminally ill people who ask for assistance in suicide change their minds when given treatment for depression and adequate palliative care.

Hendin, Herbert, Chris Rutenfrans, and Zbigniew Zylicz. "Physician-Assisted Suicide and Euthanasia in the Netherlands: Lessons from the Dutch." *Journal of the American Medical Association*, vol. 277, June 4, 1997, pp. 1,720–1,722. This article maintains that comparison of 1990 and 1995 studies of euthanasia in the Netherlands, contrary to the conclusions of the studies' authors, shows that abuses have increased and that the practice cannot be effectively regulated.

Hickman, Susan E., et al. "Hope for the Future: Achieving the Original Intent of Advance Directives." *Hastings Center Report*, vol. 35, November–December 2005, pp. S26–30. This article describes limitations of traditional advance directives and characteristics of new advance directive programs that succeed in obtaining respect for patients' wishes regarding end-of-life treatment.

Hildebrand, Adam J. "Masked Intentions." *Issues in Law and Medicine*, vol. 16, Fall 2000, pp. 143ff. Hildebrand argues that when people in a persistent vegetative state or with other profound neurological impairments who are not terminally ill are denied assisted nutrition and hydration, they are killed by starvation and dehydration, which is immoral and unethical.

Hilliard, Bryan. "Evaluating the Dissent in *State of Oregon v. Ashcroft*." *Journal of Law, Medicine and Ethics*, vol. 33, Spring 2005, pp. 142–163. Hilliard analyzes the 2004 decision by a three-judge panel of the Ninth Circuit Court of Appeals, especially the dissenting opinion of Judge J. Clifford Wallace, with which the author disagrees.

Horgan, John. "Right to Die." *Scientific American*, vol. 274, May 1996, pp. 12–13. A four-year study of terminally ill patients indicates that, in spite of the 1990 Patient Self-Determination Act, living wills and other advance directives have not had the impact for which proponents had hoped. Hospitals and physicians still frequently ignore patients' wishes as expressed in these directives, including the wish to die under certain circumstances.

Horsfall, Sara, et al. "Views of Euthanasia from an East Texas University." *Social Science Journal*, vol. 38, October 2001, pp. 617–629. About 75 percent of students at an east Texas university favored euthanasia, a proportion similar to that found in the general public. Such a high degree of support in a conservative geographic area suggests growing overall approval of euthanasia and other forms of assisted death.

Hull, Richard T. "The Case For: Physician-Assisted Suicide." *Free Inquiry*, vol. 23, Spring 2003, pp. 35–36. Hull rebuts four common arguments against assisted suicide.

Hurst, Samia A., and Alex Mauron. "Assisted Suicide and Euthanasia in Switzerland: Allowing a Role for Non-Physicians." *British Medical Journal*, vol. 326, February 1, 2003, pp. 271–273. This article describes the history and current status of assisted suicide in Switzerland: It is legally condoned and does not have to be performed by physicians.

Hwang, Karen. "Attitudes of Persons with Physical Disabilities toward Physician-Assisted Death." *Journal of Disability Policy Studies*, vol. 16, Summer 2005, p. 16. Some people with disabilities fear and oppose physician-assisted death, but others do not see themselves as exceptionally vulnerable to coercion. They find the views of activist groups such as Not Dead Yet to be patronizing and threatening to their autonomy.

"'I'd Far Rather Pick My Moment to Die.'" *Hospital Doctor*, November 24, 2005, p. 16. The arrest of British physician Michael Irwin for assisting the suicide of a terminally ill friend highlights attitudes toward assisted suicide and euthanasia in the United Kingdom.

Jochemsen, Henk. "Dutch Court Decisions on Nonvoluntary Euthanasia Critically Reviewed." *Issues in Law and Medicine*, vol. 13, Spring 1998, pp. 447ff. Jochemsen focuses on recent decisions that allow euthanasia to be performed on infants with disabilities. The author claims that such decisions potentially endanger the lives of all incompetent persons.

Journal of Law, Medicine, and Ethics, vol. 24, Fall 1996. The issue is almost entirely devoted to physician-assisted suicide. It covers legal, regulatory, medical, and ethical issues.

Kamisar, Yale. "The Reasons So Many People Support Physician-Assisted Suicide—And Why These Reasons Are Not Convincing." *Issues in Law and Medicine*, vol. 12, Fall 1996, pp. 113–131. The author offers rebuttals to common arguments in favor of assisted suicide. Kamisar contends that physician-assisted suicide cannot be safely regulated and should remain illegal.

Annotated Bibliography

————. "Some Non-Religious Views Against Proposed 'Mercy-Killing' Legislation." *Minnesota Law Review*, vol. 42, 1958, pp. 969ff. This is a famous essay in which a renowned legal scholar gives reasons for opposing the legalization of euthanasia and related acts, including physician-assisted suicide and withholding or withdrawal of life-sustaining medical treatment.

Kaplan, Kalman J., et al. "An Update on the Kevorkian-Reding 93 Physician-Assisted Deaths in Michigan." *Omega*, vol. 40, February 2000, pp. 209ff. More than two-thirds of the people assisted to kill themselves were women, including five of the six who showed no signs of illness at autopsy. Later killings showed increased routinization, including use of a "suicide machine," and a move from assisted suicide to euthanasia.

Kass, Leon R., and Nelson Lund. "Courting Death: Assisted Suicide, Doctors, and the Law." *Commentary*, vol. 102, December 1996, pp. 17–29. This article critiques the legal reasoning in two appellate court decisions that declared state laws against assisted suicide unconstitutional and argues that the Supreme Court should uphold such laws.

Keizer, Garret. "Life Everlasting: The Religious Right and the Right to Die." *Harper's Magazine*, vol. 310, February 2005, pp. 53–61. Keizer questions the motives of groups that oppose physician-assisted suicide.

Keown, J. "The Case of Ms. B: Suicide's Slippery Slope?" *Journal of Medical Ethics*, vol. 28, pp. 238–239. Keown analyzes the British High Court's ruling allowing the anonymous Ms. B, a disabled woman, to have her ventilator turned off.

King, Philip. "*Washington v. Glucksberg:* Influence of the Court in Care of the Terminally Ill and Physician Assisted Suicide." *Journal of Law and Health*, vol. 15, Summer 2000, pp. 271–301. King looks at the effects of the Supreme Court's famous 1997 decision, Oregon's Death with Dignity Act, and bills introduced into Congress on care of the terminally ill, including assisted suicide. King proposes that assisted suicide, but not euthanasia, should be one option in care for the terminally ill.

Kissane, David W., Annette Street, and Philip Nitschke. "Seven Deaths in Darwin: Case Studies Under the Rights of the Terminally Ill Act, Northern Territory, Australia." *Lancet*, October 3, 1998, pp. 1,097ff. Drawing on in-depth interviews with Nitschke and other sources, the authors present case histories of the seven people who applied for physician-assisted suicide under the Northern Territory's Rights of the Terminally Ill Act during the nine months it was in effect, focusing on the decision-making process that followed their requests. Nitschke helped four of the people die.

Koch, Tom. "The Challenge of Terri Schiavo: Lessons for Bioethics." *Journal of Medical Ethics*, vol. 31, July 2005, pp. 376–378. Koch claims that the

Schiavo case represents a broader controversy involving the definitions by which bioethicists judge cases of extreme psychological and physiological limits.

————. "Life Quality vs. the 'Quality of Life': Assumptions Underlying Prospective Quality of Life Instruments in Health Care Planning." *Social Science and Medicine*, vol. 51, August 2000, pp. 419–427. Koch critiques the assumptions underlying current instruments for measuring "quality of life" that are used in health care planning, linking them to early eugenics literature and related social policies.

Kokurina, Yelena. "Life Beyond Life." *Moscow News*, vol. 4,166, March 30, 2005, pp. 1–2. Kokurina discusses Russian lawmakers' views on treatment and potential euthanasia of coma patients.

Lavery, James V., et al. "Origins of the Desire for Euthanasia and Assisted Suicide in People with HIV-1 or AIDS: A Qualitative Study." *Lancet*, vol. 358, August 4, 2001, pp. 362–367. Researchers found that the main reasons people in this group sought euthanasia or assisted suicide were disintegration with loss of physical functioning due to disease, and loss of community, in particular the inability to have close personal relationships with other people. These two losses created a sense of loss of self.

Lavi, Shai. "Euthanasia and the Changing Ethics of the Deathbed: A Study in Historical Jurisprudence." *Theoretical Inquiries in Law*, vol. 4, July 2003, n.p. Lavi describes changes in deathbed ethics during the 19th century, showing how control of dying passed from priests to physicians and then to judges and lawmakers.

Lavrikova, Irina N. "Tver Physicians: Attitudes toward Euthanasia." *Sociological Research*, vol. 39, September–October 2000, pp. 68–74. Lavrikova reports on a survey given to physicians in Tver (Russia). About a quarter of the physicians favored granting euthanasia if a patient wanted it, but 41 percent said euthanasia was justified only under limited circumstances.

Lee, Daniel E. "Physician-Assisted Suicide: A Conservative Critique of Intervention." *Hastings Center Report*, vol. 33, January–February 2003, pp. 17–20. The author personally opposes assisted suicide but believes that it should be legalized, with safeguards like those in the Oregon law.

Lefevere, Patricia, and Robert McClary. "Schiavo Autopsy Points up Need for End-of-Life Discussions." *National Catholic Reporter*, vol. 41, July 1, 2005, pp. 10–11. Terri Schiavo's autopsy will not end confusion about whether Catholic doctrine always requires use of a feeding tube to provide nutrition for a person in a persistent vegetative state.

Lens, Vicki, and Daniel Pollack. "Advance Directives: Legal Remedies and Psychosocial Interventions." *Death Studies*, vol. 24, July–August 2000, pp. 377–399. This article explores reasons why physicians often ignore directives specifying end-of-life medical choices and discusses the effects of attempts by patients and their families to seek redress for such actions through the courts.

Lester, David. "Psychological Issues in Euthanasia, Suicide and Assisted Suicide." *Journal of Social Issues*, vol. 52, Summer 1996, pp. 51ff. Lester considers judgment of decision-making competence, diagnosis of depression, and other mental health issues affecting these practices.

Lewis, Penney. "Rights Discourse and Assisted Suicide." *American Journal of Law and Medicine*, vol. 27, Spring 2001, pp. 45ff. Lewis examines the often conflicting rights-based claims advanced in favor of assisted suicide, as well as critiques of such claims that have become popular in recent years.

Lindsay, Ronald A. "Should We Impose Quotas? Evaluating the 'Disparate Impact' Argument against Legalization of Assisted Suicide." *Journal of Law, Medicine and Ethics*, vol. 30, Spring 2002, pp. 6–17. Lindsay analyzes and rejects the argument that legalization of assisted suicide will have a disproportionate negative effect on vulnerable groups such as the disabled, the elderly, and the poor.

Lo, Bernard. "End-of-Life Care after Termination of SUPPORT." *Hastings Center Report*, vol. 25, June 1995 (special supplement), pp. S6–S8. Lo indicates that even after an extensive program to improve communication between terminally ill patients and health care professionals and increase compliance with advance directives, patients' wishes regarding end-of-life care were frequently ignored.

Longmore, Paul K. "Policy, Prejudice, and Reality: Two Case Studies of Physician-Assisted Suicide." *Journal of Disability Policy Studies*, vol. 16, pp. 38–45. The situation of two quadriplegic ventilator users who requested assistance with suicide in 1989 shows the discriminatory elements of public policy, health care delivery, and social services that make some disabled people's lives unendurable. Until such conditions are improved, legalizing assisted suicide will be dangerous to the disabled.

Lund, Nelson. "Why Ashcroft Is Wrong on Assisted Suicide." *Commentary*, vol. 113, February 2002, pp. 50–55. The author favors discouragement of assisted suicide but feels that John Ashcroft's attempt to use the Controlled Substances Act for that purpose undermines a fundamental constitutional principle.

Magnusson, Roger S. "Euthanasia: Above Ground, below Ground." *Journal of Medical Ethics*, vol. 30, October 2004, pp. 441–446. Argues that legalization of euthanasia would be safer than prohibition because it would allow the process to be regulated.

———. "'Underground Euthanasia' and the Harm Minimization Debate." *Journal of Law, Medicine and Ethics*, vol. 32, Fall 2004, pp. 486–495. Reports on the unregulated, idiosyncratic "underground" provision of assisted death by health care providers working with HIV/AIDS patients in Australia and California.

Marquet, R. L., et al. "Twenty-five Years of Requests for Euthanasia and Physician Assisted Suicide in Dutch General Practice: Trend Analysis." *British Medical Journal*, vol. 327, July 26, 2003, pp. 201–202. This article investigates the effect of increasing acceptance on the number of and underlying reasons for requests for euthanasia and assisted suicide from 1977 to 2001. The article concludes that fear that lives of increasing numbers of patients would end through medical intervention, without their consent or before all palliative care options were exhausted, is not justified.

Marzen, Thomas J. "*Wendland v. Wendland:* Pressing the Euthanasia Envelope." *National Right to Life News*, vol. 28, June 2001, n.p. Marzen holds that if the California Supreme Court allows the feeding tube of Robert Wendland, a minimally conscious man, to be removed, all patients with mental disabilities will be in danger of involuntary euthanasia.

Mathes, Michele M. "Assisted Suicide and Nursing Ethics." *MedSurg Nursing*, vol. 13, August 2004, pp. 261–264. Mathes discusses the ethics of nurses assisting patients' suicide, including position statements of the American Nurses Association and others.

———. "Terri Schiavo and End-of-Life Decisions: Can Law Help Us Out?" *MedSurg Nursing*, vol. 14, June 2005, pp. 200–202. Lawsuits such as those in the Terri Schiavo case distort the human narratives from which the legal actions spring, and legal instruments (advance directives) are not always clear. Conversations with friends and relatives are the best ways to make one's wishes about end-of-life care known.

———. "Withholding and Withdrawing Artificial Nutrition and Hydration—A Legal Perspective." *MedSurg Nursing*, vol. 9, October 2000, pp. 270ff. Mathes examines the legal issues involved in withholding or withdrawing artificial provision of food and water.

Mayo, David J., and Martin Gunderson. "Vitalism Revitalized: Vulnerable Populations, Prejudice, and Physician-Assisted Death." *Hastings Center Report*, vol. 32, July–August 2002, pp. 14–22. This article claims that legalization of physician-assisted suicide would not put disabled people at any greater risk than the risk that already exists in current policies about end-of-life care.

Mazzeo, Kathryn E. "The Right to Die versus the Right to Live, Who Decides?" *Albany Law Review*, vol. 66, Fall 2002, pp. 263–287. Mazzeo discusses current New York statutes, case law, and pending legislation that affect surrogate decision-making about end-of-life care, especially for developmentally disabled and other noncompetent people.

Annotated Bibliography

McInerney, Fran. "'Requested Death': A New Social Movement." *Social Science and Medicine*, vol. 50, January 2000, pp. 137–154. McInerney uses a socio-historical approach to argue that issues such as euthanasia and assisted suicide are part of an international social movement, which the author calls the "requested death movement."

McKenzie, David. "Church, State, and Physician-Assisted Suicide." *Journal of Church and State*, vol. 46, Autumn 2004, pp. 787–809. McKenzie discusses the rulings of the Ninth Circuit Court of Appeals and the U.S. Supreme Court in the case of *Washington v. Glucksberg* (1997). McKenzie argues that the Supreme Court's decision unconstitutionally advances the views of the Christian faith and violates a legitimate liberty interest of the people.

Meier, Diane E. "A Change of Heart on Assisted Suicide." *New York Times*, April 24, 1998. The author, a geriatrics specialist, says she used to support legalization of assisted suicide for terminally ill people but no longer does so because she believes that legalized assisted suicide would be used as a cheap substitute for better palliative care for the dying.

Meilaender, Gilbert. "Gilbert Meilaender." *First Things*, August–September 2004, pp. 35–38. Meilaender maintains that Robert Orr (in another article in the same issue) does not provide convincing reasons to believe that withdrawing feeding and hydration from a person in a persistent vegetative state can be moral.

Miller, Franklin G., Joseph J. Fins, and Lois Snyder. "Assisted Suicide Compared with Refusal of Treatment: A Valid Distinction?" *Annals of Internal Medicine*, vol. 132, March 21, 2000, pp. 470ff. This article uses three illustrative cases to defend the claim that there is a valid distinction between assisted suicide and refusal of medical treatment.

Miller, Pamela J. "Life after Death with Dignity: The Oregon Experience." *Social Work*, vol. 45, May 2000, pp. 263ff. Miller offers a framework for examining and evaluating the effects of Oregon's Death with Dignity Act.

Miller, Robert T. "The Legal Death of Terri Schiavo." *First Things*, May 2005, pp. 14–16. Miller claims that the Schiavo case produced injustice, even though Terri Schiavo's legal rights were never violated; problems arose not because the courts ignored the law but because they followed it.

Minnesota Law Review, vol. 82, April 1998. The entire issue is devoted to legal and other aspects of physician-assisted suicide, including consideration of important court cases in the right-to-die movement.

Mitchell, C. Ben. "Of Euphemisms and Euthanasia." *Omega*, vol. 40, February 2000, pp. 255ff. Mitchell compares euphemisms used by Nazi physicians to redefine medicalized killing with those used by contemporary supporters of such killing. Mitchell concludes that consistent application of euphemisms weakens arguments against assisted killing.

Mitchell, Kay, and R. Glynn Owens. "National Survey of Medical Decisions at End of Life Made by New Zealand General Practitioners." *British Medical Journal*, vol. 327, July 26, 2003, pp. 202–203. This article reports that palliative care was available in 85 percent of cases of physician-assisted death in New Zealand, suggesting that the care did not meet the patients' needs.

Morrison, R. S., and D. E. Meier. "Managed Care at the End of Life." *Trends in Health Care, Law and Ethics*, vol. 10, 1995, pp. 91–96. This article discusses the effect of managed care and cost control on availability and quality of palliative care for the terminally ill.

Murphy, Christie. "DNR: Did Helen Still Want to Die?" *Medical Economics*, vol. 79, May 24, 2002, pp. 50–51. Case study of a patient who initially said she did not want to be kept alive with a ventilator but changed her mind.

Muskin, Philip R. "The Request to Die: Role for a Psychodynamic Perspective on Physician-Assisted Suicide." *Journal of the American Medical Association*, vol. 279, January 28, 1998, pp. 323–328. Muskin stresses that a patient's request for help in dying should be met with extended discussion to determine the psychological reasons for the request.

Mystakidou, Kyriaki, et al. "The Evolution of Euthanasia and Its Perceptions in Greek Culture and Civilization." *Perspectives in Biology and Medicine*, vol. 48, Winter 2005, pp. 95–104. Feelings about euthanasia in modern Greece are influenced by the attitudes of ancient Greece, where the practice was accepted, as well as those of Christianity, which rejects it.

Ogden, Russel D. "Non-Physician Assisted Suicide: The Technological Imperative of the Deathing Counterculture." *Death Studies*, vol. 25, July 2001, pp. 387ff. This article reports on the second Self-Deliverance New Technology Conference, held in Seattle, Washington, in November 1999, as an example of a sophisticated and expanding movement of non-medical providers of death.

O'Neill, C., et al. "Physician and Family Assisted Suicide: Results from a Study of Public Attitudes in Britain." *Social Science and Medicine*, vol. 57, August 15, 2003, pp. 721–731. Data from British Social Attitude Surveys taken between 1983 and 1994 show a slight increase in support for physician-assisted suicide. Support for physician assistance in suicide was much greater than support for family assistance. Age and strength of religious affiliation were significant predictors of opposition to legalization of assisted suicide.

Onwuteaka-Philipsen, Bregje D., and Gerrit van der Wal. "A Protocol for Consultation of Another Physician in Cases of Euthanasia and Assisted

Suicide." *Journal of Medical Ethics*, vol. 27, October 2001, pp. 331–337. The protocol provided guidelines regarding four important aspects of consultation: independence, expertise, tasks, and judgment of the consultant. Most consultants considered the protocol useful to some extent.

Onwuteaka-Philipsen, Bregje D., et al. "Euthanasia and Other End-of-Life Decisions in the Netherlands in 1990, 1995, and 2001." *Lancet*, vol. 362, August 2, 2003, pp. 395 ff. This article concludes that demand for physician-assisted death has not risen among patients or physicians since 1995.

Orr, Robert D. "Ethics and Life's Ending: An Exchange." *First Things*, August–September 2004, pp. 31–35. Orr concludes that in many cases, use of a feeding tube should be optional, even for people of faith.

Osgood, Nancy. "Assisted Suicide and Older People—A Deadly Combination: Ethical Problems in Permitting Assisted Suicide." *Issues in Law and Medicine*, vol. 10, Spring 1995, pp. 415–435. Osgood maintains that if physician-assisted suicide is legalized, chronically ill or even possibly healthy old people will be pressured into killing themselves.

Otto, Randall E. "Bottom of the Slope." *Commonweal*, vol. 122, May 19, 1995, pp. 5–6. The author cites recent cases in the Netherlands that, in his opinion, show that safeguards in that country's right-to-die law have been violated, leading to euthanasia for those who are not terminally or even physically ill and for some who have not consented to the procedure.

Parks, Jennifer A. "Why Gender Matters to the Euthanasia Debate." *Hastings Center Report*, vol. 30, January 2000, pp. 30ff. Parks claims that cultural views of women as not fully rational agents lead physicians to refuse women's requests for aid in dying more often than they refuse men's requests. The less social power an individual woman has, the less likely she is to have her death requests taken seriously.

Parris, Matthew. "I Am Not in Principle against Killing People, but Talk of the 'Right to Die' Is Humbug." *Spectator*, vol. 291, January 25, 2003, p. 10. Legalization and consequent state regulation of euthanasia could lead to abuses.

Peruzzi, Nico, Andrew Canapary, and Bruce Bongar. "Physician-Assisted Suicide: The Role of Mental Health Professionals." *Ethics and Behavior*, vol. 6, 1996, pp. 353–366. Many studies indicate that depression is both common and linked to suicide, but primary care physicians, untrained in psychiatry, are seldom able to detect it. Authors assert that mental health professionals should be regularly consulted following requests for assisted suicide to identify depression and other possibly treatable problems. They also list ethical principles that apply to this area.

Pestaner, Joseph P. "End-of-Life Care: Forensic Medicine v. Palliative Medicine." *Journal of Law, Medicine and Ethics*, vol. 31, Fall 2003, pp. 365–377. Palliative care providers are unlikely to be prosecuted for providing overtreatment that hastens death, as long as their care meets usual standards.

"Physician-Assisted Suicide and Euthanasia in the Netherlands: A Report to the House Judiciary Subcommittee on the Constitution." *Issues in Law and Medicine*, vol. 14, Winter 1998, pp. 301–324. This piece reports how judicial arguments in the Netherlands during the past 23 years have led from toleration of physician-assisted suicide for competent, terminally ill adults to termination of patients' lives without consent.

"Physician-Assisted Suicide: Balancing Medical Ethics and Individual Rights." *Congressional Digest*, vol. 77, November 1998. The entire issue is devoted to pro and con opinions on physician-assisted suicide, including a discussion of whether the House of Representatives should approve the Lethal Drug Abuse Prevention Act.

"The Policeman's Dilemma: Euthanasia." *Economist*, vol. 377, October 15, 2005, p. 59US. This article describes debate over a British bill that, if passed, would legalize assisted suicide for terminally ill adults.

Quill, Timothy E. "Death and Dignity—A Case of Individualized Decision Making." *New England Journal of Medicine*, vol. 324, March 7, 1991, pp. 691–694. This article, which describes how Quill helped a terminally ill woman named Diane kill herself, helped to ignite the public debate on physician-assisted suicide in the 1990s.

Quill, Timothy E., and Christine K. Cassel. "Professional Organizations' Position Statements on Physician-Assisted Suicide." *Annals of Internal Medicine*, vol. 138, February 4, 2003, pp. 208–211. This article recommends that medical organizations take a neutral position on this contentious issue.

Quill, Timothy E., Bernard Lo, and Dan W. Brock. "Palliative Options of Last Resort: A Comparison of Voluntarily Stopping Eating and Drinking, Terminal Sedation, Physician-Assisted Suicide, and Voluntary Active Euthanasia." *Journal of the American Medical Association*, vol. 278, December 17, 1997, pp. 2,099–2,104. Four methods by which terminally ill people can end life with the help of their physicians are compared from medical and ethical standpoints. Authors see patient consent as a more important ethical criterion than whether the physician's role is active or passive.

Rachels, James. "Active and Passive Euthanasia." *New England Journal of Medicine*, vol. 292, January 9, 1975, pp. 78–80. Classic essay in which the author, a well-known philosopher, claims there is no significant distinction between passive and active euthanasia.

Radtke, Richard. "A Case against Physician-Assisted Suicide." *Journal of Disability Policy Studies*, vol. 16, Summer 2005, pp. 58–60. Drawing on his own experience as a disabled person, the author claims that the unsupportive environment created by a prejudiced society leads disabled people to underestimate their potential quality of life and therefore, in some cases, seek assisted suicide. He calls for development of a community support network that helps disabled people develop socially as well as mentally.

Rao, Jagannadha. "Legal Issues Relating to the Limitation of Life Support." *Indian Journal of Critical Care Medicine*, vol. 9, April–June 2005, n.p. Rao reviews laws on assisted suicide, euthanasia, and withdrawal of life-sustaining treatments in various countries.

Reed-Purvis, Julian. "From 'Mercy Death' to Genocide." *History Review*, March 2003, pp. 36–40. The author examines the way in which the Nazis' policy of euthanizing the mentally and physically handicapped dovetailed with their increasingly radical plans to create a "master race."

Rich, Ben A. "The Ethics of Surrogate Decision Making." *Western Journal of Medicine*, vol. 176, March 2002, pp. 127–129. Rich considers the implications of the California Supreme Court's August 2001 decision in *Wendland v. Wendland* for the law and ethics of surrogate decision making. Rich stresses the importance of making written directives.

Rietjens, Judith A. C., et al. "A Comparison of Attitudes towards End-of-Life Decisions: Survey among the Dutch General Public and Physicians." *Social Science and Medicine*, vol. 61, October 15, 2005, pp. 1,723–1,732. A greater percentage among the general public in the Netherlands supports assisted suicide and euthanasia than among physicians.

"The Right to Die." *The Bulletin with Newsweek*, vol. 120, September 24, 2002, p. 26. This article provides brief summaries of the legal status of euthanasia in different countries.

Ripley, Amanda. "The Debate Won't Die." *Time International*, vol. 162, November 24, 2003, p. 49. Prosecutors and the French public are debating whether the mother and doctor of Vincent Humbert, a man left severely disabled by an auto accident, committed a criminal act when they euthanized him in September 2003 after his repeated pleas for death.

Rivera, Seth, et al. "Motivating Factors in Futile Clinical Interventions." *Chest*, vol. 119, June 2001, pp. 1,944ff. Families were responsible for insisting on treatment later deemed futile in about two-thirds of surveyed cases in which futile treatment was given; physicians, sometimes motivated by fear of liability, accounted for the rest. The authors recommend bioethics consultations when treatment seems likely to be futile.

Robinson, Simon. "Europe's Way of Death." *Time International*, vol. 165, April 4, 2005, p. 28. Many Europeans accept euthanasia under some circumstances, but they differ on how to regulate it.

Rock, Melanie. "Discounted Lives? Weighing Disability When Measuring Health and Ruling on 'Compassionate' Murder." *Social Science and Medicine*, vol. 51, August 2000, pp. 407–417. Rock maintains that the politics of "suffering" as defined in discussions of the Robert Latimer euthanasia case and in the Disability-Adjusted Life Year scale reflect a valorization of the "normal" body in much of social science literature.

Rogatz, Peter. "The Positive Virtues of Physician-Assisted Suicide." *The Humanist*, vol. 61, November–December 2001, pp. 31–34. The fundamental principles of patient autonomy and physicians' duty to relieve suffering support legalization of physician-assisted suicide.

Rojas, Raimundo. "Spotlight on the Americas: Euthanasia in Colombia." *National Right to Life News*, vol. 28, June 2001, n.p. A decision of the Colombian Supreme Court in 1997 appeared to legalize euthanasia in that country, but later action by the Colombian Senate leaves citizens some legal protection against direct killing.

Roosevelt, Margaret. "Choosing Their Time." *Time*, vol. 165, April 4, 2005, p. 31. Oregon's assisted suicide law is becoming more accepted by physicians, patients, and the public, but whether other states will follow Oregon's example remains unclear.

Roscoe, Lori A., et al. "A Comparison of Characteristics of Kevorkian Euthanasia Cases and Physician-Assisted Suicides in Oregon." *Gerontologist*, vol. 41, August 2001, pp. 439ff. Women who are divorced or never married seem unusually likely to seek euthanasia as the result of illness, even if the illness is not terminal.

Rudden, Lawrence. "Death and the Law." *World and I*, vol. 18, May 2003, pp. 255ff. Rudden claims that Attorney General John Ashcroft's challenge to Oregon's assisted suicide law violates both individual patients' rights and states' rights.

Rurup, Mette L., et al. "A 'Suicide Pill' for Older People." *Death Studies*, vol. 29, July–August 2005, pp. 519–534. There has been debate in the Netherlands about whether a (hypothetical) "suicide pill" should be made available to older people. Relatives of patients who had died after euthanasia were most in favor of this idea, followed by the general population. Physicians were least in favor of the proposal.

Ryan, Christopher James, and Miranda Kaye. "Euthanasia in Australia— The Northern Territory Rights of the Terminally Ill Act." *New England Journal of Medicine*, vol. 334, February 1, 1996, pp. 326–328. Describes safeguards and other features of the Rights of the Terminally Ill Act, passed in Australia's Northern Territory in May 1995.

Schneider, Carl E. "All My Rights." *Hastings Center Report*, vol. 32, July–August 2002, pp. 10–12. Schneider analyzes the ruling of the European Court of Human Rights in the Diane Pretty case, which went against Pretty.

———. "Hard Cases." *Hastings Center Report*, vol. 28, March–April 1998, pp. 24–26. Schneider describes the widely publicized case of Robert Latimer, a Saskatchewan (Canadian) farmer who killed his 12-year-old severely handicapped daughter, Tracy. Although Latimer said he killed Tracy to relieve her of suffering, he was convicted of second-degree murder and sentenced to a minimum of 10 years in prison.

———. "Hard Cases and the Politics of Righteousness." *Hastings Center Report*, vol. 35, May–June 2005, pp. 24–27. Schneider looks at the Schiavo case with sympathy rather than condemnation for Terri Schiavo's parents and their supporters. The case highlights major but largely undiscussed changes in the valuation of human life in the United States.

Seay, Gary. "Do Physicians Have an Inviolable Duty Not to Kill?" *Journal of Medicine and Philosophy*, vol. 26, February 2001, pp. 75ff. Seay rebuts four types of argument offered in support of this conclusion.

Shannon, Thomas A. "Killing Them Softly with Kindness." *America*, vol. 185, October 15, 2001, p. 16. Shannon examines expansions of the new Dutch law permitting euthanasia and assisted suicide that the author finds disturbing, such as the extension of the right to request euthanasia to minors and people undergoing strictly mental suffering.

———. "Physician-Assisted Suicide: Ten Questions." *Commonweal*, vol. 123, June 1, 1996, pp. 16–17. The author asks 10 thoughtful questions about physician-assisted suicide to encourage debate on the subject.

Shannon, Thomas A., and James J. Walter. "Artificial Nutrition, Hydration: Assessing Papal Statement." *National Catholic Reporter*, vol. 40, April 16, 2004, pp. 9–10. The pope's recent statement that artificial nutrition and hydration must always be provided goes against traditional Catholic teaching and may not be effective in its aim of preventing euthanasia.

———. "Assisted Nutrition and Hydration and the Catholic Tradition." *Theological Studies*, vol. 66, September 2005, pp. 651–662. The author maintains that in the past 25 years there has been an undesirable shift in Catholic moral thinking from evaluating medical treatments (including life-sustaining care) in terms of burdens and benefits to the patient to evaluating treatments in terms of abstract principles (deontology).

Shapiro, Joseph P. "Euthanasia's Home: What the Dutch Experience Can Teach Americans about Assisted Suicide." *U.S. News & World Report*, vol. 122, January 13, 1997, pp. 24ff. The author maintains that the system of euthanasia practiced in the Netherlands probably would not work in the United States because of differences in culture and provision of health care.

Shaw, A. B. "Two Challenges to the Double Effect Doctrine: Euthanasia and Abortion." *Journal of Medical Ethics*, vol. 28, April 2002, pp. 102–104. The doctrine of double effect makes little sense when applied to euthanasia. Decisions about euthanasia are actually based more on pragmatic considerations than on ethical issues.

Shibler, Ann V. "Defying the Death Culture." *New American,* vol. 21, May 16, 2005, pp. 27–28. Kate Adamson-Klugman, who recovered from a major stroke, defends severely disabled people's right to life in an interview.

Short, Bradford William. "History 'Lite' in Modern American Bioethics." *Issues in Law and Medicine,* vol. 19, Summer 2003, pp. 45-76. Short claims that prominent European early modern moral philosophers sometimes cited by supporters of euthanasia and assisted suicide in fact believed in an inalienable right to life.

Silveira, Maria J., et al. "Patients' Knowledge of Options at the End of Life." *Journal of the American Medical Association,* vol. 284, November 15, 2000, pp. 2,483ff. A survey suggests that many U.S. citizens are not adequately informed about end-of-life issues, including euthanasia and physician-assisted suicide.

Singer, Peter. "Freedom and the Right to Die." *Free Inquiry,* vol. 22, Spring 2002, pp. 16–17. Arguments against euthanasia make more sense as arguments for safeguards to prevent errors and abuses.

———. "Ms. B and Diane Pretty: A Commentary." *Journal of Medical Ethics,* vol. 28, August 2002, pp. 234–235. The article claims that the distinction between Ms. B, who was seeking withdrawal of life-sustaining medical treatment, and Diane Pretty, who asked for assistance in suicide, is not defensible morally and that both women should have been allowed to die as they wished.

———. "Voluntary Euthanasia: A Utilitarian Perspective." *Bioethics,* vol. 17, October 2003, pp. 526–541. Singer reviews ethical arguments concerning voluntary euthanasia and physician-assisted suicide from a utilitarian perspective.

Slowther, A. "The Case of Ms. B and the 'Right to Die.'" *Journal of Medical Ethics,* vol. 28, August 2002, p. 243. Slowther provides details on the case of Ms. B, a disabled British woman who asked that her ventilator be turned off.

Smith, Iain Duncan. "It Looks Like Euthanasia to Me." *Spectator,* vol. 296, October 23, 2004, p. 189. The Mental Capacity Bill, being considered by Parliament in Britain, would permit withholding of food and water from severely incapacitated people—a painful way of hastening death.

Smith, Wesley J. "Why Secular Humanism Is Wrong: About Assisted Suicide." *Free Inquiry,* vol. 23, Spring 2003, pp. 31–32. The most compelling arguments against permitting assisted suicide are secular: money, abuses, alternatives, and abandonment.

Sneiderman, Barney, and Raymond Deutscher. "Dr. Nancy Morrison and Her Dying Patient: A Case of Medical Necessity." *Health Law Journal,* vol. 10, Annual 2002, pp. 1–30. The authors emphasize that Morrison's patient was already dying and that life support had been stopped before she gave him a fatal injection. They call her action compassionate and say that she should not have been charged as a criminal.

Snyder, Lois, and Daniel P. Sulmasy. "Physician-Assisted Suicide." *Annals of Internal Medicine*, vol. 135, August 7, 2001, pp. 209–216. This article explains why the American College of Physicians and American Society of Internal Medicine do not support the legalization of physician-assisted suicide.

Somerville, Margaret. "The Case against: Euthanasia and Physician-Assisted Suicide." *Free Inquiry*, vol. 23, Spring 2003, pp. 33–34. One major reason to oppose euthanasia is based on the principle that it is almost always wrong for one human being to kill another. The other is utilitarian: The harms and risks of legalization—to individuals, to society, and to medicine—far outweigh any benefits.

Spindelman, Marc. "A Dissent from the Many Dissents from Attorney General Ashcroft's Interpretation of the Controlled Substances Act." *Issues in Law and Medicine*, vol. 19, Summer 2003, pp. 3–44. Spindelman rejects the states' rights arguments advanced in opposition to Ashcroft's position as reflecting bad politics that liberals should reject.

Steinbock, B. "The Case for Physician Assisted Suicide: Not (Yet) Proven." *Journal of Medical Ethics*, vol. 31, April 2005, pp. 235–241. The author argues that changes in law and social policy concerning assisted suicide should be based not on individual cases but on the general need for physician-assisted suicide as weighed against the risks of mistake and abuse.

Stephens, Ronald L. "The Moral Meaning of Morphine Drips: A Modern Shibboleth Denied." *Midwest Quarterly*, vol. 43, Spring 2002, pp. 346–363. Moral arguments about use of morphine in euthanasia are based on the belief that morphine drips usually or always shorten life—a view that the author says is outmoded and erroneous.

Stringham, Edward, and Ben Parizek. "End of Life Decisions and the Maximization of Length of Life." *Journal of Social, Political, and Economic Studies*, vol. 30, Summer 2005, pp. 193–202. The authors argue that investing in resources in health care at earlier stages in life and allowing patients more say in determining the time of their death would result in a greater overall length of life.

SUPPORT Principal Investigators. "A Controlled Trial to Improve Care for Seriously Ill Hospitalized Patients: The Study to Understand Prognoses and Preferences for Outcomes and Risks of Treatment (SUPPORT)." *Journal of the American Medical Association*, vol. 274, November 22–29, 1995, pp. 1,591–1,598. This landmark study showed that, even after implementation of an extensive program to improve communication between patients and health care professionals, patients' wishes and advance directives were often ignored.

Swarte, Nikkie B., et al. "Effects of Euthanasia on the Bereaved Family and Friends: A Cross Sectional Study." *British Medical Journal*, vol. 327, July 26, 2003, pp. 189–192. The families and friends of cancer patients who died by euthanasia in the Netherlands coped better with grief symptoms and post-traumatic stress reactions than those of similar patients who died naturally.

"A Symposium on Physician-Assisted Suicide." *Duquesne Law Review*, vol. 35, 1996. The entire issue is devoted to legal aspects of physician-assisted suicide.

"Symposium on Physician-Assisted Suicide." *Ethics*, vol. 109, April 1999. The entire issue is devoted to this subject, presenting and critiquing legal and moral arguments for and against the practice.

Tännsjö, Torbjörn. "Moral Dimensions." *British Medical Journal*, vol. 331, September 24, 2005, pp. 689–691. After considering euthanasia from the moral perspectives of deontology, basic moral rights, and utilitarianism, the author concludes that euthanasia should be permitted in a few restricted situations.

Taylor, Keith. "Was Dr. Kevorkian Right?" *Free Inquiry*, vol. 23, Spring 2003, pp. 29–30. Taylor holds that people should be allowed to decide whether their lives are worth living.

Teisseyre, Nathalie, Etienne Mullet, and Paul Clay Sorum. "Under What Conditions Is Euthanasia Acceptable to Lay People and Health Professionals?" *Social Science and Medicine*, vol. 60, January 15, 2005, pp. 357–368. A survey demonstrated that laypeople and health professionals in France evaluated hypothetical scenarios involving requests for euthanasia in the same way, placing most emphasis on the extent of requests by the patient.

"Terminal Sedation vs. PAS: Difference Just Semantics?" *Medical Ethics Advisor*, August 1, 2005, n.p. Rule-based ethics are likely to distinguish between the two, but situational evaluations probably will not.

Thompson, Brendan A. "Final Exit." *Vanderbilt Journal of Transnational Law*, vol. 33, October 2000, pp. 1,035ff. Thompson explores the double-effect rule that now unofficially permits euthanasia in Britain and concludes that physician-assisted suicide should be legalized so that it can be precisely regulated.

Tolson, Jay. "Wrestling with the Final Call." *U.S. News & World Report*, vol. 138, April 4, 2005, p. 22. The Terri Schiavo case may disturb the widespread consensus that removing feeding tubes from patients in a persistent vegetative state is ethical.

Tournay, Anne E., and Douglas S. Diekema. "Withdrawal of Medical Treatment in Children." *Western Journal of Medicine*, vol. 173, December 2000, pp. 407ff. This piece summarizes situations in which withdrawal or with-holding of treatment in pediatric intensive care units may be justified. Such actions account for between 28 percent and 65 percent of deaths in these units.

Townsend, Liz. "British Health Service Doctors Accused of Involuntary Euthanasia." *National Right to Life News*, vol. 27, June 2000, n.p. Allegations that National Health Service physicians are performing involuntary euthanasia on disabled and elderly patients in Britain are causing great controversy.

————. "Nitschke 'Assists' in Death of Non-Terminal Patient." *National Right to Life News*, vol. 29, June 2002, p. 7. This is a pro-life view of the suicide of Australian Nancy Crick.

————. "Proponents Now Want 'Suicide Pill.'" *National Right to Life News*, vol. 29, April 2002, n.p. Voluntary euthanasia societies in the Netherlands and Australia have proposed that such a pill be made available.

Trotter, Griffin. "The Social Aspects of Assisted Suicide." *Health Care Ethics*, vol. 4, Fall 1996, pp. 2–3. Trotter discusses the societal, as opposed to moral, medical, or legal, aspects of physician-assisted suicide.

Tulsky, James A., Ralph Ciampa, and Elliott J. Rosen. "Responding to Legal Requests for Physician-Assisted Suicide." *Annals of Internal Medicine*, vol. 132, March 21, 2000, pp. 494ff. This article provides a framework and vocabulary for physicians to use when responding to requests for assisted suicide where such action is legal.

Valco, Nancy. "A Lethal Evolution." *First Things*, December 2001, pp. 21–24. Valco maintains that withdrawal of life-supporting treatment from people in a persistent vegetative state is incompatible with Catholic religious values and decries the acceptance of such action in some Catholic hospitals.

Van den Haag, Ernest. "Make Mine Hemlock." *National Review*, vol. 47, June 12, 1995, pp. 60ff. Van den Haag holds that there are no valid reasons for a secular government to keep a competent adult from committing suicide. Van den Haag claims that society should establish guidelines for assisted suicide and then give people, especially the disabled, the right to end their lives.

Van der Heide, Agnes, et al. "End-of-Life Decision-Making in Six European Countries: Descriptive Study." *Lancet*, vol. 362, August 2, 2003, pp. 345ff. This article investigates frequency and characteristics of end-of-life decision-making practices in Belgium, Denmark, Italy, the Netherlands, Sweden, and Switzerland.

Van der Maas, Paul J., et al. "Euthanasia, Physician-Assisted Suicide, and Other Medical Practices Involving the End of Life in the Netherlands, 1990–1995." *New England Journal of Medicine*, vol. 335, November 28, 1996, pp. 1,699–1,705. An update of the Netherlands' famous Remmelink

Report shows little change in the country's practices regarding euthanasia and physician-assisted suicide between 1991 and 1995. Authors maintain that the data do not support the accusation that physicians in that country are moving down a slippery slope.

Van der Maas, Paul J., Loes Pijnenborg, and Johannes J. M. van Delden. "Changes in Dutch Opinions on Active Euthanasia, 1966 Through 1991." *Journal of the American Medical Association*, vol. 273, May 10, 1995, pp. 1,411ff. This article examines changes in public opinion on the issue of active euthanasia in the Netherlands and changes in opinion that occurred among a representative sample of Dutch physicians during their medical practice.

Van Gend, David. "Nancy Crick's Death Not in Vain." *Human Life Review*, vol. 28, Summer 2002, pp. 87–88. Van Gend holds that the suicide of Nancy Crick, an Australian woman, in 2002 should have been prevented, and Philip Nitschke should be prosecuted for assisting her death.

Wasserman, Jason, et al. "A Scale to Assess Attitudes toward Euthanasia." *Omega*, vol. 51, November 2005, pp. 229–237. Offers a systematically designed scale to measure attitudes toward different types of euthanasia.

Welie, Jos V. M. "Why Physicians? Reflections on the Netherlands' New Euthanasia Law." *Hastings Center Report*, vol. 32, January–February 2002, pp. 42–45. Dutch legalization of euthanasia in 2001 clarifies a previously murky legal situation, but no one has explained why the law is justified in giving physicians a privilege of killing that is denied to others.

Wellman, Carl. "A Legal Right to Physician-Assisted Suicide Defended." *Social Theory and Practice*, vol. 29, January 2003, pp. 19–38. Wellman proposes that state (rather than federal) laws should recognize a set of statutory rights to request or not request, obtain or not obtain, and use or not use assistance provided by a physician to commit suicide.

———. "A Moral Right to Physician-Assisted Suicide." *American Philosophical Quarterly*, vol. 38, July 2001, pp. 271–286. This article asserts that people should have the moral liberties to request, obtain, and use assistance in dying. Wellman describes moral duties that provide protective perimeters for these liberties.

Werth, James L., Jr. "Concerns about Decisions Related to Withholding/Withdrawing Life-Sustaining Treatment and Futility for Persons with Disabilities." *Journal of Disability Policy Studies*, vol. 16, Summer 2005, pp. 31–37. Withdrawal of life-sustaining treatment can be supported by the same arguments applied to assisted suicide and may be more dangerous to disabled people because it is more likely to be applied against their will when resource allocation issues become important.

Werth, James L., Jr., and Judith R. Gordon. "*Amicus Curiae* Brief for the United States Supreme Court on Mental Health Issues Associated with

Annotated Bibliography

'Physician-Assisted Suicide.'" *Journal of Counseling and Development*, vol. 80, Spring 2002, pp. 160–172. This article describes and reprints a brief presented to the Supreme Court in 1996 by the American Counseling Association and others, supporting the right to assisted dying.

Werth, James L., Jr., and Daniel J. Holdwick, Jr. "A Primer on Rational Suicide and Other Forms of Hastened Death." *Counseling Psychologist*, vol. 28, July 2000, pp. 511–539. Provides an overview of the major mental health issues involved in evaluating requests for hastened death.

Werth, James L., Jr., and Howard Wineberg. "A Critical Analysis of Criticisms of the Oregon Death with Dignity Act." *Death Studies*, vol. 29, January–February 2005, pp. 1–27. This piece asserts that criticisms of the assisted-suicide law are unfounded.

White, Stephen W. "Euthanasia Jurisprudence and Physician-Assisted Suicide: What Did *Glucksberg* Teach Us?" *Journal of the Alabama Academy of Science*, vol. 75, July 2004, pp. 214–224. White discusses the theory of law as it applies to physicians' role in hastening the death of terminally ill people at their request. White concludes that, contrary to the decisions of the Second and Ninth Circuit Courts, physician-assisted death should be explicitly regulated by federal law.

Wiley, Lindsay F. "Assisted Suicide: Court Strikes down Ashcroft Directive." *Journal of Law, Medicine and Ethics*, vol. 30, Fall 2002, pp. 459–460. Wiley provides background on the early stages of the *Oregon v. Ashcroft* case.

Williams, Daniel. "Peaceful End Fires Euthanasia Debate." *Time International*, vol. 159, June 3, 2002, p. 18. This is a nonpartisan report of Australian Nancy Crick's suicide.

Wineberg, Howard, and James L. Werth, Jr. "Physician-Assisted Suicide in Oregon: What Are the Key Factors?" *Death Studies*, vol. 27, July 2003, pp. 501–518. This piece examines previously reported data on assisted suicide in Oregon. The article concludes that desire for control and autonomy appear to be the chief factors in requests for assisted dying.

Wolfson, Jay. "Erring on the Side of Theresa Schiavo." *Hastings Center Report*, vol. 35, May–June 2005, pp. 16–19. The author, the court-appointed guardian (guardian *ad litem*) for Terri Schiavo, supports courts' and Michael Schiavo's conclusions that Terri Schiavo was in a persistent vegetative state.

Worthen, Laura T., and Dale E. Yeatts. "Assisted Suicide: Factors Affecting Public Attitudes." *Omega*, vol. 42, March 2001, pp. 115ff. A survey of people in Denton, Texas, examined the effects of demographic factors, ideological factors, and individuals' caregiving experiences on their attitudes toward assisted suicide. Age, gender, and caregiving experience were not correlated with particular attitudes, but situational factors (for instance, whether a person was suffering pain) and commitment to certain values (such as the belief that suffering has meaning) did predict attitudes toward assisted suicide.

Wright, Walter. "Historical Analogies, Slippery Slopes, and the Question of Euthanasia." *Journal of Law, Medicine and Ethics*, vol. 28, Summer 2000, pp. 176ff. Wright asserts that supporters of euthanasia's legalization need to provide evidence that such action would not lead to Nazi-style abuses.

Ziegler, Stephen J. "Physician-Assisted Suicide and Criminal Prosecution: Are Physicians at Risk?" *Journal of Law, Medicine and Ethics*, vol. 33, Summer 2005, pp. 349–358. Ziegler concludes that prosecutors seldom proceed against physicians who assist in patients' deaths, even where such actions are illegal.

Ziegler, Stephen J., and Robert A. Jackson. "Who's Not Afraid of Proposal B?" *Politics and the Life Sciences*, vol. 23, March 2004, pp. 42–48. Exit polls made after Michigan voters rejected Proposal B, a citizen initiative that would have legalized physician-assisted suicide, in 1998 showed that many voters who would have been expected to favor the proposal nonetheless voted against it. This result suggests that obtaining passage of similar measures in other states may be difficult.

INTERNET/WEB DOCUMENTS

American Dietetic Association. "Ethical and Legal Issues in Nutrition, Hydration, and Feeding." Available online. URL: http://www.eatright.org/cps/rde/xchg/ada/hs.xsl/nutrition_8060_ENU_HTML.htm. Posted in 2002. This site discusses ethical issues involved in withdrawing nutrition and hydration and cites legal cases that have affected decision making in this area. The site affirms the patient's right to self-determination as the overriding principle and stresses that registered dietitians should work with the health care team to make nutrition, hydration, and feeding recommendations in individual cases.

American Geriatrics Society Ethics Committee. "Physician-Assisted Suicide and Voluntary Active Euthanasia." Available online. URL: http://www.americangeriatrics.org/products/positionpapers/vae94.shtml. Last updated in November 2002. A position paper from this organization holds that these activities should not be legalized and physicians should not participate in them, but physicians may provide aggressive palliative care that has the side effect of hastening death.

American Pain Foundation. "Pain Management for End of Life." Available online. URL: http://www.painfoundation.org/page.asp?file=EOL/intro.

htm. Last updated in 2005. This site discusses advance directives, resources, and emotional, legal, and ethical concerns.

Back, Tony. "End-of-Life Issues." University of Washington School of Medicine. Available online. URL: http://depts.washington.edu/bioethx/topics/eol.html. Last updated on February 22, 1999. This site considers such issues as the definition of a "good death," how to know when someone is dying, what physicians need to know about hospice and care for the dying, and how physicians who care for the dying can deal with their own emotions.

Beauchamp, Thomas, and Rita Marker. "Physician Assisted Dying: Pro and Con." San Diego Hospice. Available online. URL: http://ethics.sandiego.edu/video/Hospice/PAS/index.html. Posted on March 21, 2001. This is a video of a question-and-answer session at a conference on medical ethics and the humanities in end-of-life care. Beauchamp favors assisted dying; Marker opposes it.

Braddock, Clarence H., III. "Do-Not-Resuscitate Orders." University of Washington School of Medicine. Available online. URL: http://depts.washington.edu/bioethx/topics/dnr.html. Last updated on February 22, 1999. This site discusses when cardiopulmonary resuscitation (CPR) should be administered and when withheld, how to judge a patient's quality of life in the context of deciding whether to resuscitate, when to write do-not-resuscitate (DNR) orders, and what to do if a patient is incompetent or if family members disagree with a patient's wishes.

———. "Termination of Life-Sustaining Treatment." University of Washington School of Medicine. Available online. URL: http://depts.washington.edu/bioethx/topics/termlife.html. Last updated on February 22, 1999. This site discusses when discontinuing life-sustaining treatments is justifiable, what types of treatment may be discontinued, when competent patients may refuse treatment, and what physicians can do if a patient is incompetent or if competence is in doubt.

Braddock, Clarence H., III, and Mark R. Tonelli. "Physician-Assisted Suicide." University of Washington School of Medicine. Available online. URL: http://depts.washington.edu/bioethx/topics/pas.html. Last updated on February 22, 1999. This site considers the relationship between physician-assisted suicide and euthanasia, arguments for and against physician-assisted suicide, medical and lay opinions about assisted suicide, and what to do if a patient requests assistance in suicide.

Burgdorf, Robert L., Jr. "Assisted Suicide: A Disability Perspective." National Council on Disability. Available online. URL: http://www.nightingalealliance.org/pdf/A_Disability_Perspective.pdf. Reissued on June 9, 2005. This is the position paper of this government agency, which concludes that the dangers of legalizing assisted suicide outweigh any benefits for disabled people, especially in a climate of health care rationing and insufficient funding to help the disabled live independently in their homes and communities.

Cantor, Norman L. "The Relation between Autonomy-Based Rights and Profoundly Disabled Persons." Rutgers University Law School. Available online. URL: http://law.bepress.com/cgi/viewcontent.cgi?article=1010& context=rutgersnewarklwps. Posted in 2004. This site discusses the difficult issue of applying autonomy-based rights to never-competent people. Cantor concludes that some states' requirement of clear statements of wishes before discontinuing life-sustaining treatment of dying people leaves never-competent people in a legal and medical limbo and limits their right to have surrogates make decisions for them.

Coleman, Diane. "Assisted Suicide and Disability: Another Perspective." American Bar Association. Available online. URL: http://www.abanet. org/irr/hr/winter00humanrights/colemand.html. Accessed on February 9, 2006. This site maintains that assisted suicide and euthanasia will be used as lethal forms of discrimination against the disabled.

Corbet, Barry. "Physician Assisted Death: Are We Asking the Right Questions?" *New Mobility*, May 2003. Also available online. URL: http://www. notdeadyet.org/docs/pad.html. Accessed on February 9, 2006. A disabled writer views the issue in terms of personal preference, as a disability issue, and as public policy and concludes that, at present, physician-assisted death presents too many possibilities for abuse to be safely legalized.

Dignity in Dying. "The Problems with the Current Law." Available online. URL: http://www.dignityindying.org.uk/information/factsheets.asp?id=84. Accessed on February 8, 2006. This site criticizes Britain's Suicide Act (1961), which prohibits assistance in suicide, claiming that the law produces "uncertain and arbitrary" treatment of people who assist in suicide. This group would like to see the law replaced with one that explicitly permits assistance in the suicide of mentally competent, terminally ill adults who are suffering unbearably and request such help.

Disability Rights Commission. "Assisted Dying Policy Statement." Available online. URL: http://www.drc-gb.org/library/policy/health_and_ independent_living/assisted_dying_policy_statemen.aspx. Posted in October 2005. This is a statement of a British government committee, commenting on the Assisted Dying for the Terminally Ill Bill. It holds that legalizing assisted dying would set back disability rights considerably and potentially would heighten discrimination against disabled people.

Freer, Jack P., and Elizabeth G. Clark, "The Living Will: A Guide to Health Care Decision Making." State University of New York, Buf-

falo. Available online. URL: http://wings.buffalo.edu/faculty/research/
bioethics/lwill.html. Posted in 1994. This site defines terms, circumstances and types of health care usually discussed in advance directives,
types of advance directives, and the importance of communicating
wishes to family and physicians.

Fulton, Gere B., and Donald E. Saunders, Jr. "Who Speaks for Robert
Wendland?" University of South Carolina, Institute for Public Service
and Policy Research, *Public Policy and Practice,* vol. 1, October 2001.
Available online. URL: http://ipspr.sc.edu/ejournal/medicaltreatdec.asp.
Posted in 2001. This site summarizes *Wendland v. Wendland,* a case decided by the California Supreme Court in August 2001, involving a family dispute over whether a feeding tube should be removed from a
minimally conscious man. The article recommends advance directives,
especially powers of attorney for health care, as a way of avoiding such
disputes.

Gillis, Christina M. "Seeing the Difference: Conversations on Death and
Dying." University of California, Berkeley, Doreen B. Townsend Center
for the Humanities. Available online. URL: http://townsendcenter.
berkeley.edu/pubs/OP24_SeeingtheDiff.pdf. Posted in June 2000. This
site brings together the perceptions of clinicians, humanists, and artists
and explores the boundaries and connections among these perspectives.

Golden, Marilyn. "Why Assisted Suicide Must Not Be Legalized." Disability
Rights Education and Defense Fund. Available online. URL: http://disweb.
org/cda/issues/pas/goldenl.html. Accessed on February 17, 2006. This site
maintains that if assisted suicide is legalized, disabled people will be pressured to kill themselves so that health care providers can save money.
Golden claims that safeguards are unavoidably inadequate.

Hamlon, Kathi. "Euthanasia and Assisted-Suicide Measures in the United
States (1988–2005)." International Task Force on Euthanasia and Assisted Suicide. Available online. URL: http://www.internationaltaskforce.
org/usa.htm. Last updated in 2005. This is a brief chronology of the issues, divided by state and year.

Hendin, Herbert. "Aging and Care-Giving: Lessons on Assisted Suicide
from the Oregon and Netherlands Experiences." President's Council on
Bioethics. Available online. URL: http://www.bioethics.gov/transcripts/
march05/session1.html. Posted on March 3, 2005. This is a transcript of
a speech made to the President's Council on Bioethics, plus subsequent
discussion. Hendin warns against assisted suicide.

Hinman, Lawrence M. "Decisions at the End of Life." University of San
Diego Ethics Updates. Available online. URL: http://ethics.sandiego.
edu/presentations/AppliedEthics/Euthanasia/index_files/frame.htm.

Posted on February 21, 2001. This powerpoint presentation covers distinctions among types of euthanasia and views of euthanasia from the standpoint of several philosophies.

Hospice Foundation of America. "Living with Grief: Ethical Dilemmas at the End of Life." Available online. URL: http://www.hospicefoundation.org/teleconference/2005/default.asp. Posted in 2005. This record of the proceedings of a conference held in 2005 includes several case studies and other articles on the ethics of end-of-life care, discussion of laws related to end-of-life care, and ideas about handling family conflicts about care decisions.

House of Lords. "Assisted Dying for the Terminally Ill Bill." United Kingdom Parliament. Available online. URL: http://www.publications.parliament.uk/pa/ld200506/ldbills/036/06036.i.html. Last updated on November 10, 2005. This is the text of the controversial bill discussed by Parliament in Britain in October–November 2005, which would legalize assisted suicide for the terminally ill if passed.

House of Lords Select Committee on the Assisted Dying for the Terminally Ill Bill. "Assisted Dying for the Terminally Ill Bill." United Kingdom Parliament. Available online. URLs: http://www.publications.parliament.uk/pa/ld200405/ldselect/ldasdy/86/86i.pdf; http://www.publications.parliament.uk/pa/ld200405/ldselect/ldasdy/86/86ii.pdf; and http://www.publications.parliament.uk/pa/ld200405/ldselect/ldasdy/86/86iii.pdf. All posted on April 4, 2005. Reports (HL 86-1, 86-2, and 86-3) of the committee reviewing the Assisted Dying for the Terminally Ill Bill. Committee members had strongly differing views and presented safeguards they felt should be required if assisted dying is legalized.

Hurst, Rachel. "Assisted Suicide and Disabled People—A Briefing Paper." Disability Awareness in Action. Available online. URL: http://www.daa.org.uk/assisted_suicide.htm. Accessed on February 8, 2006. This paper claims that ill and disabled people need better treatment, not assistance in suicide, and that legalization of assisted suicide would put disabled people at risk.

Jecker, Nancy S. "Futility." University of Washington School of Medicine. Available online. URL: http://depts.washington.edu/bioethx/topics/futil.html. Last updated on February 22, 1999. This article defines the concept of medical futility, compares it with the related concepts of rationing and experimental intervention, and discusses who decides whether a treatment is futile and what to do if doctor and patient or family disagree about whether a treatment is futile.

John Paul II. "Evangelium Vitae." Vatican web site. Available online. URL: http://www.vatican.va/holy_father/john_paul_ii/encyclicals/documents/hf_jp-ii_enc_25031995_evangelium-vitae_en.html. Posted on March 25,

1995. This is the text of the encyclical in which the Pope speaks on the sanctity of life and voices opposition to euthanasia.

Lane, Bob, and Richard Dunstan. "Euthanasia: The Debate Continues." Malaspina University-College. Available online. URL: http://www.mala. bc.ca/www/ipp/euthanas.htm. Last updated in 2001. Two 1995 papers describe opposing philosophical viewpoints on euthanasia.

Last Acts. "Means to a Better End: A Report on Dying in America Today." Robert Wood Johnson Foundation. Available online. URL: http://www. rwjf.org/files/publications/other/meansbetterend.pdf. Posted in November 2002. A state-by-state study concludes that no state offers more than mediocre end-of-life care.

Lorenz, Karl, and Joanne Lynn. "End-of-Life Care and Outcomes." Agency for Healthcare Research and Quality, U.S. Department of Health and Human Services. Available online. URL: http://www.ahrq.gov/downloads/ pub/evidence/pdf/eolcare/eolcare.pdf. Posted in December 2004. This is a report on attempts to answer key questions about end-of-life care by means of a comprehensive search of the medical literature. The authors found that satisfaction and quality of care were associated with pain management, communication, practical support, and enhanced caregiving. They offer recommendations for future research.

Marker, Rita L. "Assisted Suicide and Death with Dignity: Past, Present, and Future." International Task Force on Euthanasia and Assisted Suicide. Available online. URL: http://www.internationaltaskforce.org/ rpt2005_TOC.htm. Last updated in 2005. This report covers U.S. right-to-die organizations, public opinion, assisted suicide in Oregon, and euthanasia and assisted suicide in Australia, the Netherlands, Belgium, and other countries. The article is found on the site of a group that opposes euthanasia and assisted suicide.

National Consensus Project for Quality Palliative Care. "Clinical Practice Guidelines for Quality Palliative Care." American Academy of Hospice and Palliative Medicine. Available online. URL: http://www.aahpm.org/ NCPguidelines.pdf. Accessed on February 8, 2006. This article describes core levels of palliative care, the need for expansion of palliative care services, and physical, psychological, social, and legal aspects of palliative care.

National Public Radio. "The End of Life: Exploring Death in America." Available online. URL: http://www.npr.org/programs/death. Posted in 1998. This series of 20 radio broadcasts made in 1997 and 1998 discusses death-related topics including palliative medicine, the double effect, doctors and death, suicide, and do-not-resuscitate orders. The web site includes transcripts, resources, and bibliography.

New York State Task Force on Life and the Law. "When Death Is Sought: Assisted Suicide and Euthanasia in a Medical Context." New York State Department of Health. Available online. URL: http://www.health.state. ny.us/nysdoh/provider/death.htm. Last updated in 2001. This is a revision of an influential 1994 report, stressing the dangers that could accompany the legalization of assisted suicide. The site makes recommendations for public policy and medical standards.

Oregon Department of Human Services. "Eighth Annual Report on Oregon's Death with Dignity Act." Available online. URL: http://egov.oregon. gov/DHS/ph/pas/docs/year8.pdf. Posted on March 9, 2006. Summary and statistics about people who took advantage of the controversial law through 2005.

Pearlman, Robert A. "Advance Care Planning." University of Washington School of Medicine. Available online. URL: http://depts.washington. edu/bioethx/topics/adcare.html. Last updated on February 22, 1999. Pearlman discusses the goals of advance care planning, how advance care planning differs from advance directives, and how physicians can discuss this subject with patients and family members.

Physicians Committee for Responsible Medicine. "Physician-Assisted Suicide and Capital Punishment: What Role Should Physicians Play?" Available online. URL: http://www.pcrm.org/resources/education/ society/society4.html. Accessed on February 16, 2006. This article briefly reviews arguments for and against physician participation in suicide of terminally or incurably ill people and presents three vignettes for consideration.

Pitre, Thomas M., N. Gregory Hamilton, and William Toffler. "Lessons from Oregon." Physicians for Compassionate Care Educational Foundation. Available online. URL: http://www.pccef.org/articles/art29Lessons-FromOregon.htm. Posted in 2004. This article focuses on what authors see as the dangers of legalized assisted suicide in Oregon.

Public Agenda. "Right to Die." Available online. URL: http://www.public-agenda.org/issues/frontdoor.cfm?issue_type=right2die. Posted in 2005. This issue guide includes an overview, fact file, discussion guides, quick takes, sources and resources, people's chief concerns, bills and proposals, red flags, polling organizations, and selection criteria.

Public Broadcasting System. "Before I Die." Thirteen (WNET New York). Available online. URL: http://www.thirteen.org/bid. Posted on April 22, 1997. This Public Broadcasting System (PBS) television special explores the medical, ethical, and social issues surrounding end-of-life care in the United States. Web site includes transcript and additional material by health writer Janet Firshein.

Sacred Congregation for the Doctrine of the Faith. "Declaration on Euthanasia." Catholic Information Network. Available online. URL: http://www.cin.org/vatcong/euthanas.html. Posted on May 5, 1980. This is the text of an important statement of Catholic doctrine, opposing euthanasia.

Sandeen, Peg. "Supreme Court Rules 6-3 in Favor of Oregon's Landmark Law." Death with Dignity National Center. Available online. URL: http://www.deathwithdignity.org/historyfacts/gonzalesvoregon.asp. Posted on January 17, 2006. The head of a group that supports the Oregon law permitting physician-assisted suicide comments on the Supreme Court's 2006 *Gonzales v. Oregon* ruling.

Schneiderman, Lawrence, and Sue Rubin. "Medical Futility and Non-Beneficial Treatments." San Diego Hospice. Available online. URL: http://ethics.sandiego.edu/video/Hospice/Futility/index.html. Posted on March 21, 2001. This is the video of a question-and-answer session at a conference on medical ethics and the humanities in end-of-life care.

Standing Senate Committee on Social Affairs, Science and Technology. "Quality End-of-Life Care: The Right of Every Canadian." Canadian Parliament. Available online. URL: http://www.parl.gc.ca/36/2/parlbus/commbus/senate/com-e/upda-e/rep-e/repfinjun00-e.htm. Posted in June 2000. Updates a 1995 report, "Of Life and Death." The site evaluates progress made by 2000 in fulfilling the recommendations of the earlier report and makes further recommendations. It discusses the need for a national strategy on end-of-life care.

Stevens, Kenneth R. "The Consequences of Physician-Assisted Suicide Legalizaton." Physicians for Compassionate Care Educational Foundation. Available online. URL: http://www.pccef.org/articles/art42UofO.htm. Posted on October 11, 2005. Stevens criticizes the concept of assisted suicide and its implementation in Oregon.

Tonelli, Mark R. "Advance Directives." University of Washington School of Medicine. Available online. URL: http://depts.washington.edu/bioethx/topics/advdir.html. Last updated on February 22, 1999. Tonelli discusses what types of advance health care directives are available, why they are important in medical care, their legal status, and how to talk about them with patients and family members.

United Nations Human Rights Committee. "Concluding Observations of the Human Rights Committee: Netherlands." Available online. URL: http://www.unhchr.ch/tbs/doc.nsf/0/dbab71d01e02db11c1256a950041d732?OpenDocument&Highlight=0,euthanasia. Posted on August 27, 2001. This article expresses numerous concerns about recent changes in Netherlands law explicitly permitting euthanasia, including the killing of handicapped newborns by medical personnel and allowing minors to request euthanasia.

Young, Robert. "Voluntary Euthanasia." Stanford Encyclopedia of Philosophy. Available online. URL: http://plato.stanford.edu/entries/euthanasia-voluntary. Updated in 2002. Young presents conditions for candidacy for voluntary euthanasia, moral cases for and against voluntary euthanasia, and bibliography and resources.

CHAPTER 8

ORGANIZATIONS AND AGENCIES

The following entries include organizations, both in the United States and abroad, that are devoted to furthering or blocking physician-assisted suicide and/or euthanasia; organizations that take a position for or against these activities as part of a larger purpose; and organizations devoted to or taking part in related activities, such as hospice/end-of-life care or distribution and promotion of advance health care directives. In keeping with the widespread use of the Internet and e-mail, the web site (URL) address and e-mail address are given first when available, followed by phone number and postal address.

American Academy of Hospice and Palliative Medicine
URL: http://www.aahpm.org
E-mail: aahpm@aahpm.org
Phone: (847) 375-4712
4700 W. Lake Avenue
Glenview, IL 60025
International organization of physicians dedicated to the advancement of palliative care of patients with terminal illness.

American Civil Liberties Union (ACLU)
URL: http://www.aclu.org
Phone: (212) 549-2585
125 Broad Street
18th Floor
New York, NY 10004
Supports people's right to make choices about their lives. Has sup-

ported challenges to laws against assisted suicide.

American Foundation for Suicide Prevention
URL: http://www.afsp.org
E-mail: inquiry@afsp.org
Phone: (888) 333-AFSP
120 Wall Street
22nd Floor
New York, NY 10005
Supports research and education on depression and suicide; opposes legalization of physician-assisted suicide.

American Geriatrics Society
URL: http://www. americangeriatrics.org
E-mail: info@americangeriatrics. org

Phone: (212) 308-1414
The Empire State Building
350 Fifth Avenue
Suite 801
New York, NY 10118
This is an organization of health care providers dedicated to improving the health and well-being of older adults. The group opposes physician participation in suicide or euthanasia but accepts aggressive palliative care that may shorten life.

American Life League
URL: http://www.all.org
Phone: (540) 659-4171
P.O. Box 1350
Stafford, VA 22555
Believes that all human life is sacred and opposes legalization of euthanasia.

American Medical Association
 (AMA)
URL: http://www.ama-assn.org
Phone: (800) 621-8335
515 N. State Street
Chicago, IL 60610
The AMA opposes physician-assisted suicide and euthanasia for terminally ill people and supports improvement in palliative care.

American Nurses Association
 (ANA)
URL: http://www.nursingworld.
 org
Phone: (800) 274-4262
8515 Georgia Avenue
Suite 400
Silver Spring, MD 20910

The ANA, the largest professional organization representing registered nurses in the United States, opposes physician-assisted suicide and euthanasia.

American Pain Foundation
URL: http://www.
 painfoundation.org
E-mail: info@painfoundation.org
Phone: (888) 615-7246
201 North Charles Street
Suite 710
Baltimore, MD 21201-4111
The foundation tries to improve the quality of life of people with pain by raising public awareness, providing practical information, promoting research, and advocating to increase access to effective pain management.

Americans Disabled for
 Attendant Programs Today
 (ADAPT)
URL: http://www.adapt.org
E-mail: adapt@adapt.org
Phone: (303) 733-9324
201 South Cherokee
Denver, CO 80223
The group works to obtain attendant care and other support that will allow disabled people to live productively in their communities, as an alternative to nursing home confinement or euthanasia/assisted suicide.

Americans for Better Care of
 the Dying
URL: http://www.abcd-caring.org

E-mail: info@abcd-caring.org
Phone: (703) 647-8505
1700 Diagonal Road
Suite 635
Alexandria, VA 22314
Dedicated to social, professional, and policy reform to improve the care system for patients with serious or terminal illness so that they can live meaningfully until death.

American Society of Law, Medicine, and Ethics
URL: http://www.aslme.org
E-mail: info@aslme.org
Phone: (617) 262-4990
765 Commonwealth Avenue
Suite 1634
Boston, MA 02215
Acts as a forum for discussion of issues including euthanasia and assisted suicide.

Americans United for Life
URL: http://www.unitedforlife.org
E-mail: info@aul.org
Phone: (312) 492-7234
310 South Peoria
Suite 300
Chicago, IL 60607
Works to promote awareness of the sacredness of all life, including the lives of newborns, the elderly, and comatose patients. Lobbies against legalization of euthanasia.

Association for Death Education and Counseling
URL: http://www.adec.org
E-mail: info@adec.org
Phone: (847) 509-0403
60 Revere Drive
Suite 500
Northbrook, IL 60062
Dedicated to improving the quality of death education and death-related counseling and caregiving.

The Association for Persons with Severe Handicaps (TASH)
URL: http://www.tash.org
Phone: 410-828-8274
29 W. Susquehanna Avenue
Suite 210
Baltimore, MD 21204
International association of people with disabilities, their family members, and advocates fighting to achieve full inclusion of all people in all aspects of society. Opposes withholding nutrition and hydration from disabled infants or incapacitated adults on the basis of surrogates' "substituted judgment."

Canadian Physicians for Life
URL: http://www.physiciansforlife.ca
E-mail: info@physiciansforlife.ca
Phone: (613) 728-5433
P.O. Box 1289
Ottawa, ON K0A 2Z0
Canada
Dedicated to the respect and ethical treatment of every human being, regardless of age or infirmity. Opposes physician-assisted suicide.

Center for Practical Bioethics
URL: http://www.
practicalbioethics.org
E-mail: bioethic@
practicalbioethics.org
Phone: (800) 344-3829
Herzfeld Building
11 Main Street
Suite 500
Kansas City, MO 64105-2116
The Center raises questions on and responds to ethical issues in health and health care, including end-of-life decisions and pain management. It helps patients and families, healthcare professionals, policymakers, and corporate leaders develop reasoned, real-world responses to complex ethical issues.

Compassion and Choices
URL: http://www.
compassionandchoices.org
E-mail: info@
compassionandchoices.org
Phone: (800) 247-7421
P.O. Box 101810
Denver, CO 80250-1810
Formed by the merger of Compassion in Dying and End-of-Life Choices (formerly the Hemlock Society) in January 2005, Compassion and Choices works to improve care and expand choice at the end of life. The group aggressively pursues legal reform to promote pain care, make advance directives more enforceable, and legalize physician aid in dying.

Compassionate Healthcare
Network
URL: http://www.
chninternational.com

E-mail: chn@intergate.ca/
Phone: (604) 582-3844
11563 Bailey Crescent
Surrey, BC V3V 2V4
Canada
Opposes euthanasia and assisted suicide and favors advance directives and improvement in palliative care.

Death with Dignity National
Center
URL: http://www.
deathwithdignity.org
Phone: (503) 228-4415
520 SW 6th Avenue
Suite 1030
Portland, OR 97204
Promotes a comprehensive, humane response system of care for terminally ill patients and works to increase such patients' choices and autonomy. Serves as an information resource on right-to-die issues.

Dignitas
URL: http://www.dignitas.ch
E-mail: dignitas@dignitas.ch
Phone: (+41) 44 980 44 59
Postfach 9
CH 8127 Forch
Switzerland
Dignitas, headquartered in Zurich, helps to set up suicides of members (including non-Swiss members willing to travel to Switzerland) who are incurably ill and wish to die. Such action is legal in Switzerland.

Dignity in Dying
URL: http://www.
dignityindying.org.uk

E-mail: info@dignityindying.org.
uk
Phone: (0870) 777 7868
13 Prince of Wales Terrace
London W8 5PG
United Kingdom
Formerly called the British Voluntary Euthanasia Society, this group campaigns for wider choices at the end of life, including legalization of assisted dying for competent, incurably ill adults who request it. The organization also distributes advance directives.

Disability Awareness in Action
URL: http://www.daa.org.uk
E-mail: info@daa.org.uk
46 The Parklands
Hullavington, Wiltshire
SN14 6DL
United Kingdom
Phone: + 44 (0) 1666 837 671
International human rights network run for and by disabled people, focusing on disabled people in developing countries. The group publishes resource kits and a monthly newsletter, the *Disability Tribune*.

**Disability Rights Education and
Defense Fund**
URL: http://www.dredf.org
E-mail: dredf@dredf.org
Phone: (800) 348-4232
2212 Sixth Street
Berkeley, CA 94710
Works to further the civil rights and liberties of disabled people through legislation, litigation, advocacy, technical assistance, and education. Opposes euthanasia of disabled infants.

**Dutch Voluntary Euthanasia
Society**
(Nederlandse Vereniging
vooreen Vrijwillige
Levenseinde, NVVE)
URL: http://www.
nvve.nl/nvve/home.
asp?pagnaam=homepage
Phone: (+31) 0900-6060606
Postbus 75331
1070 AH Amsterdam
The Netherlands
The society aims for social acceptance of a broad range of free choices at the end of life, including assisted suicide and voluntary euthanasia.

Dying with Dignity
URL: http://www.
dyingwithdignity.ca
E-mail: info@dyingwithdignity.
ca
Phone: (800) 495-6156
55 Eglinton Avenue East
Suite 802
Toronto, Ontario M4P 1G8
Canada
Canadian organization concerned with the quality of dying. Advises patients about their right to choose health care options at the end of life and provides advocacy if needed; distributes advance health care directives; works for legal changes to support advance directives and permit voluntary, physician-assisted dying.

**European Association of
Palliative Care**
URL: http://www.eapcnet.org
Phone: (+39) 02 2390 3390

c/o National Cancer Institute
Milano
Via Venezian 1
20133 Milano
Italy
Aims to promote palliative care in Europe and to act as a focus for all those who work, or have an interest, in the field of palliative care at the scientific, clinical, and social levels.

Euthanasia Prevention Coalition BC
URL: http://www.epc.bc.ca
E-mail: info@epc.bc.ca
Phone: (604) 794-3772
103-1075 Marine Drive
Suite 126
North Vancouver, BC
V7P 3T6
Canada
Opposes legalization or promotion of euthanasia and assisted suicide. Believes euthanasia to be murder, even if the person consents to or requests the action. Advises on alternative methods of relieving suffering.

Euthanasia Research and Guidance Organization (ERGO)
URL: http://www.finalexit.org
E-mail: ergo@efn.org
Phone: (541) 998-1873
24829 Norris Lane
Junction City, OR 97448-9559
Advises terminally ill people and their families about euthanasia. Supports choice and, if necessary, aid in dying. Founded by Derek Humphry.

Focus on the Family
URL: http://www.family.org
Phone: (800) 232-6459
[no street address required]
Colorado Springs, CO 80995
Pro-life organization that strongly opposes assisted suicide and euthanasia.

Growth House, Inc.
URL: http:// www.growthhouse. org
E-mail: info@growthhouse.org
Phone: (415) 863-3045
Works to improve the quality of compassionate care for the dying as an alternative to assisted suicide or euthanasia.

Hastings Center
URL: http://www. thehastingscenter.org
E-mail: mail@thehastingscenter. org
Phone: (845) 424-4040
21 Malcolm Gordon Road
Garrison, NY 10524-4125
Addresses fundamental ethical issues in health, medicine, and the environment, including euthanasia and physician-assisted suicide.

Hospice Education Institute
URL: http://www.hospiceworld. org
E-mail: info@hospiceworld.org
Phone: (207) 255-8800
3 Unity Square
P.O. Box 98
Machiasport, MN 04655-0098
Teaches health care professionals and the public about hospice care

and pain control for the terminally ill and works to improve end-of-life care.

Hospice Foundation of America
URL: http://www.
 hospicefoundation.org
E-mail: info@hospicefoundation.
 org
Phone: (800) 854-3402
1621 Connecticut Avenue, NW
Suite 300
Washington, DC 20009
The foundation conducts programs of professional development, public education, and research, and provides information and publications on health policy issues. Programs for the public assist individual consumers of health care who are coping with issues related to caregiving, terminal illness, and grief.

Human Life International
URL: http://www.hli.org
E-mail: hli@hli.org
Phone (800) 549-5433
4 Family Life Lane
Front Royal, VA 22630
Believes that euthanasia and assisted suicide are morally unacceptable.

HumanLifeMatters
URL: http://www.
 humanlifematters.com
E-mail: humanlifematters@shaw.
 ca
Phone: (780) 929-9231
4417 51 Street
Beaumont, AB T4X 1C8
Canada

This ministry for helping local churches effectively integrate people with disabilities provides information about disability rights and end-of-life issues, including assisted suicide and euthanasia, which the group opposes.

**International Task Force on
 Euthanasia and Assisted
 Suicide**
URL: http://
 internationaltaskforce.org
Phone: (740) 282-3810
P.O. Box 760
Steubenville, OH 43952
Opposes all forms of euthanasia and tries to influence the public, legislators, and the courts to ban them.

Jews for Life
URL: http://www.jewsforlife.org
This group believes that the current "pro-choice" position of mainstream liberal Jewish organizations is antithetical to traditional Jewish teachings. Opposes euthanasia.

Living/Dying Project
URL: http://www.livingdying.
 org
E-mail: info@livingdying.org
Phone: (415) 456-3915
P.O. Box 357
Fairfax, CA 94978-0357
This group offers spiritual support for people facing life-threatening illness and those who care for them, as well as educational services for health care providers and the general public.

National Council for Palliative
  Care
URL: http://www.ncpc.org.uk
E-mail: enquiries@ncpc.org.uk
Phone: (020) 7697 1520
The Fitzpatrick Building
188-194 York Way
London N7 9AS
United Kingdom
This is an umbrella organization for all those involved in providing, commissioning, and using hospice and palliative care services in England, Wales, and Northern Ireland. Publishes a bimonthly magazine, a monthly e-mail briefing, and regular topical briefing bulletins and publications.

National Council on Disability
URL: http://www.ncd.gov
E-mail: ncd@ncd.gov
Phone: (202) 272-2004
1331 F Street, NW
Suite 850
Washington, DC 20004
This is an independent federal agency making recommendations to the president and Congress to enhance the quality of life for all Americans with disabilities and their families.

National Hospice and Palliative
  Care Organization
URL: http://www.nho.org/
  templates/1/homepage.cfm
E-mail: nhpco_info@nhpco.org
Phone: (703) 837-1500
1700 Diagonal Road
Suite 625
Alexandria, VA 22314

Dedicated to promoting and maintaining quality care for terminally ill people and their families and to making hospice an integral part of the health care system in the United States.

National Right to Life
  Committee
URL: http://www.nrlc.org
E-mail: nrlc@nrlc.org
Phone: (202) 626-8800
512 Tenth Street, NW
Washington, DC 20004
Opposes euthanasia and physician-assisted suicide.

Not Dead Yet
URL: http://www.notdeadyet.
  org
E-mail: ndycoleman@aol.com
Phone: (708) 209-1500
7521 Madison Street
Forest Park, IL 60130
National grassroots disability rights organization that opposes legalization of physician-assisted suicide and euthanasia because it believes such a move presents great risks to disabled and chronically ill people.

Ohio Right to Life Society
URL: http://www.ohiolife.org
E-mail: life@ohiolife.org
Phone: (614) 864-5200
2238 S. Hamilton Road
Suite 200
Columbus, OH 43232-2000
Opposes all forms of euthanasia as violations of the sanctity of life.

Park Ridge Center for Health, Faith, and Ethics
URL: http://www.
parkridgecenter.org
Phone: (837) 384-3507
205 West Touhy Avenue
Suite 203
Park Ridge, IL 60068-4202
Explores the relationship between religious faith, ethics, and health care. Facilitates debate on topics such as euthanasia and physician-assisted suicide.

Physicians for Compassionate Care Educational Foundation (PCCEF)
URL: http://www.pccef.org
Phone: (503) 533-8154
P.O. Box 6042
Portland, OR 97228-6042
The PCCEF affirms an ethic based on the principle that all human life is inherently valuable and that the physician's roles are to heal illness, alleviate suffering, and provide comfort for the sick and dying. The organization opposes physician assistance in suicide.

ProLife Alliance
URL: http://www.prolife.org.uk
E-mail: info@prolife.org.uk
Phone: (020) 7581-6939
P.O. Box 13395
London SW3 6XE
United Kingdom
This group strongly opposes any form of euthanasia or assisted suicide, including discontinuation of artificially provided food and fluids. Accepts discontinuation of burdensome medical treatment and use of pain medication in line with the principle of "double effect," however.

Right to Die Society of Canada
URL: http://www.righttodie.ca
E-mail: contact-rtd@righttodie.ca
Phone: (416) 535-0690
145 Macdonell Avenue
Toronto, ON M6R 2A4
Canada
Respects the right of any mature person who is chronically or terminally ill to choose the time, place, and manner of his or her death. Helps patients through the dying process.

Supportive Care Coalition
URL: http://www.
supportivecarecoalition.org
Phone: (503) 215-5053
c/o Providence Health and Services
4805 NE Glisan Street
Suite 2E07
Portland, OR 97213-2933
A coalition of Catholic health care providers and service organizations dedicated to promoting cultural change that embraces supportive care, compassionate relief of suffering and pain, and symptom management for helping people living with life-threatening illness.

World Federation of Right to Die Societies
URL: http://www.finalexit.org/world.fed.html
E-mail: ergo@efn.org

Phone: (541) 998-1873
c/o ERGO
24829 Norris Lane
Junction City, OR 97448-9559
Group of societies in different countries that support the right of the terminally ill to choose the time and manner of their death.

World Institute on Disability
URL: http://www.wid.org

E-mail: wid@wid.org
Phone: (510) 763-4100
510 16th Street
Suite 100
Oakland, CA 94612
A nonprofit research, training, and public policy center promoting the civil rights and full societal inclusion of people with disabilities.

PART III

APPENDICES

APPENDIX A

U.S. SUPREME COURT RULING: *CRUZAN V. DIRECTOR, MISSOURI DEPARTMENT OF HEALTH* 497 U.S. 261 (1990)

[Extract. Footnotes and most case citations omitted]
Chief Justice Rehnquist delivered the opinion of the Court. . . .
[review of facts of the case omitted]
We granted certiorari to consider the question of whether Cruzan has a right under the United States Constitution which would require the hospital to withdraw life-sustaining treatment from her under these circumstances.

At common law, even the touching of one person by another without consent and without legal justification was a battery. Before the turn of the century, this Court observed that "[n]o right is held more sacred, or is more carefully guarded, by the common law, than the right of every individual to the possession and control of his own person, free from all restraint or interference of others, unless by clear and unquestionable authority of law." *Union Pacific R. Co. v. Botsford*, 141 U.S. 250, 251 (1891). This notion of bodily integrity has been embodied in the requirement that informed consent is generally required for medical treatment. Justice Cardozo, while on the Court of Appeals of New York, aptly described this doctrine: "Every human being of adult years and sound mind has a right to determine what shall be done with his own body; and a surgeon who performs an operation without his patient's consent commits an assault, for which he is liable in damages." *Schloendorff v. Society of New York Hospital*, 211 N.Y. 125, 12930, 105 N.E. 92, 93 (1914). The informed consent doctrine has become firmly entrenched in American tort law.

The logical corollary of the doctrine of informed consent is that the patient generally possesses the right not to consent, that is, to refuse treatment. Until about 15 years ago and the seminal decision in *In re Quinlan*, 70 N.J. 10, 355 A. 2d 647, cert. denied sub nom., *Garger v. New Jersey*, 429 U.S. 922 (1976), the number of right-to-refuse-treatment decisions were relatively few. Most of the earlier cases involved patients who refused medical treatment forbidden by their religious beliefs, thus implicating First Amendment rights as well as common law rights of self-determination. More recently, however, with the advance of medical technology capable of sustaining life well past the point where natural forces would have brought certain death in earlier times, cases involving the right to refuse life-sustaining treatment have burgeoned.

In the Quinlan case, young Karen Quinlan suffered severe brain damage as the result of anoxia, and entered a persistent vegetative state. Karen's father sought judicial approval to disconnect his daughter's respirator. The New Jersey Supreme Court granted the relief, holding that Karen had a right of privacy grounded in the Federal Constitution to terminate treatment. Recognizing that this right was not absolute, however, the court balanced it against asserted state interests. Noting that "the State's interest weakens and the individual's right to privacy grows as the degree of bodily invasion increases and the prognosis dims," the court concluded that the state interests had to give way in that case. The court also concluded that the "only practical way" to prevent the loss of Karen's privacy right due to her incompetence was to allow her guardian and family to decide "whether she would exercise it in these circumstances."

After *Quinlan*, however, most courts have based a right to refuse treatment either solely on the common law right to informed consent or on both the common law right and a constitutional privacy right. In *Superintendent of Belchertown State School v. Saikewicz*, 373 Mass. 728, 370 N.E. 2d 417 (1977), the Supreme Judicial Court of Massachusetts relied on both the right of privacy and the right of informed consent to permit the withholding of chemotherapy from a profoundly-retarded 67-year-old man suffering from leukemia. Reasoning that an incompetent person retains the same rights as a competent individual "because the value of human dignity extends to both," the court adopted a "substituted judgment" standard whereby courts were to determine what an incompetent individual's decision would have been under the circumstances. Distilling certain state interests from prior case law—the preservation of life, the protection of the interests of innocent third parties, the prevention of suicide, and the maintenance of the ethical integrity of the medical profession—the court recognized the first interest as paramount and noted it was greatest when an affliction was curable, "as opposed to the State interest where, as here, the issue is not whether, but when, for how long, and at what cost to the individual [a] life may be briefly extended."

In *In re Storar* 52 N.Y. 2d 363, 420 N.E. 2d 64, cert. denied, 454 U.S. 858 (1981), the New York Court of Appeals declined to base a right to refuse treatment on a constitutional privacy right. Instead, it found such a right "adequately supported" by the informed consent doctrine. . . . In the . . . Storar case, a 52-year-old man suffering from bladder cancer had been profoundly retarded during most of his life. Implicitly rejecting the approach taken in *Saikewicz*, the court reasoned that due to such life-long incompetency, "it is unrealistic to attempt to determine whether he would want to continue potentially life prolonging treatment if he were competent." As the evidence showed that the patient's required blood transfusions did not involve excessive pain and without them his mental and physical abilities would deteriorate, the court concluded that it should not "allow an incompetent patient to bleed to death because someone, even someone as close as a parent or sibling, feels that this is best for one with an incurable disease."

Many of the later cases build on the principles established in *Quinlan*, *Saikewicz* and *Storar/Eichner*. For instance, in *In re Conroy*, 98 N.J. 321, 486 A. 2d 1209 (1985), the same court that decided Quinlan considered whether a nasogastric feeding tube could be removed from an 84-year-old incompetent nursing-home resident suffering irreversible mental and physical ailments. While recognizing that a federal right of privacy might apply in the case, the court, contrary to its approach in *Quinlan*, decided to base its decision on the common-law right to self-determination and informed consent.

On balance, the right to self-determination ordinarily outweighs any countervailing state interests, and competent persons generally are permitted to refuse medical treatment, even at the risk of death. Most of the cases that have held otherwise, unless they involved the interest in protecting innocent third parties, have concerned the patient's competency to make a rational and considered choice.

Reasoning that the right of self-determination should not be lost merely because an individual is unable to sense a violation of it, the court held that incompetent individuals retain a right to refuse treatment. It also held that such a right could be exercised by a surrogate decisionmaker using a "subjective" standard when there was clear evidence that the incompetent person would have exercised it. Where such evidence was lacking, the court held that an individual's right could still be invoked in certain circumstances under objective "best interest" standards. Thus, if some trustworthy evidence existed that the individual would have wanted to terminate treatment, but not enough to clearly establish a person's wishes for purposes of the subjective standard, and the burden of a prolonged life from the experience of pain and suffering markedly outweighed its satisfactions, treatment could be terminated under a "limited-objective" standard. Where no trustworthy evidence existed, and a person's suffering would make the administration of life-sustaining treatment inhumane, a "pure-objective" standard could be used to terminate treatment. If none of these conditions obtained, the court held it was best to err in favor of preserving life.

The court also rejected certain categorical distinctions that had been drawn in prior refusal-of-treatment cases as lacking substance for decision purposes: the distinction between actively hastening death by terminating treatment and passively allowing a person to die of a disease; between treating individuals as an initial matter versus withdrawing treatment afterwards; between ordinary versus extraordinary treatment; and between treatment by artificial feeding versus other forms of life-sustaining medical procedures. As to the last item, the court acknowledged the "emotional significance" of food, but noted that feeding by implanted tubes is a "medical procedur[e] with inherent risks and possible side effects, instituted by skilled health-care providers to compensate for impaired physical functioning" which analytically was equivalent to artificial breathing using a respirator.

In contrast to *Conroy*, the Court of Appeals of New York recently refused to accept less than the clearly expressed wishes of a patient before permitting the exercise of her right to refuse treatment by a surrogate decisionmaker. *In re Westchester County Medical Center on behalf of O'Connor*, 531 N.E. 2d 607 (1988) (O'Connor). There, the court, over the objection of the patient's family members, granted an order to insert a feeding tube into a 77-year-old woman rendered incompetent as a result of several strokes. While continuing to recognize a common-law right to refuse treatment, the court rejected the substituted judgment approach for asserting it

> *because it is inconsistent with our fundamental commitment to the notion that no person or court should substitute its judgment as to what would be an acceptable quality of life for another. Consequently, we adhere to the view that, despite its pitfalls and inevitable uncertainties, the inquiry must always be narrowed to the patient's expressed intent, with every effort made to minimize the opportunity for error.*

The court held that the record lacked the requisite clear and convincing evidence of the patient's expressed intent to withhold life-sustaining treatment. . . .

[additional cases omitted]

Appendix A

As these cases demonstrate, the common-law doctrine of informed consent is viewed as generally encompassing the right of a competent individual to refuse medical treatment. Beyond that, these decisions demonstrate both similarity and diversity in their approach to decision of what all agree is a perplexing question with unusually strong moral and ethical overtones. State courts have available to them for decision a number of sources—state constitutions, statutes, and common law—which are not available to us. In this Court, the question is simply and starkly whether the United States Constitution prohibits Missouri from choosing the rule of decision which it did. This is the first case in which we have been squarely presented with the issue of whether the United States Constitution grants what is in common parlance referred to as a "right to die." We follow the judicious counsel of our decision in *Twin City Bank v. Nebeker*, 167 U.S. 196, 202 (1897), where we said that in deciding "a question of such magnitude and importance . . . it is the [better] part of wisdom not to attempt, by any general statement, to cover every possible phase of the subject."

The Fourteenth Amendment provides that no State shall "deprive any person of life, liberty, or property, without due process of law." The principle that a competent person has a constitutionally protected liberty interest in refusing unwanted medical treatment may be inferred from our prior decisions. In *Jacobson v. Massachusetts*, 197 U.S. 11, 2430 (1905), for instance, the Court balanced an individual's liberty interest in declining an unwanted smallpox vaccine against the State's interest in preventing disease. Decisions prior to the incorporation of the Fourth Amendment into the Fourteenth Amendment analyzed searches and seizures involving the body under the Due Process Clause and were thought to implicate substantial liberty interests. . . .

Just this Term, in the course of holding that a State's procedures for administering antipsychotic medication to prisoners were sufficient to satisfy due process concerns, we recognized that prisoners possess "a significant liberty interest in avoiding the unwanted administration of antipsychotic drugs under the Due Process Clause of the Fourteenth Amendment." *Washington v. Harper*, U.S., (1990) . . . Still other cases support the recognition of a general liberty interest in refusing medical treatment. . . .

But determining that a person has a "liberty interest" under the Due Process Clause does not end the inquiry; "whether respondent's constitutional rights have been violated must be determined by balancing his liberty interests against the relevant state interests." *Youngberg v. Romeo*, 457 U.S. 307, 321 (1982). . . .

Petitioners insist that under the general holdings of our cases, the forced administration of life-sustaining medical treatment, and even of artificially-delivered food and water essential to life, would implicate a competent person's liberty interest. Although we think the logic of the cases discussed above would embrace such a liberty interest, the dramatic consequences involved in refusal of such treatment would inform the inquiry as to whether the deprivation of that interest is constitutionally permissible. But for purposes of this case, we assume that the United States Constitution would grant a competent person a constitutionally protected right to refuse life-saving hydration and nutrition.

Petitioners go on to assert that an incompetent person should possess the same right in this respect as is possessed by a competent person. . . .

The difficulty with petitioners' claim is that in a sense it begs the question: an incompetent person is not able to make an informed and voluntary choice to exercise a hypothetical right to refuse treatment or any other right. Such a "right" must be exercised for her, if at all, by some sort of surrogate. Here, Missouri has in effect recognized that under certain circumstances a surrogate may act for the patient in electing to have hydration and nutrition withdrawn in such a way as to cause death, but it has established a procedural safeguard to assure that the action of the surrogate conforms as best it may to the wishes expressed by the patient while competent. Missouri requires that evidence of the incompetent's wishes as to the withdrawal of treatment be proved by clear and convincing evidence. The question, then, is whether the United States Constitution forbids the establishment of this procedural requirement by the State. We hold that it does not.

Whether or not Missouri's clear and convincing evidence requirement comports with the United States Constitution depends in part on what interests the State may properly seek to protect in this situation. Missouri relies on its interest in the protection and preservation of human life, and there can be no gainsaying this interest. As a general matter, the States—indeed, all civilized nations—demonstrate their commitment to life by treating homicide as serious crime. Moreover, the majority of States in this country have laws imposing criminal penalties on one who assists another to commit suicide. We do not think a State is required to remain neutral in the face of an informed and voluntary decision by a physically-able adult to starve to death.

But in the context presented here, a State has more particular interests at stake. The choice between life and death is a deeply personal decision of obvious and overwhelming finality. We believe Missouri may legitimately seek to safeguard the personal element of this choice through the imposition of heightened evidentiary requirements. It cannot be disputed that the Due Process Clause protects an interest in life as well as an interest in refusing life-sustaining medical treatment. . . . A State is entitled to guard against potential abuses . . . [W]e [also] think a State may properly decline to make judgments about the "quality" of life that a particular individual may enjoy, and simply assert an unqualified interest in the preservation of human life to be weighed against the constitutionally protected interests of the individual.

In our view, Missouri has permissibly sought to advance these interests through the adoption of a "clear and convincing" standard of proof to govern such proceedings. . . . "This Court has mandated an intermediate standard of proof 'clear and convincing evidence' when the individual interests at stake in a state proceeding are both 'particularly important' and 'more substantial than mere loss of money.'" *Santosky v. Kramer*, 455 U.S. 745, 756 (1982). . . .

We think it self-evident that the interests at stake in the instant proceedings are more substantial, both on an individual and societal level, than those involved in a run-of-the-mine civil dispute. But not only does the standard of proof reflect the importance of a particular adjudication, it also serves as "a societal judgment about how the risk of error should be distributed between the litigants." *Santosky*, supra, 455 U.S. at 755. The more stringent the burden of proof a party must bear, the more that party bears the risk of an erroneous decision. We believe that Missouri may permissibly place an increased risk of an erroneous decision on those seeking to terminate an incompetent individual's life-sustaining treatment. . . . An erroneous decision to withdraw life-sustaining treatment . . . is not susceptible of correction. . . .

In sum, we conclude that a State may apply a clear and convincing evidence standard in proceedings where a guardian seeks to discontinue nutrition and hydration of a person diagnosed to be in a persistent vegetative state. We note that many courts which have adopted some sort of substituted judgment procedure in situations like this, whether they limit consideration of evidence to the prior expressed wishes of the incompetent individual, or whether they allow more general proof of what the individual's decision would have been, require a clear and convincing standard of proof for such evidence. . . .

The Supreme Court of Missouri held that in this case the testimony adduced at trial did not amount to clear and convincing proof of the patient's desire to have hydration and nutrition withdrawn. In so doing, it reversed a decision of the Missouri trial court which had found that the evidence "suggest[ed]" Nancy Cruzan would not have desired to continue such measures, but which had not adopted the standard of "clear and convincing evidence" enunciated by the Supreme Court. The testimony adduced at trial consisted primarily of Nancy Cruzan's statements made to a housemate about a year before her accident that she would not want to live should she face life as a "vegetable," and other observations to the same effect. The observations did not deal in terms with withdrawal of medical treatment or of hydration and nutrition. We cannot say that the Supreme Court of Missouri committed constitutional error in reaching the conclusion that it did. . . .

No doubt is engendered by anything in this record but that Nancy Cruzan's mother and father are loving and caring parents. If the State were required by the United States Constitution to repose a right of "substituted judgment" with anyone, the Cruzans would surely qualify. But we do not think the Due Process Clause requires the State to repose judgment on these matters with anyone but the patient herself. Close family members may have a strong feeling—a feeling not at all ignoble or unworthy, but not entirely disinterested, either—that they do not wish to witness the continuation of the life of a loved one which they regard as hopeless, meaningless, and even degrading. But there is no automatic assurance that the view of close family members will necessarily be the same as the patient's would have been had she been confronted with the prospect of her situation while competent. All of the reasons previously discussed for allowing Missouri to require clear and convincing evidence of the patient's wishes lead us to conclude that the State may choose to defer only to those wishes, rather than confide the decision to close family members.

The judgment of the Supreme Court of Missouri is Affirmed. [Notes omitted]

APPENDIX B

OREGON DEATH WITH DIGNITY ACT ORS 127.800–897, 1994

SECTION I

GENERAL PROVISIONS

1.01 Definitions The following words and phrases, whenever used in this Act, shall have the following meanings:

(1) "Adult" means an individual who is 18 years of age or older.

(2) "Attending physician" means the physician who has primary responsibility for the care of the patient and treatment of the patient's disease.

(3) "Consulting physician" means the physician who is qualified by specialty or experience to make a professional diagnosis and prognosis regarding the patient's disease.

(4) "Counseling" means a consultation between a state licensed psychiatrist or psychologist and a patient for the purpose of determining whether the patient is suffering from a psychiatric or psychological disorder, or depression causing impaired judgment.

(5) "Health care provider" means a person licensed, certified, or otherwise authorized or permitted by the law of this State to administer health care in the ordinary course of business or practice of a profession, and includes a health care facility.

(6) "Incapable" means that in the opinion of a court or in the opinion of the patient's attending physician or consulting physician, a patient lacks the ability to make and communicate health care decisions to health care providers, including communication through persons familiar with the patient's

manner of communicating if those persons are available. Capable means not incapable.

(7) "Informed decision" means a decision by a qualified patient, to request and obtain a prescription to end his or her life in a humane and dignified manner, that is based on an appreciation of the relevant facts and after being fully informed by the attending physician of:

(a) his or her medical diagnosis;

(b) his or her prognosis;

(c) the potential risks associated with taking the medication to be prescribed;

(d) the probable result of taking the medication to be prescribed;

(e) the feasible alternatives, including, but not limited to, comfort care, hospice care and pain control.

(8) "Medically confirmed" means the medical opinion of the attending physician has been confirmed by a consulting physician who has examined the patient and the patient's relevant medical records.

(9) "Patient" means a person who is under the care of a physician.

(10) "Physician" means a doctor of medicine or osteopathy licensed to practice medicine by the Board of Medical Examiners for the State of Oregon.

(11) "Qualified patient" means a capable adult who is a resident of Oregon and has satisfied the requirements of this Act in order to obtain a prescription for medication to end his or her life in a humane and dignified manner.

(12) "Terminal disease" means an incurable and irreversible disease that has been medically confirmed and will, within reasonable medical judgment, produce death within six (6) months.

SECTION 2

WRITTEN REQUEST FOR MEDICATION TO END ONE'S LIFE IN A HUMANE AND DIGNIFIED MANNER

2.01 Who may initiate a written request for medication

An adult who is capable, is a resident of Oregon, and has been determined by the attending physician and consulting physician to be suffering from a terminal disease, and who has voluntarily expressed his or her wish to die, may make a written request for medication for the purpose of ending his or her life in a humane and dignified manner in accordance with this Act.

2.02 Form of the written request

(1) A valid request for medication under this Act shall be in substantially the form described in Section 6 of this Act, signed and dated by the patient and witnessed by at least two individuals who, in the presence of the patient, attest that to the best of their knowledge and belief the patient is capable, acting voluntarily, and is not being coerced to sign the request.

(2) One of the witnesses shall be a person who is not:

(a) A relative of the patient by blood, marriage or adoption;

(b) A person who at the time the request is signed would be entitled to any portion of the estate of the qualified patient upon death under any will or by operation of law; or

(c) An owner, operator or employee of a health care facility where the qualified patient is receiving medical treatment or is a resident.

(3) The patient's attending physician at the time the request is signed shall not be a witness.

(4) If the patient is a patient in a long term care facility at the time the written request is made, one of the witnesses shall be an individual designated by the facility and having the qualifications specified by the Department of Human Resources by rule.

SECTION 3

SAFEGUARDS

3.01 attending physician responsibilities

The attending physician shall:

(1) Make the initial determination of whether a patient has a terminal disease, is capable, and has made the request voluntarily;

(2) Inform the patient of:

(a) his or her medical diagnosis;

(b) his or her prognosis;

(c) the potential risks associated with taking the medication to be prescribed;

(d) the probable result of taking the medication to be prescribed;

(e) the feasible alternatives, including, but not limited to, comfort care, hospice care and pain control.

(3) Refer the patient to a consulting physician for medical confirmation of the diagnosis, and for determination that the patient is capable and acting voluntarily;

(4) Refer the patient for counseling if appropriate pursuant to Section 3.03;

(5) Request that the patient notify next of kin;

(6) Inform the patient that he or she has an opportunity to rescind the request at any time and in any manner, and offer the patient an opportunity to rescind at the end of the 15 day waiting period pursuant to Section 3.06;

(7) Verify, immediately prior to writing the prescription for medication under this Act, that the patient is making an informed decision;

(8) Fulfill the medical record documentation requirements of Section 3.09;

(9) Ensure that all appropriate steps are carried out in accordance with this Act prior to writing a prescription for medication to enable a qualified patient to end his or her life in a humane and dignified manner.

3.02 Consulting Physician Confirmation

Before a patient is qualified under this Act, a consulting physician shall examine the patient and his or her relevant medical records and confirm, in writing, the attending physician's diagnosis that the patient is suffering from a terminal disease, and verify that the patient is capable, is acting voluntarily and has made an informed decision.

3.03 Counseling Referral

If in the opinion of the attending physician or the consulting physician a patient may be suffering from a psychiatric or psychological disorder, or depression causing impaired judgment, either physician shall refer the patient for counseling. No medication to end a patient's life in a humane and dignified manner shall be prescribed until the person performing the counseling determines that the person is not suffering from a psychiatric or psychological disorder, or depression causing impaired judgment.

3.04 Informed decision

No person shall receive a prescription for medication to end his or her life in a humane and dignified manner unless he or she has made an informed decision as defined in Section 1.01(7). Immediately prior to writing a prescription for medication under this Act, the attending physician shall verify that the patient is making an informed decision.

3.05 Family notification

The attending physician shall ask the patient to notify next of kin of his or her request for medication pursuant to this Act. A patient who declines or is unable to notify next of kin shall not have his or her request denied for that reason.

3.06 Written and oral requests

In order to receive a prescription for medication to end his or her life in a humane and dignified manner, a qualified patient shall have made an oral request and a written request, and reiterate the oral request to his or her attending physician no less than fifteen (15) days after making the initial oral request. At the time the qualified patient makes his or her second oral request, the attending physician shall offer the patient an opportunity to re-scind the request.

3.07 Right to rescind request

A patient may rescind his or her request at any time and in any manner without regard to his or her mental state. No prescription for medication under this Act may be written without the attending physician offering the qualified patient an opportunity to rescind the request.

3.08 Waiting periods

No less than fifteen (15) days shall elapse between the patient's initial and oral request and the writing of a prescription under this Act. No less than 48 hours shall elapse between the patient's written request and the writing of a prescription under this Act.

3.09 Medical record documentation requirements

The following shall be documented or filed in the patient's medical record:

(1) All oral requests by a patient for medication to end his or her life in a humane and dignified manner;

(2) All written requests by a patient for medication to end his or her life in a humane and dignified manner;

(3) The attending physician's diagnosis and prognosis, determination that the patient is capable, acting voluntarily and has made an informed decision.

(4) The consulting physician's diagnosis and prognosis, and verification that the patient is capable, acting voluntarily and has made an informed decision;

(5) A report of the outcome and determinations made during counseling, if performed;

(6) The attending physician's offer to the patient to rescind his or her request at the time of the patient's second oral request pursuant to Section 3.06; and

(7) A note by the attending physician indicating that all requirements under this Act have been met and indicating the steps taken to carry out the request, including a notation of the medication prescribed.

3.10 Residency requirements

Only requests made by Oregon residents, under this Act, shall be granted.

3.11 Reporting requirements

(1) The Health Division shall annually review a sample of records main-tained pursuant to this Act.

(2) The Health Division shall make rules to facilitate the collection of information regarding compliance with this Act. The information collected shall not be a public record and may not be made available for inspection by the public.

(3) The Health Division shall generate and make available to the public an annual statistical report of information collected under Section 3.11(2) of this Act.

3.12 Effect on construction of wills, contracts and statutes

(1) No provision in a contract, will or other agreement, whether written or oral, to the extent the provision would affect whether a person may make or rescind a request for medication to end his or her life in a humane and dignified manner, shall be valid.

(2) No obligation owing under any currently existing contract shall be conditioned or affected by the making or rescinding of a request, by a person, for medication to end his or her life in a humane and dignified manner.

3.13 Insurance or annuity policies

The sale, procurement, or issuance of any life, health, or accident insurance or annuity policy or the rate charged for any policy shall not be conditioned upon or affected by the making or rescinding of a request, by a person, for medication to end his or her life in a humane and dignified manner. Neither shall a qualified patient's act of ingesting medication to end his or her life in a humane and dignified manner have an effect upon a life, health, or accident insurance or annuity policy.

3.14 Construction of act

Nothing in this Act shall be construed to authorize a physician or any other person to end a patient's life by lethal injection, mercy killing or active euthanasia. Actions taken in accordance with this Act shall not, for any purpose, constitute suicide, assisted suicide, mercy killing or homicide, under the law.

SECTION 4

IMMUNITIES AND LIABILITIES

4.01 Immunities

Except as provided in Section 4.02:

(1) No person shall be subject to civil or criminal liability or professional disciplinary action for participating in good faith compliance with this Act. This includes being present when a qualified patient takes the prescribed medication to end his or her life in a humane and dignified manner.

(2) No professional organization or association, or health care provider, may subject a person to censure, discipline, suspension, loss of license, loss of privileges, loss of membership or other penalty for participating or refusing to participate in good faith compliance with this Act.

(3) No request by a patient for or provision by an attending physician of medication in good faith compliance with the provisions of this Act shall

constitute neglect for any purpose of law or provide the sole basis for the appointment of a guardian or conservator.

(4) No health care provider shall be under any duty, whether by contract, by statute or by any other legal requirement to participate in the provision to a qualified patient of medication to end his or her life in a humane and dignified manner. If a health care provider is unable or unwilling to carry out a patient's request, the health care provider shall transfer, upon request, a copy of the patient's relevant medical records to the new health care provider.

4.02 Liabilities

(1) A person who without authorization of the patient willfully alters or forges a request for medication or conceals or destroys a rescission of that request with the intent or effect of causing the patient's death shall be guilty of a Class A felony.

(2) A person who coerces or exerts undue influence on a patient to request medication for the purpose of ending the patient's life, or to destroy a rescission of such a request, shall be guilty of a Class A felony.

(3) Nothing in this Act limits further liability for civil damages resulting from other negligent conduct or intentional misconduct by any persons.

(4) The penalties in this Act do not preclude criminal penalties applicable under other law for conduct which is inconsistent with the provisions of this Act.

SECTION 5

SEVERABILITY

5.01 Severability

Any section of this Act being held invalid as to any person or circumstance shall not affect the application of any other section of this Act which can be given full effect without the invalid section or application.

SECTION 6

FORM OF THE REQUEST

6.01 Form of the request

A request for a medication as authorized by this Act shall be in substantially the following form:

REQUEST FOR MEDICATION TO END MY LIFE IN A HUMANE AND DIGNIFIED MANNER

I, _____, am an adult of sound mind.

I am suffering from _____, which my attending physician has determined is a terminal disease and which has been medically confirmed by a consulting physician.

I have been fully informed of my diagnosis, prognosis, the nature of medication to be prescribed and potential associated risks, the expected result, and the feasible alternatives, including comfort care, hospice care and pain control.

I request that my attending physician prescribe medication that will end my life in a humane and dignified manner.

INITIAL ONE:

___ I have informed my family of my decision and taken their opinions into consideration.

___ I have decided not to inform my family of my decision.

___ I have no family to inform of my decision.

I understand that I have the right to rescind this request at any time.

I understand the full import of this request and I expect to die when I take the medication to be prescribed.

I make this request voluntarily and without reservation, and I accept full moral responsibility for my actions.

Signed:_____

Dated: _____

DECLARATION OF WITNESSES

We declare that the person signing this request:

(a) Is personally known to us or has provided proof of identity;

(b) Signed this request in our presence;

(c) Appears to be of sound mind and not under duress, fraud or undue influence;

(d) Is not a patient for whom either of us is attending physician.

_____ Witness 1/

Date

_____ Witness 2/

Date

Note: One witness shall not be a relative (by blood, marriage or adoption) of the person signing this request, shall not be entitled to any portion of the person's estate upon death and shall not own, operate or be employed at a health care facility where the person is a patient or resident. If the patient is an inpatient at a health care facility, one of the witnesses shall be an individual designated by the facility.

APPENDIX C

U.S. NINTH CIRCUIT COURT EN BANC RULING COMPASSION IN DYING ET AL. V. STATE OF WASHINGTON 79 F. 3RD 790 (9TH CIR. 1996)

[Extract. Footnotes and most case citations omitted]
[Stephen] REINHARDT, Circuit Judge:

I.

This case raises an extraordinarily important and difficult issue. It compels us to address questions to which there are no easy or simple answers, at law or otherwise. It requires us to confront the most basic of human concerns—the mortality of self and loved ones—and to balance the interest in preserving human life against the desire to die peacefully and with dignity. People of good will can and do passionately disagree about the proper result, perhaps even more intensely than they part ways over the constitutionality of restricting a woman's right to have an abortion. Heated though the debate may be, we must determine whether and how the United States Constitution applies to the controversy before us, a controversy that may touch more people more profoundly than any other issue the courts will face in the foreseeable future.

Today, we are required to decide whether a person who is terminally ill has a constitutionally-protected liberty interest in hastening what might otherwise be a protracted, undignified, and extremely painful death. If such an interest exists, we must next decide whether or not the state of Washington may constitutionally restrict its exercise by banning a form of medical assistance that is frequently requested by terminally ill people who wish to die. We first conclude that there is a constitutionally-protected liberty interest in determining the time and manner of one's own death, an interest that must be weighed against the state's legitimate and countervailing interests, especially those that relate to the preservation of human life. After balancing the competing interests, we conclude by answering the narrow question before us: We hold that insofar as the Washington statute prohibits physicians from prescribing life-ending medication for use by terminally ill, competent adults who wish to hasten their own deaths, it violates the Due Process Clause of the Fourteenth Amendment.

II. PRELIMINARY MATTERS AND HISTORY OF THE CASE [OMITTED]

III. OVERVIEW OF LEGAL ANALYSIS: IS THERE A DUE PROCESS VIOLATION?

In order to answer the question whether the Washington statute violates the Due Process Clause insofar as it prohibits the provision of certain medical assistance to terminally ill, competent adults who wish to hasten their own deaths, we first determine whether there is a liberty interest in choosing the time and manner of one's death—a question sometimes phrased in common parlance as: Is there a right to die? Because we hold that there is, we must then determine whether prohibiting physicians from prescribing life-ending medication for use by terminally ill patients who wish to die violates the patients' due process rights.

The mere recognition of a liberty interest does not mean that a state may not prohibit the exercise of that interest in particular circumstances, nor does it mean that a state may not adopt appropriate regulations governing its exercise. Rather, in cases like the one before us, the courts must apply a balancing test under which we weigh the individual's liberty interests against the relevant state interests in order to determine whether the state's actions are constitutionally permissible. . . .

As Justice O'Connor explained in her concurring opinion in *Cruzan*, the ultimate question is whether sufficient justification exists for the intrusion by the government into the realm of a person's "liberty, dignity, and freedom." *Cruzan*, 497 U.S. at 287, 289 (O'Connor, J., concurring). If the balance favors the state, then the given statute—whether it regulates the exercise of a due process liberty interest or prohibits that exercise to some degree—is constitutional. If the balance favors the individual, then the statute—whatever its justifications—violates the individual's due process liberty rights and must be declared unconstitutional, either on its face or as applied. Here, we conclude unhesitatingly that the balance favors the individual's liberty interest.

IV. IS THERE A LIBERTY INTEREST?

. . .[W]e endeavor to conduct an objective analysis of a most emotionally-charged of topics. In doing so, we bear in mind the second Justice Harlan's admonition in his now-vindicated dissent in *Poe v. Ullman*, 367 U.S. 497, 543 (1961):

> [T]he full scope of the liberty guaranteed by the Due Process Clause cannot be found in or limited by the precise terms of the specific guarantees elsewhere in the Constitution. This 'liberty' is not a series of isolated points pricked out in terms of the taking of property; the freedom of speech, press, and religion; the right to keep and bear arms; the freedom from unreasonable searches and seizures; and so on. It is a rational continuum which, broadly speaking, includes a freedom from all substantial arbitrary impositions and purposeless restraints, . . . and which also recognizes, what a reasonable and sensitive judgment must, that certain interests require particularly careful scrutiny of the state needs asserted to justify their abridgment.

Applying Justice Harlan's teaching, we must strive to resist the natural judicial impulse to limit our vision to that which can plainly be observed on the face of the document before us, or even that which we have previously had the wisdom to recognize. . . .

In examining whether a liberty interest exists in determining the time and manner of one's death, we begin with the compelling similarities between right-to-die cases and abortion cases. In the former as in the latter, the relative strength of the competing interests changes as physical, medical, or related circumstances vary. In right-to-die cases the outcome of the balancing test may differ at different points along the life cycle as a person's physical or medical condition deteriorates, just as in abortion cases the permissibility of restrictive state legislation may vary with the progression of the pregnancy. Equally important, both types of cases raise issues of life and death, and both arouse similar religious and moral concerns. Both also present basic questions about an individual's right of choice. . . .

In deciding right-to-die cases, we are guided by the Court's approach to the abortion cases. *Casey* in particular provides a powerful precedent, for in that case the Court had the opportunity to evaluate its past decisions and to determine whether to adhere to its original judgment. . . . [T]he fundamental message of that case lies in its statements regarding the type of issue that confronts us here: "These matters, involving the most intimate and personal choices a person may make in a lifetime, choices central to personal dignity and autonomy, are central to the liberty protected by the Fourteenth Amendment." *Casey*, 112 S.Ct. at 2807.

A. DEFINING THE LIBERTY INTEREST AND OTHER RELEVANT TERMS

The majority opinion of the three-judge panel that first heard this case on appeal defined the claimed liberty interest as a "constitutional right to aid in killing oneself." *Compassion In Dying*, 49 F.3d at 591. However, the subject we must initially examine is not nearly so limited. Properly analyzed, the first issue to be resolved is whether there is a liberty interest in determining the time and manner of one's death. We do not ask simply whether there is a liberty interest in receiving "aid in killing oneself" because such a narrow interest could not exist in the absence of a broader and more important underlying interest—the right to die. In short, it is the end and not the means that defines the liberty interest.

The broader approach we employ in defining the liberty interest is identical to the approach used by the Supreme Court in the abortion cases. In those cases, the Court initially determined whether a general liberty interest existed (an interest in having an abortion), not whether there was an interest in implementing that general liberty interest by a particular means (with medical assistance). . . . In this case, our analysis is necessarily the same. First we must determine whether there is a liberty interest in determining the time and manner of one's death; if so, we must then examine whether Washington's ban on assisted suicide unconstitutionally restricts the exercise of that liberty interest.

While some people refer to the liberty interest implicated in right-to-die cases as a liberty interest in committing suicide, we do not describe it that way. We use the broader and more accurate terms, "the right to die," "determining the time and manner of one's death," and "hastening one's death" for an important reason. The liberty interest we examine encompasses a whole range of acts that are generally not considered to constitute "suicide." Included within the liberty interest we examine, is for example, the act of refusing or terminating unwanted medical treatment. . . .

B. THE LEGAL STANDARD

There is no litmus test for courts to apply when deciding whether or not a liberty interest exists under the Due Process Clause. Our decisions involve difficult judgments regarding the conscience, traditions, and fundamental tenets of our nation. We must sometimes apply those basic principles in light of changing values based on shared experience. Other times we must apply them to new problems arising out of the development and use of new technologies. In all cases, our analysis of the applicability of the protections of the Constitution must be made in light of existing circumstances as well as our historic traditions.

Historically, the Court has classified "fundamental rights" as those that are "implicit in the concept of ordered liberty," *Palko v. Connecticut,* 302 U.S. 319, 325–26 (1937). . . .

In recent years, the Court has spoken more frequently of substantive due process interests than of fundamental due process rights. . . . The Court has also recently expressed a strong reluctance to find new fundamental rights. . . .

Under the Court's traditional jurisprudence, those classified as fundamental rights cannot be limited except to further a compelling and narrowly tailored state interest. See *Collins,* 112 S.Ct. at 1068. Other important interests, such as the liberty interest in refusing unwanted medical treatment, are subject to a balancing test that is less restrictive, but nonetheless requires the state to overcome a substantial hurdle in justifying any significant impairment. . . .

Although in determining the existence of important rights or liberty interests, the Court examines our history and experience, it has stated on a number of occasions that the limits of the substantive reach of the Due Process Clause are not frozen at any point in time. . . .

In *Casey,* the Court made it clear that the fact that we have previously failed to acknowledge the existence of a particular liberty interest or even that we have previously prohibited its exercise is no barrier to recognizing its existence. In discussing a woman's liberty interest in securing an abortion, the Casey Court stated that pregnancy involves "suffering [that] is too intimate and personal for the State to insist, without more, upon its own vision of the woman's role, however dominant that vision has been in the course of our history and culture." *Casey,* 112 S.Ct. at 2807. . . .

C. HISTORICAL ATTITUDES TOWARD SUICIDE [OMITTED]

D. CURRENT SOCIETAL ATTITUDES

Clearly the absence of a criminal sanction alone does not show societal approbation of a practice. Nor is there any evidence that Americans approve of suicide in general. In recent years, however, there has been increasingly widespread support for allowing the terminally ill to hasten their deaths and avoid painful, undignified, and inhumane endings to their lives. Most Americans simply do not appear to view such acts as constituting suicide, and there is much support in reason for that conclusion.

Polls have repeatedly shown that a large majority of Americans—sometimes nearing 90 percent—fully endorse recent legal changes granting terminally ill patients, and sometimes their families, the prerogative to accelerate their death by refusing or terminating treatment. Other polls indicate that a majority of Americans favor doctor-assisted suicide for the terminally ill. . . .

Our attitudes toward suicide of the type at issue in this case are better understood in light of our unwritten history and of technological developments. Running beneath the official history of legal condemnation of physician-assisted suicide is a strong undercurrent of a time-honored but hidden practice of physicians helping terminally ill patients to hasten their deaths. According to a survey by the American Society of Internal Medicine, one doctor in five said he had assisted in a patient's suicide. . . .

The debate over whether terminally ill patients should have a right to reject medical treatment or to receive aid from their physicians in hastening their deaths has taken on a new prominence as a result of a number of developments. . . .

The now recognized right to refuse or terminate treatment and the emergent right to receive medical assistance in hastening one's death are inevitable consequences of changes in the causes of death, advances in medical science, and the development of new technologies. Both the need and the capability to assist individuals end their lives in peace and dignity have increased exponentially.

E. PRIOR COURT DECISIONS

Next we examine previous Court decisions that delineate the boundaries of substantive due process. We believe that a careful examination of these decisions demonstrates that there is a strong liberty interest in determining how and when one's life shall end, and that an explicit recognition of that interest follows naturally, indeed inevitably, from their reasoning.

The essence of the substantive component of the Due Process Clause is to limit the ability of the state to intrude into the most important matters of our lives, at least without substantial justification. In a long line of cases, the Court has carved out certain key moments and decisions in individuals' lives and placed them beyond the general prohibitory authority of the state. The Court has recognized that the Fourteenth Amendment affords constitutional protection to personal decisions relating to marriage, procreation, family relationships, child rearing and education, and intercourse for purposes other than procreation. The Court has recognized the right of individuals to be free from government interference in deciding matters as personal as whether to bear or beget a child and whether to continue an unwanted pregnancy to term.

A common thread running through these cases is that they involve decisions that are highly personal and intimate, as well as of great importance to the individual. Certainly, few decisions are more personal, intimate or important than the decision to end one's life, especially when the reason for doing so is to avoid excessive and protracted pain. Accordingly, we believe the cases . . . provide strong general support for our conclusion that a liberty interest in controlling the time and manner of one's death is protected by the Due Process Clause of the Fourteenth Amendment.

While the cases we have adverted to lend general support to our conclusion, we believe that two relatively recent decisions of the Court, *Planned Parenthood v. Casey*, 112 S.Ct. 2791 (1992) and *Cruzan v. Director, Missouri Dept. of Health*, 497 U.S. 261 (1990), are fully persuasive, and leave little doubt as to the proper result.

F. LIBERTY INTEREST UNDER *CASEY*

In *Casey*, the Court surveyed its prior decisions . . . and then said:

> *These matters, involving the most intimate and personal choices a person may make in a lifetime, choices central to personal dignity and autonomy, are central to the liberty protected by the Fourteenth Amendment. At the heart of liberty is the right to define one's own concept of existence, of meaning, of the universe, and of the mystery of human life. Beliefs about these matters could not define the attributes of personhood were they formed under compulsion of the State.*

The district judge in this case [Barbara Rothstein] found the Court's reasoning in *Casey* "highly instructive" and "almost prescriptive" for determining "what liberty interest may inhere in a terminally ill person's choice to commit suicide." *Compassion In Dying*, 850 F. Supp. at 1459. We agree.

Like the decision of whether or not to have an abortion, the decision how and when to die is one of "the most intimate and personal choices a person may make in a lifetime," a choice "central to personal dignity and autonomy." A competent terminally ill adult, having lived nearly the full measure of his life, has a strong liberty interest in choosing a dignified and humane death rather than being reduced at the end of his existence to a childlike state of helplessness, diapered, sedated, incontinent. How a person dies not only determines the nature of the final period of his existence, but in many cases, the enduring memories held by those who love him.

Prohibiting a terminally ill patient from hastening his death may have an even more profound impact on that person's life than forcing a woman to carry a pregnancy to term. . . .

G. LIBERTY INTEREST UNDER *CRUZAN*

In *Cruzan*, the Court considered whether or not there is a constitutionally-protected, due process liberty interest in terminating unwanted medical treatment. The Court said that an affirmative answer followed almost inevitably from its prior decisions holding that patients have a liberty interest in refusing to submit to specific medical procedures. . . .

Cruzan stands for the proposition that there is a due process liberty interest in rejecting unwanted medical treatment, including the provision of food and water by artificial means. Moreover, the Court majority clearly recognized that granting the request to remove the tubes through which Cruzan received artificial nutrition and hydration would lead inexorably to her death. Accordingly, we conclude that *Cruzan*, by recognizing a liberty interest that includes the refusal of artificial provision of life-sustaining food and water, necessarily recognizes a liberty interest in hastening one's own death.

H. SUMMARY

Casey and *Cruzan* provide persuasive evidence that the Constitution encompasses a due process liberty interest in controlling the time and manner of one's death—that there is, in short, a constitutionally recognized "right to die." Our conclusion is strongly influenced by, but not limited to, the plight of mentally competent, terminally ill adults. We are influenced as well by the plight of others, such as those whose existence is reduced to a vegetative state or a permanent and irreversible state of unconsciousness.

Our conclusion that there is a liberty interest in determining the time and manner of one's death does not mean that there is a concomitant right to exercise that interest in all circumstances or to do so free from state regulation. To the contrary, we explicitly recognize that some prohibitory and regulatory state action is fully consistent with constitutional principles.

In short, finding a liberty interest constitutes a critical first step toward answering the question before us. The determination that must now be made is whether the state's attempt to curtail the exercise of that interest is constitutionally justified.

V. RELEVANT FACTORS AND INTERESTS

To determine whether a state action that impairs a liberty interest violates an individual's substantive due process rights we must identify the factors relevant to the case at hand, assess the state's interests and the individual's liberty interest in light of those factors, and then weigh and balance the competing interests. The relevant factors generally include: 1) the importance of the various state interests, both in general and in the factual context of the case; 2) the manner in which those interests are furthered by the state law or regulation; 3) the importance of the liberty interest, both in itself and in the context in which it is being exercised; 4) the extent to which that interest is burdened by the challenged state action; and, 5) the consequences of upholding or overturning the statute or regulation.

A. THE STATE'S INTERESTS

We analyze the factors in turn, and begin by considering the first: the importance of the state's interests. We identify six related state interests involved in the controversy before us: 1) the state's general interest in preserving life; 2) the state's more specific interest in preventing suicide; 3) the state's interest in avoiding the involvement of third parties and in precluding the use of arbitrary, unfair, or undue influence; 4) the state's interest in protecting family members and loved ones; 5) the state's interest in protecting the integrity of the medical profession; and, 6) the state's interest in avoiding adverse consequences that might ensue if the statutory provision at issue is declared unconstitutional. . . .
[discussion of state interests omitted]

VI. APPLICATION OF THE BALANCING TEST AND HOLDING

Weighing and then balancing a constitutionally-protected interest against the state's countervailing interests, while bearing in mind the various consequences of the decision, is quintessentially a judicial role. . . .

The liberty interest at issue here is an important one, and in the case of the terminally ill, is at its peak. Conversely, the state interests, while equally important in the abstract, are for the most part at a low point here. . . .

The state has chosen to pursue its interests by means of what for terminally ill patients is effectively a total prohibition, even though its most important interests could be adequately served by a far less burdensome measure [that is, regulation]. The consequences of rejecting the as-applied challenge would be disastrous for the terminally ill, while the adverse consequences for the state would be of a far lesser order. This, too, weighs in favor of upholding the liberty interest.

We consider the state's interests in preventing assisted suicide as being different only in degree and not in kind from its interests in prohibiting a number of other medical practices that lead directly to a terminally ill patient's death. Moreover, we do not consider those interests to be significantly greater in the case of assisted suicide than they are in the case of those other medical practices, if indeed they are greater at all. . . . In this case, the state has wide power to regulate, but it may not ban the exercise of the liberty interest, and that is the practical effect of the program before us. Accordingly, . . . we hold that the "or aids" provision of Washington statute RCW 9A.36.06 is unconstitutional as applied to terminally ill competent adults who wish to hasten their deaths with medication prescribed by their physicians. . . .

VII. CONCLUSION

We hold that a liberty interest exists in the choice of how and when one dies, and that the provision of the Washington statute banning assisted suicide, as applied to competent, terminally ill adults who wish to hasten their deaths by obtaining medication prescribed by their doctors, violates the Due Process Clause. . . .

There is one final point we must emphasize. Some argue strongly that decisions regarding matters affecting life or death should not be made by the courts. Essentially, we agree with that proposition. In this case, by permitting the individual to exercise the right to choose we are following the constitutional mandate to take such decisions out of the hands of the government, both state and federal, and to put them where they rightly belong, in the hands of the people. We are allowing individuals to make the decisions that so profoundly affect their very existence—and precluding the state from intruding excessively into that critical realm. The Constitution and the courts stand as a bulwark between individual freedom and arbitrary and intrusive governmental power. Under our constitutional system, neither the state nor the majority of the people in a state can impose its will upon the individual in a matter so highly "central to personal dignity and autonomy," *Casey*, 112 S.Ct. at 2807. Those who believe strongly that death must come without physician assistance are free to follow that creed, be they doctors or patients. They are not free, however, to force their views, their religious convictions, or their philosophies on all the other members of a democratic society, and to compel those whose values differ with theirs to die painful, protracted, and agonizing deaths.

AFFIRMED

APPENDIX D

U.S. SECOND CIRCUIT COURT RULING
TIMOTHY E. QUILL ET AL. V. DENNIS C. VACCO
80 F. 3RD 716 (2ND CIR. 1996)

[Extract. Footnotes and most case citations omitted]
[Roger J.] MINER, Circuit Judge.
[background of case omitted]

DISCUSSION

I. JUSTICIABILITY

As they did in the district court, the state defendants contend on appeal that this action does not present a justiciable case or controversy. We reject this contention. . . . The physician plaintiffs have good reason to fear prosecution in New York County.

II. SUBSTANTIVE DUE PROCESS

Plaintiffs argue for a right to assisted suicide as a fundamental liberty under the substantive component of the Due Process Clause of the Fourteenth Amendment. This Clause assures the citizenry that any deprivation of life, liberty or property by a state will be attended by appropriate legal processes. However,

Appendix D

despite the language of the Due Process Clause of the . . . Fourteenth Amendment, which appears to focus only on the processes by which life, liberty, or property is taken, the cases are legion in which th[at] Clause ha[s] been interpreted to have substantive content, subsuming rights that to a great extent are immune from . . . state regulation or proscription. Among such cases are those recognizing rights that have little or no textual support in the constitutional language. Bowers v. Hardwick, *478 U.S. 186, 191 (1986).*

Rights that have no textual support in the language of the Constitution but qualify for heightened judicial protection include fundamental liberties so "implicit in the concept of ordered liberty" that "neither liberty nor justice would exist if they were sacrificed." *Palko v. Connecticut*, 302 U.S. 319, 325–26 (1937). Fundamental liberties also have been described as those that are "deeply rooted in this Nation's history and tradition." *Moore v. City of East Cleveland*, 431 U.S. 494, 503 (1977). It is well settled that the state must not infringe fundamental liberty interests unless the infringement is narrowly tailored to serve a compelling state interest. The list of rights the Supreme Court has actually or impliedly identified as fundamental, and therefore qualified for heightened judicial protection, include . . . the right to privacy. The right of privacy has been held to encompass personal decisions relating to marriage, procreation, family relationships, child rearing and education, contraception and abortion. While the Constitution does not, of course, include any explicit mention of the right of privacy, this right has been recognized as encompassed by the Fourteenth Amendment's Due Process Clause. Nevertheless, the Supreme Court has been reluctant to further expand this particular list of federal rights, and it would be most speculative for a lower court to do so.

In any event, the Supreme Court has drawn a line, albeit a shaky one, on the expansion of fundamental rights that are without support in the text of the Constitution. . . .

[T]he statutes plaintiffs seek to declare unconstitutional here cannot be said to infringe upon any fundamental right or liberty. . . . [T]he right contended for here cannot be considered so implicit in our understanding of ordered liberty that neither justice nor liberty would exist if it were sacrificed. Nor can it be said that the right to assisted suicide claimed by plaintiffs is deeply rooted in the nation's traditions and history. Indeed, the very opposite is true. . . . Although neither suicide nor attempted suicide is any longer a crime in the United States, 32 states, including New York, continue to make assisted suicide an offense. Clearly, no "right" to assisted suicide ever has been recognized in any state in the United States. . . .

We therefore decline the plaintiffs' invitation to identify a new fundamental right, in the absence of a clear direction from the Court whose precedents we are bound to follow. . . .

III. EQUAL PROTECTION

According to the Fourteenth Amendment, the equal protection of the laws cannot be denied by any State to any person within its jurisdiction. This constitutional guarantee simply requires the states to treat in a similar manner all individuals who are similarly situated. But disparate treatment is not necessarily a denial of the equal protection guaranteed by the Constitution. The Supreme Court has described the wide discretion afforded to the states in establishing acceptable classifications:

> *The Equal Protection Clause directs that "all persons similarly circumstanced shall be treated alike." But so too, "[t]he Constitution does not require things which are different in fact or opinion to be treated in law as though they were the same." The initial discretion to determine what is "different" and what is "the same" resides in the legislatures of the States. A legislature must have substantial latitude to establish classifications that roughly approximate the nature of the problem perceived, that accommodate competing concerns both public and private, and that account for limitations on the practical ability of the State to remedy every ill. In applying the Equal Protection Clause to most forms of state action, we thus seek only the assurance that the classification at issue bears some fair relationship to a legitimate public purpose.* Plyler v. Doe, 457 U.S. 202, 216 (1982). . . .

Applying the foregoing principles to the New York statutes criminalizing assisted suicide, it seems clear that: 1) the statutes in question fall within the category of social welfare legislation and therefore are subject to rational basis scrutiny upon judicial review; 2) New York law does not treat equally all competent persons who are in the final stages of fatal illness and wish to hasten their deaths; 3) the distinctions made by New York law with regard to such persons do not further any legitimate state purpose; and 4) accordingly, to the extent that the statutes in question prohibit persons in the final stages of terminal illness from having assistance in ending their lives by the use of self-administered, prescribed drugs, the statutes lack any rational basis and are violative of the Equal Protection Clause.

The right to refuse medical treatment long has been recognized in New York. In 1914 Judge Cardozo wrote that, under New York law, "[e]very human being of adult years and sound mind has a right to determine what shall be done with his own body." *Schloendorff v. Society of New York Hosp.,*

Appendix D

211 N.Y. 125, 129 (1914). In 1981, the New York Court of Appeals held that this right extended to the withdrawal of life-support systems. *In re Eichner* (decided with *In re Storar*), 52 N.Y.2d 363, cert. denied, 454 U.S. 858 (1981). . . .

After these cases were decided, the New York legislature placed its imprimatur upon the right of competent citizens to hasten death by refusing medical treatment and by directing physicians to remove life-support systems already in place. . . .

The concept that a competent person may order the removal of life-support systems found Supreme Court approval in *Cruzan v. Director, Missouri Dep't of Health*, 497 U.S. 261 (1990). . . .

In affirming the Missouri Supreme Court, the United States Supreme Court stated: "The principle that a competent person has a constitutionally protected liberty interest in refusing unwanted medical treatment may be inferred from our prior decisions." The Court noted that the inquiry is not ended by the identification of a liberty interest, because there also must be a balancing of the state interests and the individual's liberty interests before there can be a determination that constitutional rights have been violated. Id. at 279. The Court all but made that determination in the course of the following analysis:

> *Petitioners insist that under the general holdings of our cases, the forced administration of life-sustaining medical treatment, and even of artificially-delivered food and water essential to life, would implicate a competent person's liberty interest. Although we think the logic of the cases discussed above would embrace such a liberty interest, the dramatic consequences involved in refusal of such treatment would inform the inquiry as to whether the deprivation of that interest is constitutionally permissible. But for purposes of this case, we assume that the United States Constitution would grant a competent person a constitutionally protected right to refuse life-saving hydration and nutrition.*

The Court went on to find that Missouri allowed a surrogate to "act for the patient in electing to have hydration and nutrition withdrawn in such a way as to cause death," subject to "a procedural safeguard to assure that the action of the surrogate conforms as best it may to the wishes expressed by the patient while competent." The Court then held that the procedural safeguard or requirement imposed by Missouri—the heightened evidentiary requirement that the incompetent's wishes be proved by clear and convincing evidence—was not forbidden by the United States Constitution.

In view of the foregoing, it seems clear that New York does not treat similarly circumstanced persons alike: those in the final stages of terminal illness who are on life-support systems are allowed to hasten their deaths by directing the removal of such systems; but those who are similarly situated, except for the previous attachment of life-sustaining equipment, are not allowed to hasten death by self-administering prescribed drugs. The district judge has identified "a difference between allowing nature to take its course, even in the most severe situations, and intentionally using an artificial death-producing device." *Quill*, 870 F. Supp. at 84. But Justice Scalia, for one, has remarked upon "the irrelevance of the action-inaction distinction," noting that "the cause of death in both cases is the suicide's conscious decision to 'pu[t] an end to his own existence.'" *Cruzan*, 497 U.S. at 296–297. . . .

Indeed, there is nothing "natural" about causing death by means other than the original illness or its complications. The withdrawal of nutrition brings on death by starvation, the withdrawal of hydration brings on death by dehydration, and the withdrawal of ventilation brings about respiratory failure. By ordering the discontinuance of these artificial life-sustaining processes or refusing to accept them in the first place, a patient hastens his death by means that are not natural in any sense. It certainly cannot be said that the death that immediately ensues is the natural result of the progression of the disease or condition from which the patient suffers.

Moreover, the writing of a prescription to hasten death, after consultation with a patient, involves a far less active role for the physician than is required in bringing about death through asphyxiation, starvation and/or dehydration. Withdrawal of life support requires physicians or those acting at their direction physically to remove equipment and, often, to administer palliative drugs which may themselves contribute to death. The ending of life by these means is nothing more nor less than assisted suicide. It simply cannot be said that those mentally competent, terminally-ill persons who seek to hasten death but whose treatment does not include life support are treated equally.

A finding of unequal treatment does not, of course, end the inquiry, unless it is determined that the inequality is not rationally related to some legitimate state interest. The burden is upon the plaintiffs to demonstrate irrationality. At oral argument and in its brief, the state's contention has been that its principal interest is in preserving the life of all its citizens at all times and under all conditions. But what interest can the state possibly have in requiring the prolongation of a life that is all but ended? Surely, the state's interest lessens as the potential for life diminishes. And what business is it of the state to require the continuation of agony when the result is imminent and inevitable? What concern prompts the state to interfere with a mentally competent patient's "right to define [his] own concept of existence, of meaning, of the universe, and of the mystery of human life," *Planned*

Parenthood v. Casey, 112 S. Ct. 2791, 2807 (1992), when the patient seeks to have drugs prescribed to end life during the final stages of a terminal illness? The greatly reduced interest of the state in preserving life compels the answer to these questions: "None."

A panel of the Ninth Circuit attempted to identify some state interests in reversing a district court decision holding unconstitutional a statute of the state of Washington criminalizing the promotion of a suicide attempt. *Compassion in Dying v. Washington*, 49 F.3d 586 (9th Cir. 1995). The plaintiffs in the Washington case contended for physician-assisted suicide for the terminally-ill, but the panel majority found that the statute prohibiting suicide promotion furthered the following: the interest in denying to physicians "the role of killers of their patients"; the interest in avoiding psychological pressure upon the elderly and infirm to consent to death; the interest of preventing the exploitation of the poor and minorities; the interest in protecting handicapped persons against societal indifference; the interest in preventing the sort of abuse that "has occurred in the Netherlands where . . . legal guidelines have tacitly allowed assisted suicide or euthanasia in response to a repeated request from a suffering, competent patient." The panel majority also raised a question relative to the lack of clear definition of the term "terminally ill."

The New York statutes prohibiting assisted suicide, which are similar to the Washington statute, do not serve any of the state interests noted, in view of the statutory and common law schemes allowing suicide through the withdrawal of life-sustaining treatment. Physicians do not fulfill the role of "killer" by prescribing drugs to hasten death any more than they do by disconnecting life-support systems. Likewise, "psychological pressure" can be applied just as much upon the elderly and infirm to consent to withdrawal of life-sustaining equipment as to take drugs to hasten death. There is no clear indication that there has been any problem in regard to the former, and there should be none as to the latter. In any event, the state of New York may establish rules and procedures to assure that all choices are free of such pressures. With respect to the protection of minorities, the poor and the non-mentally handicapped, it suffices to say that these classes of persons are entitled to treatment equal to that afforded to all those who now may hasten death by means of life-support withdrawal. In point of fact, these persons themselves are entitled to hasten death by requesting such withdrawal and should be free to do so by requesting appropriate medication to terminate life during the final stages of terminal illness.

As to the interest in avoiding abuse similar to that occurring in the Netherlands, it seems clear that some physicians there practice nonvoluntary euthanasia, although it is not legal to do so. The plaintiffs here do not argue for euthanasia at all but for assisted suicide for terminally-ill, mentally

competent patients, who would self-administer the lethal drugs. It is difficult to see how the relief the plaintiffs seek would lead to the abuses found
in the Netherlands. . . .

Finally, it seems clear that most physicians would agree on the definition of "terminally ill," at least for the purpose of the relief that plaintiffs
seek. . . .

The New York statutes criminalizing assisted suicide violate the Equal
Protection Clause because, to the extent that they prohibit a physician from
prescribing medications to be self-administered by a mentally competent,
terminally-ill person in the final stages of his terminal illness, they are not
rationally related to any legitimate state interest.

CONCLUSION

We reverse the judgment of the district court and remand for entry of judgment in favor of the plaintiffs in accordance with the foregoing.

APPENDIX E

U.S. SUPREME COURT RULING: *WASHINGTON STATE V. GLUCKSBERG* 117 S. CT. 2258 (1997)

[Extract. Footnotes and most case citations omitted.]

Chief Justice Rehnquist delivered the opinion of the Court.

The question presented in this case is whether Washington's prohibition against "caus[ing]" or "aid[ing]" a suicide offends the Fourteenth Amendment to the United States Constitution. We hold that it does not....

[background of case omitted]

I

[following history section is considerably shortened]

...We begin, as we do in all due process cases, by examining our Nation's history, legal traditions, and practices.... In almost every State—indeed, in almost every western democracy—it is a crime to assist a suicide. The States' assisted suicide bans are not innovations. Rather, they are longstanding expressions of the States' commitment to the protection and preservation of all human life.... [F]or over 700 years, the Anglo American common law tradition has punished or otherwise disapproved of both suicide and assisting suicide.... And the prohibitions against assisting suicide never contained exceptions for those who were near death. Rather,

[t]he life of those to whom life ha[d] become a burden—of those who [were] hopelessly diseased or fatally wounded—nay, even the lives of criminals condemned to death, [were] under the protection of law, equally as the lives of

279

those who [were] in the full tide of life's enjoyment, and anxious to continue to live. Blackburn v. State, 23 Ohio St. 146, 163 (1872). . . .

Because of advances in medicine and technology, Americans today are increasingly likely to die in institutions, from chronic illnesses. Public concern and democratic action are therefore sharply focused on how best to protect dignity and independence at the end of life, with the result that there have been many significant changes in state laws and in the attitudes these laws reflect. Many States, for example, now permit "living wills," surrogate health care decisionmaking, and the withdrawal or refusal of life sustaining medical treatment. At the same time, however, voters and legislators continue for the most part to reaffirm their States' prohibitions on assisting suicide. . . .

Against this backdrop of history, tradition, and practice, we now turn to respondents' constitutional claim.

II

The Due Process Clause guarantees more than fair process, and the "liberty" it protects includes more than the absence of physical restraint. . . . . The Clause also provides heightened protection against government interference with certain fundamental rights and liberty interests. . . . In a long line of cases, we have held that, in addition to the specific freedoms protected by the Bill of Rights, the "liberty" specially protected by the Due Process Clause includes the rights to marry, to have children, to direct the education and upbringing of one's children, to marital privacy, to use contraception, to bodily integrity, and to abortion. We have also assumed, and strongly suggested, that the Due Process Clause protects the traditional right to refuse unwanted lifesaving medical treatment.

But we "ha[ve] always been reluctant to expand the concept of substantive due process because guideposts for responsible decisionmaking in this unchartered area are scarce and open ended." *Collins*, 503 U.S., at 125. By extending constitutional protection to an asserted right or liberty interest, we, to a great extent, place the matter outside the arena of public debate and legislative action. We must therefore "exercise the utmost care whenever we are asked to break new ground in this field," ibid., lest the liberty protected by the Due Process Clause be subtly transformed into the policy preferences of the members of this Court.

Our established method of substantive due process analysis has two primary features: First, we have regularly observed that the Due Process Clause specially protects those fundamental rights and liberties which are, objectively, "deeply rooted in this Nation's history and tradition," and "implicit in the concept of ordered liberty," such that "neither liberty nor justice would exist if they were sacrificed." *Palko v. Connecticut*, 302 U.S. 319, 325, 326 (1937). Second, we have required in substantive due process cases a "careful description" of the asserted fundamental liberty interest. Our Nation's history, legal traditions, and practices thus provide the crucial "guideposts for responsible decisionmaking" that direct and restrain our exposition of the Due Process Clause. As we stated recently in *Flores*, the Fourteenth Amendment "forbids the government to infringe . . . 'fundamental' liberty interests at all, no matter what process is provided, unless the infringement is narrowly tailored to serve a compelling state interest." 507 U.S., at 302. . . .

Turning to the claim at issue here, the Court of Appeals stated that "[p]roperly analyzed, the first issue to be resolved is whether there is a liberty interest in determining the time and manner of one's death," 79 F. 3d, at 801, or, in other words, "[i]s there a right to die?," id., at 799. Similarly, respondents assert a "liberty to choose how to die" and a right to "control of one's final days," *Brief for Respondents* 7, and describe the asserted liberty as "the right to choose a humane, dignified death," id., at 15, and "the liberty to shape death," id., at 18. As noted above, we have a tradition of carefully formulating the interest at stake in substantive due process cases. For example, although *Cruzan* is often described as a "right to die" case, see 79 F. 3d, at 799; post, at 9 (Stevens, J., concurring in judgment) (*Cruzan* recognized "the more specific interest in making decisions about how to confront an imminent death"), we were, in fact, more precise: we assumed that the Constitution granted competent persons a "constitutionally protected right to refuse lifesaving hydration and nutrition." *Cruzan*, 497 U.S., at 279; id., at 287 (O'Connor, J., concurring) ("[A] liberty interest in refusing unwanted medical treatment may be inferred from our prior decisions"). The Washington statute at issue in this case prohibits "aid[ing] another person to attempt suicide," Wash. Rev. Code §9A.36.060(1) (1994), and, thus, the question before us is whether the "liberty" specially protected by the Due Process Clause includes a right to commit suicide which itself includes a right to assistance in doing so.

We now inquire whether this asserted right has any place in our Nation's traditions. Here, as discussed above, we are confronted with a consistent and almost universal tradition that has long rejected the asserted right, and continues explicitly to reject it today, even for terminally ill, mentally competent adults. To hold for respondents, we would have to reverse centuries of legal doctrine and practice, and strike down the considered policy choice of almost every State. . . .

Respondents contend, however, that the liberty interest they assert is consistent with this Court's substantive due process line of cases, if not with this Nation's history and practice. Pointing to *Casey* and *Cruzan*, respondents read our jurisprudence in this area as reflecting a general tradition of "self sovereignty," *Brief of Respondents* 12, and as teaching that the "liberty" protected by the Due Process Clause includes "basic and intimate exercises of personal autonomy," id., at 10; see *Casey*, 505 U.S., at 847 ("It is a promise of the Constitution that there is a realm of personal liberty which the government may not enter"). According to respondents, our liberty jurisprudence, and the broad, individualistic principles it reflects, protects the "liberty of competent, terminally ill adults to make end of life decisions free of undue government interference." *Brief for Respondents* 10. The question presented in this case, however, is whether the protections of the Due Process Clause include a right to commit suicide with another's assistance. With this "careful description" of respondents' claim in mind, we turn to *Casey* and *Cruzan*. . . .

Respondents contend that in *Cruzan* we "acknowledged that competent, dying persons have the right to direct the removal of life sustaining medical treatment and thus hasten death," *Brief for Respondents* 23, and that "the constitutional principle behind recognizing the patient's liberty to direct the withdrawal of artificial life support applies at least as strongly to the choice to hasten impending death by consuming lethal medication," id., at 26. Similarly, the Court of Appeals concluded that "*Cruzan*, by recognizing a liberty interest that includes the refusal of artificial provision of life sustaining food and water, necessarily recognize[d] a liberty interest in hastening one's own death." 79 F. 3d, at 816.

The right assumed in *Cruzan*, however, was not simply deduced from abstract concepts of personal autonomy. Given the common law rule that forced medication was a battery, and the long legal tradition protecting the decision to refuse unwanted medical treatment, our assumption was entirely consistent with this Nation's history and constitutional traditions. The decision to commit suicide with the assistance of another may be just as personal and profound as the decision to refuse unwanted medical treatment, but it has never enjoyed similar legal protection. Indeed, the two acts are widely and reasonably regarded as quite distinct. See *Quill v. Vacco*, post, at 5–13. In *Cruzan* itself, we recognized that most States outlawed assisted suicide— and even more do today—and we certainly gave no intimation that the right to refuse unwanted medical treatment could be somehow transmuted into a right to assistance in committing suicide. 497 U.S., at 280.

Respondents also rely on *Casey*. There, the Court's opinion concluded that "the essential holding of *Roe v. Wade* should be retained and once again reaffirmed." *Casey*, 505 U.S., at 846. . . . [I]n reaching this conclusion, the opinion discussed in some detail this Court's substantive due process tradition of interpreting the Due Process Clause to protect certain fundamental rights and "personal decisions relating to marriage, procreation, contraception, family relationships, child rearing, and education," and noted that many of those rights and liberties "involv[e] the most intimate and personal choices a person may make in a lifetime."

The Court of Appeals, like the District Court, found *Casey* "'highly instructive'" and "'almost prescriptive'" for determining "'what liberty interest may inhere in a terminally ill person's choice to commit suicide'": "Like the decision of whether or not to have an abortion, the decision how and when to die is one of 'the most intimate and personal choices a person may make in a lifetime,' a choice 'central to personal dignity and autonomy.'" 79 F. 3d, at 813–814.

Similarly, respondents emphasize the statement in *Casey* that:

> *At the heart of liberty is the right to define one's own concept of existence, of meaning, of the universe, and of the mystery of human life. Beliefs about these matters could not define the attributes of personhood were they formed under compulsion of the State.* Casey, *505 U.S., at 851.* Brief for Respondents *12.*

By choosing this language, the Court's opinion in *Casey* described, in a general way and in light of our prior cases, those personal activities and decisions that this Court has identified as so deeply rooted in our history and traditions, or so fundamental to our concept of constitutionally ordered liberty, that they are protected by the Fourteenth Amendment. . . . That many of the rights and liberties protected by the Due Process Clause sound in personal autonomy does not warrant the sweeping conclusion that any and all important, intimate, and personal decisions are so protected, and *Casey* did not suggest otherwise.

The history of the law's treatment of assisted suicide in this country has been and continues to be one of the rejection of nearly all efforts to permit it. That being the case, our decisions lead us to conclude that the asserted "right" to assistance in committing suicide is not a fundamental liberty interest protected by the Due Process Clause. The Constitution also requires, however, that Washington's assisted suicide ban be rationally related to legitimate government interests. This requirement is unquestionably met here. As the [appeals] court . . . recognized, Washington's assisted suicide ban implicates a number of state interests. . . .

First, Washington has an "unqualified interest in the preservation of human life." *Cruzan,* 497 U.S., at 282. The State's prohibition on assisted suicide, like all homicide laws, both reflects and advances its commitment to this interest. . . . The Court of Appeals . . . recognized Washington's interest in protecting life, but held that the "weight" of this interest depends on the "medical condition and the wishes of the person whose life is at stake." Washington, however, has rejected this sliding scale approach and, through its assisted suicide ban, insists that all persons' lives, from beginning to end, regardless of physical or mental condition, are under the full protection of the law. . . . As we have previously affirmed, the States "may properly decline to make judgments about the 'quality' of life that a particular individual may enjoy," *Cruzan*, 497 U.S., at 282. This remains true, as *Cruzan* makes clear, even for those who are near death.

Relatedly, all admit that suicide is a serious public health problem, especially among persons in otherwise vulnerable groups. . . . The State has an interest in preventing suicide, and in studying, identifying, and treating its causes. . . .

Those who attempt suicide—terminally ill or not—often suffer from depression or other mental disorders. . . . Research indicates . . . that many people who request physician assisted suicide withdraw that request if their depression and pain are treated. . . . [B]ecause depression is difficult to diagnose, physicians and medical professionals often fail to respond adequately to seriously ill patients' needs. Thus, legal physician assisted suicide could make it more difficult for the State to protect depressed or mentally ill persons, or those who are suffering from untreated pain, from suicidal impulses.

The State also has an interest in protecting the integrity and ethics of the medical profession. In contrast to the Court of Appeals' conclusion that "the integrity of the medical profession would [not] be threatened in any way by [physician assisted suicide]," the American Medical Association, like many other medical and physicians' groups, has concluded that "[p]hysician assisted suicide is fundamentally incompatible with the physician's role as healer." American Medical Association, *Code of Ethics* §2.211 (1994). . . . And physician assisted suicide could, it is argued, undermine the trust that is essential to the doctor-patient relationship by blurring the time-honored line between healing and harming.

Next, the State has an interest in protecting vulnerable groups—including the poor, the elderly, and disabled persons—from abuse, neglect, and mistakes. The Court of Appeals dismissed the State's concern that disadvantaged persons might be pressured into physician assisted suicide as "ludicrous on its face." We have recognized, however, the real risk of subtle coercion and undue influence in end-of-life situations. . . . If physician assisted suicide were permitted, many might resort to it to spare their families the substantial financial burden of end-of-life health care costs.

The State's interest here goes beyond protecting the vulnerable from coercion; it extends to protecting disabled and terminally ill people from prejudice, negative and inaccurate stereotypes, and "societal indifference."

49 F. 3d, at 592. The State's assisted suicide ban reflects and reinforces its policy that the lives of terminally ill, disabled, and elderly people must be no less valued than the lives of the young and healthy, and that a seriously disabled person's suicidal impulses should be interpreted and treated the same way as anyone else's. . . .

Finally, the State may fear that permitting assisted suicide will start it down the path to voluntary and perhaps even involuntary euthanasia. The Court of Appeals struck down Washington's assisted suicide ban only "as applied to competent, terminally ill adults who wish to hasten their deaths by obtaining medication prescribed by their doctors." Washington insists, however, that the impact of the court's decision will not and cannot be so limited. *Brief for Petitioners* 44–47. If suicide is protected as a matter of constitutional right, it is argued, "every man and woman in the United States must enjoy it." *Compassion in Dying*, 49 F. 3d, at 591. The Court of Appeals' decision, and its expansive reasoning, provide ample support for the State's concerns. The court noted, for example, that the "decision of a duly appointed surrogate decision maker is for all legal purposes the decision of the patient himself"; that "in some instances, the patient may be unable to self-administer the drugs and . . . administration by the physician . . . may be the only way the patient may be able to receive them,"; and that not only physicians, but also family members and loved ones, will inevitably participate in assisting suicide. Thus, it turns out that what is couched as a limited right to "physician assisted suicide" is likely, in effect, a much broader license, which could prove extremely difficult to police and contain. Washington's ban on assisting suicide prevents such erosion. . . .

We need not weigh exactingly the relative strengths of these various interests. They are unquestionably important and legitimate, and Washington's ban on assisted suicide is at least reasonably related to their promotion and protection. We therefore hold that Wash. Rev. Code §9A.36.060(1) (1994) does not violate the Fourteenth Amendment, either on its face or "as applied to competent, terminally ill adults who wish to hasten their deaths by obtaining medication prescribed by their doctors."

***

Throughout the Nation, Americans are engaged in an earnest and profound debate about the morality, legality, and practicality of physician assisted suicide. Our holding permits this debate to continue, as it should in a democratic society. The decision of the en banc Court of Appeals is reversed, and the case is remanded for further proceedings consistent with this opinion.

It is so ordered.

NEW YORK STATE V. QUILL 117 S. CT. 2293 (1997)

[Extract. Footnotes and most case citations omitted.]

Chief Justice Rehnquist delivered the opinion of the Court.

In New York, as in most States, it is a crime to aid another to commit or attempt suicide, but patients may refuse even lifesaving medical treatment. The question presented by this case is whether New York's prohibition on assisting suicide therefore violates the Equal Protection Clause of the Fourteenth Amendment. We hold that it does not. . . .

[background of case omitted]

The Equal Protection Clause commands that no State shall "deny to any person within its jurisdiction the equal protection of the laws." This provision creates no substantive rights. Instead, it embodies a general rule that States must treat like cases alike but may treat unlike cases accordingly. . . . If a legislative classification or distinction "neither burdens a fundamental right nor targets a suspect class, we will uphold [it] so long as it bears a rational relation to some legitimate end." *Romer v. Evans*, 517 U.S. (1996).

New York's statutes outlawing assisting suicide affect and address matters of profound significance to all New Yorkers alike. They neither infringe fundamental rights nor involve suspect classifications. . . . These laws are therefore entitled to a "strong presumption of validity." *Heller v. Doe*, 509 U.S. 312, 319 (1993).

On their faces, neither New York's ban on assisting suicide nor its statutes permitting patients to refuse medical treatment treat anyone differently than anyone else or draw any distinctions between persons. Everyone, regardless of physical condition, is entitled, if competent, to refuse unwanted lifesaving medical treatment; no one is permitted to assist a suicide. . . .

The Court of Appeals, however, concluded that some terminally ill people—those who are on life support systems—are treated differently than those who are not, in that the former may "hasten death" by ending treatment, but the latter may not "hasten death" through physician assisted suicide, 80 F. 3d, at 729. This conclusion depends on the submission that ending or refusing lifesaving medical treatment "is nothing more nor less than assisted suicide." Ibid. Unlike the Court of Appeals, we think the distinction between assisting suicide and withdrawing life sustaining treatment, a distinction widely recognized and endorsed in the medical profession and in our legal traditions, is both important and logical; it is certainly rational. . . . The distinction comports with fundamental legal principles of causation and intent. First, when a patient refuses life-sustaining medical treatment, he dies from an underlying fatal disease or pathology; but if a patient ingests lethal medication prescribed by a physician, he is killed by that medication. . . .

Furthermore, a physician who withdraws, or honors a patient's refusal to begin, life-sustaining medical treatment purposefully intends, or may so intend, only to respect his patient's wishes and "to cease doing useless and futile or degrading things to the patient when [the patient] no longer stands to benefit from them." *Assisted Suicide in the United States*, Hearing before the Subcommittee on the Constitution of the House Committee on the Judiciary, 104th Cong., 2d Sess., 368 (1996) (testimony of Dr. Leon R. Kass). The same is true when a doctor provides aggressive palliative care; in some cases, painkilling drugs may hasten a patient's death, but the physician's purpose and intent is, or may be, only to ease his patient's pain. A doctor who assists a suicide, however, "must, necessarily and indubitably, intend primarily that the patient be made dead." Id., at 367. Similarly, a patient who commits suicide with a doctor's aid necessarily has the specific intent to end his or her own life, while a patient who refuses or discontinues treatment might not. . . .

The law has long used actors' intent or purpose to distinguish between two acts that may have the same result. . . . Put differently, the law distinguishes actions taken "because of" a given end from actions taken "in spite of" their unintended but foreseen consequences. *Feeney*, 442 U.S., at 279. . . .

Given these general principles, it is not surprising that many courts, including New York courts, have carefully distinguished refusing life-sustaining treatment from suicide. . . .

Similarly, the overwhelming majority of state legislatures have drawn a clear line between assisting suicide and withdrawing or permitting the refusal of unwanted lifesaving medical treatment by prohibiting the former and permitting the latter. . . .

This Court has also recognized, at least implicitly, the distinction between letting a patient die and making that patient die. In *Cruzan v. Director, Mo. Dept. of Health*, 497 U.S. 261, 278 (1990), we concluded that "[t]he principle that a competent person has a constitutionally protected liberty interest in refusing unwanted medical treatment may be inferred from our prior decisions," and we assumed the existence of such a right for purposes of that case. But our assumption of a right to refuse treatment was grounded not, as the Court of Appeals supposed, on the proposition that patients have a general and abstract "right to hasten death," 80 F. 3d, at 727–728, but on well-established, traditional rights to bodily integrity and freedom from unwanted touching. In fact, we observed that "the majority of States in this country have laws imposing criminal penalties on one who assists another to commit suicide." *Cruzan* therefore provides no support for the notion that refusing life-sustaining medical treatment is "nothing more nor less than suicide."

For all these reasons, we disagree with respondents' claim that the distinction between refusing lifesaving medical treatment and assisted suicide is "arbitrary" and "irrational." Granted, in some cases, the line between the two may not be clear, but certainty is not required, even were it possible. Logic and contemporary practice support New York's judgment that the two acts are different, and New York may therefore, consistent with the Constitution, treat them differently. By permitting everyone to refuse unwanted medical treatment while prohibiting anyone from assisting a suicide, New York law follows a longstanding and rational distinction.

New York's reasons for recognizing and acting on this distinction—including prohibiting intentional killing and preserving life; preventing suicide; maintaining physicians' role as their patients' healers; protecting vulnerable people from indifference, prejudice, and psychological and financial pressure to end their lives; and avoiding a possible slide towards euthanasia—are discussed in greater detail in our opinion in *Glucksberg*, ante. These valid and important public interests easily satisfy the constitutional requirement that a legislative classification bear a rational relation to some legitimate end.

The judgment of the Court of Appeals is reversed.

It is so ordered.

APPENDIX F

TABLES AND GRAPHS

CHANGES IN SUPPORT FOR ASSISTED SUICIDE, 1950–2003

Responses in the United States to the question, "When a person has a disease that cannot be cured, do you think doctors should be allowed by law to end the patient's life by some painless means if the patient requests it, or not?"

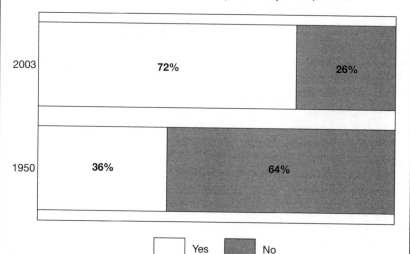

2003	72%	26%
1950	36%	64%

☐ Yes ▨ No

Source: Gallup Organization, January 1950, June 2003. Reprinted in Public Agenda, "Right to Die: Quick Takes," URL: http://www.publicagenda.org/issues/angles_graph.cfm?issue_type=right2die&id=233&graph=majpropdiesupportRF.jpg.
© Infobase Publishing

NUMBER OF PRESCRIPTION RECIPIENTS AND DEATHS UNDER
THE OREGON DEATH WITH DIGNITY ACT, BY YEAR, 1998–2005

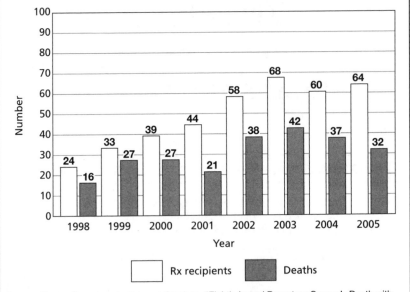

Source: Oregon Department of Human Services, "Eighth Annual Report on Oregon's Death with Dignity Act," March 9, 2006, p. 4. URL: http://egov.oregon.gov/DHS/ph/pas/docs/year8.pdf.

© Infobase Publishing

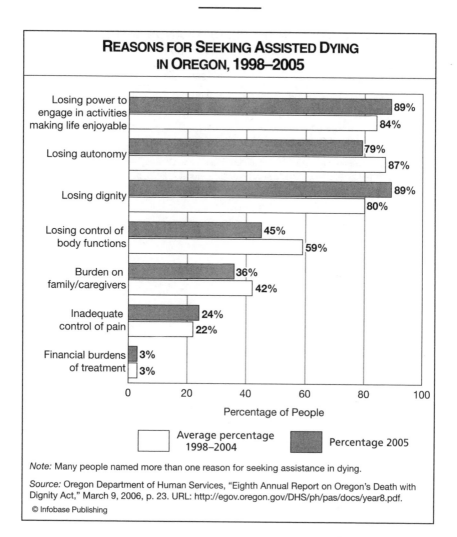

REASONS FOR SEEKING ASSISTED DYING IN OREGON, 1998–2005

Losing power to engage in activities making life enjoyable — 89% / 84%

Losing autonomy — 79% / 87%

Losing dignity — 89% / 80%

Losing control of body functions — 45% / 59%

Burden on family/caregivers — 36% / 42%

Inadequate control of pain — 24% / 22%

Financial burdens of treatment — 3% / 3%

Percentage of People — 0, 20, 40, 60, 80, 100

Average percentage 1998–2004 | Percentage 2005

Note: Many people named more than one reason for seeking assistance in dying.

Source: Oregon Department of Human Services, "Eighth Annual Report on Oregon's Death with Dignity Act," March 9, 2006, p. 23. URL: http://egov.oregon.gov/DHS/ph/pas/docs/year8.pdf.

© Infobase Publishing

ASSISTED DYING IN THE NETHERLANDS IN THE YEARS
1990, 1995, AND 2001

Euthanasia Requests/Deaths	1990	1995	2001
Number of requests for euthanasia or assisted suicide	8,900	9,700	9,700
Deaths from euthanasia as a percentage of total deaths	1.7	2.4	2.6

Source: Onwuteaka-Philipsen, Bregje D., et al. "Euthanasia and Other End-of-Life Decisions in the Netherlands in 1990, 1995, and 2001." *Lancet,* vol. 362, August 2, 2003, pp. 395ff.

INDEX

Locators in **boldface** indicate main topics. Locators followed by *c* indicate chronology entries. Locators followed by *b* indicate biographical entries. Locators followed by *g* indicate glossary entries. Locators followed by *t* indicate graphs/tables.

A

ableism 148*g*

abortion
  Compassion in Dying et al. v. State of Washington 81–82, 84, 85
  Quinlan case 69
  Roe v. Wade 14, 31–32, 78, 79, 99

ACLU. *See* American Civil Liberties Union

An Act for the Relief of Parents of Theresa Marie Schiavo 40

active euthanasia 4, 148*g*

Adkins, Janet 25, 121*c*, 133*b*

Adler, John 108–109

advance directive (health care directive) 148*g*
  Advance Planning and Compassionate Care Act 127*c*
  American Medical Association 119*c*
  Americans with 59
  Cruzan v. Director, Missouri Department of Health 24, 75, 121*c*
  do-not-resuscitate order 59
  durable power of attorney 16–17
  Glucksberg v. Washington State 93
  living will 16, 115*c*–117*c*

National Conference of Commissioners on Uniform State Laws 122*c*

Sandra Day O'Connor 24

and patient medical records 59

Patient Self-Determination Act 24, 65, 66, 121*c*

Quinlan case 71, 72

Respecting Choices in Wisconsin 59

Schiavo case 106, 126*c*

Uniform Health Care Decisions Act 122*c*

Wendland v. Wendland 41, 103

Advance Planning and Compassionate Care Act 127*c*

Advocates for the Developmentally Disabled 22

aging population 56

aid in dying 148*g*

AIDS epidemic 18

Alexander, Leo 10

ALS. *See* amyotrophic lateral sclerosis

Alzheimer's disease 29, 121*c*

AMA. *See* American Medical Association

American Academy of Hospice and Palliative Medicine 233

American Academy of Pediatrics 20

American Bar Association 71

American Civil Liberties Union (ACLU) 233
  Bouvia v. Superior Court ex rel. Glenchur 22, 72
  Schiavo case 39, 106

American Foundation for Suicide Prevention 35, 233

American Geriatrics Society 233–234

American Hospital Association 116*c*

American Life League 234

American Medical Association (AMA) 234
  advance directive 119*c*
  Compassion in Dying et al. v. State of Washington 83
  end-of-life care 127*c*
  Glucksberg v. Washington State 100
  opposition to Lethal Drug Abuse Prevention Act 36
  persistent vegetative state 119*c*
  reverses position on persistent vegetative state 17

American Nurses Association (ANA) 234

Index

Index

Index

299

Index

301

Index

Index

Index

Index

Index